A HISTORY OF THE AMERICAN WORKER

1933–1941

A CARING SOCIETY

By Irving Bernstein

THE NEW DEAL COLLECTIVE BARGAINING POLICY

ARBITRATION OF WAGES

EMERGENCY DISPUTES AND NATIONAL POLICY
(WITH OTHERS)

*

A History of the American Worker

THE LEAN YEARS
1920–1933

TURBULENT YEARS
1933–1941

A CARING SOCIETY
1933–1941

A History of the American Worker
1933–1941

A Caring Society

THE NEW DEAL, THE WORKER,
AND
THE GREAT DEPRESSION

Irving Bernstein

*

ILLUSTRATED

Houghton Mifflin Company · Boston
1985

Library of Congress Cataloging in Publication Data

Bernstein, Irving, date
A caring society.

Bibliography: p.
Includes index.
1. Labor and laboring classes — United States — 1914– . 2. Labor policy — United States — History. 3. Unemployment — United States — History. I. Title. II. Title: History of the American worker, 1933–1941.
HD8072.B365 1985 362.8′5′0973 84-25129
ISBN 0-395-33116-1

Printed in the United States of America

V 10 9 8 7 6 5 4 3 2 1

The author gratefully acknowledges permission to quote from the following sources:

Hard Times: An Oral History of the Great Depression by Studs Terkel (New York: Pantheon, a Division of Random House, Inc., 1970).

The New Economics: Keynes' Influence on Theory and Public Policy, edited by Seymour E. Harris (New York: Knopf, 1947).

Out of This Furnace (Boston: Little, Brown, 1941).

U.S.A., Volume 3 (pages 456–61 and 559–61) by John Dos Passos. Copyright 1930, 1937, 1946 by John Dos Passos and Houghton Mifflin Company. Copyright © renewed 1958, 1960, 1974 by Houghton Mifflin Company.

Panic: A Play in Verse by Archibald MacLeish. Copyright 1935 by Archibald MacLeish. Copyright © renewed 1963 by Archibald MacLeish. Reprinted by permission of Houghton Mifflin Company.

To
Fritzi

*

A Caring Society
is a book from the research program of
the Institute of Industrial Relations,
University of California, Los Angeles.

*

Contents

	Preface	xi
	Prologue: Adrift	1
One	Relief: A National Policy	17
Two	The Social Security Act	43
Three	WPA	72
Four	The Dilemma of Unemployment	86
Five	Fair Labor Standards	116
Six	Social Programs in Action	146
Seven	Images of the Worker	189
Eight	Watershed	275
	Notes	309
	Index	327
	Photographs follow page 178	

Preface

NUMEROLOGY NEVER INTERESTED ME until I struggled to complete this third volume of a trilogy. I then became obsessed with the number three. As a third child and a third son, I had cause to worry. Would the trimester ever end with the act of literary birth? Would the trireme carrying the manuscript sink in a storm within the three-mile limit of its destination? Would I be convicted of trigamy (said to be more fun than bigamy) under the Sherman Act and be required to pay treble damages? Would the tritium (atomic mass 3) in the hydrogen bomb cause it to explode and thereby bring the world to an end? Would readers accuse me of writing tripe and trivia? Someone who should know told me that there was a tradition in Italian literature of writers of trilogies not finishing the third volume. This was the stuff of bad dreams, which, fortunately, are behind me. *A Caring Society* is a palpable fact.

American labor history and American society were profoundly changed by the Great Depression and the New Deal. This trilogy recounts that transformation. *The Lean Years,* after some background on the twenties, deals with the desperate period between 1929 and 1933. *Turbulent Years* tells the story of the extraordinary growth of unionism and collective bargaining between the arrival of the New Deal on March 4, 1933, and Pearl Harbor on December 7, 1941. *A Caring Society,* concerned with the same time span, narrates the dilemma of unemployment and its consequences, including the response of a compassionate and popular government. The system the New Deal erected in the thirties became the basis for the American version of the welfare state. In Chapter Seven I have analyzed the remarkable emergence of the image of the worker in the arts, particularly in fiction, drama, painting and sculpture, photography, and folk song. The final chapter summarizes and weighs the major developments of the period.

This volume is intended to stand on its own feet (all three?) and to be read by itself. For those who have the time, however, I think there is much to be gained by reading the three books consecutively. Certain themes and leading figures recur.

In a project of this size and duration, of course, I have incurred enormous obligations to others, some of which I want to acknowledge here. The largest is to the University of California, Los Angeles, particularly to the Institute of Industrial Relations, which supported the research and writing for many years, and to UCLA's superb library system, which provided me with so many useful materials. I also want to thank the numerous librarians and archivists at many other institutions who gave generously of their time and resources. Four experts associated with the University of California read the manuscript critically and offered many suggestions for its improvement — Benjamin Aaron, professor of law at UCLA, Paul Bullock, research economist at UCLA, David Brody, professor of history at Davis, and Clark Kerr, president emeritus of the University. I want to express special gratitude to my editors at Houghton Mifflin, book people who take bookmaking seriously: Ruth K. Hapgood and Anita McClellan for encouragement and support, and Lois M. Randall for a thorough editorial scouring of the manuscript. Sharon Geltner, coordinator at the Institute of Industrial Relations, prepared the index. Errors and shortcomings that remain, of course, are my responsibility.

Irving Bernstein

Sherman Oaks,
California

A HISTORY OF THE AMERICAN WORKER

1933–1941

A CARING SOCIETY

Prologue

Adrift

AMERICANS, Thomas Wolfe wrote, are "a nomad race," vagrant floaters adrift in a sea of loneliness. They are obsessed by "the hunger for voyages, the hunger that haunts Americans." Wolfe, himself a rover, wore out his short life in ceaseless wandering in search of an irretrievable home.

Woody Guthrie, the minstrel of the migrants of the thirties, opened his autobiography in this fashion:

> I could see men of all colors bouncing along in the boxcar. We stood up. We laid down. We piled around on each other. We used each other for pillows. I could smell the sour and bitter sweat soaking through my own khaki shirt and britches, and the work clothes, overhauls and soggy, dirty suits of the other guys. My mouth was full of some kind of gray mineral dust that was about an inch deep all over the floor. . . . Our car was a rough rider, called by hoboes a "flat wheeler."
>
> "We would hafta git th' only goddam flat wheeler on th' whole dam train!" a heavy-set boy . . . beside me [said].
>
> "Beats walkin'!" I [said].[1]

1

Paul S. Taylor was a professor of economics at the University of California in Berkeley in the thirties. He had been interested in the problems of American agriculture, in farm labor, in Mexican labor in the United States, particularly in agriculture. His wife, Dorothea Lange, was a gifted photographer. Early in 1935, the Division of Rural Rehabilitation of the California Emergency Relief Administration asked Taylor to take a look at rural relief in that state to see what could be done about it. The discovery Taylor made is best told in his own words to the Tolan Committee:

> I got in a car and started down the highway. I went to the pea harvest, where the migrants were at work in the fields.
>
> I drove from the San Luis Obispo country down to Pomona and the pea fields at Calipatria and the Imperial Valley, and I had not gone far before I realized that something fundamental was happening in our rural sections. I had seen, years before, a great number of Mexican agricultural laborers. I was astounded to find that within the course of 4 or 5 years the complexion of the labor supply was enormously changed. Here I saw pea pickers from Vermont, Oklahoma, Arkansas, and Texas, and on the cars gathered around the fields licenses from other States.
>
> The Mexicans were still there, but proportionately fewer than I had been accustomed to a very short time before. As I went down the highways, I saw more and more dilapidated cars, obviously filled with families with all their household possessions. They had trailers, bedding, stoves, and so forth; and where they were pulled up by the roadside to fix a tire, or tinker with the engine, or to get gas and oil, I stopped my car, too. I talked with them; asked where they came from; asked why they came. The first answers were: "Blowed out," "burned out," "dried out."

Taylor had discovered the Dust Bowl and its victims, the Okies, the Arkies, the Mizoos, and others, who were making the trek to California.

He returned later on other trips to follow their trails backward. Dorothea Lange accompanied him and photographed the migrants. The Taylors went to the California Department of Agriculture inspection station at Fort Yuma on the Arizona border to watch the cars and speak to the occupants. Taylor asked "by which routes they had come, from what counties of what States, and then I worked eastward, always with the flow coming west as I drove east." In the Texas Panhandle he learned that it was more than the dust in the Great Plains that drove people out. He came to a virtually abandoned village, the buildings boarded up. At the gas station he asked the attendant why the people had left. "The answer came immediately: 'Why, it is the tractors.' " Machines were displacing men in American agriculture.

By the end of the decade, migration was recognized as a national problem of the first magnitude. Taylor persuaded John H. Tolan, a member of the House of Representatives from California, that there should be a congressional investigation. On April 22, 1940, Tolan got the House to create the Select Committee to Investigate the Interstate Migration of Destitute Citizens and became its chairman. The Tolan Committee held hearings, which fill ten volumes, throughout the nation between July 29, 1940, and February 26, 1941, and issued its report on April 3, 1941. The testimony and the studies provide a penetrating insight into the tragic impact of the Great Depression upon the lives of the millions of Americans who were compelled to move.[2]

2

Historically, Americans had always been what Wolfe called them, "a nomad race." The New World was discovered, explored, and settled by wanderers. Men on the move pushed the frontier westward to the Pacific. From the inception of settlement, Europeans and some others in very large numbers emigrated to the colonies and, later, to the United States. Mobility within the country was, if anything, even greater. These were, on the whole, migrations sustained by hope. People moved on the expectation of improving their fortunes. In the thirties, by contrast, hope yielded to despair. The push displaced the pull. Folks migrated not so much because they expected life to be better elsewhere, but because they could no longer bear to stay home. Often there was nothing in the new place and they were forced to move on again, and again. For many, wandering became aimless, undertaken for its own sake.

No one ever counted the number of migrants of the Great Depression. The Tolan Committee made a stab at it for one year. Using data collected on some nonagricultural employed workers under the new old-age pension and unemployment-insurance systems and adjusting for their dependents, the Committee estimated that 4 million people outside agriculture had made interstate moves during 1937. To this figure the Committee added 1 million persons connected with farming. Its hunch was that this total for 1937, 5 million, was "greater in most of the preceding years, smaller in some of those that followed." This suggests that perhaps 50 million migrations between states took place during the decade, a staggering figure even if one discounts for the fact that many individuals would be counted more than once.

Those who were well-off frequently complained that the migrants were inferior people, bums, or hoboes. Given the size of the movement, this could hardly have been correct. Ethnically, the migrants were much like their critics. A Department of Labor study in 1937 reached this conclusion: "The workers who migrate across state lines are predominantly native white Americans." Considering all migrants, a very large proportion moved as families, and among farm people families were in the majority. Bertha McCall, the director of the National Travelers Aid Association, said that the "transient population differs very little from the average static population." The former were "ordinary citizens seeking opportunity." Helen Gahagan Douglas, the actress and congresswoman who visited many migrant camps in California, reported: "They are the same kind of American stock as the people who helped build up the Middle and Far West regions of this great country." Mrs. Franklin D. Roosevelt, who looked into camps all over the nation, said that those who moved were often "the finer people" who had "adventure in their souls." She found them of "good stock" and was struck by "the beauty of some of the children" and their "bright minds."

The great migration of the thirties was a special case of poverty. The income levels of the migrants, of course, were extremely low. A study of migratory-casual industrial workers showed median annual earnings of $400 in 1933 and 1934, for industrial and agricultural workers combined, $275 in 1933 and $220 in 1934. More than half of the 1,700,000 migrants who registered under social security had an income in 1937 of less than $700. Seasonal workers in agriculture, the Labor Department reported in 1937, averaged about $300 annually per single man and $400 per family.

Such destitution had a severe impact upon standards of living, especially on health. Life on the road was often characterized by an inadequate and/or unbalanced diet, sometimes even hunger and malnutrition, by exposure to the elements, by bad water and sanitation, and by poor or no medical care and hospitalization. Migrants were especially susceptible to the communicable and filth-borne diseases. They suffered from high rates of digestive ailments, pulmonary tuberculosis, local infections, gonorrhea, syphilis, and malaria. In fact, many communities considered them a menace to the public health.

The United States suffered a severe erosion of its housing capital during the decade, and transients got the worst of it. Those who migrated to the northern cities, as many southern blacks did, found themselves in the most dilapidated homes those communities offered. Others lived in hastily thrown-together camps, in shack towns, in jungles, or in the streets or fields. Squatting sometimes created towns. In 1934 the Los Angeles County community that was to become Bell Gardens had virtually no residents; migrant squatters raised its population to 26,000 by 1940.

Perhaps the most poignant impact of migration was upon the education of children. An itinerant child, of course, cannot attend school regularly. The inevitable consequence is interrupted learning. A Farm Security Administration study of 407 migrant families showed that 84 percent of the youngsters were held back at least one grade by age fourteen; for those of Mexican extraction the figure was 88.4 percent.

Established communities, regarding the migrants as offensive and threatening, rejected them. Thus, the police often ran them out of town, the cities and states frequently denied them relief, and communities segregated them from the permanent residents. In 1936 Los Angeles Police Chief James E. Davis deployed 150 of his officers along California's borders with Arizona, Nevada, and Oregon in a "bum blockade" to bar migrants from reaching the city. But establishment fear occasionally produced help. Mrs. Douglas reported that the Las Vegas hotels left their first floors open at night so that transients might sleep in the gambling casinos rather than climb to the second floor and disturb the paying guests. While the migrant's labor was welcome to bring in a crop, he and his family were not. Rejection and segregation of the migrants, Mrs. Douglas said, "sets them apart as a class." By the end of the decade a subculture of migratory destitution was emerging and Woody Guthrie was its voice.[3]

3

The Tolan Committee, in addition to taking the testimony of experts, listened to the stories of the migrants themselves, scores of them. Some were extremely interesting:

*

In 1898 Marvin Montgomery's family — he was one of seven children — had moved from a farm in Arkansas to a farm in the Cherokee

Nation in Indian Territory near Sallisaw. His father worked it for ten years. They then crossed the river to the Choctaw side, to another farm near what would become Stigler after the Territory became the State of Oklahoma. Marvin Montgomery tilled the land there for thirty years, married, and produced four children, three boys and a girl.

In the midthirties Oklahoma was struck by the drought and the wind. The Dust Bowl was no place for a farmer. "It just got so hard, such a hard get-by," Montgomery said. "I just drug along. . . . It was just a hard old going. . . . I wanted to change countries to see if I couldn't find something better." He decided to move to California. It was not for the climate or for the relief. "It was work, was what I was really looking for."

On December 29, 1937, Montgomery loaded his family and their belongings into his 1929 Hudson Super-Six. He had $53 in his pocket. The Montgomerys struck out for the West Coast via Fort Worth and El Paso. Usually they slept in tourist camps, paying about a dollar and a half at night. Sometimes, instead, they drove through the night to save the money. The eight-year-old Hudson had two breakdowns and burned an awful lot of oil. "I got to where I had to blindfold it to get it past a filling station."

The money ran out in Arizona and they stopped for five weeks in Eloy to pick cotton. Montgomery and the children worked in the fields and together earned $4 or $5 a day. All six slept in a 12-by-14-foot tent. On February 8, 1938, they crossed the line into California at Yuma.

The old Hudson got the Montgomerys to the San Joaquin Valley. They stayed briefly near Wasco and then settled in at the Farm Security Administration camp at Shafter. "I hoed beets some," Montgomery said, "hoed some cotton, and I picked up spuds." The children worked alongside him.

For nine months at Shafter the family lived in a 14-by-16-foot tent. Montgomery paid rent of 10 cents a day, $3 a month. He also owed $4 a month in work. "I always got that off my chest the first of the month." This impressed Bob Hardy, the camp manager, and, when a house became available, he told Montgomery about it. The family moved into a two-room house, with water, electricity, and a garden plot. The rent was $8.20 a month. After a year in California Montgomery could vote, and his family became eligible for relief — $52 a month. The children went to school. Harvey, who was seventeen, was starting the ninth grade. He remembered Oklahoma, all right, but "I would rather stay out here." His father was "waiting for something to break."

*

John McCrae got out of high school in Lancaster, New York, near Buffalo, in 1925. He went to work for the New York Central Railroad in the stockroom, lived at home, and bought a car. In 1929 the railroad closed the plant and laid him off. "I could not find employment at that time, and having trouble with my stepfather, who is very hard to get along with, I was just compelled to leave home." He spent the next eleven years on the road, visiting forty-three states. He drove his own car for a couple of years, and after that, "I hitchhiked most of the time."

At first McCrae had the urge to travel. He picked up odd jobs to pay for seeing the country. Then he decided to settle down and find steady work. Jobs were extremely scarce, he had no trade, and he was handicapped by poor eyesight. Occasionally he would find casual work in hotels or restaurants or in construction. The best he did was to work for almost a year on building a new boiler house in a steel mill in Youngstown, Ohio. In the summers of 1939 and 1940, he was second cook at a children's camp in the Berkshires in western Massachusetts for $45 a month and keep.

When the federal Transient Bureau was operating, he stayed in its camps in Springfield, Illinois, Kansas City, and Springfield, Missouri. "They were very good," he said. He was supplied with food and clothing, and he could stay as long as he wished provided he worked a few hours a day. During the winters he tried to find a restaurant job. In his travels he met thousands of people "just about the same way I am, . . . willing to work." He also ran into many people who had been "dried out on the farms and were going to other States looking for work." McCrae had never applied for relief. He had not lived anywhere long enough to meet the residency requirements except for Youngstown, where he did not need help.

In late November 1940 he went to Baltimore to look for work in the hotels and restaurants. None was available and he had no place to stay. He moved to Washington and, when he appeared before the Tolan Committee in December, he was living at the local Transient

Bureau. He liked the city and would remain there if he could find a steady job. "Otherwise I will just have to keep going until I do find something where I can settle down."

*

Guy F. Gulden was born on a farm in 1891 in Nebraska, Gosper County, in the southwest part of the state. His schooling ended with the eighth grade. When he was nineteen, he started farming for himself on 320 acres rented from his father. He married and there were two children, both of whom died. In 1920 Gulden moved to Colorado. He learned the plasterer's trade, joined the union, and worked as a plasterer for six years.

But Gulden's first love was the land. In 1926 he returned to the canyon country in Gosper County to farm. The area was naturally dry and no irrigation water was available. During World War I, the farmers had plowed up the bottoms of the canyons and later heavy rains and winds had washed and blown the topsoil out. Gulden had 240 acres, but only 90 were level; the rest was broken up. He raised corn and had a fair crop in 1930, less in 1931. The next year he worked for another farmer. In 1933 he returned to his own place, but the crop was "not much." There was a devastating drought in 1934 that "just blowed me out. I had 160 acres of corn, and some cane, and feed, and I sold the whole damned business for $7.50." He also sold one hundred starving cows to the government for $18.

Gulden now had about $100 in cash and he and his wife moved to Idaho. He found work as a farmhand. He got $45, a place to live, a quart of milk a day, and a little patch where he "raised a few beans." After two and a half years the man he worked for traded for a farm in Oregon and the Guldens moved with him. It did not work out and, after six months, they decided to leave. For three years, Gulden said, "me and the Missus" had argued over where to go. He had read about some run-down farms in upstate New York. "I figured that they get more rain there and I could build them up." Mrs. Gulden preferred California. "She talked me into coming out here," he said. "I thought this was the darndest desert I ever saw when I came out here." They settled in Las Lomas, near Watsonville, in October 1937.

Since coming to California, Gulden had picked cotton, had built three or four houses, had worked for a trucker. His wife had done housework and worked pretty steady. With the help of an FHA loan,

Gulden had built himself a 22-by-26-foot house on two and three-quarter acres outside Watsonville. The Guldens had an annual income of about $400. The payments on the house loan came to $14.56 a month and "sometimes it was kind of tough." But the Guldens had not applied for relief.

*

Karen and Kathryn Lee were born in Kansas City. Their mother remarried when they were small children. The stepfather, according to Karen, "used to drink a lot . . . and was a reckless driver." In 1934 he kicked the girls out of the house. Karen was fourteen, Kathryn twelve. Later they read in the newspaper that their parents had been killed in an automobile accident. Kathryn thought it happened because her stepfather was drunk.

The girls went to St. Louis, though they knew no one there. They found jobs doing housework in the early mornings and evenings and went to school during the days. After two and a half years Karen had completed three and a half years of high school and Kathryn had reached the eighth grade. Karen said, "My ambition was to become a doctor, but I think that is out now."

In 1936 they lost their jobs in St. Louis and took to the road for the next four years. They hitchhiked all over the country, getting rides mostly from truck drivers. If they were in a town when the sun went down, they would go to a park for the night. "We never slept," Karen said. "We just stayed out. . . . We were afraid of tramps." Occasionally they found work cleaning house or as waitresses in restaurants or taverns.

In the summer of 1940 the Lee girls were back in St. Louis, jobless. Someone said there was plenty of work in Chicago and they hitched up. On a Sunday afternoon in August they were in Douglas Park when a policeman picked them up. The police took them to an emergency home run by the Salvation Army, where the Tolan Committee found them. They did not want to go back to either Kansas City or St. Louis. "I want to be anywhere where I think I will be able to find a decent job," Karen said. "Right now, I think I would scrub steps."

*

The Thomas family was from St. Louis. Mr. Thomas was an unemployed electrician. There were five children in 1934, three boys and two girls, and another girl would come along in a few years. The family was on relief — $11 a week for groceries — and it was hard to get by. All the children were sick; Selby had sinus trouble and a mastoid operation and Janet had heart trouble. Mrs. Thomas was told to take them out of school to board them in the country, but she did not have the money.

In October 1934 the Thomases decided to leave St. Louis because of the children's health. They sold their furniture for $30 and purchased a 1927 Buick for $25. After they bought five gallons of gas, they had 65 cents in cash. They set out for Arizona. Mr. Thomas sold corn medicine along the way. Sometimes they slept in cabins when they had the money, but usually the children slept in the car and the parents on army cots under a tarpaulin. The two older boys were musical, playing the violin and the guitar. Mrs. Thomas recounted,

> After we arrived at Del Rio [Texas] we parked on a street in front of a church and I had the children practicing their music as usual, which they did every day. They were playing church pieces, sacred pieces, and the lady in a shoeshop came out and invited them in her shop to play for her husband. When her husband heard them she asked me if I would let them go to a friend of hers that owned a cafe. I told her if she would wait until my husband came back to the car I would ask him, which she did. She met me about the same time my husband did and asked him for permission for the children to go and he finally decided they should go up and play.
>
> She said that if they didn't pick up any money she would pay them for the trouble of going up there.
>
> When they went to this cafe they collected 90 cents. That encouraged the children and the lady persuaded us to let them go around and see if they couldn't pick up some more money. They collected around $6 that night, enough to carry us across the desert and mountains, and we went on to Bisbee, Ariz.

The Thomas family now had a formula for financing its travels. Alberta Thomas continued,

> They would go into cafes at first when they were smaller, and barber shops and garages or any places where they would think anybody would be interested in music, and ask them for permission to play. When they got permission to play they played.

For the next six years the family lived off the music of the two boys. They moved constantly, visiting forty-two states. After Arizona, they drove east to Pennsylvania, then back to St. Louis and out west to

Cheyenne and the Pacific Coast, again, Arizona and Missouri, then Texas and Florida. Thomas looked for work in these states and found none. He built a trailer, which made sleeping more comfortable. For a short time the girls attended school in Florida. But the charge — $3 for tuition and $6.70 for books — was too steep. For the most part Mrs. Thomas gave the children "their lessons." Since she had only finished the seventh grade herself, they were not up with other youngsters of the same age. "But," she said, "I taught them to the best of my ability what I knew."

At one point in their travels the Thomases decided to settle down. They made a $15 payment on a 40-acre tract near Higdon, Missouri, which was priced at $200. It was rolling land with cutover timber that had to be cleared. At first they lived in the trailer. Then they built a one-room log cabin and later added a room to it. They tried to farm, but, as Mrs. Thomas said, "We just couldn't make a go of it." They returned to the road and to the boys' musical earnings.

When Mrs. Thomas appeared before the Tolan Committee in Washington in December 1940, things had begun to turn up. Mr. Thomas had just gotten a job with a coal company in Washington at $30 a week and so could not testify. The two older boys were entertaining in night clubs in the District of Columbia and Virginia. The family now had a 1938 Ford V-8, though it had recently been in a wreck. They lived in the Alexandria Tourist Camp in their trailer. All the children were in good health. Several had started school in Alexandria in September, though held back a year. When asked whether she preferred to migrate or to settle down, Mrs. Thomas said, "I would rather live a normal life with my family."

*

Jane Maxwell, who was black, was born in Savannah in 1916. She could not have received much of an education because she began to work when she was twelve or thirteen. She did housework, not sleeping in, for which she got $1.25 a week, sometimes $1.50 a week. When Congressman Tolan asked how she could live on $1.50 a week, Jane replied, "I do not know; that was all I could make." She got married in 1932 and had a baby the next year. Her husband deserted her a month after the boy was born and she had not seen him for eight years. Jane lived with her mother, who looked after the child while she worked. The grandmother and the son were frequently sick.

They were living on the west side of Savannah when a woman on the east side told Jane in 1937 about a black man who could get her a job in New York. She agreed to pay him $17.50 — $2.50 down and $15 out of her first month's earnings. He drove her and seven other black women to New York in his car. They arrived on a Friday. On Saturday she started work on a sleeping-in job in Manhattan. Jane did "housework and cleaning and washing for the kids." She got $30 a month. After a couple of months Jane lost this job because the family left for Brooklyn. She moved to Harlem and found another job. She sent for her mother and child, who came up on the bus. Both were sick.

When Jane appeared before the Tolan Committee in July 1941, she had been out of work for some time. She received $16.85 and her mother got $8 in relief every two weeks. She paid $22 a month for rent. It was a struggle. "I make it do until I can do better." She was looking for a job. Jane preferred New York to Savannah. "I could not make a living there."

*

Roy Hulm was born in Russia in 1892 and came to the United States in 1910. His wife, Frances, was ten years younger and came from Pequot, Minnesota. Roy had finished high school and a two-year business course; Frances had three years of high school and had taught for a year. They had eleven children.

In 1932 the Hulms moved from North Dakota to a rented farm near Meadow, South Dakota. It was the beginning of the drought and, as Frances said, "We lost everything." For the next four or five years they were on relief in South Dakota. Early in 1937 Roy was on the WPA at $44 a month. He thought he had some kind of connection with Governor William Langer of North Dakota and went to see him in Bismarck. According to Roy, Langer promised him a job at $125 a month and told him to come back later. Upon returning to South Dakota, Roy asked the relief authorities there to finance his family's move. The Hulms were transported by car and their furniture by truck, arriving in Bismarck on June 26, 1937. Roy did not get the job. For more than a year, South Dakota provided relief to the Hulms though they lived in North Dakota. Frances worked in a laundry while Roy waited.

In August 1938, when Roy applied for relief in North Dakota, he was refused. A welfare worker came to the door on a Saturday evening to inform the Hulms that they would be shipped back to South Dakota, and on Monday morning the family and their possessions were trucked to the border town of Lemmon. North Lemmon was in North Dakota and, across the tracks, South Lemmon was in South Dakota. The Hulms were deposited just across the railroad, but the South Dakota police, who wanted them to return to Bismarck, would not let them out of the vehicle. When the children got hungry after several hours, Frances persuaded the police to buy them supper. Later she got them to put the family up for the night at the hotel. Early the next morning they were awakened, put back in a truck, and hauled off to Bismarck. The North Dakota police promptly turned them back, dropping them and their furniture this time in North Lemmon. The North Dakota policeman gave them a $5 bill and ordered them to cross the tracks into South Dakota. They walked over. The chief of police in South Lemmon told them to go right back to North Dakota. They refused to return. South Dakota relented and allowed them to stay for a week or two. Then back the Hulms went to North Dakota.

The plight of the Hulms, which gained a certain notoriety in the Dakotas, led to a good deal of litigation over which state and which county was liable for the relief they received. When Roy and Frances appeared before the Tolan Committee in Lincoln, Nebraska, in September 1940, the family was in Bismarck and Roy was on the WPA. Their case was an item in the chamber of horrors of what could happen to people under the state-residency laws. When Congressman Tolan asked Frances whether she favored a uniform statute, she said, "There should be something done so that a person doesn't have to be treated like a dog."

*

Thomas Benjamin Harrison Higgenbottom was a kind of itinerant farmer. He had farmed in many parts of Oklahoma — in the Indian Territory in the central east, near Slick, close to Muskogee, outside Tahlequah, several places in Wagoner County — and over in Kansas. He had seven children living; the eighth had died. "I always get the children to help me," he said. "If I am out in the field, my shadow amounts to a whole lot." His wife tended to the house.

When the government cut his cotton acreage in 1933, there was not enough work for everyone, so a couple of the older boys left to "go hunt us a job." In 1936 the drought hit Wagoner County hard. All Higgenbottom got from his land was "a few potatoes" that kept "us from starving to death." In the fall he went off to Texas to pick cotton, but that didn't work out. He was back in Oklahoma for the winter, which was very cold. Two to three hundred chickens, a mule, and a cow starved. "That doesn't look good to a farmer." He decided to put in one more crop. "This is our last crop," he said. "I will never see anything else that I have starve to death." He made the crop and sold out.

In the latter part of 1937, with about $40 in cash, Higgenbottom loaded his wife, the five younger children, and their belongings into his 1929 Model A Ford roadster. Higgenbottom had heard that there was good cotton country around Gilbert, Arizona. He drove west on Route 66 through Amarillo and on into Arizona. Generally, the Higgenbottoms slept in tourist cabins for 75 cents or $1 a night. When they got to Gilbert, the picking was pretty much over, but they did a little work for $4 a day. The first of 1938 Higgenbottom got a construction job on a dam at Mormon Flat. In July the family went to Eloy to pick cotton. Eight of them lived in a 12-by-14-foot tent in "a mighty filthy camp." Since the Higgenbottoms did not associate with blacks or Mexicans and there were several hundred of them in the main camp, they moved out into the desert. It was very dusty and they had to carry water a long way. There were no sanitary facilities and they needed to change clothes in the brush. In January 1939 smallpox broke out, and the folks who were picking cotton, Higgenbottom said, were "scabby as goats." The rancher fired anyone who got smallpox. The head of one of his girls, Higgenbottom said, "was a solid scab." The health authorities quarantined the camp for three weeks.

The Higgenbottoms then went to Avondale, Arizona, to pick cotton. They lived in a tin shack with a dirt floor. After a couple of weeks Mrs. Higgenbottom saw a woman picking lice off her children. "We loaded right away," Higgenbottom said, "and got out as quick as we could."

They crossed over into California on February 12, 1939. Their first stop was at a Farm Security Administration tent camp at Calipatria in the Imperial Valley. There was no rent. "We had showers," he said.

"There wasn't no papers blowing around and everything was just kept clean."

The Higgenbottoms became California migratory farm laborers, "fruit tramps." They picked peas and cherries near Beaumont, worked in the tomatoes and hay near Thornton, picked apricots outside San Jose, and then moved on to Visalia, back to Calipatria, to Thornton. From time to time they went on relief. When Higgenbottom appeared before the Tolan Committee in Los Angeles on September 28, 1940, his family was living in a two-room house on a farm north of Fresno. "I am figuring," he said, "on trying to stay there another year and farm."[4]

4

Lewis Andreas practiced medicine in Chicago. He was interested in helping people in trouble. In 1932 he was a founder of the city's first group practice medical center. He looked after the workers who got shot up by the police at the Republic Steel plant on the far South Side on Memorial Day, 1937.

During the worst part of the Great Depression, Dr. Andreas told Studs Terkel, "there was a feeling of perplexity." He recalled "an ominous march down Michigan Avenue."

> A very silent, scraggly march of the unemployed. Nobody said anything. Just a mass of people flowing down that street. In their minds, I think, a point was reached: We're not gonna take it any more. I remember it particularly because of the silence. No waving of banners, no enthusiasm. An undercurrent of desperation.
>
> It was the hopeful voice of F.D.R. that got things out of the swamps. He didn't have much to offer, but it was enough. He was a guy flexible enough to understand the need for experiments, for not being rigid and for making people feel there was somebody who gave a damn about them.[5]

One

Relief: A National Policy

IT WAS A SCANDAL IN THE THIRTIES that no one knew how many people were out of work because no reliable statistics existed. Robert R. Nathan, among others, worked up some estimates for the years 1929–1935.

In 1933 President Roosevelt had established a high-level consultative body, the National Emergency Council, with which he met from time to time. At the meeting on January 28, 1936, Nathan's unemployment estimates were discussed and a question arose as to the author's location. No one knew.

Roosevelt was handed a note. He turned to Secretary of Commerce Roper and said, "Oh, ho, Dan." He then read, "Robert R. Nathan, Chief of Income Section, Division of Economic Research, Commerce Department."

Roper replied, "I presume I got him through the NRA. . . . What was the sentence that was pronounced on him?"

Roosevelt: "To quit figuring!"[1]

1

Nathan, in fact, constructed his estimates for the Committee on Economic Security for its use in drafting the unemployment insurance provisions of the Social Security Act of 1935. He calculated that average monthly joblessness in 1933 was 13,176,000. For the first quarter the monthly figures were as follows: January — 14,492,000; February — 14,597,000; March — 15,071,000. The Bureau of Labor

Statistics' retrospective annual estimate for 1933, derived by another method, was 12,830,000. The BLS also later reported that the civilian labor force in 1933 consisted of 51,590,000 persons. Applying Nathan's data, therefore, 25.5 percent of the labor force was out of work in 1933, 29.2 percent in the high month, March. The BLS showed 24.9 percent of the labor force unemployed in 1933. Nineteen thirty-three was the worst year, and March was the worst month, for joblessness in the history of the United States.

But these statistics measured only the more serious part of the problem of unemployment. During the Great Depression, the Hoover Administration, industry, and many labor unions adopted a policy of work-sharing. Although no one knows how many millions of wage earners with jobs were on short time, there is no doubt that there were a great many. The experience of the United States Steel Corporation may be instructive. In 1929 the corporation had 224,980 full-time employees. Their number shrank to 211,055 in 1930, to 53,619 in 1931, to 18,938 in 1932, and to zero on April 1, 1933. All those who remained on the payroll on this last date were part-time workers, and they were only half as numerous as those employed full time in 1929.

Massive joblessness had a profound social and emotional impact upon the American people. The movement of population, historically a response to economic opportunity, changed drastically when opportunity dried up. Immigration from abroad virtually ceased and the long-term shift from farm to city slowed significantly. Transiency took their place — the worker adrift in a sea of unemployment, sailing rudderless without home port or destination. Studs Terkel caught the memories of people on the move. Dynamite Garland was a little girl of a working-class family in Cleveland. Her father lost his job. "I remember," Dynamite recalled, "all of a sudden we had to move." Louis Banks, a black from Arkansas, said, "A man had to be on the road. Had to leave his wife, had to leave his mother, leave his family just to try to get money to live on." Joe Morrison, who came from the coal country of southwestern Indiana, saw a lot of kids wandering, "looking for jobs, looking for excitement." But he was surprised to see "women riding freight trains. That was unheard of." Dynamite's family, which lived in a cold garage for seven years, reserved Sunday for fantasy. There were lots of houses for sale or for rent. They would pile into the Model A and go "house hunting." "You'd go look and see where you could put this and where you could put that, and this is gonna be my room. I knew where I was gonna have my horse in the barn." The transient in a cruel and ironic sense became the hero of the Great Depression, the symbol of a floundering America —John Dos Passos's Vag in *U.S.A.*, John Steinbeck's Tom Joad in *The Grapes of Wrath,* Woody Guthrie singing, "My poor feet has traveled a hot dusty road," the haunting Okie faces in Dorothea Lange's photographs.

No one wanted this "hero." He wound up in the jungle, in the junk-pile Hooverville with its Prosperity Road, Hard Times Avenue, and Easy Street. Peggy Terry told Terkel that, one day in Oklahoma City, her father told the kids he wanted to show them something and took them to the Hooverville. It was ten miles wide and ten miles long and "incredible." People lived in "old, rusted-out car bodies. I mean that was their home." Some made shacks out of orange crates. "One family with a whole lot of kids were living in a piano box." A couple with seven children "lived in a hole in the ground."

Existing physically was painful. Many people were continually hungry and some starved. Peggy Terry recalled a day when she and her sister had nothing to eat but a few biscuits and a jar of mustard. They ate so much mustard that they got sick and could never again stand it. John Beecher, a social worker in the South, saw the relief authorities in Ainsley, Alabama, put salt-pork gravy in a baby bottle and the child was sucking at the nipple. Dr. Lewis Andreas, who practiced medicine in Chicago, remembered,

> People starved on the street and on streetcars. I knew a resident at People's Hospital. Every day, he told me, somebody would faint on a streetcar. They'd bring him in, and they wouldn't ask any questions. . . . They knew what it was. Hunger. When he regained consciousness, they'd give him something to eat. People were flopping on the streets from hunger.

Most of the United States is cold in the winter, in some areas extremely cold. People on the road struggled to keep warm and sometimes spent the winter months in Florida or the Southwest. Those who remained at home often were unable to afford fuel. Jane Yoder, who lived in a mining town in Illinois, told Terkel of being "just desperate to be warm." Her sister, Katie, got a heavy coat in Chicago and Jane, who was jealous, sneaked it out of the closet for her own use. "I can remember being cold, just shivering," Jane recalled, "and came home, and nothing to do but go to bed, because if you went to bed, then you put the coat on the bed and you got warm." The destitute stole coal, tapped gas mains, and put jumpers on electric wires to go around the meters.

Many people were unable to make payments on their homes or to pay rent, and were evicted by mortgage-holders and landlords. Cars, furniture, and appliances were repossessed. Harry Hartman, who was a bailiff in Chicago, had a heart. He told Terkel that he would overlook the beds, report that "the mattress was full of cockroaches," say that a box of shirts was "partly full." People would weep when their possessions were taken away. Judge Samuel A. Heller sat on the Landlords and Tenants Court in Chicago and heard 400 eviction cases a day. The defendants had received five-day notices to pay the rent or be dispossessed. There was no legal defense. The people were "desperate and frightened." They cried and fainted in the courtroom. Judge Heller stretched the law. He gave them ten days plus an extra day for each child. Later he gave everybody thirty days prior to dispossession. The real estate people did not like Judge Heller.

The family as an institution took a fearful beating. The marriage and birth rates fell sharply, causing the unusually small "Depression generation." Elsa Ponselle, a Chicago schoolteacher, was going with a commercial artist and expected to get married. "Suddenly he was laid off. . . . And he just disappeared." Ray Wax, a restless entrepreneur, told Terkel that he had had "a serious affair" and had then run away. "You lived in a fear of responsibility for another person. You backed off when someone got close." Desertions were common, and children were parceled out to relatives and friends. Alcoholism increased, and stealing, as noted, became widespread. Ed Paulsen, who was on the road, said, "Everybody was a criminal. You stole, you cheated." This created a "coyote mentality":

> You were a predator. You had to be. The coyote is crafty. He can be fantastically courageous and a coward at the same time. . . . I grew up where they were hated, 'cause they'd kill sheep. . . . They're mean. But how else does a coyote stay alive? He's not as powerful as a wolf. He has a small body. He's in such bad condition, a dog can run him down.

He's not like a fox. A coyote is nature's victim as well as man's. We were coyotes in the thirties, the jobless.

Peggy Terry "felt so bad" because the children got nothing for Christmas. "Not an orange, not an apple — nothing." She stole the pretty box with the big red ribbon off the piano at church. It turned out to be a scarf for the piano. Want drove both single and married women into prostitution. Slim Collier, who lived in Waterloo, Iowa, told Terkel of a man in the neighborhood whose wife was a part-time prostitute. He could afford store-bought cigarettes, while others rolled their own.

The Depression undermined the husband-father in his culturally expected role as breadwinner, a point that Terkel's interviewees made repeatedly. Slim Collier's father, who was a tool-and-die maker at the John Deere tractor plant in Waterloo, was laid off when Slim was seven. "All of a sudden, my father, who I saw only rarely, was around all the time." An energetic man, he could not stand idleness. He invented work for himself, became irritated when the child played, and took Slim to the woodshed. Eventually they quarreled and the boy left home. Bob Leary's father spent two years painting the house to try to keep his self-respect. Larry Van Dusen, who was the oldest boy and whose father was a skilled carpenter, had a feeling of his father's failure, and they had bitter fights. Dr. Nathan Ackerman, a psychiatrist, went to Pennsylvania to observe the impact of prolonged unemployment upon coal miners. The men

> hung around street corners and in groups. They gave each other solace. They were loath to go home because they were indicted, as if it were their fault for being unemployed. A jobless man was a lazy good-for-nothing. The women punished the men for not bringing home the bacon, by withholding themselves sexually. By belittling and emasculating the men, undermining their paternal authority, turning to the eldest son. Making the eldest son the man of the family. These men suffered from depression. They felt despised, they were ashamed of themselves. They cringed, they comforted one another. They avoided home.

Perhaps the most serious impact was upon the morale of the American people. The depression of the spirit was more severe than that of the economy. "Society was no longer a comfortable abstraction,"

Alfred Kazin wrote, "but a series of afflictions." The novelist Martha Gellhorn, who made confidential field investigations for the Federal Emergency Relief Administration, wrote from Massachusetts to Harry Hopkins, the administrator:

> Now about the unemployed themselves. The picture is so grim that whatever words I use will seem hysterical and exaggerated. . . . I find them all in the same shape — fear, fear driving them into a state of semi-collapse; cracking nerves; and an overpowering terror of the future. I haven't been in one home that hasn't offered me the spectacle of a human being driven beyond his or her power of endurance and sanity.

This was the dominant theme of the people who talked to Terkel. It was evident in the imagery: there were "no road signs"; there was "no better tomorrow"; the man who was out of work was "walking upside-down"; "everything that wasn't nailed down was coming loose." Everyone was scared. General Robert E. Wood, a top executive of Sears, Roebuck, had to lay off thousands of people. The women in the halls were "terrified." He had to fire an Italian girl, the only one working in a family of ten, who was "frightened to death." Elsa Ponselle said the Depression was "a way of life for me" for ten years. She thought it would go on "forever and ever and ever. That people would always live in fear of losing their jobs." Herman Shumlin, the Broadway producer, watched the faces of the men in the breadlines. "I'd see that flat, opaque, expressionless look which spelled . . . human disaster." They had lost their jobs, homes, and families. "And worse than anything else, lost belief in themselves." Dr. Ackerman found that the jobless suffered from "an excess of guilt." Virginia Durr was horrified because the fundamentalist preachers in Alabama told the unemployed that God was punishing them and causing their children to starve because of their sins. "And the people believed it."

The position of black people was special. Most of them had never known anything but hard times. "The Negro," Clifford Burke told Terkel, "was born in depression." The Great Depression "only became official when it hit the white man." Burke knew a middle-class black who tried to pass as white and killed himself when he lost his stocks. This was unusual. A black man might take his life over a woman or get killed in a fight, "but when it came to the financial end of it, there were so few who had anything."[2]

2

Unemployment on this vast scale overwhelmed the existing relief resources — private agencies and local and state governments. The first halting step toward federal responsibility, the Emergency Relief and Construction Act of 1932, was seriously inadequate in amount and administratively defective by providing only for short-term loans to the states through the Reconstruction Finance Corporation (RFC). New York State, which had the best relief system in the nation, was helping only one fourth of its million destitute families in January 1933. A family of five in a coal county in western Pennsylvania was subsisting on $1.97 a week. By the early months of 1933, virtually everyone who knew anything about the problem agreed with the testimony of Professor Sumner H. Slichter of Harvard before the Senate Subcommittee on Manufactures: "The need for national assistance, by this time, has become . . . self-evident."

When Franklin D. Roosevelt became President on March 4, 1933, one of his most urgent tasks was to devise a new federal relief policy. It would join two streams of development — the actual experience of New York State under Roosevelt's leadership as governor and the proposals that had been considered in the Congress during the preceding year, particularly the La Follette–Costigan bill.

Roosevelt, who had been a believer in local responsibility for relief, had changed his position in 1931 in the face of the mass joblessness that afflicted his state. He called the legislature into special session on August 28 and said:

> Our Government is not the master but the creature of the people. The duty of the State toward the citizens is the duty of the servant to its master. . . .
>
> One of these duties of the State is that of caring for those of its citizens who find themselves the victims of such adverse circumstance as makes them unable to obtain even the necessities for mere existence without the aid of others. . . .
>
> To these unfortunate citizens aid must be extended by Government, not as a matter of charity, but as a matter of social duty.

The legislature responded, and Roosevelt created the Temporary Emergency Relief Administration (TERA). He persuaded his unwilling old friend, Jesse Isador Straus, president of R. H. Macy & Co., to become chairman. Straus wanted a competent executive director and invited William Hodson of the Russell Sage Foundation. Hodson declined and suggested Harry Hopkins of the Tuberculosis and Health Association. Hopkins accepted at once. A year later, when Straus resigned, Hopkins became chairman. Thus, in the year and a half before Roosevelt became President, Hopkins set up and ran the nation's foremost relief program. He also won Roosevelt's respect for his formidable administrative skills along with his permanent friendship.

In December 1931, Senators Edward P. Costigan of Colorado and Robert M. La Follette, Jr., of Wisconsin had introduced separate bills that would have made large federal grants to the states for unemployment relief. They were referred to the Subcommittee on Manufactures, of which La Follette was chairman, were joined into a single bill, and became the subject of hearings that focused national attention upon unemployment and dramatized the plight of the jobless. During 1932 the La Follette–Costigan bill failed to pass, but mounting political pressure for it forced Congress and President Hoover to add a provision to the bill creating the RFC to grant modest loans to the states for unemployment relief. The funds would run out in the spring of 1933. Costigan and La Follette, supported by Senator Robert F. Wagner of New York, were not put off by this compromise. La Follette resumed hearings in January 1933 as worsening unemployment increased the pressure for federal action. Hopkins was the subcommittee's star witness.

His testimony elaborated the program he had already recommended to Roosevelt on December 14, 1932:

1. Grants-in-aid to the states; no loans.
2. The federal government should deal only with the states.
3. Funds of two types —
   a. direct grants to the states
   b. free funds to be allotted at the discretion of the administrator.
4. Administration by an independent agency modeled on TERA. Not the RFC.
5. An appropriation of $600 million to $1 billion.

Shortly after Roosevelt's inauguration, Hopkins and his friend Hodson came to Washington. Roosevelt, busy with the banking and farm crises, could not see them. Hopkins called Frances Perkins, the new Secretary of Labor. She met them at the Women's University

Club, which was so crowded that they talked in a cramped "hole under the stairs." Hopkins and Hodson laid out their plan for federal grants for unemployment relief. "I was impressed," Miss Perkins wrote, "by the exactness of their knowledge and the practicality of their plan." She arranged for them to see the President at once. He reacted similarly and called in Senators Wagner, La Follette, and Costigan to put the proposal into a bill.

The measure, to become known as the Federal Emergency Relief Act, incorporated the points Hopkins had made in his December 14, 1932, letter to Roosevelt — establishment of a Federal Emergency Relief Administration (FERA), direct grants to the states, and some funds reserved at the discretion of the administrator. The RFC would be no more than paymaster. But Roosevelt was tighter with funds than Hopkins wanted; he approved $500 million.

This was the Hundred Days, and Roosevelt could get whatever he wanted from Congress. While conservative Republicans warned that the Republic would collapse, the Senate voted for the measure 55 to 17 on March 30, and the House 326 to 42 three weeks later. The President signed the emergency relief bill on May 12, 1933.

Roosevelt had no trouble in choosing an administrator. As a courtesy, he asked Governor Herbert H. Lehman of New York to release Hopkins. Lehman, who shared the President's admiration for Hopkins, asked him why he had to pick a man from New York when he had the whole country to select from. But Roosevelt prevailed. On May 22 Harry Hopkins came down to Washington.[3]

3

Hopkins was born, the fourth in a family of five children, on August 17, 1890, in Sioux City, Iowa. People who knew the parents would later say that he combined their opposite characteristics: His father was salty, easygoing, shiftless, and sporting; his mother had stern missionary zeal centered on the Methodist Church. When Harry was a boy, the family moved about the Midwest a good deal as his father searched for success in business. The elder Hopkins finally settled in Grinnell, Iowa, running a harness shop. Harry, after he became famous, liked to call himself the harnessmaker's boy from Iowa.

He attended Grinnell College, where he was active in campus politics and was a notable practical joker. In his studies, he did well with the two professors he respected and indifferently with the others. He graduated in 1912.

Hopkins intended to go into the newspaper business in Bozeman, Montana. But he was offered a job working with poor children at Christadora House, a settlement, in New York City and jumped at the opportunity to see the big city. It turned out to be more than city lights. Hopkins, who said, "I'd never seen a Jewish boy before in my life," was exposed to slum life on the Lower East Side. He became deeply involved in social work, in alleviating the lot of the disadvantaged. He moved on later to the Association for Improving the Condition of the Poor, the Board of Child Welfare, the Red Cross during World War I (after rejection by the armed forces for defective vision), the Milbank Memorial Fund, the New York Tuberculosis and Health Association, and TERA. As *Fortune* said of him in 1935:

> The fact is that Harry Hopkins knows little of this world's work except charity; ever since 1912 he has been living next door to acute human need. Almost his entire maturity has been spent with one or another New York organization concerned with the poverty and sickness and desperation of a city where poverty, sickness and desperation are more thickly concentrated than anywhere else in the Western world.

Though not professionally trained, Hopkins became a professional social worker. In the thirties he would become the social workers' social worker and would put that profession on the map.

His first marriage, which produced three children, ended in a messy divorce in the twenties. He remarried happily, had another child, and then suffered the death of his second wife in 1937.

Hopkins, despite his great energy, was continually at war with bad health. Dr. Jacob A. Goldberg, who worked with him at the Tuberculosis Association, said, "You could mark him down as an ulcerous type. He was intense, seeming to be in a perpetual nervous ferment — a chain smoker and black coffee drinker." He seems to have consumed large quantities of pills, and the Hopkins "papers" that went to the Roosevelt Library after his death contained enough medications to stock a small pharmacy. Admiral Ross T. McIntire, the President's physician, said, "Our biggest job is to keep Harry from ever feeling completely well. When he thinks he's restored to health he goes out on the town — and from there to the Mayo Clinic." One drink was usually enough to put him away and he was always underweight, even cadaverous. Roosevelt worried about the health of this "half-man." He sent Hopkins two dollars when he gained two pounds, but warned him not to put on more than fifty pounds "because Popper has not got more than 50$." The two dollar bills were still clipped to the note when Hopkins died, and the estate was not much bigger.

Hopkins was almost indifferent to money, seldom earning much and never accumulating any. His pay was cut severely when he took over the federal relief program in 1933. When he got a little ahead, time and health permitting, he ran off to fashionable night spots or to the races ($2 window). It would be flattering to describe his clothes as plain; his shirts usually needed washing and his suits bagged at his bony knees and elbows. Though Hopkins was one of the most powerful men in the nation, he did not display that fact. Ernie Pyle wrote: "And that old office of yours, Mr. Hopkins, good Lord, it's terrible. It's so little in the first place, and the walls are faded and water pipes run up the walls and your desk doesn't even shine. But I guess you don't care."

One needed only to look into those intense dark eyes to recognize that this was a man of "piercing understanding," the words of the citation that accompanied the Distinguished Service Medal bestowed on Hopkins at the end of the war. His biographer, Robert E. Sherwood, thought the phrase exceptionally apt because it caught "the penetrating sharpness of his mind and the relentless, tireless drive that was behind it." Winston Churchill told Hopkins that he wanted to put him in the House of Lords as "Lord Root of the Matter."

Hopkins must have been one of the greatest administrators, though unorthodox, who ever served the government of the United States. He had an exceptional capacity for stripping a complex problem to its essentials and of devising a solution that worked. All this with great speed. He enjoyed nothing more than cutting through red tape. His bird-dog nose could smell incompetence and corruption a mile away. He gave and he received personal loyalty to a remarkable degree. Arthur Krock said that he could weave a "magic personal spell" over people, which he did over the President, but especially over women. When Wendell Willkie asked Roosevelt why he kept Hopkins, whom Willkie distrusted, Roosevelt replied,

> Someday you may well be sitting here where I am now as President of the United States. And when you are, you'll be looking at that door over there and knowing that practically everybody who walks through it wants something out of you. You'll learn what a lonely job this is, and you'll discover the need for somebody like Harry Hopkins who asks for nothing except to serve you.

The people Hopkins hired at FERA were exceptionally able. Even more important, they agreed with him, they respected him, they loved him, and they gave him their best.

Though Hopkins was not anti-intellectual, he put people into two categories, the "talkers" and the "doers," and he proudly classed himself among the latter. Thus, he rarely expressed his personal philosophy. There is, however, an unusual impromptu speech he delivered to the students at Grinnell in 1939. "Growing up in this town, moving to the East, and having been almost every place in this Union, I have grown to have a tremendous affection and love for this country — the fields — the land — and the people." But America's most important asset was its democratic system of government. It was threatened from within by "great and powerful interests" that sought to buy control and from without by the "hate and fear sweeping the world." "It doesn't belong to anybody but the people of America." Hopkins could not see how the United States could "continue to exist as a democracy of 10,000,000 or 12,000,000 people unemployed. It just can't be done." There was "no reason why the people of America should dwell in poverty."[4]

4

During the Hundred Days in the spring of 1933, Roosevelt started three major programs to lift the nation out of the Great Depression: The National Recovery Administration (NRA), headed by General Hugh S. Johnson, was intended to stimulate business; the Public Works Administration (PWA), under Secretary of the Interior Harold L. Ickes, would spur heavy construction; and the Agricultural Adjustment Administration (AAA), led by George N. Peek, would try to revive agriculture. While the President hoped that all these programs would succeed, he recognized that they would not eliminate unemployment and the suffering of the jobless in the near future. Thus, there was urgent need for the Federal Emergency Relief Administration headed by Hopkins.

The President swore the administrator in on May 22. Within an hour Hopkins was in his office at the Walker-Johnson Building organizing the new agency, surrounded by packing cartons, files, typewriters, and workmen shoving furniture around. Within two hours he approved over $5 million in grants from the matching fund to Colorado, Illinois, Iowa, Michigan, Mississippi, Ohio, and Texas. The United States now had a genuine unemployment relief program and it was moving.

Since Hopkins intended the states and their subdivisions to assume the basic responsibility for administration and he wanted the jobless to get virtually all the relief money, he recruited a very small Washington headquarters staff. It came to only 121 people with a total monthly payroll of $22,000. Hopkins had considerable latitude in selecting personnel because FERA was exempt from civil service requirements. Aubrey Williams was second in command and was in charge of the Division of Relations with States. He was a soft-spoken Alabamian who had fought in World War I, had stayed in France to take a doctorate at the University of Bordeaux, and had then become a leading social work administrator in the Midwest. Jacob Baker headed the Works Division. He was a thick-set engineer with a varied background in mining, steel, electric power, schoolteaching, and publishing. Corrington Gill ran the Division of Research, Statistics, and Finance. He had studied economics and statistics at the University of Wisconsin, had been a newspaper reporter, and had organized the statistical work for the Hoover Administration's relief program. Hopkins also recruited a number of the nation's leading social workers — Frank Bane, Sherrard Ewing, and Rowland Haynes, among others.

In the hectic early months Hopkins and his lieutenants wrestled with problems that had never been faced before. While the policies they evolved were intended to deal with an immediate crisis, they would have a significant long-run impact, particularly upon the welfare provisions of the Social Security Act of 1935. The basic FERA policies were the following:

First, this federal-state program was exclusively public and the intention was to restrict it to unemployment relief. This meant that private charitable organizations whose funds had been depleted could not gain support from FERA. Similarly, state and local categorical programs, for example, to aid the aged, children, or the infirm, were ineligible for assistance. Finally, Hopkins insisted that each state establish an emergency relief administration solely concerned with helping the unemployed. Following New York's lead in 1931, most of the states had set up relief programs, but many were handled by existing welfare agencies. The latter were required to change and states that had no agencies were compelled to establish them.

Second, in administration, FERA sought to fence out politics, to professionalize the relief process, and to maintain reasonably uniform national standards. These goals were only partly attained. The desperate need for speed, the propensity of state and local politicians to treat federal funds as pork barrel, and the enormous differences in governmental systems and standards between the states joined to undermine their achievement. Although the statute gave Hopkins the sanction of federalizing an ineffectual state administration, its exercise, occasionally resorted to, was in itself an admission of failure. Politics and patronage oozed into the joints of state and local relief administrations. While Hopkins, with Roosevelt's backing, won some well-publicized battles with several governors and senators, his small staff could hardly win a war on so many fronts. FERA was a social work program and an effort was made to staff the agency with professionals. This was moderately successful in urban areas where social workers were available; but in smaller communities there were few professionals, there was an insistence upon hiring local people, and there was a tendency to give jobs to the unemployed regardless of qualification. The attempt to establish national standards was an agonizing struggle. Some states had a tradition of strong county government and filtered down relief administration, often with unhappy results; other states had weak counties and kept administration centralized. The disparity in standards was appalling. The average monthly relief grant per family in May 1933 ranged from $3.86 in Mississippi to $33.22 in New York. Many states stoutly resisted taxing themselves or borrowing in order to match federal funds, and several southern states never did either. Hopkins quietly made money available in the South, on the theory that this was the only way to prevent mass starvation among blacks.

Third, according to the FERA rule, eligibility for relief covered "all needy unemployed persons and/or their dependents" and included those employed or with resources whose incomes were "inadequate to provide the necessities of life." The rule continued, "There shall be no discrimination because of race, religion, color, noncitizenship, political affiliation, or because of membership in any special or selected group." This broad regulation was revolutionary in its impact and was the source of sharp controversy. Millions of blacks, who had been denied access to government at all levels, suddenly became eligible for federal relief. They took advantage of the opportunity and in the process switched political allegiance from the Republican to the Democratic Party. The middle-class jobless were also eligible. The work-relief programs developed for professionals, intellectuals, and artists became the subjects of press attack. Under the policy, strikers qualified for assistance. In the bitter and often violent labor disputes of the early New Deal, employers attacked Hopkins for allegedly financing strikes in their plants. The FERA answered that its obligation was to help those who merited relief, that participation in a work stoppage was irrelevant to a finding of need.

Fourth, the FERA regulation declared that those eligible "shall receive sufficient relief to prevent physical suffering and to maintain minimum living standards." This implied that the needy would receive food, shelter, fuel and utilities, clothing, and medical care, at least. Given the enormous size of the program and the shortage of funds, this was an unrealizable objective. As Hopkins later said, "We have never given adequate relief." Day-to-day administration compelled a sharpening of priorities. In most localities this meant that food was supplied first to prevent starvation, and if anything was left, some other "necessities" were covered. Urban dwellers usually got an allowance for fuel; those in rural areas were expected to cut wood. Gas or kerosene for cooking was normally covered. At the outset there was no provision for rent unless the family was evicted, which occurred frequently, and in which case FERA paid one month's rent on new quarters. The agency covered medicine, occasionally doctor bills, but not hospital costs. Clothing was provided mainly by the renovation of hand-me-downs in work-relief sewing rooms.

Fifth, FERA sought to provide relief in cash in order to preserve the morale and dignity of the recipient in permitting him to make his own spending decisions. But, again, this was an impossible goal to achieve, particularly at the outset of the program. Many local agencies issued food orders, especially to grocers who offered discounts. In numerous towns, commissaries were set up in warehouses and reliefers waited in long lines for surplus food that FERA bought from the Department of Agriculture. During the first year, even a large number of those who were on work relief and, presumably, earned wages were paid in kind.

Sixth, FERA policy allowed for both "direct relief" and "work relief." But Hopkins and his staff recognized that Americans, perhaps especially the jobless, were committed to the work ethic, hated the "dole," and wanted to earn their money. Thus, FERA in principle much preferred work relief. Baker's division devised an immense number and variety of local work programs, some useful, some "make-work," and some having aspects of forced labor. Work relief got FERA into the complex problem of wage determination. The early wage standard was a "fair rate," which was interpreted mainly as the prevailing local wage for common labor. This meant that black reliefers in the rural South got as little as 10 cents an hour. Later FERA raised the minimum wage to 30 cents an hour.

FERA was an immense peacetime mobilization of people and resources under forced draft. The economics of Harry Hopkins, Ickes said, consisted of an urge "to feed the hungry, and Goddam fast." Gill made a "relief census" for October 1933, the sixth month of the program. It showed that 3 million families, a total of 12.5 million persons, one tenth of the nation's population, depended on unemployment relief. Four states provided one third of this number — New York, Illinois, Pennsylvania, and Ohio. But the highest proportion of a state's population on relief was in the South — one fourth in Florida and one fifth in South Carolina and West Virginia. Relief families were larger on the average than others, which meant that an unusually large number of children depended on public assistance. This was also true of the aged. Blacks, who were only one tenth of the general population, made up one sixth of all persons on relief.

While FERA, of course, was a national program, it was actually administered at the local level. Hopkins, who wanted to keep an eye on these programs, hired a sharp newspaperwoman, Lorena A. Hickok, to travel about the country and report on particular conditions. She was later joined by the novelist Martha Gellhorn. Their letters illuminate the underside of American life in the early New

Deal period, and Hopkins would sometimes send an especially interesting one to Roosevelt. Since, as has already been noted, there were sharp differences between states, to say nothing of cities and counties, it is difficult to generalize. But Lorena Hickok's report on New York covering the period October 2–12, 1933, reveals the relief program in action in the nation's largest city.

New York, she wrote, "is struggling today with the biggest community relief job on earth — the biggest job ever undertaken by any city since the world began." It was trying to provide food, clothing, shelter, and medical care for "1,250,000 men, women, and children wholly dependent on public funds for their subsistence." Many others — some thought 1 million — should be on relief. They were on "thin ice, barely existing." "The magnitude of the relief job . . . and its complexities are breath-taking." One city block would have 200 families that required support. Those in need were of all nationalities, of all levels of education, from all occupational classes. "There they are, all thrown together into a vast pit of human misery, from which a city, dazed, still only half awake to the situation, is trying to extricate them."

"I have a feeling that the job is being done better than anyone would have a right to expect." But it was not good. The fundamental problem, "towering above all others," was lack of money. Financing was triangular — one third each from the federal, state, and city governments — with $6.3 million in August and a goal of $10 million a month. The last week of the month, when the money ran out, was called a "foodless holiday." The investigators themselves went unpaid. This unwanted holiday had broken morale more than anything else. Complaints about bad administration were usually traceable to lack of funds.

> Let me try to tell you what happens when you apply for relief in New York City.
>
> You go first to a schoolhouse in your neighborhood designated as a precinct Home Relief office. If you are the kind of person the government really should be interested in helping, you go there only as the last resort. You have used up all your resources and have strained the generosity of your relatives and your friends to the breaking point. Your credit is gone. You couldn't charge a nickel's worth at the grocery store. You owe several months' rent. The landlord has lost his patience and is threatening to throw you out. Maybe you've already gone through an eviction or two. . . . The chances are you've been hungry

> for some time. And now there's no food in the house. You've simply got to do something.
>
> If your children happen to attend the school where you must go to apply for relief, it just makes it that much tougher. . . .
>
> There will be a policeman around — maybe several. A lot more would be there inside of three minutes if you caused any commotion. . . .
>
> If you get by the policeman — and some people, I have been told, take one look at him, lose their courage, and turn around and go home — you have to tell some man at the door what you're there for. If you've got any pride, it hurts. And maybe he isn't any too patient. He's on relief himself, perhaps totally unqualified temperamentally for the job and worried about how he's going to make ends meet if he doesn't get his pay check next week.
>
> There's a maze of stairs, the atmosphere, the "smell" of a schoolhouse. For a moment, perhaps, your mind runs back to the time when you were going to school — years before the depression and all the trouble it brought you. You hate all this.
>
> You go into a room filled with people. Up at the front a line of makeshift desks, where interviewers are taking down the stories of relief applicants. You sit down on a bench in the back of the room. And there you wait, wondering if they're going to make you sell the radio, which wouldn't bring in enough to feed the family two days.
>
> You're apt to wait a long time — and it doesn't improve your morale. Eventually you get your turn. Maybe the questions aren't so bad, but you hate answering them, just the same. If the person asking the questions were sympathetic and tactful, qualified by experience and temperament for the job, it might not be so bad. But the person asking those questions is just another victim of the depression like yourself. He's apt to be without experience or training. Possibly he hates the job — and hates you because you're part of it. He, too, may be worried about next week's pay check.
>
> Finally, you get out — and go home and wait. An investigator will call at your home — another "somebody on work relief," who got the job because he needed a job and not because he was qualified for it — and asks more questions.
>
> Eventually, the idea is that you'll have some sort of work relief job.

In August the average relief given per family was $23. This meant that virtually everything was spent on food, which had risen in price. There was nothing for rent, and evictions had risen to "an alarming rate." Medical care, utilities, fuel, carfare, and other little necessary expenses were not covered. Lorena Hickok visited a woman who was trying to heat milk for her two children. The gas for the stove had been shut off and she could not use a borrowed electric grill because the fuses had blown and the landlord refused to replace them. She was burning newspapers under the pan.

There was almost no relief for unmarried people. Mary Simkhovitch of Greenwich House said single women were "just discards." Three to six of them would live in one room on the earnings of the woman with a job, "just managing to keep alive." They could no longer afford the YWCA or the settlement houses. Simkhovitch had marched in an unemployment parade to City Hall the other day.

Politics, clearly, was a problem in relief administration. The *World-Telegram* had run an exposé asserting that Tammany Hall had relief locked up. Hickok thought this an exaggeration, though the machine and the Catholic Church were influential. She did not see much evidence of misuse of funds, and she thought lack of money a much more serious problem than political influence.

Hickok closed her letter to Hopkins with field evidence on the health, physical and emotional, of the jobless. A public health nurse had seen a relief family of ten in which eight members had T.B. A case supervisor was disturbed about "queer complexes and nervous disorders" because so many people had been "stretched beyond the breaking point." A settlement-house kindergarten teacher found the children "excitable and high-strung." She thought it due to "the distress at home."[5]

5

The jobless and those who ministered to them were especially sensitive to the weather. They looked forward to the warmth of spring and the dog days of summer; fall made them uneasy and they dreaded the cold of winter. The winter of 1932–1933 had been absolutely harrowing and could not be put out of mind. Even if economic recovery had been going well in the fall of 1933, Hopkins and his people at FERA would have had to be edgy as they contemplated the prospective winter months, which, in fact, were to be unusually cold, reaching 56° below zero in New England. But things were *not* going well.

There had been a "boomlet" during the summer, but the air had gone out of it by Labor Day. The NRA, despite General Johnson's pyrotechnics, was simply not generating a significant business recovery and expansion of employment. It had caused higher prices, which businessmen and some consumers had anticipated during the summer and had hedged against by forward buying. PWA was inherently a long-term program: The Grand Coulee Dam on the Columbia River, the All-American Canal in Southern California, the Triborough Bridge and the Midtown-Hudson Tunnel in New York City, and the highway from the Shenandoah to the Great Smokies could not be built or the electrification of the Pennsylvania Railroad between Wilmington and Washington be completed in a few months. Ickes's insistence that these and other projects must be carefully planned and honestly carried out added nothing to the speed at which they were set in motion.

Winfield Riefler, who had been the chief economist for the Federal Reserve Board, prepared weekly economic analyses for Roosevelt's National Emergency Council. The analysis for August 22, 1933, was cheerful and stressed a counterseasonal increase in industrial production. The tone of the September 12 report was "on the one hand this and on the other hand that." Riefler wrote on October 3, "September closed with a note of apprehension in the air." On September 27, Secretary of the Treasury William H. Woodin had five cabinet members and their wives to dinner. Afterward, Ickes confided to his diary, the men went upstairs for coffee, cigars, and serious talk. Woodin, who had been away ill during much of the summer, had been very optimistic about the economy before he left. "Last night he was worried and frankly said so. He doesn't like the situation. . . . The financial men in New York were all down in the mouth. . . ." Marriner S. Eccles, the imaginative Utah banker who made a Keynesian analysis of the economic collapse before Keynes and who was to become chairman of the Federal Reserve Board, was convinced that there was a "Roosevelt Depression" in the fall of 1933.

The deepening gloom, of course, quickly reached FERA headquarters. The staff, particularly Williams, was convinced that it was necessary to develop a large emergency work-relief program that would be labor intensive and would stimulate purchasing power in order to tide the nation over the winter. Hopkins agreed, but he was doubtful of his ability to persuade Roosevelt. Such a proposal was certain to arouse conservative opposition, but more important politically, the American Federation of Labor would probably come out against it for providing work to reliefers that might be performed by union members.

Hopkins arrived in Chicago by rail on Saturday, October 28, to lunch with President Robert Maynard Hutchins of the University of Chicago and to attend a football game. Frank Bane, who had been working with Williams, and Louis Brownlow, the head of the Public Administration Clearing House, met him at the station and strongly urged the emergency program. Hopkins was impressed but said he could not figure out a way to get over the labor hurdle with Roosevelt. When he got to Kansas City, he received a call from Williams in Madison, Wisconsin. The latter had consulted with John R. Commons, the noted labor historian at the University of Wisconsin, who had dug up an 1898 statement by Samuel Gompers advocating a work-relief program for the unemployed, exactly what FERA was hoping to develop. Hopkins immediately arranged to see Roosevelt upon his return to Washington. The President accepted the idea at once. He asked Hopkins how many jobs he would create, and was told about 4 million. Roosevelt said that meant $400 million and that Hopkins ought to get it from the unexpended PWA balance.

On the weekend of November 4–5, Hopkins gathered Bane, Brownlow, Williams, Baker, Gill, and several others at the Powhatan Hotel in Washington and they drew up the plans for the Civil Works Administration (CWA). At noon on Monday, November 6, Hopkins met with Secretaries Perkins, Wallace, and Ickes at the Interior Department. He wanted to put 2 million people to work by November 15 and another 2 million by December 1, a spectacular schedule. There would be triangular funding — roughly equal amounts from the FERA and PWA and lesser contributions by the states and municipalities. They agreed, Ickes wrote, that "we really are in a very critical condition and that something drastic and immediate ought to be done." While Ickes was suspicious of Hopkins and thought the proposal "would put a serious crimp in the balance of our public works fund," he agreed to give CWA $400 million.

The President issued the executive order creating the Civil Works Administration on November 8, 1933. On November 11, Hopkins, Ickes, and their staffs met to draw up lines of demarcation between PWA and CWA and to fix standards for the latter. They agreed that CWA projects would be on force account with the government as employer, that is, no contracts would be let to private construction firms. Thus, the undertakings would be secondary; there would be no construction of buildings, sewers, waterworks, incinerators, or bridges. The reliefers would work 30 hours a week and would receive PWA pay scales.

In effect, the FERA, including the state relief administrations, turned itself into the CWA. The reorganization was completed by November 15. While Hopkins failed to achieve his fantastic employment schedule, he did not miss by much. On December 9, 2.3 million persons were employed on civil works and the goal of 4 million was reached around December 15. This speed was made possible by dropping the means test for eligibility. At the peak in January 1934, there were 4,264,000 people at work on CWA projects. Liquidation began in mid-February and CWA officially closed down on July 14, 1934.

The achievements of CWA were impressive. It helped bring the nation through a rugged winter with no significant unrest, in fact, with a sharp rise in morale among the jobless, who much preferred work relief to direct relief. The cost was relatively low, approximately $1 billion: $825 million in federal funds from FERA and PWA and $175 million from the states and localities. About three fourths of these expenditures went for wages, helping to support purchasing power, and about one fourth for other things, including materials. The 180,000 projects included many that added to the country's stock of capital equipment — 500,000 miles of secondary roads, 40,000 schoolhouses built or improved, thousands of playgrounds, almost 500 new and 500 improved airports. CWA also developed parks, cleared waterways, attacked insect pests, built swimming pools, and put scholars, writers, and artists to work in literary and cultural endeavors. Finally, the CWA experience was to prove useful later in developing the Works Progress Administration.

But there were shortcomings. The haste with which people were put to work meant that many were assigned to ill-conceived projects and engaged in what the hostile press called "leaf-raking." Similarly, Hopkins was unable to prevent political interference and graft in many localities, though he exposed and attacked it when he found it. Finally, the PWA wage scales that CWA paid proved unworkable in the South.

Hopkins's objective was a wage-and-hour structure that would give CWA workers enough income to live on, but not enough to undermine their incentive to take private employment. The original wage scales for manual labor were as follows:

	SOUTH	CENTRAL	NORTH
Skilled	$1.00	$1.10	$1.20
Unskilled	.40	.45	.50

The clerical and white-collar weekly rates were $12 in the South, $15 in the central zone, and $18 in the North (including the West). Manual workers could work maxima of 30 hours weekly and 8 hours daily. The clerical week was no more than 39 hours. In the South the unskilled rate of 40 cents was higher than many workers received in private employment, and the differential was widened in many localities by the overclassification of workers as skilled, entitling them to the $1 rate. There were howls of protest from southern employers and politicians. In addition, the high wages drained off CWA funds rapidly. Thus, in January 1934, Hopkins cut the workweek to 24 hours in cities and 15 hours in rural areas. On March 2, CWA junked the wage scale and paid a flat 30 cents an hour unless the prevailing wage was higher.

Despite these failings, Searle F. Charles has written, "CWA stands out in all American history as one of the greatest peacetime administrative feats ever completed." The army was much interested in learning from it for the purpose of wartime mobilization and assigned a Corps of Engineers officer to study CWA. Lieutenant Colonel John C. H. Lee wrote:

> The accomplishments of the C.W.A. were possible through the arduous efforts of the young administrator and the group of able young assistants which he has assembled and inspired. They have worked daily long into the night with a morale easily comparable to that of a war emergency. These assistants address Mr. Hopkins fondly as "Harry." There is no rigidity or formality in their staff conferences with him, yet he holds their respect, confidence, and seemingly whole-souled cooperation. Practically all have had active experience in social welfare or other work of a relief nature. Insofar as such a class of workers was available, Mr. Hopkins has assembled a corps of professionals for the fulfillment of the President's relief program.
>
> On the whole, it is apparent that the mission of the Civil Works Administrator had been accomplished by 15 February 1934. His program had put over four million persons to work, thereby directly benefiting probably twelve million people otherwise dependent upon direct relief. The program put some seven hundred million dollars into general circulation. Such losses as occurred were negligible, on a percentage basis, and even those losses were probably added to the pur-

> chasing power of the country. Thus, Mr. Hopkins' loose fluidity of organization was justified by the results achieved. It enabled him to engage for employment in two months nearly as many persons as were enlisted and called to the colors during our year and a half of World War mobilization, and to disburse to them weekly, a higher average rate of wages than Army or Navy pay.[6]

6

As the CWA was phased out in the spring of 1934, FERA took over its uncompleted projects and itself launched many new ones. Thus, FERA now became a predominantly work-relief program. The hastily contrived "leaf-raking" projects of 1933 gave way to careful planning and an increasing number of unemployed architects, engineers, technicians, and others with special skills were engaged in this effort. When FERA went out of business in the summer of 1935, it had completed almost 240,000 projects at a cost of $1.3 billion. The monthly average number employed was 2 million and the top of 2,446,000 was reached in January 1935.

The accomplishments in 1934–1935 were impressive: 5000 new public buildings, 30 percent of them schools; 200,000 miles of roads and 44,000 miles of highways built or repaired; 7000 bridges; 2700 miles of sanitary and storm sewers; 9000 miles of drainage, irrigation, and other ditches; 2000 miles of levees; 1000 miles of water mains; 400 pumping stations; 2000 playgrounds; 800 parks; over 350 swimming pools; more than 4000 athletic fields. In addition, FERA workers processed 195 million pounds of meat and preserved 60 million pounds of fruits and vegetables. They manufactured 1 million articles of infant wear, 3.5 million dresses, over 1 million shirts, 1,250,000 mattresses, 5 million pillow cases, and 4 million sheets. The food and textile products were distributed to families on relief. FERA gave over 1 million immunization shots against typhoid, smallpox, diphtheria, and scarlet fever. It taught more than half a million people to read and write. It also provided a substantial amount of job training and a fair amount of cultural activity.

Two of these activities proved especially controversial — production-for-use and white-collar projects. Hopkins, recognizing that the jobless needed mattresses, took 250,000 bales of surplus cotton from the Agricultural Adjustment Administration, bought ticking in the open market, and put unemployed women to work sewing mattresses by hand in abandoned factories. They were then given to the destitute. The National Association of Manufacturers denounced this as "socialism," competing with the free enterprise system. Hopkins observed that the poor needed mattresses and had no money with which to buy them. The conservative press, exploiting deep-seated anti-intellectualism in the United States, had a field day with projects involving teachers, artists, and scholars. Nothing enraged Hopkins more. "They are damn good projects. . . . Some people make fun of people who speak a foreign language and dumb people criticize something they don't understand — God damn it!" He pointed out that painters and ditch-diggers shared the need to eat.

In the latter stages of FERA, old-line Democratic politicians increasingly sought to exploit the relief organizations in their states to their own political advantage and kept Hopkins constantly at bay. He fought skirmishes and battles with, among others, Vice President John Nance Garner of Texas, Senator Theodore Bilbo of Mississippi, Senator Pat McCarran of Nevada, Senator James E. Murray of Montana, and Governor Martin L. Davey of Ohio. Davey, who was the most arrogant of the lot, took over the state relief administration. Hopkins, with Roosevelt's support, federalized the Ohio agency. Davey threatened that he would have Hopkins arrested if he set foot in the state. Hopkins promptly went to Cleveland and nothing happened.[7]

7

Roosevelt and Hopkins had regarded FERA as an emergency program that they hoped would soon work itself out of business. But by the spring of 1934, it was evident that the country would continue to confront massive unemployment and that more permanent legislation to relieve the jobless must be planned. Two other important proposals were in a similar state. The movement to establish a system of unemployment insurance had picked up steam between 1932, when Wisconsin enacted the first state law, and early 1934, when Senator Robert F. Wagner of New York and Representative David J. Lewis of Maryland introduced a bill that the Department of Labor had drafted. Senator Clarence C. Dill of Washington and Representative William P. Connery, Jr., of Massachusetts had proposed legislation in 1932 to establish a system of old-age pensions. By the spring of 1934, the House had passed the Dill-Connery bill and the Senate Pensions Committee had reported it favorably.

Roosevelt, while committed in principle to all three ideas, was dissatisfied with details of both legislative proposals and felt that there should be a comprehensive review of economic security within the executive branch before Congress took any action. Hopkins, Miss Perkins, and Assistant Secretary of Labor Arthur J. Altmeyer, who was fully familiar with the Wisconsin experience, drafted an executive order that the President issued on June 29, 1934, creating the Committee on Economic Security. It was to study the problem of security broadly and report to the President with legislative proposals by December 1, 1934. FERA would provide the funding.[8]

Two

The Social Security Act

In 1912 Charles McCarthy, head of the Wisconsin Legislative Reference Department, wrote *The Wisconsin Idea.* During the Progressive Era, Wisconsin led all the other states in pioneering reform, in becoming, as Theodore Roosevelt noted in the introduction to the volume, "a laboratory for wise experimental legislation aiming to secure the social and political betterment of the people as a whole." There were, McCarthy pointed out, two basic reasons for this. One was bold and vigorous political leadership, notably in the person of Robert M. La Follette, who was governor and later United States senator. The other was the close and effective relationship between the state government and the state university in the drafting and administration of the laws. An appendix to McCarthy's book lists dozens of members of the University of Wisconsin faculty who also served the state in their many fields of specialization. Among them was "J. R. Commons. Professor of political economy."

John R. Commons was the embodiment of the Wisconsin Idea and a good deal else besides. If he had a weakness, it was a penchant for abstruse thinking at the juncture of economics and law, which he hitched to a prolix style of prose. It is uncertain whether anyone has ever fully understood *The Legal Foundations of Capitalism* or *Institutional Economics, Its Place in Political Economy.* But these products of his later years may be forgiven, except, perhaps, by the publisher, in someone whose other accomplishments were so formidable.

Commons was one of the trinity of great American institutional economists of the first part of the twentieth century, along with Thorstein Veblen and Wesley C. Mitchell. An early romance with orthodox economic theory ended when Wesleyan University fired him from his first teaching job because his students were bored by the subject's empty formalism. Commons's mind and style were wholly inductive, working from the particular to the general. With the help of his students at the University of Wisconsin, he ran a gigantic vacuum cleaner that picked up facts and documents about American economic institutions. One monument was *A Documentary History of American Industrial Society,* published in eleven volumes in 1910–1911. Another, by "John R. Commons and Associates," was the standard *History of Labour in the United States,* the first two volumes of which appeared in 1918 and the last two by 1935. Commons was as interested in generalizing from as in gathering particular facts. His essays contain many illuminating insights, particularly into American economic history.

Veblen and Mitchell were essentially intellectual. Commons differed in that for him thought and action were inseparable. Since he considered the unbridled capitalism of his time, given his democratic value system, inequitable and dangerous, he thrust himself into many movements for its reform. He was a founder in 1906 of the American Association for Labor Legislation (AALL), which pushed workmen's compensation, industrial safety, unemployment insurance, and old-age pensions. John B. Andrews, who led the AALL from 1908 to 1943, had been one of his students. Commons, of course, worked closely with La Follette and the Progressive Movement in Wisconsin in drafting and administering that state's labor and social legislation. He was a pioneer, a man who was invariably off launching a new project. Like George Washington, he acquired a "father" image. He became the "father" of American labor history and the "father" of the first social insurance system to emerge, workmen's compensation.

While his intellectual and institutional output was remarkable, Commons's most lasting contribution was the people he trained and inspired. Over his many years of teaching at Madison he attracted an extraordinary group of students. With the New Deal, the Wisconsin Idea went national. It was not just that Bob La Follette, Jr., sat in his father's seat in the Senate and was the leading spokesman, along with Senators Wagner and Costigan, for labor and social legislation or that his brother Phil, the governor of Wisconsin, had called the legislature into special session to enact the nation's first unemployment insurance law in 1932 (Commons had written the original version in 1921, his student Paul Raushenbush had redrafted it in 1931, and another student, Assemblyman Harold M. Groves, had introduced the bill). It was also because the nation was now, at last, ready to give serious consideration to ideas that John R. had advanced a generation earlier and because many of the people who knew most about these matters were his former students.

It was no coincidence that Miss Perkins asked Arthur J. Altmeyer to become assistant secretary of labor in 1934 and almost at once put him in charge of work related to the Committee on Economic Security, which she chaired. Altmeyer was from Wisconsin, had taken his Ph.D. with Commons, and had been his research assistant. In the twenties he had been secretary of the Wisconsin Industrial Commission, charged with administering the state's labor laws. He had never forgotten a point Commons had made with him: "Administration is legislation in action." Altmeyer was a superb administrator and he would become, as will be noted later, the architect of that administrative masterpiece, the social security system of the United States.

Nor was it a coincidence that Altmeyer placed a call to Madison on July 24, 1934, to offer the chairman of the Economics Department at the University of Wisconsin, Edwin E. Witte, the executive directorship of the Committee on Economic Security. Witte, characteristically, was on the job in the Walker-Johnson Building in Washington on July 26. He, of course, had been a student of Commons. Witte was now forty-seven, extremely energetic, utterly dedicated, direct and self-effacing in manner. He had served on the Wisconsin Industrial Commission, had been head of the Wisconsin Legislative Reference Library for eleven years, which gave him insight into the legislative process, and had been active in the American Association for Labor Legislation. He was a scholar of distinction and had published a basic study, *The Government in Labor Disputes,* in 1932. With the possible exception of Felix Frankfurter, he was the nation's leading authority on the labor injunction and had helped draft the Norris–La Guardia Act of 1932. Altmeyer's choice was flawless.[1]

1

Insecurity for the wage earner and his family is a characteristic of all capitalist industrial societies. The principal risks are loss of income arising from unemployment; the inability to obtain or to perform work because of old age; incapacity for employment due to illness off the job; accidents or sickness caused by the job that lead to loss of income, medical costs, and, in some cases, the need for rehabilitation; support for mothers and children as a consequence of loss of the male breadwinner; and a basic disability for employment arising out of a handicap, such as blindness. With the development of industrialism during the nineteenth century, the number of persons in need in these categories rose significantly in all the advanced nations. There was early realization that many of these risks could be mitigated by application of the insurance principle. At the outset, particularly in Europe, but also in the United States, such programs were private, instituted by insurance companies, trade unions, and progressive employers. However, private plans were seriously defective in a variety of ways, among them low benefit payments and severely restricted coverage.

Thus, in Europe there emerged early on the realization that the state must establish systems of *social* insurance to protect the worker and his family against the hazards of industrial life. The most dramatic innovations occurred, first, in Bismarck's Germany in 1883 with comprehensive health insurance and in 1884 with workmen's compensation and, second, in Britain under the Lloyd George government in 1911 with unemployment insurance. Over the years these nations extended their systems and Europe as a whole followed their lead, as did Australasia and, to a lesser extent, Latin America. By the time of the Great Depression, therefore, almost all of the world's industrial nations had reasonably comprehensive social insurance programs covering the risks of industrial life.

The United States was the exception. Leaving aside the complexities of the federal system and constitutional impediments imposed by a hostile judiciary, the fundamental obstacle was an ingrained philosophical commitment to individualism, or, as Roy Lubove has phrased it by adapting an old trade-union term, "the constraints of voluntarism." This ideology was expressed in a variety of precepts: a man was out of work because he was lazy; children bore the responsibility for looking after their aged parents; doctors under a fee-for-service system provided free or low-cost care for the poor; local charities tended to the indigent and the handicapped; the employer's task was to produce goods and sell them at a profit, not to look after the welfare of his employees; workers, Gompers taught, must rely upon their own unions and reject the advice of intellectuals and the authority of a hostile government. At a more general level, "compulsory" social insurance deprived man of his individual freedom. Even worse, it was an "alien" import, which during World War I was identified with the enemy, Germany. At the same time, it smacked of "Marxian socialism."

The social insurance movement in the United States began during the Progressive Era with the establishment of the American Association for Labor Legislation in 1906. At the outset, AALL concentrated on the most obvious, dramatic, and politically amenable issue, industrial injury and disease. Starting in 1911, a number of the more advanced states enacted workmen's compensation laws and the federal government improved the statute covering its own employees. The Association also pushed the industrial safety movement in industry in order to prevent job-related accidents and disease. Commons and Andrews sought to "Americanize" the compensation laws by introducing the principle of experience or merit rating, that is, offering the employer the incentive of a lower premium if he prevented injuries and illnesses.

Having enjoyed a good deal of success with workmen's compensation, AALL next moved to establish state health insurance programs on the German model. Since this was the period of World War I, the timing could not have been worse. Organized medicine became aroused and fought these proposals, particularly in bitter legislative battles in New York and California. The American Medical Association won a total victory over the American Association for Labor Legislation. Not only did the doctors realize their own formidable political power, they also dealt a devastating blow to the entire social insurance movement. The latter lapsed into inactivity in the hostile decade of the twenties, excepting only modest stirring in the area of old-age pensions. The number of old people was now very large, their proportion of the population was increasing, and their financial needs were serious. The Fraternal Order of Eagles urged the enactment of state pension laws, and Abraham Epstein directed the campaign. In 1927 he founded the American Association for Old Age Security. By the end of the decade eight states had passed laws that allowed their counties to pay pensions, two of which provided for some state financial aid.

The Great Depression reenergized the impulse for social insurance. Massive joblessness, widespread poverty, and general financial insolvency sharpened the needs. Most obvious was the call for unemployment insurance either as an alternative or as a supplement to relief; the aged, who suffered great misery, demanded old-age pensions; a rising incidence of illness was accompanied by a decreasing ability to pay for its care; many private plans went broke; and so on. Roosevelt, who sensed these needs, committed himself to both old-age pensions and unemployment insurance in 1930, and Miss Perkins had been a supporter of comprehensive social insurance much earlier. Wisconsin, as noted above, enacted the Groves bill in 1932. Ohio, though it failed to take action, in the same year brought out a basic study of unemployment insurance, known as the "Ohio plan," which reflected the work of a noted authority, I. M. Rubinow, and a former student of Commons, William M. Leiserson. In 1932, as well, the AFL broke with the Gompers tradition and supported unemployment insurance. The Democratic platform in 1932 endorsed state unemployment and old-age insurance systems. With the New Deal, serious proposals for federal unemployment and old-age programs were introduced into Congress and became the subjects of hearings. The volume and quality of research increased markedly, both inside and outside the universities. Aside from the older authorities, like Commons and his followers, including Andrews as well as Rubinow, a new group of experts emerged. Epstein published a basic study, *Insecurity: A Challenge to America,* in 1933. Groups led by Alvin H. Hansen at the University of Minnesota, Paul H. Douglas at the University of Chicago, and Bryce W. Stewart at Industrial Relations Counselors, Inc., worked and published on unemployment insurance. Edgar L. Sydenstricker of the Milbank Memorial Fund concentrated on health insurance. Barbara N. Armstrong of the University of California brought out an important book in 1932, *Insuring the Essentials.* There were, of course, many other scholars at work in these fields as well as an enormous popular literature.

By 1934, Roosevelt recognized that the time was ripe for federal action. But he insisted that the program should be comprehensive and should draw upon the experts and the knowledge now available in the United States.[2]

2

Franklin Roosevelt's attitude toward social insurance was to prove crucial to the development of the legislation. It is doubtful that any other domestic question of the thirties interested him as much or aroused so deep a personal commitment. Since he felt that the economy ultimately would recover, he regarded his early programs, like NRA, AAA, PWA, and FERA, as "emergency" arrangements that would be wiped off the statute books when they were no longer needed. The National Labor Relations Act, which Senator Wagner developed, won Roosevelt's tardy support but lay in an area peripheral to his interests. He regarded social insurance, or, as it ultimately came to be called, social security, as his principal monument to domestic innovation. And it sat at the very center of his policy interests.

He had given the social insurance issues a great deal of thought, had discussed them at length with Miss Perkins and to a lesser extent with other authorities, including the great British expert, Sir William Beveridge, involved himself closely in the drafting process, and imprinted his unmistakable stamp upon the legislation. While Roosevelt needed technical guidance, particularly on the actuarial side and on the economic consequences of massive deferred transfer payments, he constructed the grand design.

Roosevelt's original intention was that the program should be inclusive. This meant a single package that at the minimum contained old-age pensions, unemployment insurance, and categorical programs to assist those groups that were unable to provide for themselves. He also wanted to establish comprehensive health insurance until he became convinced that it was politically impossible. At the outset he entertained Hopkins's idea that work relief should be linked to unemployment compensation, though they would later be separated. Roosevelt felt that coverage should be universal, that all Americans should be entitled to these benefits. While Miss Perkins admired the boldness of the concept, she was alarmed by the administrative and financing complications. Roosevelt liked to look at the world through the eyes of the farmer from Dutchess County. He described the administrative arrangement he wanted to Miss Perkins this way:

> The system ought to be operated through the post offices. Just simple and natural — nothing elaborate or alarming about it. The rural free delivery carrier ought to bring papers to the door and pick them up after they are filled out. The rural free delivery carrier ought to give each child his social insurance number and his policy or whatever takes the place of a policy. The rural free delivery carrier ought to be the one who picks up the claim of the man who is unemployed, or the old lady who wants old-age insurance benefits.

Roosevelt coined a phrase to describe this comprehensive system — "from the cradle to the grave insurance." He was rather annoyed in 1942 when the Beveridge Plan was announced with fanfare in Britain as providing "cradle to the grave" protection.

Roosevelt insisted that the two basic systems should be self-supporting, that they should not depend upon general tax revenues. In short, they must be contributory, they must be work-related, and employers and employees must pay for the benefits the workers would receive. This appealed to him on several grounds. One was that the programs would be more acceptable politically. The other was that the worker would be entitled to his benefit as a matter of right, as something he had earned by work rather than as a handout from the government based upon a means test. While strong economic arguments for doing otherwise were advanced both in 1934 and since, Roosevelt did not consider financing an economic question. As he said after the passage of the act, "We put those payroll contributions there so as to give the contributors a legal, moral, and political right to collect their pensions and their unemployment benefits. With those taxes in there, no damn politician can ever scrap my social security program."

On June 8, 1934, the President sent a special message to Congress reviewing accomplishments and setting goals. "Among our objectives," he declared, "I place the security of men, women, and children of the Nation first." In this context he dealt with housing, the development of natural resources, and "security against the hazards and vicissitudes of life." Of this last he wrote,

> Next winter we may well undertake the great task of furthering the security of the citizen and his family through social insurance.
>
> This is not an untried experiment. Lessons of experience are available from States, from industries, and from many Nations of the civilized world. The various types of social insurance are interrelated; and I think it is difficult to attempt to solve them piecemeal. Hence, I am

looking for a sound means which I can recommend to provide at once security against several of the great disturbing factors in life — especially those which relate to unemployment and old age. I believe there should be a maximum of cooperation between States and the Federal Government. I believe that the funds necessary to provide this insurance should be raised by contribution rather than by an increase in general taxation. Above all, I am convinced that social insurance should be national in scope, although the several States should meet at least a large portion of the cost of management, leaving to the Federal Government the responsibility of investing, maintaining and safeguarding the funds constituting the necessary insurance reserves.

I have commenced to make, with the greatest care, the necessary actuarial and other studies necessary for the formulation of plans for the consideration of the 74th Congress.

This last point was of great significance. Roosevelt, Miss Perkins wrote, "was aware that 1936 was not too far away, that there might be a change of administration." He was determined that "*his* program" must be enacted in 1935. The bill must be ready when the new Congress convened in January. This put the Committee on Economic Security in a time vise; it had less than six months in which to make the basic studies, reach consensus, and draft the legislation.[3]

3

The executive order on economic security that Roosevelt issued on June 29, 1934, established a four-level arrangement. He intended that it should perform a variety of functions: first and foremost, to draft the legislation; second, to unify the interested federal agencies behind the program; third, to tap the expert resources of the government itself, markedly improved by the inflow of talent in 1933–1934; fourth, to obtain expert advice from outside the government; and, finally, to prepare the country and the Congress to accept the legislation. The setup was cumbersome, but, by and large, it served all these objectives.

The Committee on Economic Security (CES) constituted the top level and consisted of Secretary of Labor Perkins, Secretary of the Treasury Henry Morgenthau, Jr., Secretary of Agriculture Henry A. Wallace, Attorney General Homer S. Cummings, and FERA Administrator Hopkins. Miss Perkins, because of her chairmanship, her commitment, and Roosevelt's urging, was the key member. She gave this program top priority over her many other duties, assumed the basic responsibility, was faithful about attending meetings, and, in the later stages, knocked heads together to reach consensus. Morgenthau was sympathetic though not much involved. When he could not be present at meetings, he sent Treasury officials Jacob Viner or Josephine Roche in his place. Much the same can be said of Wallace; Undersecretary Rexford G. Tugwell substituted for him. Cummings never came to a meeting, but was represented by his assistant, Alexander Holtzoff, who was under instructions to vote as Miss Perkins wished. Hopkins was much interested and supportive, attended all meetings after returning from a summer trip to Europe, and provided the funds and office space for Witte's staff.

The Technical Board on Economic Security, made up of about twenty top-level government experts under the chairmanship of Altmeyer, constituted the second echelon. Among the luminaries were Murray W. Latimer, chairman of the Railroad Retirement Board; Isador Lubin, commissioner of Labor Statistics; Winfield Riefler, chairman of the Central Statistical Board and economist for the National Emergency Council; Alvin H. Hansen, chief economic analyst for the State Department; William M. Leiserson, chairman of the National Mediation Board; Harry A. Millis, member of the National Labor Relations Board; H. J. Oliphant, solicitor of the Treasury; H. R. Tolley of Agriculture; Aubrey Williams and Corrington Gill of FERA; and Thomas H. Eliot, assistant solicitor in the Labor Department and counsel to CES. The Technical Board broke itself into an executive committee and specialized groups on unemployment insurance, old-age security, public employment and relief, and medical care. Witte was in daily contact with Altmeyer and consulted regularly with these committees. Reports from outside experts and the staff as well as recommendations on policy were screened by the Technical Board before moving on to CES.

The third level was the Advisory Council. The executive order simply specified the title without defining its composition or functions. No one ever quite figured out what to do about it. The Council was established in conjunction with a public National Conference on Economic Security, held in Washington on November 14–15. The Council consisted of twenty prominent citizens from various walks of life, with President Frank P. Graham of the University of North Carolina as chairman. In Witte's view, neither the Conference nor the Council proved helpful and may even have been harmful in exposing differences in views, particularly over unemployment insurance.

The final layer consisted of Witte, his staff, and the groups of outside experts he set up to study and report on specific aspects of economic security. Witte himself participated in meetings of CES, the Technical Board, and the Council. Bryce Stewart and the research staff at Industrial Relations Counselors worked on unemployment insurance; Barbara N. Armstrong, with Murray Latimer and J. Douglas Brown of Princeton as advisers, made the study of old age; Edgar L. Sydenstricker and Dr. I. S. Falk, also of the Milbank Fund, worked on health insurance and medical care; Emerson Ross of FERA and a group from that agency prepared material on public employment; Meredith B. Givens of the Social Science Research Council headed a group that analyzed employment opportunities; Katherine Lenroot and Martha Eliott of the Children's Bureau studied the security of children; Louis H. Bean of the Department of Agriculture did some work on farmers and agricultural labor; O. S. Powell of the Federal Reserve Bank of Minneapolis and Alan R. Sweezy of the Treasury advised on the management of reserve funds; Joseph P. Harris of the University of Washington studied financing; and Thomas Eliot was concerned with constitutional and legal questions as well as with drafting the bill. There was also a statistical group and a consulting body of actuaries, the latter from the universities and industry. The timing of reports proved difficult and, in some cases, impossible. That is, CES and Witte were under an almost inflexible schedule, and several of the study groups, given the complexity of their problems and the commitments of busy people, were unable to provide written reports in time, though they advised Witte orally of their thinking. Ultimately, the important studies were delivered and, excepting health insurance, were published.

Unemployment insurance was the overriding question before CES and its subordinate bodies. As will be pointed out shortly, however, the public and Congress were much more concerned with assistance for the aged. The obvious justification for launching an unemployment compensation system was current joblessness. The Bureau of Labor Statistics later estimated unemployment in 1934 at 11,340,000.

Aside from the inherently tough policy questions raised by unemployment insurance, the existence of the Wisconsin statute and its unusual features stoked the controversy. The Commons group, the La Follette movement, and the Wisconsin Federation of Labor were extremely anxious to preserve the state law in the face of federal legislation. The Wagner-Lewis bill, introduced into Congress with Administration support in February 1934, would have done so by imposing a 5 percent federal payroll tax on employers that could be offset by contributions to a state unemployment insurance fund. The basic objective of the Wisconsin law was to prevent unemployment by offering the employer a lower contribution rate for stabilizing employment in his plant. It set up two systems: The employer might elect an individual plant reserve fund, the rate determined by his experience with unemployment, or, failing that choice, he must pay into a pooled state fund at a fixed rate. Many experts, however, were unpersuaded either that state responsibility for unemployment insurance was sound national policy or that experience rating would stabilize employment.

CES wrestled with a series of difficult policy questions. The first, as noted, was whether the system should be wholly federal or a mixed federal-state arrangement. If the latter won out, it would raise a second question: Should basic authority be conferred upon the states, as in Wagner-Lewis, or should the federal government impose national standards and pool state funds in the U.S. Treasury? Third, who should contribute: the employer alone, the employee and the employer, both in addition to the government? Fourth, should the Wisconsin example of experience rating be adopted? Finally, there were a number of other issues that, while important, did not generate so much controversy. They included the constitutionality of the statute, the contribution rate, the amount and duration of benefits, and the timing of the program.

In September, Stewart's study group at Industrial Relations Counselors reported in favor of a wholly national system, contributions from employer, employee, and the government, and an exception for entire industries and very large firms to permit them to set up independent funds. Witte, who felt himself bound by the President's June 8 message, favored a federal-state arrangement. The proposals went to the Technical Board's unemployment insurance committee, which opted for a federal system, contributions by employers and employees, and an exception for industries but not for individual employers. The executive committee of the Board made a preliminary report to CES on October 1. It preferred a national system "if constitutional"; no government contributions, contributions from the employer and "probably" the employee; at the outset only a single pooled fund, but "contracting out" by industry and firm with safeguards for the employees should be "explored"; benefit levels sufficient to support a family and payments only in cash for the exclusive purpose of unemployment insurance. CES took no action on October 1.

For the next month and a half, Stewart's group, the staff, and the Technical Board studied these questions. At this time the "subsidy" variant emerged, evidently suggested by Emerson Ross of FERA. The two versions of a federal-state system shared the features of a uniform federal tax on payrolls and of state unemployment compensation laws. They differed in the manner in which the states would finance their systems. Under the Wagner-Lewis or "offset" plan, an employer who contributed to his state system was credited with that amount against his federal tax. In the "subsidy" arrangement the federal government would grant funds to a state to pay benefits on condition that the state law met federal standards. Those who favored a national program preferred the "subsidy" plan over Wagner-Lewis because it met the President's condition that funds should be deposited in the Treasury, because it was more readily convertible into a federal program, and because it would give the federal government more control over the states. At this time, Andrews, Epstein, and half a dozen state legislative committees complained about CES delay. However, the Technical Board remained divided, and its report to CES for the latter's meeting of November 9 merely discussed the advantages of the alternatives — federal, Wagner-Lewis, and "subsidy." CES reported to Roosevelt that it opposed a wholly federal system, but did not choose between the federal-state alternatives. The President publicly adopted this recommendation in his address to the National Conference on Economic Security at the White House on November 14.

The Advisory Council, which became active in late November, did not feel bound by the President's statement and a majority endorsed a federal program. Stewart continued to hold this view and was supported widely in business circles.

CES now had to wrestle with these thorny issues. While Roosevelt had originally set a December 1 deadline, he extended it to Christmas. CES met repeatedly in December, culminating in a six-hour session at Miss Perkins's home on the evening of either December 22 or 23. It opted for a federal-state system with loose national standards that would allow the states authority over most of the important features of the program. CES came out for the "offset" system, rather than the "subsidy." Morgenthau, supported by Wallace, insisted successfully upon low contribution rates during the first two years in order not to alarm businessmen. This was in the face of strong opposition from an expert group of supporters of unemployment insurance led by Paul Kellogg of the *Survey* and Frank Graham, who argued that the benefit levels would be grossly inadequate. Roosevelt would answer that "it is a matter of finance and we cannot eat the whole cake at one meal." CES, despite Morgenthau's opposition, recommended contributions exclusively from the employer. While a majority on the Committee opposed individual employer accounts, they felt the states should be free to adopt them if they wished but they would be required to meet special standards.

Miss Perkins and Hopkins reported these recommendations orally to the President on December 24. While Witte hoped that the controversy over unemployment insurance was ended, this was not to be the case. Both Wallace and Morgenthau submitted the CES recommendations to their assistants and there were cries of anguish in Agriculture and the Treasury. Tugwell and Jerome Frank, the general counsel of AAA, insisted on a national system despite Wallace's vote for a federal-state arrangement. Witte and Frank debated this heatedly for weeks. On January 15, 1935, however, Miss Perkins got Wallace to sign the final report. The Treasury was divided. A conservative group opposed the whole security program and a liberal group thought it did not go far enough. Morgenthau was the last member of CES to sign the report, and then only after a personal appeal from the Secretary of Labor.

The drafting of a program for the aged evoked no such controversy, though it raised the formidable question of constitutionality. The problems of old people were universally recognized. The first was that their absolute number as well as their percentage of the whole population had been rising sharply and demographic projections left no doubt that these trends would continue into the future. Second, employers discriminated widely against older workers, not at age sixty-five, but at forty or forty-five, so that persons in the higher age ranges found it difficult either to get or to retain jobs. As a result, a disproportionate share of the jobless was over forty. Finally, a very large percentage of the aged were destitute, or had extremely low incomes, or had exhausted their meager savings. Old people by 1934 were in desperate condition, needed government help to take care of their needs, and were making their voices heard politically, particularly in the Townsend Movement.

The entire CES apparatus agreed that two programs were necessary. One, old-age assistance, was addressed to the present needy among the aged, those who were incapable of contributing to an annuity system and who, therefore, must be supported by the government. Several of the states already had old-age assistance laws, which, while seriously inadequate, could serve as a base for a federal-state system. The federal government out of general revenues would grant each state the same amount the latter put up, but not to exceed $15 a month per recipient, provided that it enacted an assistance law that met federal standards of administration, coverage, and adequacy.

The other and in the long run far more important program was old-age insurance. The assumption was that support for the worker during his senior years was an insurable risk provided that it was linked to employment during his productive years. He must contribute himself so that he would earn a pension as a matter of right. The employer must also contribute as a cost of production, depreciating the worker as he would a machine. The system, everyone agreed, must be wholly federal because of high mobility in the labor force, inequities that would arise between varying state systems, the difficulty of handling numerous state reserve accounts, unfairness to employers in states with high contribution rates, and the efficiency of scale in administering an essentially routine insurance operation.

CES insisted that the system must be self-supporting, that is, contributions from employees and employers must cover both the cost of pensions and of administration. Thus, it was necessary to build up a reserve in the early years by keeping income higher than outgo. This would be accomplished by placing the present needy aged under the assistance program, by deferring full pensions for those who reached old age during the early years of the program, and by keeping pension levels low. The amount of the pension would be determined by the resources of the system, not by how much it cost to live. Thus, a person wholly dependent on this benefit would subsist in poverty; he and/or his employer must set aside other funds for old age during his earning years. A death benefit would be paid to survivors.

Everyone worried about the constitutionality of this insurance system. Miss Perkins considered the constitutional problem "almost insuperable." She drew comfort from a bit of advice she received from Justice Harlan Fiske Stone at a social occasion just before CES was formed. He admired her "greatly," considering her "the first real Secretary of Labor the country has ever had." She told Stone that she hoped to develop an old-age insurance system but was very unsure of the method because, she laughed, "Your Court tells us what the Constitution permits." Stone whispered, "The taxing power of the Federal Government, my dear; the taxing power is sufficient for everything you want and need." Thereafter she insisted at CES that the fund should be built up by taxation. But, Eliot asked, while Congress had the power to tax and to spend for the general welfare, were contributions made to a compulsory retirement system taxes within the meaning of the Constitution? The Supreme Court would answer this question in 1937.

Katherine Lenroot and Martha Eliott of the Children's Bureau did the basic work on child welfare and CES accepted their recommendations. In December 1934 about 8 million persons under age sixteen were on relief, approximately 40 percent of those receiving assistance. A large portion was in families headed by women because the fathers were dead or incapacitated or had deserted. The Bureau, therefore, devised a program for what was then called mothers' pensions or mothers' assistance, known later as Aid to Families with Dependent Children. Financial assistance would allow the mother to remain at home and look after her children rather than be forced into employment. Except for a few in the South, the states already had mothers' assistance laws, but most were permissive, aid was confined primarily to widows, benefit levels tended to be very low, and administration, usually at the county level, was spotty. CES proposed a three-way matching-fund program — federal, state, and local — in which the condition of federal support would be higher standards and improved state and local administration. The cost to the federal government was estimated at $25 million annually at the outset, an amount already exceeded by FERA relief to families headed by women. CES also urged the restoration of maternal and child health services that had lapsed in 1929, financial assistance for state and local child-welfare services, and support for state programs to assist crippled children.

No one urged a program of pensions for the blind upon CES, no studies were made, and the committee made no recommendations. The provision in the statute on aid for the blind came out of the Senate Finance Committee during legislative consideration of the bill.

The thorniest question CES faced was national health insurance. Roosevelt favored such a program. Hopkins, who had worked for years in the health field, was more concerned with health insurance than with any other form of social insurance. Sydenstricker and Falk, who headed the study group, thought it much needed and were prepared to recommend a comprehensive program. But nothing could be done because of powerful opposition by the American Medical Association (AMA). Since the public generally was uninformed and apathetic, organized medicine's position became automatically supreme. For a moment it seemed that there might be a split in AMA ranks, and the American College of Surgeons actually endorsed health insurance at its 1934 convention. Roosevelt, his personal physician, Dr. Marvin McIntyre, and Witte sought to exploit this apparent opening by trying to bring organized medicine into the planning of the program. But the doctors soon closed ranks against everything. The AMA had demonstrated its political power on this issue in the states at the end of World War I, and there was not the slightest doubt that it would have similar clout in Congress in 1935. Roosevelt, Miss Perkins, Hopkins, Altmeyer, and Witte recognized that if the bill included health insurance, the Administration ran the serious risk of losing unemployment insurance, old-age pensions, and the other programs that were politically feasible. They dropped health insurance.

There was a small salvaging operation. Dr. Michael M. Davis, director of medicine for the Julius Rosenwald Fund, suggested support for public health. State programs in this area were weak in the poorer states, especially in the South. Sydenstricker and Falk accepted the Davis idea promptly. The U.S. Public Health Service was delighted, and the proposal won the support of the AMA. CES recommended a grant of $10 million: $2 million directly to the Public Health Service and $8 million to be distributed by the Service to the states to strengthen their programs.

One important question that CES did not address was work relief. Hopkins and his people at FERA, impressed with their success with CWA, were eager to put a permanent comprehensive work-relief program into the economic security bill. Miss Perkins doubted that this was sound, but she accompanied Hopkins to the White House as he made his plea. "Although Hopkins was eloquent," she wrote, "the President at once saw that this would be the very thing he had been saying he was against for years — the dole." The works bill would be handled separately.

A final issue before CES was the location of the programs the economic security bill would launch. The FERA favored creation of a new Department of Public Welfare with cabinet status that would bring together all the new arrangements, including FERA. The Department of Labor, which hoped to gain control over several of the programs, opposed this idea. Ultimately, Miss Perkins and Hopkins worked out a settlement that the other members of CES accepted: The idea of a new department was dropped; Labor would get unemployment insurance, the social insurance board that would administer old-age pensions, and the Department's Children's Bureau would receive the secondary child-welfare programs; FERA would gain old-age assistance and aid to dependent children; the U.S. Public Health Service would receive the public health program; and the Treasury would be responsible for management of the funds.

The burden of writing the bill fell upon Thomas Eliot and it was, indeed, heavy. He would be severely criticized for his work, and Eliot readily admitted that the bill "was certainly not well drafted." In his defense one may note that he was twenty-seven, that he was innocent of the legislative process, that most of the proposals were new, that several of the programs were extremely complex, that he could not really start work until the final decisions were made late in December, and that several departments, especially Treasury and Agriculture, insisted upon their own language. In the light of these circumstances, Witte, the man whom Eliot described as "a walking encyclopedia on welfare and social insurance," stoutly defended Eliot's work. Miss Perkins wrote that "he did it well."

The President's plan to present the bill to the new Congress when it convened early in January 1935 was, of course, frustrated by the wrangling over unemployment insurance. On January 4 he promised that it would be delivered within ten days. As this period closed, Miss

Perkins insisted that her reluctant fellow members of CES, Wallace and Morgenthau, sign the report and they did. Though it bore the date of January 15, it was not actually delivered to the White House until January 17, 1935. Roosevelt told the press that the delay stemmed from the fact that a paragraph in the old-age title "sounds ambiguous, as if it were going to bust the Government."

On January 17, the President submitted the Economic Security bill to Congress. He urged speed, pointing out that the states would also have to act and that forty-four legislatures would be in session in 1935. There ensued a comic opera scene over who would have the honor of attaching his name to the bill. The Senate's choice was obvious — Wagner. The House was the problem. In a meeting with the Democratic leadership, Roosevelt suggested the same names as the bill in the last session — Wagner-Lewis. Speaker Joseph W. Byrns said that this was not acceptable to Chairman Robert L. Doughton of the Ways and Means Committee. Thus, both Lewis and Doughton introduced the bill into the House; Lewis got his in first because Doughton did not have a copy and had to borrow one from Wagner; but Doughton got a lower number and so the right to call it after himself at the hearings before Ways and Means. Ultimately this proved meaningless because the statute became known neither as Wagner-Lewis nor as Wagner-Doughton. It would be called the Social Security Act.[4]

4

Francis E. Townsend, a son of the Middle Border, was born in a log cabin on a homestead farm in northern Illinois in 1867, where his family scratched out a precarious livelihood. As a child, he walked two miles to a one-room schoolhouse to learn to read out of McGuffey (some would later wonder whether he ever acquired arithmetic). In 1885 the family moved to Nebraska. The drought depressed Francis, and he left home for Southern California in 1887. He tried his hand at hay farming and failed, then worked as a farmhand on the Newhall Ranch. He moved north to the State of Washington and became a teamster, but soon lost the job. He returned to Nebraska and high school in 1890, receiving a diploma three years later. He then homesteaded in Kansas. Tired of the struggle, he sold the farm in 1898 and rode the rails to Colorado, seeking his fortune in the Cripple Creek gold rush. All he found was a mucker's job during the warm months. He then sold iron stoves to sod farmers in Kansas.

In 1899, at age thirty-one, Townsend decided to become a doctor and enrolled at the Omaha Medical College. Four years later he took a job with the town physician in Belle Fourche, a frontier railhead cowtown in the Black Hills of South Dakota. He now made a good living and married a widowed nurse. He liked the town except for the wide-open saloons and brothels. He joined in a clumsy and unsuccessful effort to clean up Belle Fourche and, at the same time, declared himself a Socialist and became the hopeless Socialist candidate for state auditor. He began a habit he would continue later — writing letters to the editor of the local paper, here about town morals and Socialism. In 1908 he moved to nearby Nisland and combined farming with medicine. The next decade was sad: the Townsends lost their twin daughters to cholera, the farm failed, and the doctor had two dangerous bouts with peritonitis.

In 1919, after serious surgery, Townsend decided that he could not face another South Dakota winter. He migrated to Long Beach, California, and started medical practice anew. It was not successful, and he was forced to sell houses and lots on the side. In 1928 he became friendly with a shrewd real estate operator, Robert Earl Clements. In 1930, luckily, Townsend got a job with the Long Beach Health Department, giving home medical service to the indigent. It proved an overpowering experience.

Long Beach was special in that it had a very high concentration of people much like Francis Townsend — white, Anglo-Saxon, Protestant (on the fundamentalist side), rural and small town folk from the Middle West, many retired farmers, small businessmen, and professional people — who had put a little money aside and had migrated to Southern California, where living was cheap, to spend their declining years in the sunshine. The Los Angeles wisecrack was that Long Beach was a "cemetery with lights." It had been founded as a temperance colony and was the site of the state horseshoe-pitching contest. They said that 150,000 people showed up on Iowa Day for the picnic in Bixby Park, including many lonely old folks from other midwestern states who wanted to find someone to talk to. Iowa jokes were the blue-plate special: When you met a stranger in Long Beach, you asked, "What part of Iowa are you from?" The town was said to be

"Iowa's seaport." The transcontinental trains on Iowa Day were supposed to run nonstop from Des Moines to Bixby Park. California's governor, Frank Merriam, was a transplanted hawkeye from Long Beach.

Southern California, including Long Beach, was a hothouse in which offbeat religions, economic panaceas, and political movements throve, some wild, some fraudulent, and some moderately practical. They said that the Lord tilted North America like a pinball machine and all the nuts rolled down into the Los Angeles Basin. It was the base for theosophy, the Occult Temple at Krotona, stereometry, New Thought, faith healing, osteopathy, chiropractic, naturopathy, Aimee Semple McPherson's Four Square Gospel, the I AM cult, Mankind United, the Agabeg Occult Church, Technocracy, the Utopian Society, Upton Sinclair's EPIC Movement, Ham and Eggs, $25-Every-Monday, $30-Every-Thursday. "It is significant," Carey McWilliams noted, that the Townsend Movement "should have been launched in Long Beach."

As Townsend made his rounds of the needy for the Health Department, he was shocked by what he found. The medical problems, as is characteristic of the elderly, were very serious. But more impressive to Townsend was their economic misery. Many who held jobs had lost them. The stock market crash had wiped out equities. Bank failures had swallowed up savings accounts. Real estate holdings had plummeted in value. These people, his people, were in poverty and were consumed by fear. Townsend, who was now sixty-six, began to think about what could be done to help them, and he thought he found an answer.

The Townsend Movement's official version of the "creation," almost certainly apocryphal, ran as follows: One morning, as he looked out the window, the doctor was startled to observe three old women rummaging for food in a garbage can.

> A torrent of invectives tore out of me, the big blast of all the bitterness that had been building in me for years. I swore and I ranted, and I let my voice bellow with wild hatred I had for things as they were.
>
> My wife came a-running.
>
> "Doctor! Doctor!" She's always called me doctor, ". . . oh, you mustn't shout like that. All the neighbors will hear you!"
>
> "I want all the neighbors to hear me!" I roared defiantly. "I want God almighty to hear me! I'm going to shout till the whole country hears!"

What happened, doubtless, was more prosaic. Nostrums were bobbing about to explain and provide remedies for economic disaster, the old-age pension panacea among them. Dr. Townsend picked it up and set about refining it. He would have time. Effective October 2, 1933, he lost his job at the Health Department. He revived his old habit of writing letters to the editor. Over a period of five months beginning with September 30, 1933, the Long Beach *Press Telegram* published a series of his letters in which he laid out the Townsend Plan.

The government would provide $200 a month to every person aged sixty or over who was not a habitual criminal, on condition that he or she retire and spend the pension within a month. The system would be financed by a sales tax, later changed to a transactions tax. Townsend sought to achieve two objectives: The first was to provide for the elderly. The second, as he titled his September 30 letter, was a "Cure for Depressions." Old people would be removed from competition in the labor market, providing jobs for younger workers. More important, the aggregate spending of $2 or $3 billion monthly would stimulate business and restore prosperity.

The idea, of course, was economically preposterous. For years Townsend tried to find a reputable economist to endorse it and never succeeded. Among its shortcomings, as Paul Douglas pointed out, were these: About half the national income would be given to less than one tenth of the population. The immense tax would lead to a staggering increase in prices, seriously eroding real earnings. Pensions would be paid irrespective of need, so that John D. Rockefeller and Henry Ford would become beneficiaries. There would be no aggregate increase in purchasing power, but merely a transfer from those taxed to those pensioned. The Townsend Plan had no significance as an economic proposal. Rather, it became the basis for an important political and quasi-religious movement.

The immediate response to Townsend's letters was so great as to astonish him. In November 1933 he decided to devote full time to promotion of the Plan and began to circulate petitions. Thousands of people signed up. The doctor needed help and went to his old friend, Clements. That promoter, smelling a rising market, immediately came on board. On January 24, 1934, they incorporated as Old Age Revolving Pensions, Ltd (OARP). Since the California law required three signatories, the doctor became president, his brother Walter, the silent partner, was vice president, and Clements became secretary-treasurer. In fact, Townsend (the "Founder") and Clements (the "Co-Founder") owned the Townsend Plan. Clements, who called the Movement "the racket," later admitted to a congressional investigating committee that he had picked up $79,000 by the time of his resignation in mid-1936.

OARP formed Townsend Clubs in Southern California and people swarmed in. The Movement quickly spread throughout the Far West, then to the Middle West, and more slowly to the East and the South. Most members were old folks, but there were also a good many younger people who hoped the Plan would lift the support of their parents off their backs. Townsend and Clements established a private corporation, which they alone owned, to publish a weekly newspaper, called *The Modern Crusader* in 1934 and the *Official Townsend Weekly* in 1935 and thereafter. It specialized in patent medicine ads for bladder pills and gland stimulators that promised the purchaser that he or she would "Live 100 Years" or get "Married at 120." OARP seems to have kept no statistics during its early years, and the Founders grossly exaggerated the size of the membership and the number of clubs. But there can be no doubt that both grew phenomenally in 1934–1935. Clements said in a moment of moderation on April 2, 1936, that the membership was something over 2 million in about 7000 clubs.

Supporters of the Plan called it "the crusade," and club meetings had the evangelical style of the revival tent. Fundamentalist preachers entered into the leadership. The delegates to the 1935 national convention were described as "just folks . . . Methodist picnic people." Some said the doctor was a latter-day Jesus Christ. Townsend himself liked to compare the Movement with the rise of Christianity and promised that it would establish the universal brotherhood of man on earth. The singing of hymns was part of the club ritual. Meetings closed with

> Onward, Townsend soldiers,
> Marching as to war,
> With the Townsend banner
> Going on before.

Our devoted leaders
Bid depression go;
Join them in the battle,
Help them fight the foe.

Some thought Townsendism was heir to the fundamentalist temperance movement, particularly the Anti-Saloon League, now that Prohibition had been repealed.

Like the League, the Townsend Movement was more than a quasi-religious crusade; it was also a political lobby. Townsendism had political power in part because old people had a high propensity to vote and were distributed fairly uniformly in all the states and congressional districts. A bill proposing the Plan was introduced into Congress in 1935, and Townsend and other leaders testified before both the House Ways and Means and Senate Finance committees in its support and against Roosevelt's Economic Security bill. Townsendites were instructed to vote for candidates who backed the Plan and to write letters to members of Congress, which they did on a huge scale. In the West in particular, a few candidates came out for the pension scheme, and more important, a large number of congressmen became frightened.

The political impact of the Townsend Movement in 1934–1935 is clear. It had no effect upon the substantive old-age assistance or insurance provisions of the Administration bill. But the doctor's appearance before the congressional committees and the flood of mail and press attention that went with it pushed the other features of the bill into the background. "The effect created," Witte wrote, "was that the real issue became the Townsend plan or the economic security bill." Virtually all members of Congress thought the doctor's proposal would wreck the country, but the pressure demanded that they do something for old people, and they, therefore, had no alternative but to vote for the old-age provisions of the Administration bill. While many, perhaps a majority, opposed unemployment insurance and the welfare features, the President insisted on a package. This guaranteed that the other proposals would also make it through Congress. Thus, the Townsend Movement was a potent political force in the passage of the Social Security Act.[5]

5

Since the President demanded speed, the House Ways and Means Committee and the Senate Finance Committee held concurrent hearings, the former from January 21 to February 12, the latter from January 22 to February 20, 1935. Substantially the same witnesses appeared before both. Witte bore the brunt of defending and, especially, explaining the complex measure to Congress. He was supported by a large number of Administration spokesmen, members of CES, and technical experts.

Two rival measures were introduced. The first, of course, was the Townsend Plan, and the doctor and several of his advisers testified in its behalf. His appearances received great advance publicity, he attracted the biggest audiences, and he got front-page coverage in the press. The members of both committees cut Townsend to pieces, particularly by showing the defects in the transactions tax and by exposing the questionable organizational and financial features of OARP. The other was the Lundeen bill, which would have established a national unemployment-insurance system covering everyone over eighteen who was out of work. It would also have provided sickness, accident, and maternity coverage. The benefits would be financed entirely by the government out of tax revenues. Mary Van Kleeck of the Russell Sage Foundation was the author and the Communist Party the principal backer. Neither measure generated significant support in Congress, though the Townsend Plan, as noted, created indirect pressure for the Administration bill.

Organized labor was ambivalent. The AFL had not participated in drafting the economic security measure, was not much interested in the substantive proposals, was concentrating its legislative energies upon enactment of Senator Wagner's National Labor Relations bill, and was having a momentary strain in its relations with the Roosevelt Administration. While President William Green testified in a generally favorable manner before both committees, he was sufficiently critical to create the public impression of opposition. In later stages of the legislative process the AFL quietly urged senators friendly to the labor movement to vote for the bill.

Industry was divided. The National Association of Manufacturers took a hard line in opposition. The United States Chamber of Commerce, though proposing changes, was on the whole favorable. The

National Retail Dry Goods Association supported the bill because merchants expected that it would increase their business. Marion B. Folsom of the Eastman Kodak Company, though anxious to preserve the integrity of his firm's insurance programs, much impressed the Senate committee with his favorable testimony.

The deliberations of the Ways and Means Committee following the hearings were crucial in the legislative history. While the substantive provisions were not changed significantly, the bill was reorganized and completely redrafted, including a change in title.

Thomas Eliot wrote later that legislative drafting requires "foreseeing every possible question . . . and eliminating every ambiguity." He learned this from "a tense, caustic redheaded Yankee," Middleton Beaman, the legislative counsel of the House of Representatives. As the Ways and Means Committee read the bill, paragraph by paragraph, Beaman's "terrierlike" questions forced the members to anticipate and avoid problems that might arise in the future. Fred Vinson, later Chief Justice of the United States, was "the dominant influence" on Ways and Means.

The Committee reported a much improved bill to the House. Eliot wrote, "I was a wiser young man than I had been three months before . . . thanks to Mr. Beaman, a much humbler one. I was also exhausted."

Beaman's prodigious efforts improved the clarity and effectiveness of the bill and enhanced its chances of being held constitutional. This redrafting, of course, took time and delayed the Committee's report until April 5.

The Ways and Means Committee also changed the measure's name from the Economic Security Act to the Social Security Act. The introduction of this term evokes curiosity, and Altmeyer has explored it. On a trip to Colombia many years after passage of the law, he learned that Simon Bolivar, "The Great Liberator," had made a memorable address in Angostura in 1819 in which he said that the most perfect system of government produces, among other things, "the greatest amount of social security." This is no more than a historical footnote, because the Ways and Means Committee had no knowledge of the statement. During the hearings, Green employed the term and the *Washington Post* referred to the "social-security bill." More important, evidently, was the influence of Abraham Epstein. While the index of his book *Insecurity, A Challenge to America,* published in 1933, does not list "social security," he used the term in the text. He also employed it in his testimony before the Committee. This, doubtless, was because he had changed the name of his organization in 1933, reflecting its wider scope, from the American Association for Old Age Security to the American Association for Social Security. Since Epstein was out of money, this allowed him to use the same letterheads by striking out "Old Age" and substituting "Social." Later, the term spread throughout the world to describe comprehensive systems of social insurance. Ironically, in the United States, usage narrowed the meaning to old-age pensions.

The House debated the bill from April 11 to 19 under a rule that permitted unrestricted amendments, and many were offered. The most important was to put the entire cost of old-age assistance on the federal government, and it was easily defeated. Both the Townsend Plan and the Lundeen bill were proposed as substitutes. Each got only about fifty votes, in both cases mainly from Representatives who opposed any legislation rather than from supporters. The House passed the Social Security bill on April 19 by an overwhelming vote of 371 to 33. The nay votes came mainly from conservatives plus a handful of Townsend and Lundeen backers.

The Senate Finance Committee, because it was busy with other matters, did not reach social security until May. Since its membership was heavily weighted with southern conservatives, the Administration anticipated difficulties. This was compounded on May 6, when the Supreme Court in a five-to-four decision in the *Alton Railroad* case held the Railroad Retirement Act, which established a compulsory old-age pension system for employees of Class I railways, an unconstitutional exercise of the power of Congress to regulate interstate commerce. But the Committee chairman, Senator Pat Harrison of Mississippi, though himself little interested in the bill, was eager to please Roosevelt and employed his formidable legislative skills in guiding the measure through. An opinion of the Attorney General stated that the *Alton Railroad* case did not necessarily make any provision of the social security bill unconstitutional. The deliberations of the Finance Committee saw the emergence of an important amendment, proposed by Senator Bennett Champ Clark of Missouri. The insurance brokers, who, according to Witte, engaged in "a vast amount of lobbying," sought to breach the exclusive government old-age pension system by allowing for the contracting-out of private annuities to insurance companies. While there were many arguments against Senator Clark's proposal, the one Roosevelt stressed was that private insurance companies would skim off low-risk young workers and "unload the old people on the Government." The Clark Amendment failed of passage by a tie vote. The Finance Committee reported the bill out on May 20.

Senate consideration took place between June 14 and 19. The fight was over the Clark Amendment, which was now made more attractive by requiring that private annuity plans must meet a variety of federal safeguards. Senator Clark presented his arguments skillfully and the Senate adopted the amendment 51 to 35. The chamber then passed the Social Security bill by the commanding vote of 76 to 6.

In conference the Clark Amendment was the decisive issue. Since the House conferees insisted on its deletion and the Senate members on its retention, the Committee simply referred it back to the two chambers. In conference, as well, the Perkins-Hopkins agreement on the location of the new programs fell apart. Congress was unwilling to give them either to the Department of Labor or to FERA. The Social Security Board was to be an independent agency and would even administer aid for dependent children.

The battle over the Clark Amendment delayed passage for almost a month. The ultimate compromise was to enact the law without this provision, but, since the old-age pension system would not go into effect until 1937, a joint legislative committee would be created to report to Congress on contracting-out in 1936. The House passed the bill on August 8 and the Senate the next day, in both cases without a roll call. The President signed the Social Security Act with some ceremony on August 14, 1935. "If the Senate and the House of Representatives in this long and arduous session," he said, "had done nothing more than pass this Bill, the session would be regarded as historic for all time."[6]

6

"One of the few permissible generalizations about American politics," James MacGregor Burns has written, "had been that a President's party loses some strength during non-presidential or off-year elections." Nineteen thirty-four was an exception, and for good reasons. One was Roosevelt's extraordinary personal popularity and towering leadership in the political arena. In most districts a candidate who was *for* the President and his New Deal had an automatic advantage over his rival. Samuel Lubell has described the second as "the revolt of the city," or, in Raymond Moley's phrase, the triumph of population over acreage. Franklin Roosevelt and his Democratic Party directed their appeal basically to the urban masses — unionizing workers, the jobless on relief, the "new" immigrants from southern and eastern Europe and their children, Catholics, Jews, and blacks. The American political process was being transformed. In Lubell's solar-system image, the Democratic Party was rising as the sun and the Republican Party was setting as the moon.

On the Saturday before the 1934 election, Postmaster General James A. Farley, who had good cause to consider himself an astute political prognosticator, sent Roosevelt a prediction of a massive Democratic victory. He said that Democrats would capture twenty-six of the thirty-five senatorial races, including a shattering of the historic Republican bastion of Pennsylvania. He thought the Democrats would hold their ground in the House. The President considered Farley's predictions recklessly optimistic. In fact, they were cautious. Democratic strength in the Senate rose from 59 to 69 and in the House from 313 to 322. Arthur Krock wrote in the *New York Times* that Roosevelt's New Deal had won "the most overwhelming victory in the history of American politics."

The convening of the Seventy-Fourth Congress in 1935 would open the road to significant legislative changes. On a fine November day, Harry Hopkins drove to the racetrack at Laurel, Maryland, with Aubrey Williams and several other members of his staff. Exhilarated by the election returns and the prospects, Hopkins said suddenly, "Boys — this is our hour. We've got to get everything we want. . . . Now or never. Get your minds to work on developing a complete ticket." They retired to the St. Regis Hotel in New York to draft a program. The day before Thanksgiving, with a memorandum in his pocket, Hopkins headed south to see Roosevelt at Warm Springs, Georgia.[7]

Three

WPA

IF, when Harry Hopkins went to Warm Springs to spend Thanksgiving of 1934 with the President, he expected quick approval for a new federal unemployment relief policy, he was sadly disappointed. "Franklin Roosevelt," Frances Perkins has written, "was not a simple man. . . . He was the most complicated human being I ever knew." While he had a capacity for bold and decisive action, which he had demonstrated dramatically during the Hundred Days, he had an equal talent for vacillation, a quality, she pointed out, that "exasperated those associates of his who expected 'crystal clear' and unwavering decisions."

This latter characteristic of Roosevelt's was nowhere more evident than in the development of an unemployment relief program in 1934–1935. In part this arose from extremely tough policy questions, which will be set forth shortly. But it also stemmed from his desire to retain the goodwill and some harmony between two of his most trusted, loyal, and competent lieutenants who were feuding bitterly, Hopkins, the Relief Administrator, and Ickes, the Public Works Administrator. Roosevelt simply could not be firm with people he liked.

Robert E. Sherwood recounts a story to illustrate this. Early in the war, when he headed the Office of War Information, Sherwood returned from a long overseas airplane trip, which had been bumpy. Visiting Roosevelt at Shangri-la, the President's retreat in the Maryland hills, he shook his head to relieve the pressure in his ears. The President asked what the trouble was and Sherwood told him that the flight had been rough.

"I didn't know you'd been away," he said. "What did you go there for?"

I explained that there had been trouble in our outpost office and I had gone to fire the man in charge of it. I hastened to add, to the President of the United States, that the man in question was not in any way disloyal or corrupt — merely not the right personality for the particular job. Roosevelt looked at me with that expression of wide-eyed innocence that he could always assume and asked, "And did you fire him?"

"Yes, sir," I said.

His face now expressed wondering incredulity.

"How did you do it?" he asked.

My answer was pretty lame. "Well, sir — I just asked the man up to my hotel room, and then I said to him, 'Jack — I — I'm terribly sorry, but — I've got to ask for your resignation.' Fortunately, he was very decent about the whole thing and resigned."

Roosevelt now had an expression of open amazement and said, "I can't believe it. I can't believe you had the courage to fire anybody. I thought you were a complete softy — like me."[1]

1

Roosevelt's vacillation over unemployment relief policy went on at least from early September 1934, when Hopkins urged him to abolish FERA and launch a $5 billion public works program, to September 13, 1935, when he granted a decisive budget allocation that made the Works Progress Administration supreme. That year was an ordeal.

The basic problem was that there were a great many policy problems. Some, fortunately, were easily resolved. The first was that the federal "dole" must be abolished. While FERA sought to push work relief over direct relief, it had only partly succeeded. The immediate need to feed the hungry, budget constraints, and local preference for the cheaper arrangement in a decentralized administrative system combined to preserve direct relief. Roosevelt, who was wholly committed to the work ethic, found the dole philosophically obnoxious. He said to Congress on January 4, 1935:

> The lessons of history, confirmed by the evidence immediately before me, show conclusively that continued dependence upon relief induces a spiritual and moral disintegration fundamentally destructive of the national fibre. To dole out relief in this way is to administer a narcotic, a subtle destroyer of the human spirit. It is inimical to the dictates of sound policy. It is in violation of the traditions of America. Work must be found for the able-bodied but destitute workers.
>
> The Federal Government must and shall quit this business of relief.

A Gallup Poll a few years later showed that the American people overwhelmingly agreed. The fact that the National Association of Manufacturers and the U.S. Chamber of Commerce preferred direct relief because it was less costly and eliminated competition by the public sector hardly impressed Roosevelt. By 1935, he was at war with business.

Getting rid of the dole assumed that the relief population was divisible into two categories — the employables and the unemployables. In his January 4 address the President approximated their numbers as 3.5 million who were able to work and 1.5 million who were not. These figures seem low. FERA studies for 1935 showed that over 11 million persons were out of work and relief was being given to 5 million families, which included over 6 million workers. Corrington Gill estimated that 80 percent of the jobless were employable and that 20 percent were unemployable, mainly because of old age, but also due to physical or mental handicaps or to the situation of mothers who had to look after their children. The Administration assumed that the Social Security Act would provide for most of the unemployables by old-age assistance, pensions for the blind, and aid to dependent children. Any categories not covered would become the responsibility of state and local government. Thus, the federal government's residual obligation was to provide *work* for the employables.

The second easy decision was to abolish FERA. Its Administrator was the first to suggest it. Hopkins had told Gill when he hired the economist in 1933 that he expected to become "the most unpopular man in America." "One of the disagreeable things I will have to do," Hopkins said, "will be to keep reminding the American public of the serious problem of unemployment and destitution, and they won't want to hear it." The word *Emergency* in the title of the agency was all right in 1933, when it could be linked to Hoover. But in 1935, with a presidential election in the offing, it could rub off on Roosevelt. Instead, the President and Hopkins talked about "Progress." Jim Townsend, the Democratic chairman in Dutchess County, told the President that 15 to 20 percent of the relief workers were "chiselers." Roosevelt figured it must be equally bad in the rest of the country. The conservative press had succeeded in creating the public impression that a reliefer who "worked" was either "boondoggling" or "raking leaves." A temporary agency, conveniently, could be put out of business in a hurry.

The third clear decision was to make the new program wholly federal. The FERA experience with state and local administration had not been ennobling. The people at the top in Washington were in an awkward position to find out what was going on at the level of actual delivery of relief to recipients — the locality. And, when they did learn, they were often annoyed to discover that it sometimes involved politics or corruption or the dole. Hopkins spent a large share of his energies containing these tendencies. He felt strongly that a centralized administration would diminish these problems. Roosevelt was concerned that the exposure of widespread dishonesty might embarrass his Administration.

But from this point forward all the questions became tough. The first was to choose the better means of reviving business and stimulating employment among two competing analyses of the Depression. One held that the basic problem was stagnation in the heavy industries due to a very low rate of private investment. The remedy was a massive public works program with a high ratio of materials costs to labor costs. While providing limited direct employment, big public projects would create jobs indirectly by raising the demand for steel, cement, copper, lumber, and other basic materials. The other analysis held that the fundamental difficulty was the inadequacy of aggregate demand. The solution was a large number of short-term public projects with a high ratio of direct labor to material costs. This would provide jobs for millions of the unemployed, thereby stimulating mass purchasing power. In 1934–1935 the principal American theoretical spokesman for this view was Marriner Eccles, whom Roosevelt had appointed to the Federal Reserve Board in 1934. But FERA was the fountainhead of this thinking at the policy level. On his visit to Europe in the summer of 1934, Hopkins had been much impressed with Scandinavian public works. During the fall his staff worked intensively on programs that would link public works and public employment. In 1936 this analysis would reach full theoretical development when John Maynard Keynes published *The General Theory of Employment, Interest, and Money.*

The second difficult question, closely related to the first, was whether the stress should be on producing public works for their own sake or because they created jobs for the unemployed. Here the conflict between Ickes and Hopkins was sharpest. As Public Works Administrator, Ickes sought to build up the nation's stock of capital equipment and to beautify the land. He pushed dams, highways, bridges, tunnels, schoolhouses, and other public buildings, along with facilities for the armed forces. Such projects required careful planning and engineering. Many months and sometimes years elapsed before they generated a significant volume of employment. As Relief Administrator, Hopkins was eager to use public works to make jobs for those out of work, as he had with CWA. PWA projects took too long and, even after the wait, the demand was often for skills that the unemployed did not have. Further, the location of these capital improvements did not match up well with the concentrations of the jobless. The most effective way to help the unemployed was to pay them wages directly.

Third, should the method of financing emphasize government expenditures that would not be recoverable or self-liquidating projects? Roosevelt much preferred the latter and Ickes shared his view. Hopkins hired an outside consultant in the fall of 1934 to examine the possibilities. Many types of works were potentially capable of recovering their costs — highways, bridges, rural electrification, housing, railway improvements, and water systems, among others. But they must be PWA-type projects. FERA sought to justify its programs in these terms by watering down the meaning of self-liquidation, by suggesting the avoidance of the payment of interest, and by proposing low wages as well as prices for materials that were below NRA code levels. No one was impressed. A CWA-type program and self-liquidation were inherently contradictory.

The fourth tough area consisted of a group of questions related to employment. Should only persons on relief be eligible for jobs on public works? Such a policy would have the advantages of helping the neediest, of diminishing the relief load, and of being relatively cheap. But there were serious shortcomings: Those among the jobless who were not on relief would be denied public employment; the skill mix and location of the relief population did not match the labor needs of works projects; and white-collar and professional people formed a special problem. Another employment question was whether the work should be performed under force account, that is, with the government as employer, or through private contractors.

The former, of course, would give the government far more control over employment policies, including costs. Closely related to this was wage policy. Under contracting, it would become the prevailing wage, namely, the rates contractors and the building trades unions negotiated. If performed by force account, the government could fix wages below those in private employment in order to maintain the incentive to work in the private sector, but still sufficient to provide a minimum standard of living, the "security wage." A related question under force account was whether the significant wage was, on the one hand, the hourly rate or, on the other, weekly or monthly earnings. If the latter, this raised the problem of the number of allowable hours of work. The construction industry and the building trades unions, of course, strongly urged contracting and the prevailing wage.

Fifth, what would be the duration of the program? The answer depended upon when one expected the private sector to recover. The predominant view at FERA and in many other quarters, both sophisticated and naive, was that the Depression, which in 1935 was already six years old, would continue for a long time. This assumption argued for a "permanent" public-works–public-employment policy to absorb the unemployed. Long-term budgeting would have a favorable impact on the economy and would allow for larger projects. But this was a politically dangerous proposition because it admitted that the New Deal had failed to revive the private economy. The Republicans were certain to use this argument in the 1936 presidential election, even if the program was budgeted on a year-to-year basis.

The final difficult decision was the administrative arrangement. The answers to the preceding questions would determine the outcome here. If the analysis stressed revival of the heavy industries, a massive public works program for its own sake, self-liquidation, contracting out, and the prevailing wage, the funds and the authority must go to Ickes and PWA. If the choice was to revive aggregate demand, to create jobs quickly, to have government underwrite the costs, to operate by force account, and to establish a "security wage," Hopkins and the agency that succeeded FERA would be the winner.

Roosevelt was torn over these questions. He talked about them at length with visitors who streamed in to see him. He had many meetings with Ickes and Hopkins, sometimes bringing in Morgenthau and Daniel Bell, the Director of the Budget, to deal with financing. Roosevelt's political instinct and humanity told him that Hopkins was right, that it was necessary to provide public work swiftly for the employables among the jobless. But his heart was with Ickes on major public works. While he had no Napoleonic ambition to enshrine himself in stone, he thought the country desperately needed to build up its capital stock. Roosevelt and Ickes, for example, would lovingly discuss the route of a great transcontinental highway. While the President did not hesitate to run up the national debt when he thought it necessary, he was an old-fashioned believer in the balanced budget and would always be uncomfortable with the Keynesian analysis. Finally, as an admitted "softy," Roosevelt hated to choose between Ickes and Hopkins. He had great confidence in both and found hurting either extremely painful.[2]

2

The President's uncertainty was evident in the bill he submitted to Congress on January 21, 1935. On several counts it can only be described as amazing. For one, it would have authorized the largest peacetime appropriation in American history to that time, $4,880,000,000. Although the $880 million consisted of unexpended balances under previous appropriations, the $4 billion of new money was itself a record. Second, the two key people in the Administration, Hopkins and Ickes, had not been consulted. Bell of the Budget Bureau had been in charge of drafting and his principal adviser was Clinton M. Hester of the Treasury. Third, the bill was only two pages long. Finally, it proposed that this large sum should be used "in the discretion and under the direction of the President" to promote the general welfare, to provide relief from unemployment, to remedy economic maladjustments, to alleviate distress, and to improve living and working conditions. With this vagueness Roosevelt deferred answering all of the tough questions he faced.

The House Appropriations Committee held hearings for only a few hours and illuminated nothing. The Senate Appropriations Committee spent three days on hearings. Both Hopkins and Ickes appeared and merely revealed their own puzzlement. The latter confessed that he had not read the bill till the day he testified. Admiral C. J. Peoples, chief of the Treasury's Procurement Division, was the apparent Administration spokesman. He did not know how the money would be spent or who would be in charge. Peoples stressed self-liquidation, even going so far as to suggest that the government would sell gasoline to recover the cost of highways, a notion that hardly appealed to senators who favored private industry.

Nevertheless, on January 24, despite some restiveness, the House easily passed the bill in virtually the form presented by a vote of 329 to 78. In the Senate the opposition was much stronger, consideration continued for two months, and five significant amendments were advanced.

First, the Associated General Contractors (AGC), with AFL support, sought to maximize contract as opposed to force-account works. The AGC proposed an amendment that the Senate adopted saying, "Wherever practicable in the carrying out of the provisions of this joint resolution, full advantage shall be taken of the facilities of private enterprise."

The greatest controversy arose over the second point, wage policy. The AFL, speaking on behalf of its building trades affiliates, strongly urged the prevailing over the security wage. While the latter was not specified in the bill, it was obvious that persons on work relief would be paid less than union rates. The AFL proposal was narrowly defeated in the House by the argument that the President opposed it. The Federation made its main stand in the upper house. Senator Pat McCarran of Nevada introduced an amendment that would have required that rates "shall not be less than the prevailing rates of wage paid for work of a similar nature . . . in the city, town, village, or other civil division of the State in which the work is located." McCarran, invited to attend a meeting of the AFL Executive Council, regaled the union leaders with a sentimental saga of his humble beginnings as a sheepherder. President William Green strongly supported the amendment, arguing that a security wage would drag the prevailing wage down. He also urged the affiliated unions to back the McCarran proposal. Corrington Gill pointed out that a requirement to pay the prevailing wage would increase the cost of the program by over $2 billion. The Senate Committee at first approved the amendment and then rejected it. After a bitter debate, the Senate itself adopted McCarran's proposal on February 21 by a vote of 44 to 43. The White House announced that Roosevelt would veto the bill. The amendment was recommitted. The ultimate compromise was that the President would fix wages that would "not affect adversely or otherwise tend to decrease the going rate of wages paid for work of a similar nature."

The private utilities proposed the third amendment. Frightened by the establishment of the Tennessee Valley Authority in 1933, they sought to prohibit further development of public power with the ingenious device that construction projects under this bill must commit at least 50 percent of their expenditures to direct labor. Ickes pointed out that this would put PWA "out of business." It would eliminate rural electrification, slum clearance, and grade crossings, along with most other kinds of works. There was talk of reducing the figure to 33⅓ percent, but Ickes thought the result would be almost equally devastating. The ratio finally was cut to 25 percent. While this was still wrong in principle, Ickes wrote, "we could operate under this language and I came to the conclusion that I would not be justified in opposing such a compromise."

The fourth amendment, again proposed by McCarran, vented senatorial distaste for Hopkins and his staff. FERA's earlier victories over the politicians now turned into defeat. Any administrator who held a job paying $5000 or more must be appointed by the President and *confirmed* by the Senate. The upper house adopted the amendment without debate, and the House, after some grumbling, went along.

The final amendment reflected strong antiwar sentiment in the United States in 1935. Roosevelt had used PWA to build up the armed forces, particularly the Navy, which constructed the carriers *Yorktown* and *Enterprise,* four heavy cruisers, and many destroyers, submarines, and airplanes. Aside from the fact that some senators considered increased military expenditures unwarranted in any case, many others thought it improper to spend for military equipment funds that were appropriated for relief and civil public works. The restriction forbade the use of these funds for "munitions, warships, or military or naval material." But the appropriation might be employed for construction or improvement of military posts, forts, camps, cemeteries, and like areas.

The resolution with these principal changes was then passed by both houses and signed by the President on April 8, 1935. The title was the Emergency Relief Appropriation Act of 1935.[3]

3

In the concluding months of 1934, when the works program was being drafted, Hopkins and Ickes had teamed up reasonably well. At that stage the President insisted that they jointly outline the plan and indicate how the money would be spent, without going into the administrative arrangement. They reached agreement only on bland generalities. Morgenthau, who needed to know the specific costs, who thought one man should be in charge, and who preferred Hopkins to Ickes, made his annoyance known to Roosevelt.

After the turn of the year Ickes became upset because the President in his annual message to Congress said that he planned to coordinate control over public works and relief. "I am at a loss to understand what he has in mind," Ickes wrote in his diary. The uncertainty was more than he could bear and he unleashed his unrivaled capability to anticipate the worst. He thought Roosevelt would put either Donald R. Richberg or Admiral Peoples over him and Hopkins. Richberg had been Ickes's detested law partner. "Hopkins and I would do the work and he would get the credit. He is good at that." Peoples was without either "imagination" or "character." If the President made either boss, it would be a sign of "lack of confidence in me."

On January 7, Ickes went to see Hopkins, who was laid up with the flu. Hopkins was as much in the dark as Ickes, but they agreed that working for either Richberg or Peoples would be intolerable. Ickes said he would support creation of a new welfare department with Hopkins as secretary and would turn over several bureaus from the Department of the Interior. In the alternative, Ickes would make Hopkins Deputy Administrator of Public Works in charge of supplying relief labor to PWA projects. Hopkins, doubtless amused by these clumsy machinations, allowed Ickes to think that he was making progress.

The Senate's slowness in passing the works bill allowed for a two-month delay in which the President need not face up to the administrative decisions. Hopkins sweated; Ickes tortured himself and talked, both to his diary and to friends, of withdrawing as Administrator of PWA. Hopkins described him as the " 'great resigner' — anything doesn't go his way, threatens to quit. He bores me." By March the White House could stall no longer. The President instructed Bell to persuade Hopkins and Ickes to agree on an administrative scheme. Bell reported back, hardly to Roosevelt's surprise, that he had failed. The President began to play with organization charts, shifting agencies and administrators about in boxes. He was moving toward a rather unkempt troika: on one side, a work-relief program under Hopkins; on the other, public works under Ickes along with an amorphous assortment of other programs, including low-cost housing, rural electrification, highways, agricultural relief and the Civilian Conservation Corps; and in the middle, an ill-defined peacekeeping mission. The last was exceedingly troublesome. For a while Roosevelt toyed with the idea of heading it himself. Morgenthau suggested Joseph P. Kennedy, who was chairman of the Securities and Exchange Commission, but Kennedy said he could not work with Ickes. The choice finally narrowed to Frank Walker, the New Deal's official man-in-the-middle. Everyone recognized that Walker had no personal ambitions, that he liked all the contestants, and that he dearly aspired for equal love from every one of them. As Hopkins said in a sardonic attack on Ickes, "The fellow that is making all the trouble around here is Walker. . . . Blame Walker. That is one of the things he is here for, to be blamed for everything."

In a series of executive orders between April 30 and June 26, 1935, Roosevelt more or less established this arrangement. The Division of Applications and Information was placed in the National Emergency Council, and Walker was named director of both the Division and the Council. The Advisory Committee on Allotments consisted of representatives from PWA, the National Emergency Council, the Budget Bureau, the Treasury, the Reconstruction Finance Corporation, and the National Resources Board, with Ickes as chairman. The Works Progress Division under Hopkins received a large assortment of co-ordinating and research duties along with, as caboose, the duty to "recommend and carry on small useful projects designed to assure a maximum of employment in all localities." That was all the authority Hopkins needed. He also arranged to have the name of his agency changed in one of the orders from "Division" to "Administration." This made the acronym WPA. Ickes was convinced that he deliberately scrambled PWA to confuse the public with the initials.

The summer of 1935 started as a race between Hopkins and Ickes for power and money, but it soon became a runaway. Roosevelt insisted that the relief appropriation must be used primarily for quick job creation. Here WPA, which stressed on-site employment, had a great advantage over PWA, which had to invest heavily in off-site materials and equipment. In addition, Hopkins far surpassed Ickes at administrative infighting. The order said that WPA must not undertake a construction job costing over $25,000. Hopkins broke up big projects into little ones to fit this requirement. WPA was supposed to supply PWA with relief labor and Hopkins would drag his feet when he needed the workers himself. Hopkins described his methods in a discussion with Charles E. Merriam:

> There are two kinds of administrators — gentlemen and go-getters. When a gentleman learns that his appropriation is being cut by the Bureau of the Budget, he accepts it. But I'm no gentleman. If my appropriation is ever being cut, I simply call up the White House and ask the President to issue a stop order, saying that I will go over in a few days and explain why. Then I never go over. That is how a go-getter always beats a gentleman.
>
> What happens when two go-getters compete against each other?
>
> Then I pretend to be a gentleman, and, when the other fellow finds out, it is too late.

Ickes's *Secret Diary* for the summer of 1935 makes painful reading. On August 31, his wife, Anna, was killed in an automobile accident on the Taos road near Santa Fe, New Mexico. More relevant to the present purpose, he lost out to Hopkins. He saw WPA as "a glorified CWA program," consisting of a miscellany of "trivial and ephemeral" projects that would be inefficiently run and wide open to corruption. "I begged him [the President] not to involve himself too intimately with a program that . . . I didn't believe could succeed." He was certain that WPA would cost Roosevelt the 1936 election. As Hopkins increased his lead, Ickes became "thoroughly disheartened" and talked again about resigning. While at the outset he felt that Walker would mediate their disputes fairly, he later became convinced that Walker favored Hopkins and "there is no use arguing any proposition before him." In late August, the conflict broke in the press and a *Washington Star* headline read, "ICKES IS SHORN OF PWA POWER." He was incensed and once more decided to resign. Roosevelt told him that the newspapers were "cockeyed" and he should not be "childish."

In mid-September, Ickes wrote, the PWA-WPA battle was "smoldering in the newspapers." He was pleased that the papers he saw said he was for "desirable public works" while Hopkins was for "boondoggling." The press wrote of a "showdown" at Hyde Park.

In fact, Roosevelt had invited Ickes, Hopkins, and Walker, among others, to his family place on the Hudson on September 12. They had, Ickes wrote, "a very pleasant dinner, with movies and some talk afterward." He shared a room with Walker, who warned him "that his wife said he was a terrible snorer." "All I can say about Frank is that he fully lived up to the advance notices of his prowess." During the "intermissions" Ickes turned over "onto my good ear."

The next day the President brought the whole group into the library. They proceeded to allocate funds, and it was a devastating experience for Ickes, despite his howls of protest. Though PWA had petitions for projects costing over $2 billion, it received only $200 million. WPA got the lion's share.

The Hyde Park allocation meeting sealed Hopkins's victory. By the fall of 1935 the WPA organization was firmly established, and in December, 2,667,000 persons were employed on its projects. In February 1936 the number passed 3 million. As of December 31, 1935, $4,236,981,642 had been allocated under the Emergency Relief Appropriation Act. WPA and FERA got $2,098,618,999. The PWA grant was $445 million, the Bureau of Public Roads got $500 million, the CCC $523 million, and a number of other federal agencies received lesser amounts. The American economy recovered significantly between mid-1935 and mid-1937 and unemployment declined sharply. Many thought that this injection of federal spending, particularly by WPA, was the basic reason for the improvement.[4]

4

Before Ickes left Hyde Park, the President invited both Ickes and Hopkins to join him on a sea voyage. Ickes would go out by train with Roosevelt to Nevada to dedicate the just completed Boulder Dam. They would then proceed to San Diego to board the cruiser *Houston* for a leisurely fishing and sightseeing trip down the Pacific Coast, through the Panama Canal, and then across the Caribbean to Charleston, South Carolina. A holiday at sea always revived Roosevelt, and he thought Ickes might benefit, too.

Ickes wrote, "I really don't feel like going on that trip with the President." He admitted that he was "desperately tired," that his morale was low, that he was worried about raising the money for the inheritance taxes on his wife's estate, and that he was afraid he would get seasick and sunburned. In San Diego he almost missed the sailing. His spirits lifted as soon as he was at sea. His quarters were "quite luxurious," the food, excepting the coffee, was excellent, and off Cerros Island he caught a 12-pound yellowtail, the record for the day. He countered the Pacific swells by crawling into his bunk and he stayed in the shade to protect his skin. Ickes noted with some pleasure that Hopkins got both seasick and burned. At the Canal he bought three Panama hats and the Scot in him glowed over the fact that they would have cost far more in the States. The ship's paper, *The Blue Bonnet,* carried a story, "Buried at Sea," that seemed as though Roosevelt had been the author:

> The feud between Hopkins and Ickes was given a decent burial today. With flags at half-mast . . . the President officiated at the solemn ceremony which we trust will take these two babies off the front page for all time. Hopkins was dressed in his immaculate blues, browns, and whites, his fine figure making a pretty sight with the moon-drifted sea in the foreground. Ickes wore his conventional grays, Mona Lisa smile and carried his stamp collection.
>
> The ceremony, tho brief, was impressive. Hopkins expressed regret at the unkind things Ickes had said about him — and Ickes on his part promised to make it stronger — only more so — as soon as he could get a stenographer who could take it hot. As the sun burst through the fading moonlight bathing all . . . the two feudists turned facing the sea to pledge their fealty. It was soon over. The President gave them a hearty slap on the back — pushing them both into the sea. "Full steam ahead," ordered the President.

Ickes thought the story "hilarious." When they landed at Charleston, he wrote, "I am glad I took this trip." He had had a chance and a rest and "I badly needed them." He had not slept so well in months. The company was fine. Even "Harry Hopkins fitted in well with his easy manners and keen wit."[5]

Four

The Dilemma of Unemployment

STUDS TERKEL talked to Noni Saarinen, who had come to the United States from Finland in 1921 and had settled in Chicago. Her husband, a painter, could not find work during the Depression. Noni took a job as a housemaid, and he stayed home to look after their boy. "He said he's walking upside-down. . . . You start walking on the floor, and then you put yourself upside-down, how you feel. Because he couldn't provide for his family."

Edward Burgess was lucky. He had steady work at Donnelly's, the big printing shop. Burgess had a theory about how you licked unemployment: "I spotted this Studebaker in the window at Twenty-sixth and Michigan. So I says to May, let's buy that car. So we just stopped in, give 'em $600, all we had with us, and bought the car." His foreman at Donnelly's, who had bought a Ford, said, "You sure did your bit for the Depression." Burgess said, "If everybody would spend ten cents more a day than they ordinarily spent, we'd sneak out of this in a hurry."[1]

1

The estimates of the volume of unemployment in March 1933 strain credulity. Robert R. Nathan put it at 15,071,000. W. S. Woytinsky thought it was 14,300,000. The National Industrial Conference Board estimated 14,586,000. The AFL figured 15,389,000. There can be no doubt that close to 30 percent of the labor force was totally jobless.

This disaster in the labor market, combined with the demoralization of business, severe agricultural distress, and the collapse of the banking system, demanded that Roosevelt and his New Deal move decisively and immediately to revive the economy. Like Ed Burgess, almost everyone had a remedy, but in essence there were four basic policy options:

The first was to encourage business associations to restrict output and to "stabilize," that is, to raise prices. The Depression, supporters argued, showed that the competitive market system had failed; America's capacity to produce had outsped its ability to consume and prices had fallen to dangerously low levels. According to the Federal Reserve Board, manufacturing production had sunk 48 percent between 1929 and 1932; the Bureau of Labor Statistics reported that wholesale prices, excluding farm commodities, had fallen 23.4 percent over the same period. The precondition for industry cartels to allocate production and to fix prices was the suspension of the antitrust laws.

The backers of this idea were a diverse group. Many were businessmen who recoiled from the hazards of the competitive market even in good times and abhorred the "cutthroat" competition so prevalent during the Depression. The United States Chamber of Commerce was the principal lobby expressing this view. During World War I the War Industries Board (WIB) had operated such a system. Its chairman, Bernard M. Baruch, at this time a noted financier and Elder Statesman, repeatedly urged such a policy. His wartime assistant and present associate, General Hugh S. Johnson, echoed Baruch's position. Gerard Swope, the president of the General Electric Company, who had also worked for WIB, had made a notable statement on September 16, 1931, proposing a similar plan. But Swope, who was more progressive than the Chamber or Baruch, linked it to proposals to help labor — workmen's compensation, life and disability insurance, old-age pensions, and unemployment insurance. A few liberal economists, particularly Rexford G. Tugwell and George B. Galloway, would reconstruct the economy by substituting central planning for laissez-faire. They would stabilize production, prices, and employment by industry under government control.

General Johnson and Tugwell were among the main draftsmen of the National Industrial Recovery Act. Title I of that statute, signed by Roosevelt on June 16, 1933, set this policy in motion. The President named Johnson to head the National Recovery Administration (NRA).

The New Deal applied a similar logic to agriculture. The production of farm commodities had not changed significantly between 1929 and 1932, in fact, had risen slightly. But the prices farmers received had collapsed, falling 53 percent during this period. As a result, gross farm income had plummeted 54 percent. Since producing units were small, markets were competitive, and few commodity associations were effective, the NRA scheme of industry cartels was unworkable. The government would have to do the job itself. The policy took shape in the Agricultural Adjustment Act of May 12, 1933. The Department of Agriculture would make a benefit payment to each participating farmer in the seven basic commodities — wheat, cotton, field corn, hogs, rice, tobacco, and milk — for taking land out of production. The system would be financed by excise taxes at the processing level. The hope was that curtailment of output would boost farm prices. These higher prices, combined with the benefit payments, would raise farm income.

The second idea to emerge was devaluation of the dollar. Historically, American depressions had kindled interest in monetary remedies, and the Great Depression was no exception. Now formidable forces were pressing for currency manipulation. Debtors and those who suffered from falling prices, especially farmers, urged cheap money. American exporters, who sold their goods in world markets against foreign competitors who offered devalued prices, wanted equal treatment. A number of nations, notably Britain, which dramatically left the gold standard in September 1931, set precedents. The old silver slogan of the nineties, "16 to 1," stirred memories. The seven western silver-producing states presented a solid bloc of fourteen votes in the Senate in favor of coinage of the metal. Senator Elmer Thomas of Oklahoma, whose political roots wound back to the Bryan campaigns of 1896 and 1900, lent a powerful voice to "reflation" by the monetization of silver or any other means. Father Charles E. Coughlin, the Detroit priest, gathered an immense following for his demagogic preachments on cheap money. While most university economists held fast for the gold standard and the stable dollar, monetary tinkering attained a certain marginal academic respectability. Professor Irving Fisher of Yale had long urged a "compensated" dollar, that is, a flexible currency indexed to prices in order to iron out the business cycle. Fisher gained a large following in the thirties. George F. Warren, professor of agricultural economics at Cornell, suddenly vaulted into prominence with the nostrum that the price level could be jacked up by raising the price of gold.

These powerful pressures for "reflation" presented a supreme test to Roosevelt's political artistry. His performance, with one exception, was consummate. He had two objectives: The first was to devalue the dollar in order to raise prices, in the hope that this would stimulate domestic recovery. The other was to contain and undermine politically the wild-eyed monetarists, particularly Coughlin.

During the Hundred Days the government took possession of virtually the entire nation's gold hoard and forbade its export. On June 5, 1933, "gold clauses" were repudiated so that no one could demand the metal any longer in exchange for paper notes or in payment of debts. In effect, the United States abandoned the gold standard. On July 2, Roosevelt torpedoed the London Economic Conference at which the Europeans were seeking international exchange stabilization; he wanted American devaluation. In the fall of 1933, the government began to buy domestically mined gold at gradually higher prices. This venture concluded in the passage of the Gold Reserve Act on January 30, 1934, under which the President fixed the price at $35 per fine ounce. The result was the devaluation of the dollar by slightly more than 40 percent. A by-product of this operation was to transfer control over money from the big bankers, particularly the Federal Reserve Bank of New York, to the federal government.

The silver bloc, however, was too much for Roosevelt. Senator Thomas jammed through Congress an amendment to the Agricultural Adjustment Act that authorized the President to make the metal legal tender. Roosevelt delayed by buying silver at a modest rate. The pressure in the country and in Congress continued to build up, culminating in passage of the Silver Purchase Act on June 19, 1934. Under this law the government was forced to buy silver at artificially high prices and to accumulate an inventory of the metal for which it had no use. This proved a bonanza to speculators and to the western mining interests.

The third policy option was for the federal government to stimulate the construction of public works. The need was obvious because building had almost ceased. Total outlays on construction fell 77 percent between 1929 and 1933, from $12.3 billion to $2.8 billion. In the public sector the drop was 64 percent, from $3.6 to $1.3 billion. The latter was due wholly to the collapse of building by state and local governments, while the federal share expanded modestly. The construction industry was prostrate; the building trades suffered from massive unemployment; the suppliers of materials and funds to the industry saw their markets dry up. Clearly, business and employment could not recover unless construction revived.

In the context of the Great Depression the industry was of special significance for two reasons. The first was that it was big. In 1929, for example, construction accounted for 11.5 percent of gross national product and almost 5 percent of nonagricultural employment. Second, its performance historically had exacerbated the business cycle. That is, it overexpanded in good times and overcontracted in bad. Its current condition was a dismal illustration of this rule.

For many years, therefore, a few economists and policy makers during depressions had urged measures to spur public building, but with indifferent success. There had been a handful of modest experiments by the states and localities, but they could hardly solve a national problem. In 1919 Senator Kenyon had proposed a $100 million fund to stimulate public works at all governmental levels in bad times, but the bill was reported unfavorably. In 1928 Senator Wagner tried again. A much watered-down version of his bill became law in 1931, establishing the Federal Employment Stabilization Board. But it merely advised the President and had no funds to invest. President Hoover, whose primary concern was to balance the budget, staunchly opposed the expansion of public works. In 1932 Wagner forced Hoover to accept an appropriation of $300 million for federal works and $1.5 billion for self-liquidating projects, partly available to states and localities, as the price for creating the Reconstruction Finance Corporation to provide loans to private business.

By the eve of the New Deal the theory of public works had become fully articulated. Two illustrations will suffice. In Britain, which suffered the identical distress, the noted economist, John Maynard Keynes, wrote a series of articles for *The Times* of London in March 1933 that appeared shortly in a pamphlet entitled *The Means to Prosperity*. Keynes argued that public stimulation of construction was a fundamental way to revive employment. It would create jobs in the building industry and, by the "multiplier effect," would increase employment among both suppliers and those who sold consumer goods to the newly employed. The cost to the government would be far less than the outlay on contracts because the dole would decline and tax revenues would rise. In the light of this reasoning, Keynes regarded budget balancing as a form of idiocy.

Marriner S. Eccles, a Utah banker, who was known only in the intermountain area, independently worked out the same analysis. He had been shocked by the Depression and had worried over how to deal with it. In 1931 he began to express his ideas in speeches in Utah. In February 1933, Senator Pat Harrison of Mississippi, chairman of the Committee on Finance, held hearings on the economic crisis to which he invited some 200 notables to testify, including this western banker. Eccles urged a federal fund of $2.5 billion "and more if necessary" for self-liquidating government projects and loans to states and localities at low interest rates for public works. His reasoning, while less sophisticated in form than that of Keynes, stressed the same basic points — the multiplier effect and the need for government to expand rather than curb investment.

This thinking took policy shape primarily in that title of the National Industrial Recovery Act of 1933 that appropriated $3.3 billion for public works, leading to the establishment of PWA under Ickes. The relief program, insofar as it provided jobs on public facilities, was a supplement. Together, according to Arthur D. Gayer, the leading student of public works, they "constituted the most gigantic experiment ever undertaken by any country . . . to relieve business depression and to stimulate recovery through government spending on public construction."

The fourth policy alternative was to reduce the hours of labor. This was the historic remedy of the American Federation of Labor, trotted out with each depression. The theory held that there was a fixed amount of work to be performed. If this figure was divided by the number of persons with jobs plus those seeking employment, the result would yield the number of hours everyone could work in order to provide full employment. In the context of 1932–1933 this was estimated at thirty hours a week.

In November 1932, the AFL convention in Cincinnati strongly endorsed the five-day week and the six-hour day. On December 21, Senator Hugo L. Black of Alabama introduced legislation known as the thirty-hour bill. Despite its almost certain unconstitutionality, its rigidity and unworkability, and the unanimous opposition of industry, the Black bill, floating on the economic crisis, began to sail through Congress. The Senate Judiciary Committee reported favorably on March 30 and the Senate passed it by a vote of 53 to 30 on April 5, 1933. Roosevelt and Miss Perkins were convinced that the theory was unsound, while Moley and General Johnson thought the bill would wreck the country. The Administration was determined to stop it. At first the Secretary of Labor proposed comprehensive amendments. Roosevelt then went all the way. On May 1, the President came out against the thirty-hour bill, and on May 17 he offered his substitute, the National Industrial Recovery bill. Black's proposal died in the House Rules Committee.

In summary, Roosevelt's New Deal launched a three-front attack on unemployment: raising prices and wages through NRA and AAA, devaluing the dollar by, in effect, leaving the gold standard, and pumping up federal investment with public works and jobless relief. By the summer of 1933 all three programs were under way. Except insofar as hours would be reduced flexibly by industry through the NRA codes, the Administration rejected a comprehensive policy to cut hours of work. But there was a fourth policy, if one can call it that, namely, the lifting of public confidence. This was probably Franklin Roosevelt's greatest accomplishment. Arthur M. Schlesinger, Jr., put it this way:

> Through his handling of government and his handling of Congress, through his speeches and his press conference, through his style and manner as a public figure, Roosevelt projected what a more public relations–conscious age would call his image upon the country. In 1933, it was an image of fatherly purpose which reassured and unified a panicky nation.[2]

2

These policies had an immediate and salutary impact. The Department of Commerce estimate of national income payments rose from $3.5 billion in March to $4.2 billion in October 1933. The Federal Reserve Board's index of industrial production (1923–1925 = 100) spurted from 59 in March to a peak of 100 in July 1933. It remained quite high for the next three months — 91 in August, 84 in September, and 76 in October. This surge in business activity, of course, was reflected in the labor market. Nathan's monthly estimates of employment and unemployment, necessarily rough because of the inadequacy of the basic data, showed a dramatic improvement in mid-1933. His figure of the number of persons at work in March was 34,716,000. By October it had risen to 38,802,000, a gain of 4 million jobs. The Nathan estimates of those out of work fell from 15,071,000 in March to 11,176,000 in October. Thus, the unemployment rate dropped during this period from 30.3 to 22.4 percent.

Clearly, the New Deal had stopped the slide into economic disaster and for the time being had turned the system around. There can be no doubt that the main cause for this improvement was NRA. In fact, the gain during the summer of 1933 was called "the NRA boomlet." The signing of the first codes and the extraordinary hoopla in which General Johnson packaged his operation nurtured confidence. More important, businessmen, anticipating that the codes, along with devaluation of the dollar, would inflate prices, bought and produced ahead. The exceptionally high production figure for July, which could not be sustained, is evidence of this.

But by fall of 1933 the boomlet had exhausted itself. For almost two years thereafter, from October 1933 to August 1935, the American economy remained on a plateau. National income payments held fairly steady around $4.5 billion monthly. The index of industrial production moved narrowly in the 70s and 80s, far below the base period 1923–1925. Nathan's estimates of employment quite consistently ranged between 38 and 39 million. His unemployment figure hung in the neighborhood of 12 million. As a result, the fraction of the labor force out of work remained at between one fourth and one fifth.

This dismal condition, bad as it was, would have been much worse except for heavy infusions of federal funds. During this period, roughly half of Treasury expenditures were for what the Administration until mid-1935 called the "emergency" and thereafter referred to as "recovery and relief." They went mainly for agricultural assistance, for unemployment relief, and for public works. Without quite realizing what was happening, the New Deal, in responding to urgent human needs, was moving the nation into a fundamentally new relationship of government to economic life on the hinge of unemployment.[3]

3

In January 1936, Keynes published *The General Theory of Employment, Interest, and Money.* For a world groping in the dark, the book was a beacon of light. Its impact, particularly in Britain and America, was immediate and enormous, first on economists, especially the younger ones, then on shapers of public policy, and, finally, on the literate public. To describe *The General Theory* as the most important work of the Great Depression era is a gross understatement. It will probably prove to be the most significant volume in the social sciences published in the twentieth century.

Such an extravagant statement would hardly have surprised its author, whom only a fool would accuse of underestimating his own genius. Keynes completed the draft of the book in late 1934. On New Year's Day, 1935, he wrote George Bernard Shaw,

> I believe myself to be writing a book on economic theory which will largely revolutionise — not, I suppose, at once but in the course of the next ten years — the way the world thinks about economic problems. When my new theory has been duly assimilated and mixed with politics and feelings and passions, I can't predict what the final upshot will be in its effect on action and affairs. But there will be a great change, and in particular the Ricardian foundations of Marxism will be knocked away.
>
> I can't expect you, or anyone else, to believe this at the present stage. But for myself I don't merely hope what I say, — in my own mind I'm quite sure.

The famous concluding paragraph of *The General Theory,* which has given comfort to scholars, reads as follows:

> If the ideas are correct — an hypothesis on which the author himself must necessarily base what he writes — it would be a mistake, I predict, to dispute their potency over a period of time. At the present moment people are unusually expectant of a more fundamental diagnosis; more particularly ready to receive it; eager to try it out, if it should be even plausible. But apart from this contemporary mood, the ideas of economists and political philosophers, both when they are right and when they are wrong, are more powerful than is commonly understood. Indeed the world is ruled by little else. Practical men, who believe themselves to be quite exempt from any intellectual influences, are usually the slaves of some defunct economist. Madmen in authority, who hear voices in the air, are distilling their frenzy from some aca-

> demic scribbler of a few years back. I am sure that the power of vested interests is vastly exaggerated compared with the gradual encroachment of ideas. Not, indeed, immediately, but after a certain interval; for in the field of economic and political philosophy there are not many who are influenced by new theories after they are twenty-five or thirty years of age, so that the ideas which civil servants and politicians and even agitators apply to current events are not likely to be the newest. But, soon or late, it is ideas, not vested interests, which are dangerous for good or evil.

John Maynard Keynes was born in Cambridge on June 5, 1883, into one of those remarkable English families, like the Darwins and the Mills, which was distinguished, not for title or wealth, but, rather, for intellect, for scientific curiosity, for faith in reason, and for commitment to improving man's lot. His brother, in fact, married Charles Darwin's granddaughter. His father, John Neville Keynes, was a political economist of some note, the author of basic works on deductive logic and methodology in economics, as well as the chief administrator of Cambridge University. His mother, Florence Ada Keynes, was one of the first women students at Newnham College, was involved in the welfare of the town, and would become the mayor of Cambridge. His brother, Geoffrey, was a noted surgeon and Blake scholar. His sister, Margaret, married A. V. Hill, who would win the Nobel Prize in physiology.

Keynes enjoyed a happy and stimulating childhood in Cambridge, prepared at Eton, and entered King's College in 1902. It was an exceptional moment at Cambridge. Aside from being a brilliant student, particularly in mathematics and philosophy, Keynes came under the influence of the philosopher G. E. Moore, in the company of a group of extraordinary young people. Leonard Woolf wrote much later that Moore was "the only great man I have ever met or known in the world of ordinary, real life." Aside from Keynes, the students included Lytton Strachey, E. M. Forster, Woolf, Clive Bell, Duncan Grant, Desmond MacCarthy, and Thoby Stephen. The last was often visited by his beautiful and gifted sisters, Vanessa, who married Bell, and Virginia, who wed Woolf. In the years just before the First World War, Keynes and most of the others, along with the art historian Roger Fry, lived near each other in London and formed the nucleus of a loose movement called after the neighborhood, Bloomsbury.

No one has ever succeeded in defining Bloomsbury. Leonard Woolf has written,

> There have often been groups of people, writers and artists, who were not only friends, but were consciously united by a common doctrine and object, or purpose, artistic or social. The utilitarians, the Lake poets, the French impressionists, the English Pre-Raphaelites were groups of this kind. Our group was quite different. Its basis was friendship, which in some cases developed into love and marriage. The colour of our minds and thought had been given to us by the climate of Cambridge and Moore's philosophy, much as the climate of England gives one colour to the face of an Englishman while the climate of India gives a quite different colour to the face of a Tamil. But we had no common theory, system, or principles which we wanted to convert the world to; we were not proselytizers, missionaries, crusaders, or even propagandists.

While this is certainly correct, it does not go far enough. Bloomsbury, including Keynes, shared a set of common values.

One was a passion for the word, spoken and written. These people treasured the English language. They were brilliant conversationalists and controversialists; many, Keynes among them, were writers of the very first order. Second was their devotion to art. They were, of course, intimately caught up in literature and painting, and they were captivated by the ballet. The third value is a bit difficult to put, but significant: They waged a civilized revolt against the institutions and values of Victorian Britain. The received verities were, at the least, examined critically and often rejected. This process crossed the span of human experience — Empire, the Queen, classical economics, religion, sex, literature, and painting, among others. Bloomsbury welcomed the big challenge, gloried in leading the way to the new. Finally was their faith in human reason. These people, notably Keynes, believed that issues could be thought through, debated, written out in rational fashion and that the world, or at least the most important part of it, would accept the conclusions because they were intellectually defendable. This was based upon an optimistic judgment of the perfectibility of man, the notion that the mind could control the feelings.

In Woolf's sense and in possessing these values, Keynes was of Bloomsbury. But he was something more, quite different from the others: he was worldly. He was enamored of and would become much involved in large affairs — finance, business, publishing, politics, international relations. While Keynes enjoyed both his lives, he was somewhat suspect with those on either side who did not cross the line.

In 1906, Keynes took his first job in the India Office in London. The duties were not onerous. He said later that his only achievement in a two-year stint was to get one pedigreed bull to Bombay. In fact, the painful problem of the rupee aroused his interest in monetary questions and led to his first book, *Indian Currency and Finance* (1913). He also spent much time on a dissertation for King's College, which came out as the *Treatise on Probability* (1921).

While Keynes had done little economics at Cambridge, his brilliance had caught the eye of Alfred Marshall, the reigning monarch of the classical school worldwide. In 1908 Marshall retired from lecturing to allow himself more time for writing and was succeeded by the youthful A. C. Pigou. This caused an envious senior colleague to decline to lecture further and still another economist departed. There were openings for two lectureships and Keynes was offered one. He accepted, though the only certainties were £100 from Pigou's pocket and an equal amount from his father's.

Thus, Keynes returned to King's to teach economics. He considered the corpus of traditional theory slight and amenable to command in a very short time. He quickly mastered Marshall and expounded the master's ideas to his own pupils. He also worked away at probability and became editor of the *Economic Journal,* a post he would hold for thirty-three years. At the same time he shared quarters in Bloomsbury so as to be with his friends in London.

World War I shattered this pleasant arrangement. Early in 1915 Keynes went to the Treasury, in which he held several important posts. He, evidently, was primarily responsible for arranging the financing of Britain's war effort. R. F. Harrod has written, "There have been men of ripe judgment who affirmed that Keynes contributed more than any other person in civil life to winning the First World War." Early in 1918 an incident brought out the Bloomsbury in Keynes. Britain's loans to France had mounted and the French were running an unfavorable balance of payments. Degas was to hold an auction in Paris of his private collection. Keynes persuaded Chancellor of the Exchequer Bonar Law to set aside £20,000. With it he made a rich haul in modern paintings and drawings for the National Gallery. He also bought on his own account a Cézanne and an Ingres, the start of a sizable private collection.

In 1919 Keynes was the Treasury representative on the British delegation to the Paris peace conference. Positioned to observe the peacemaking from the inside, he participated energetically and with growing frustration in the drafting of the reparations provisions. He was appalled by what he called "this scene of nightmare" and thought the reparations terms of the Treaty of Versailles would undermine postwar economic stability. He resigned from the delegation, exhausted and ill, on June 5, 1919, informing Lloyd George, "I can do no more good here."

During August and September, Keynes wrote a book about the experience that was published in December 1919 as *The Economic Consequences of the Peace.* It was a devastating analysis of the treaties, written in sparkling Keynesian prose. Harrod has called it "one of the finest pieces of polemic in the English language." The book caused a sensation among both those who agreed with the argument and those who did not. Keynes, overnight, became an international celebrity.

He had a personal postwar reconversion problem. The style of life to which he aspired would be expensive, and he had almost no money. He decided to reduce his commitment to Cambridge in order to allow time for ventures in London. Keynes became a speculator in foreign currencies and made investments; he went on the board of a large insurance company. After a precarious start he became remarkably successful. He accumulated a substantial personal fortune and managed the finances of King's College spectacularly. His method was to pay no attention to insider's tips. He relied mainly upon information published in the newspapers, which he filtered into his assessments of future prospects, short- and long-term. Keynes did this work in the morning in bed and reckoned that it took half an hour a day.

He was again a resident of Bloomsbury amid the circle of his old friends. In 1921 Diaghilev brought his ballet company to London. Keynes was enchanted, especially captivated by a leading ballerina, Lydia Lopokova. He brought her into Bloomsbury. She amused his friends with her troubles with the English language: "I dislike being in the country in August, because my legs get so bitten by barristers." They were wed in 1925. While there were mutterings about Keynes marrying a dancer, Mrs. Marshall approved: "The best thing that Maynard ever did." Later, Keynes would put his shrewd manipulative mind to work in support of the arts in Britain, particularly the ballet and painting.

By now the famous Keynes character and style were fully articulated. In the conclusion of its obituary of April 22, 1946, *The Times* of London summed them up this way:

> And finally there was the man himself — radiant, brilliant, effervescent, gay, full of impish jokes. His entry into the room invariably raised the spirits of the company. He always seemed cheerful; his interests and projects were so many and his knowledge so deep that he gave the feeling that the world could not get seriously out of joint in the end while he was busy in it. He did not suffer fools gladly; he often put eminent persons to shame by making a devastating retort which left no loophole for facesaving. He could be rude. He did not expect others to bear malice and bore none himself in the little or great affairs of his life. He had many rebuffs but did not recriminate. When his projects were rejected, often by mere obstructionists, he went straight ahead and produced more projects. He was a shrewd judge of men and often plumbed the depths in his psychology. He was a humane man genuinely devoted to the cause of the common good.

In the late twenties Keynes bought a house in the country, called Tilton, that had once been in the family. He slowly built the property into a very successful farm. In 1942, when he was awarded a peerage, he became Baron Keynes of Tilton. Between 1925 and 1930 his consuming intellectual interest was the monetary question, and in the latter year he published a masterful two-volume study, *A Treatise on Money.* In many ways it prefigured *The General Theory,* particularly in distinguishing between savings and investment and in questioning the economic virtue of thrift.

While Keynes had started in economics as an expositor of Marshallian theory and held the great classicist in highest esteem (he wrote a glowing obituary in 1924), his pragmatic mind was always ready to bend orthodoxy to reality. When he stood classical theory on its head in 1936, this was no sudden discovery. His lecture at Oxford in 1924, entitled "The End of Laissez-Faire," is one sign. The letter he wrote his mother on August 9, 1914, is an even earlier one. Mrs. Keynes, in her capacity as Guardian of the Poor in Cambridge, had asked his advice on dealing with unemployment in the town. He responded,

> When money can be usefully spent on capital improvements, a large part of it going in payment of labour which *might otherwise be unemployed,* the argument for spending it is very strong. It would, for example, be

> ridiculous for the guardians to contribute to the amount of unemployment in Cambridge by refraining from useful building, and then spend money, in order to give relief, to maintain men in idleness or in relatively useless occupations.

Orthodoxy asserted quite a different remedy, if that is the proper word, namely, that jobs would be created if workers accepted lower wages. This was precisely Pigou's recommendation to the Macmillan Committee during the Great Depression.

That disaster, which Keynes thought a ridiculous and needless waste of human resources as well as a dangerous threat to democratic institutions, caused him to cast off the lines to Marshallian moorings totally. His book, he wrote, was "a struggle of escape from habitual modes of thought and expression." Now intellectually adrift, he was free to chart a new course. He could reconstruct economic theory to account for reality, appalling as it was, and to provide workable remedies.

Keynes called his work the *general* theory as a way of disposing of classical economics. While its teachings were not incorrect, they described "a special case only," a system of distribution under full employment. "So long as the classical postulates hold good, unemployment . . . cannot occur." This special case, obviously, is not "the economic society in which we actually live." Thus, to use classical economics as the basis for policy during the Great Depression would be both "misleading and disastrous."

The fundamental Keynesian postulate was that an economy could reach equilibrium at varying levels of employment, both *below* and at full employment. The actual level it would attain at any given moment was the sum of two factors: consumption and investment. "This is the essence of the General Theory of Employment." Together, consumption and investment constituted what Keynes called "effective demand." If it was insufficient, it would bring "the increase of employment to a standstill *before* a level of full employment has been reached." This explains "the paradox of poverty in the midst of plenty."

The individual, the corporation, and the government had two choices in the disposition of income — to buy goods and services for consumption or to save. "The propensity to consume," as Keynes put it, was a "subjective" decision in a wealthy society. One might choose to consume out of a variety of motives that he characterized as "Enjoyment, Shortsightedness, Generosity, Miscalculation, Ostentation and Extravagance." Or one might opt to save out of "Precaution, Foresight, Calculation, Improvement, Independence, Enterprise, Pride and Avarice."

If a given propensity to consume is assumed, policy can determine the level of employment as a function of investment. R. F. Kahn, a student of Keynes, had published an article in the *Economic Journal* in 1931 in which he established a quantitative relationship between an increase in investment and the consequent increment in employment, which he called the "multiplier." If the propensity to consume was high, the ratio was more than one to one: "small fluctuations in investment will lead to wide fluctuations in employment." With a large propensity to consume and heavy unemployment, public works will generate many more jobs than those directly created by the works themselves.

This analysis led Keynes into a playful discussion of a "wasteful" multiplier relationship. While, obviously, it was "sensible" for the community to gratify social needs by building houses, schools, roads, and the like, mankind — including, notably, statesmen and bankers — was not always distinguished for rationality. Wasteful investment in an activity like warmaking had precisely the same effect on employment. "The form of digging holes in the ground known as gold-mining, which not only adds nothing whatever to the real wealth of the world but involves the disutility of labour, is the most acceptable of all solutions." Britain, he suggested, could restore full employment "if the Treasury were to fill old bottles with banknotes, bury them at suitable depths in disused coal mines, which are then filled up to the surface with town rubbish, and leave it to private enterprise on well-tried principles of *laissez-faire* to dig the notes up again." For the ultimate in nonsense, Keynes much admired ancient Egypt because it had created employment with *two* useless activities — pyramid-building and the mining of precious metals.

A basic assumption of traditional theory was that savings were automatically invested. Keynes thought this "absurd." The act of saving, he pointed out, was a decision "not to have dinner today." One did not eat that meal tomorrow; it became economically lost. Thus, one could not rely on private savings to keep the level of investment high enough to produce full employment. If the object was to increase employment, thrift was not, as capitalism preached, a virtue. Economic growth, "so far from being dependent on the abstinence of the rich, as is commonly supposed, is more likely to be impeded by it." This conclusion undermined a basic argument in favor of the inequitable distribution of income and wealth. Keynes was quite prepared to see "the euthanasia of the rentier," in fact, thought it inevitable.

Since the rate of investment was critical in fixing the level of employment, the state must play a central role in determining "the inducement to invest." Aside from this, Keynes, who had no taste for socialism, would leave matters to individual choice and private markets. He considered the general theory "moderately conservative in its implications." In this, Keynes, of course, was correct. His system, by providing for economic growth and high employment, would allow capitalism to endure, would smooth out many of its grosser inequities, and would undermine movements for revolutionary change.

In hindsight, it is difficult to understand the jolt these ideas produced contemporaneously. Conservatives, of course, found them repugnant. Even many liberals, Franklin Roosevelt among them, were unable to get them fully down. Alvin H. Hansen, of Harvard, who would become the leading American Keynesian, needed a good deal of time for digestion. Paul A. Samuelson, who would make a fortune out of a textbook that popularized *The General Theory* and would also win the Nobel Prize in economics, wrote,

> I have always considered it a priceless advantage to have been born as an economist prior to 1936 and to have received a thorough grounding in classical economics. It is quite impossible for modern students to realize the full effect of what has been advisedly called "The Keynesian Revolution" upon those of us brought up in the orthodox tradition. What beginners today often regard as trite and obvious was to us puzzling, novel, and heretical.
>
> To have been born as an economist before 1936 was a boon — yes. But not to have been born too long before![4]

4

In the late summer of 1935, the American economy entered its first relatively substantial period of expansion since the twenties, which lasted for two years. Income payments moved upward from $4.5 billion in August 1935 to just over $6 billion in October 1937, a gain of one third. The index of industrial production (1923–1925 = 100) advanced from 87 in August 1935 to 115 in August 1937, an increase of close to one third. Nathan estimated that nonagricultural unemployment declined from about 8.5 million in the summer of 1935 to 6.25 million in mid-1937. The Bureau of Labor Statistics reported that the number at work in manufacturing industries rose from 7,236,000 in July 1935 to 9,120,000 in July 1937, a gain of almost 2 million jobs, or about one fourth. The BLS annual data for the entire civilian labor force show a rise in employment from 42,260,000 in 1935 to 46,300,000 in 1937; this is about a 4 million advance, just under one tenth. The number out of work fell from 10,610,000 in 1935 to 7,700,000 in 1937, an improvement of almost 3 million jobs, or about one fourth.

There appear to have been two basic causes for this recovery. The first was an increase in the already strong federal support for the economy. It will be recalled that Congress, at Roosevelt's urging, had passed the Emergency Relief Appropriation Act in April 1935 and that WPA and PWA were at this time pumping into the system the $4,880,000,000 the law provided. Further, early in 1936 both houses overwhelmingly passed the soldiers' bonus over the President's veto. Certificates amounting to $1.7 billion went out in June and $1.4 billion were cashed within the next six months, mainly during the summer of 1936. The second factor was a marked increase in consumption. In part this was the consequence of higher federal expenditures. But there was something more. After half a dozen years of depression the old Model A was plumb worn out and there was a big hole in the seat of the nation's pants. For those with incomes, with savings, or with access to credit, this was the time to replace consumers' goods that were no longer serviceable.

Some were carried away by the recovery and thought the nation would soon be back on solid economic ground. Secretary of the Treasury Morgenthau, who was apoplectic over the unbalanced federal budget, on August 23, 1936, handed Roosevelt the draft of a speech written in the Treasury's Research Division. It opened: "We have today reached the point where we can say with real meaning, wasn't the depression awful?" The author predicted on the basis of the current rate of recovery that within four years relief would be eliminated, the budget would be in balance, and the debt could start being retired. The President told Morgenthau that it was "great stuff," but he did not use it. Keynes, on the contrary, thought the United States was enjoying a temporary upturn of short duration that would be followed by another depression. Unfortunately — and, as usual — Keynes was right.

The boomlet was both weak and lopsided. None of the indicators reached the levels of the twenties. Two estimates of gross national product in current dollars showed that 1937 was 13 percent below 1929 and 8 percent under the 1925–1929 average. The index of income payments seasonally adjusted peaked at 91 in August 1937 compared with 100 in 1929. The index of industrial production seasonally adjusted (1923–1925 = 100) got up to 118 in March, April, and May 1937, almost reaching the monthly average of 119 in 1929. Automobile output was exceptionally high in the spring of 1937. The Dow-Jones industrials, which had averaged 311 in 1929, peaked at 184 in August 1937. The gravest weakness, of course, was employment. Here it must be borne in mind that the civilian labor force had grown from 49,180,000 persons in 1929 to 54,000,000 in 1937, an increase of 11 percent. Thus, if 1937 was to have been a year of reasonably full employment, it would have been necessary both to have replaced the 1929 jobs that had been lost and also to have created almost 5 million new jobs. Neither was accomplished. As noted above, 7,700,000 people were still out of work in 1937.

Further, the 1935–1937 boomlet was not in balance. Its main force was increased consumption. Capital expenditures by business were $11,489 million in 1929, bottomed at $2,987 million in 1933, and recovered to $8,200 million in 1937. Consumer expenditures were $73,342 million in 1929, dropped to $42,270 million in 1933, and rose to $63,000 million in 1937. Thus, by 1937, capital expenditures had recovered only 71 percent of their 1929 level in contrast with 86 percent for consumption. Hansen has stressed that investment leads a sustained recovery, that it cannot play this role if it is limited to the satisfaction of current consumption, that it must include "large bold projects, looking far into the future." But during the 1935–1937 years, "new investment in plant and equipment was geared rigorously and narrowly, to a quite unusual degree, to the immediate requirements of consumption." Businessmen shied away from long-term commitments.

The situation with regard to construction, particularly housing, was even more dismal. Average annual expenditures on residential and public construction between 1925 and 1928 were $7,368 million. They touched bottom in 1933 at $2,294 and rose to $4,400 million in 1937. This was only 60 percent of the level of the late twenties. There was a widely held view in the thirties that the nation was wearing out its old housing, that there could be no sustained recovery without a very large increase in residential construction. It did not show up during the 1935–1937 recovery.

These basic weaknesses in business investment and residential construction made the boomlet highly vulnerable. If consumption fell due to a reduction in either governmental or personal expenditures, or both, particularly for automobiles, the recovery would collapse. This is precisely what occurred.

The stock market, which had been rising continuously since March 1935, topped out in February 1937. The averages declined over the next six months at a modest though ominously steady rate. The industrial production index, seasonally adjusted, started to fall in June. Automobile output fluctuated erratically between May and October. The adjusted index of income payments leveled off in March. Factory employment behaved in like manner. Thus, by the spring of 1937 the upward thrust of the recovery had exhausted itself. For approximately six months thereafter the economy teetered precariously.

In October 1937 the nation entered a "recession" that Kenneth D. Roose has described as "without parallel for its severity in American history." The swiftness of the collapse much exceeded that which followed the crash of 1929.

On October 11, 1937, there was a very sharp take-out in the stock market. Earle Bailie, a financier whose judgment Morgenthau respected, phoned him that there was a "lack of confidence bordering almost on disorder, or you could use the word panic, if you wanted to, but that would be putting it a little strongly." Any doubts that remained were resolved on "Black Tuesday," October 19, when the market collapsed. Prices plummeted, as Morgenthau put it, "amid an hysteria resembling a mob in a theater fire." There were frantic demands that the President close the exchange. While Roosevelt declined to do so, the people in the White House were badly frightened.

Over the succeeding nine months the American economy was wrung out. National income fell 13 percent, payrolls 35 percent. Industrial production declined by one third, durables output by more than one half. The seasonally adjusted index of automobile output skidded from 142 in October 1937 to 43 in July 1938, knocking out a main prop of the recovery. Employment in manufacturing industries dropped by almost one fourth. The estimate of civilian employment declined from 46,300,000 in 1937 to 44,220,000 in 1938, a loss of over 2 million jobs. Unemployment rose from 7,700,000 to 10,390,000, an increase of more than 2.5 million.

Economists, who had been of little help in explaining the 1929 depression, rushed in to offer diagnoses of the 1937 recession. They may charitably be described as differing sharply, doubtless reflecting the basic prejudices of their authors. Roose analyzed these analyses alongside the actual economic performance and came up with three basic causes for the downturn.

Though Roose did not rank it first, Hansen, probably the keenest of the contemporary observers, stressed the dropoff in government support for the system. In the latter stages of the recovery and even after the economy began to slip, Morgenthau, whose economics was of the most orthodox sort, urged Roosevelt, Hopkins, and Ickes to reduce federal expenditures. He enjoyed a good deal of success. Further, in 1937 the new social security and unemployment insurance taxes skimmed off a significant part of the income stream. A group of economists, sensitive to the Kahn-Keynes multiplier concept, devised a system for segregating government expenditures that increased income from those that did not. Arthur D. Gayer consolidated their results on a monthly basis for the period July 1929–November 1937. They showed that average monthly income-increasing governmental expenditures were $263 million in 1935 and $335 million in 1936. By contrast, they dropped to an average of $107 million in the first six months of 1937. The slide continued into the latter part of 1937: July — $114 million; August — $35 million; September — $36 million; October — $53 million; and November — zero. The fit with the onset of the recession is so exact as to leave virtually no doubt that the retraction of governmental income-generating expenditures was the primary cause.

The second factor that Roose pointed to was the reduced profitability of investment as a result of rising costs. Corporations, that is, were unwilling to undertake long-term capital investments because they could not foresee high future returns. In the period from November 1936 to April 1937, in anticipation of increased consumer and armaments demand, commodity and raw materials prices rose sharply in world markets. In addition, in the United States wages increased markedly with new union strength based on the Wagner Act and the CIO drives in the mass-production industries.

Finally, Roose noted Federal Reserve Board action on excess reserves that caused short-term government paper to weaken. This, in turn, resulted in higher interest rates on borrowing and the decline of stock prices. Corporations had less inducement to float securities for investment. This factor, clearly, was of secondary causal importance.

The period of the 1937–1938 recession was an unrelieved disaster for the Roosevelt Administration. The international situation was desperate. The Spanish Republic was falling before Franco's fascist guns. Hitler seized Austria and Czechoslovakia and brought Britain and France to humiliation at Munich. Japanese forces penetrated deep into China and in December 1937 bombed and sank the American gunboat *Panay* in the Yangtze River. There was a gloomy consensus that World War II would soon break out. On October 21, 1937, Ickes joined Roosevelt and the English writer H. G. Wells for lunch. Wells said it would start in 1940; the President thought 1941 more likely.

The domestic scene was equally dismal. Despite his enormous victory in the 1936 presidential election, Roosevelt's position inside the country deteriorated. His prime legislative proposal in 1937, to increase the membership of the Supreme Court, was beaten decisively in the Senate, though he would gain a more liberal court in the long run. The President called Congress into special session late in the year. None of his proposals passed. The fruitless fight over the wages-and-hours bill showed that the sharp cleavage between AFL and CIO on the industrial front had now spread to the legislative chambers. The New Deal was blamed for the great contemporary strikes, particularly the sitdowns at General Motors and the bloody Little Steel confrontation. The latter led to an irreparable breach between Roosevelt and John L. Lewis. Business and the press, sensing the weakening of the New Deal, launched vigorous attacks upon the Administration. To top everything off, the country was now sliding into a major economic decline. Roosevelt, with the example of Hoover before him, needed no lessons in the politics of depression. Dan Roper, the Secretary of Commerce, was issuing cheery statements that business was basically sound. When the cabinet met on October 9, 1937, Roosevelt said testily, "Dan, I wish you would stop giving out so many Hooverish statements." Concerning Democratic prospects, the President told Ickes that "unless we have an economic recovery before 1940 no one can be elected."

During this period Roosevelt floundered. He seemed to have lost the flair for leadership. Morgenthau found him "depressed," "troubled, as yet uncertain about policy," "just treading water." Ickes, who agreed, laid it up mainly to the "terrific defeat for the President" in the court fight. At a cabinet meeting in early November 1937, Ickes felt that he had never seen Roosevelt "so anxious." The next month they sailed together into the Gulf of Mexico on the *Potomac*. The President kept mainly to himself, reading and working on his stamp collection. Ickes thought "he didn't seem at all like himself. He looked bad and he seemed listless." On March 2, 1938, Ickes wrote that "the President appears to have lost all his fight." The New Dealers were alarmed, frustrated, and defensive.

During this period of indecision three key economic ideas emerged, which Roosevelt juggled in his mind. The first was to conciliate business, in particular by trying to bring the federal budget into balance. Morgenthau was the principal spokesman for this view within the Administration, supported by Roper and Postmaster General James A. Farley. Roosevelt was ambivalent. He was infuriated by the attacks from business and feared that concessions would lead to the dismantling of the New Deal. On the other hand, he really believed in a balanced budget, had repeatedly promised to produce one, and was stung by constant reminders that he had betrayed his pledges.

The second policy option was to adopt the program that Keynes had laid out in *The General Theory*. By now the Keynesian ideas had taken root in the universities. In the winter and spring of 1938, for example, a group of young economists, mainly at Harvard, drafted a Keynesian position paper that they published as *An Economic Program for American Democracy*. There was, as well, an influential Keynesian group within the Administration. Marriner Eccles, who had long advocated these views, was now chairman of the Federal Reserve Board and restated them both in public and in a strong memorandum to Roosevelt. The nation, he wrote, was heading into a severe depression. The urgent need was an immediate spending program on public works. William O. Douglas, chairman of the Securities and Exchange Commission, proposed the establishment of a system of industrial banks to provide capital for business, especially small firms. Leon Henderson, who worked for Harry Hopkins and had predicted the slump, now recommended the resumption of large-scale government spending. Lauchlin Currie, a sophisticated economist who was an administrative assistant to the President, worked with Henderson and urged Roosevelt to stimulate housing, exports, and agriculture. There was even a knot of high-level Keynesians within the Treasury itself. Ickes, who confided to his diary in October 1937, doubtless belligerently, "I don't profess to know anything about economics," thought Roosevelt would do well to counsel with Keynes.

The relationship between Roosevelt and Keynes, however, was peculiar and strained. The economist sought acceptance of his ideas in America because he thought the United States, as the anchor of the democratic world, must make its economic ship seaworthy. Further, he felt that the President, whose mind seemed open and pragmatic, would welcome new and workable ideas. On December 31, 1933, he had published an open letter to Roosevelt in the *New York Times* to which the latter seems to have paid no heed. In June 1934 Keynes came to Washington to consult with a number of high Administration officials, Miss Perkins among them, who were eager to learn his views. He also had a talk with the President that, while agreeable, seems to have accomplished nothing. Roosevelt told Miss Perkins that Keynes had left "a whole rigamarole of figures. He must be a mathematician rather than a political economist." Keynes said to her guardedly that he had "supposed the President was more literate, economically speaking."

On February 1, 1938, Keynes, deeply disturbed about the American recession, wrote Roosevelt a long, unsolicited, and eloquent letter. While he expressed support for several New Deal policies, he attacked the retrenchment of government expenditures in 1936 — "an error of optimism" — as a basic cause of the slump. He strongly urged a heavy resumption of investment in public works and, among other things, in housing. "The handling of the housing problem has been really wicked." He stressed the importance of the housing industry to recovery because of its large size, its geographic dispersion, and the independence of its financing from the stock exchanges. He urged placing "most of the eggs in the housing basket." Keynes also thought Roosevelt had been too hard on businessmen. They should be treated as "domestic animals," not as "wolves and tigers." "If you work them into the surly, obstinate mold, of which domestic animals, wrongly handled, are so capable, the nation's burdens will not get carried to market; and in the end public opinion will veer their way."

While Roosevelt could hardly ignore the economic advice, there can be no doubt that he found the letter as a whole annoying because he asked Morgenthau, who disagreed fundamentally with Keynes, to draft the reply. It was a banal essay in bureaucratic indirection that Roosevelt dutifully signed.

James MacGregor Burns has offered a perceptive analysis of the Roosevelt-Keynes dilemma. The roadblock was Roosevelt's mind. It was "eminently operative . . . quick, keen, fast, flexible." His mental habits were "staccato." He "disdained elaborate, fine-spun theories. . . . He hated abstractions." He insisted on retaining discretion; he refused to lock himself into a long-term commitment. Keynesian economics defied these imperatives. It was an abstract theoretical system that demanded a set of long-run policies. The President's mind could not shift to that level. As a result, Burns wrote, "Roosevelt's deficiencies as an economist were as striking as his triumphs as a politician."

The third policy choice to emerge was to unfurl the old Progressive banner of attack on monopoly. It had two sources, one intellectual, the other current experience during the recession.

As Keynes had exposed the innocence and unreality of classical theory in explaining the business cycle and unemployment, another group of economists, mainly American, had stripped away the fictions of market structure. The heart of the system, the classicists held, was "free" or "perfect" competition in markets for goods and services. This assumed two polar structures — competition or monopoly. Since the latter was limited to utilities, which were "natural" monopolies, all other markets were free. In a competitive market no firm was large enough to dominate, entry was easy, and each firm was impelled by profit maximization. Free pricing was the regulator, the theory often being called the price system. The price, by moving up and down in response to the pull of demand and the push of supply, established equilibrium in the market.

A series of studies published between 1932 and 1935 demonstrated for most basic markets in the economy that the theory had no foundation in reality. A. A. Berle, Jr., and Gardiner C. Means, in *The Modern Corporation and Private Property,* showed that many markets were highly concentrated in a small number of large firms, that the trend was in this direction, and that the managers of these big corporations controlled but did not own them. Joan Robinson, a colleague of Keynes at Cambridge, in *The Economics of Imperfect Competition,* and Edward H. Chamberlain of Harvard, in *The Theory of Monopolistic Competition,* sought to adjust the theory to reality. Means, in *Industrial Prices and Their Relative Inflexibility,* demonstrated that price was not the market regulator. Read together, these studies pictured a system wholly unlike that prescribed by the nineteenth-century classicists. Many markets were not free or perfect. Their structures were neither competitive nor monopolistic; rather, they were oligopolies in which a handful of firms dominated. Entry was either difficult or impossible. Managements, while concerned with profits, were also motivated to preserve the firm and their own positions. Prices were not free; rather, as Means put it, they were "administered" by the oligopolists. Thus, price did not regulate the market. Conversely, the structure of the market determined the price. By the time of the recession, these ideas had penetrated both the universities and the New Deal, including the White House.

The Administration, as it studied the causes of the slump, became convinced that oligopoly and especially its handmaiden, administered pricing, were basic. That is, price rigidity and even increases by the heavy industries, particularly building materials, had prevented demand from rising and had held back homebuilding. Government expenditures on public works, intended to stimulate employment, had been skimmed off by rising prices. Robert H. Jackson, the assistant attorney general in charge of the Antitrust Division, was a leading spokesman for this view. Ickes, a certified Bull Mooser, took to the airwaves in a slashing attack on monopoly. Morgenthau was shocked to learn that in presumably secret competitive bidding for cement, steel, and plumbing supplies the government had received identical prices from alleged competitors. At his press conference on February 18, 1938, the President displayed charts showing the rigidity of building materials prices as contrasted with the flexibility of agricultural prices.

On March 25, 1938, the stock market sagged sickeningly. Roosevelt, who was on vacation in Warm Springs, Georgia, snapped out of his lethargy. Now, according to Henry Wallace, he was "rarin' to go." He decided on a two-pronged program, one a Keynesian increase in federal expenditures, the other an attack on industrial concentration and administered pricing.

On April 14 the President sent to Congress a program to stimulate economic recovery, and that evening he delivered a fireside chat on network radio to the American people. While he alluded briefly to the drop in government expenditures, he argued that the main cause of the recession had been overproduction. "By the autumn of 1937 the Nation . . . had stocks on hand which the consuming public could not buy because . . . purchasing power . . . had not kept pace with the production." At the same time prices of raw materials had risen so rapidly that "buyers and builders ceased to buy or to build." Business slumped and laid off workers. This problem "calls for action." He proposed three groups of measures that together would cost slightly more than $3 billion. They were as follows:

1. Work relief:	
Works Progress Administration	$1,250,000,000
Farm Security Administration	75,000,000
National Youth Administration	75,000,000
Civilian Conservation Corps	50,000,000
2. Public works:	
Public Works Administration	450,000,000
Highways	100,000,000
Flood control	37,000,000
Federal buildings	25,000,000
3. Loans from the Treasury:	
Farm Security Administration	100,000,000
Public Works Administration	550,000,000
United States Housing Authority	300,000,000

Congress passed the bill in short order, in fact, increasing the outlay to $3.75 billion, and the President signed it on June 22, 1938. WPA, which got the lion's share of the funds, began spending them at once, particularly in midwestern automobile centers, which had been hit very hard by recession unemployment, and in the South, where, according to Hopkins, people were starving. Ickes, who had remarried and had left for a European honeymoon on May 18, had gotten Roosevelt's approval for over 2000 projects before his departure. Immediately after his return, he wrote that PWA was moving ahead "under a full head of steam." Ickes noted in his diary with satisfaction: "The stock market has been booming lately."

On April 29, 1938, Roosevelt sent his second proposal to Congress: recommendations to curb monopolies and the concentration of economic power. When private power exceeds that of the state, he argued, "the liberty of a democracy is not safe." This was the road to fascism. "Among us today a concentration of private power without equal in history is growing." It impaired the effectiveness of the economic system and barred an equitable distribution of income. He set forth the statistics of concentration. "One of the primary causes of our present difficulties lies in the disappearance of price competition in many industrial fields." This was not just dangerous to small business. "Managed industrial prices mean fewer jobs."

Roosevelt proposed two measures to deal with this set of problems. The first was to strengthen enforcement of the antitrust laws, for which he requested a special appropriation of $200,000 for the Department of Justice. The other was for "a thorough study of the concentration of economic power in American industry and the effect of that concentration upon the decline of competition." He urged the establishment of a special, properly funded intergovernmental commission to make the study, and he supplied an agenda of topics for investigation. Congress responded enthusiastically to these proposals.

In 1938, when Robert H. Jackson became solicitor general, Thurman W. Arnold, formerly the mayor of Cheyenne, Wyoming, and at that time professor of law at Yale, took over the Antitrust Division. There were several ironies in the situation. The first was that the New Deal, which had suspended antitrust under NRA, was now vigorously enforcing it. The other was that Arnold, whose many redeeming qualities included a penchant for mockery, had just published *The Folklore of Capitalism.* He had ridiculed antitrust as a ceremonial moral attack on large combinations that, in fact, were not disturbed. It is a commonplace of antitrust history that the Sherman Act, which was passed in 1890, was not really enforced until Arnold took charge in 1938. He used the new funds Congress provided to hire bright and energetic young lawyers and economists who embarked on an antitrust campaign that has no equal.

Arnold's task was facilitated by the creation of the Temporary National Economic Committee, chaired by Senator Joseph O'Mahoney of Wyoming. TNEC made a massive investigation of the structure and business practices of American industry, again without precedent.

The recession, insofar as a specific month can be named, ended in June 1938. Income payments and industrial production, seasonally adjusted, turned up in June. Employment in manufacturing, seasonally adjusted, which could be expected to lag, began to improve in July. There can be no doubt that the New Deal policy, both in anticipation and in impact, was the basic cause. Here credit must go entirely, or virtually so, to the Keynesian package. While it is impossible to measure the indirect effect of vigorous antitrust investigation and enforcement on output and employment, it is a certainty that the short-run results were, at best, slight, and, more likely, none at all.

The defect in the 1938 program was its modesty. While it succeeded in turning the system around, it failed to produce even an approximation of full employment. According to Robert R. Nathan's estimates, nonagricultural unemployment declined gradually between July 1938 and September 1939, when war broke out in Europe. Thereafter, of course, the rate of increase accelerated. Starting with January 1939, broader monthly data for employment in all nonagricultural establishments became available. The annual figure for 1937 was 31,026,000 and for 1938 it was 29,209,000. By September 1939 it had risen to 31,584,000. Thereafter the pace quickened because of the war. By December 1941, when the United States entered the conflict, 38,493,000 persons were employed in nonagricultural establishments. Despite these gains, unemployment remained a serious problem. In 1938 there were 10,390,000 out of work, 19 percent of the civilian labor force. The corresponding figures for 1939 were 9,480,000 and 17.2 percent. In 1940, despite the war, they were still 8,120,000 and 14.6 percent. Even 1941 showed 5,560,000 unemployed, 9.9 percent of the civilian labor force. The New Deal in its 1938 program merely contained unemployment; it did not eliminate joblessness. Roosevelt was a most reluctant Keynesian. Only the compulsions of war forced him to spend public funds on a scale sufficient to create full employment.[5]

5

Studs Terkel asked Larry Van Dusen about his childhood during the Great Depression. His sharpest memory was of his father, a carpenter, proud of his craft, with his own set of fine tools, and "very much of an individualist, as craftsmen usually are."

Larry was the first of six children, and there was "a special feeling between the father and the oldest son." The main feeling Larry had was of his "father's failure." He couldn't understand why he was "the kid who had to put a piece of cardboard into the hole of my shoe to go to school." Occasionally his father would find a job fixing a roadbed or driving a cab. But he considered this "beneath his status" and "he'd have a fight with the boss." The old man drank. "During the Depression he drank more." Often there were "bitter quarrels between father and son." His father had "a habit of taking off" to look for work in Chicago or Topeka, leaving the family at home, "waiting and hoping." Once in a great while "heaven would break out" and he would get a week's work. Larry remembered his return with "that smell of fresh sawdust on those carpenter overalls, and the fact that Dad was home, and there was a week's wages."

But most of the time he was out of work and the family scraped along. "A craftsman like my father felt pretty silly pouring concrete for a wall on the bluffs around the K.C. railroad yards . . . when the nation needed houses and his craftsmanship could have been used."[6]

Five

Fair Labor Standards

IN 1937, the Senate Committee on Education and Labor and the House Labor Committee held joint hearings on the fair labor standards bill. On June 11, John E. Edgerton, who ran a textile mill in the South and was president of the Southern States Industrial Council, testified in opposition. Edgerton considered himself an enlightened employer. He said he was a churchgoer and employed a number of elderly women as a philanthropic gesture. But he thought a national minimum wage and maximum hour law would ruin the South in disregard of "natural laws."

A wage of $16 a week, considering layoffs, would work out to an annual income of $620 for 42 weeks. Edgerton was asked whether a family of four — a man, his wife, and two children — assuming all were healthy, could make it on $16 a week.

> EDGERTON: Well, I say, before even I could form an intelligent opinion, I would have to know the circumstances as to whether $16 will provide him with what he calls a living standard. He may be a fellow that cannot think of a living standard unless he has four glasses of beer a day or some wine, and another fellow does not have to have that.
>
> REP. WOOD: We will just leave out all of the luxuries, the beer and the wine and champagne.
>
> EDGERTON: Some people regard those as necessities.
>
> REP. WOOD: Well, some of these $16-a-week workers might drink champagne on that fabulous wage. I am just talking about a man and a wife and two healthy children, a healthy wife, healthy himself, and satisfied with a minimum of comfort. Do you think that $16 a week is sufficient for him to rear that family in the ordinary comforts of life?

. . . and give those children proper clothing and food and give them an education?

EDGERTON: Well, it depends altogether on where he lives and what he has to pay for his rent.

REP. WOOD: The most advantageous territory — do you think $16 a week is enough in the most advantageous territory?

EDGERTON: Sixteen dollars a week is enough, now, for what?

REP. WOOD: To rear that family in the ordinary comforts of life and educate the children. Do you believe that $16 a week is sufficient?

EDGERTON: I am not going to answer such a question as that.[1]

1

NRA was the federal government's first venture into the comprehensive regulation of hours, wages, and child labor. For the New Dealers, particularly the President, Secretary Perkins, and Senator Wagner, this was in part a realization of the old humanitarian Progressive dream of eradicating social evils. They recalled the sweatshops on the Lower East Side of Manhattan and the tragedy of the Triangle Shirtwaist fire. More immediately, they sought to overcome the Depression. Shorter hours, they believed, would create more jobs; higher wages would increase consumer purchasing power; and removal of children from the labor market would reserve work for unemployed adults.

Title I of the National Industrial Recovery Act provided for codes of fair competition by industry or trade. Section 7 established labor standards in two ways. In industries or trades with collective bargaining — and 7(a) encouraged its adoption — the agreement under 7(b) would determine "the standards as to the maximum hours of labor, minimum rates of pay and such other working conditions as may be necessary." A collective bargaining agreement, if approved by the President, had the effect of a code of fair competition. In the absence of bargaining, the President under 7(c) was empowered to investigate an industry's or trade's labor conditions and to promulgate "a limited code of fair competition" fixing maximum hours, minimum wages, and other conditions of employment.

This system went into effect almost immediately after the enactment of the law on June 16, 1933, particularly in two pattern-setting codes. The first, approved by Roosevelt on July 9, covered the cotton-textile industry. Mill workers were limited to forty hours weekly.

Office employees would work a forty-hour week averaged over a six-month period. Maintenance crews could be worked 10 percent longer, but would be paid time and a half for overtime. The minimum wage was $13 a week in the North and $12 in the South, but learners, outside employees, and cleaners were not covered. While existing differentials between rates above the floor were maintained, the spread between the higher rates and the minimum was not. Employment of children under sixteen years of age was prohibited. A number of other industries adopted codes with essentially the same provisions.

In late July, NRA announced the President's Re-employment Agreement, a blanket code. It established a thirty-five-hour week, later changed to forty, for blue-collar workers and forty hours for office employees. There were some exemptions. The minimum wages gave weight both to regional and size-of-community factors. It was 40 cents an hour for manual workers or the 1929 rate, provided that the latter was not less than 30 cents. The white-collar minimum ranged from $12 to $15 a week. The provision dealing with wages above the minimum was ambiguous and required later interpretation. With certain exceptions, children under sixteen were not permitted to work. This blanket code covered many industries and trades.

By February 1935, there were in effect 517 basic codes and 178 supplements, a total of 695, covering much of American industry and over 22 million workers. This massive program had a profound impact upon labor standards. Prior to the New Deal, hours and wages in the United States were characterized by a very wide dispersion, often irrational, within plants, within industries, within cities, and between towns and regions. NRA pushed standards in the direction of more rational norms, a movement that found support in rising collective bargaining.

In the late twenties, workers were on the five-day week, the five-and-a-half-day week, the six-day week, and, in some cases, the seven-day week. Almost none worked forty hours, many forty-eight, a large number over fifty, and some in excess of sixty. The average in manufacturing in 1929, according to the Census of Manufactures, was 50.6 hours. During the Depression, because work was slack and many employers instituted work-sharing, hours declined precipitously. In

1932, average weekly hours in manufacturing were 38.3 (32.6 for durables), in bituminous coal 27.2, and on Class I railroads 38.9.

Under NRA the 40-hour week became the norm, though there were many exceptions. Of the first 393 codes, 341 provided for 40 hours — 98 as the maximum, 97 by averaging, and 146 with exemptions for certain classes of employees. Twenty-nine codes established workweeks of less than 40 hours. Excluding the 11 with variable schedules, only 24 exceeded 40 hours and 15 of those were for 48. Arithmetic dictated that the 40- and 48-hour weeks would bring with them the 8-hour day. A large minority of the codes prescribed a premium rate for overtime hours, more frequently time and a third but often time and a half. It was normally paid after 40 hours weekly and not unusually after 8 hours daily.

These were emerging rather than clearly established norms. There were many exceptions. In retailing, for example, the duration of work was fixed by store hours, usually exceeding forty. Many codes removed the limits during peak and seasonal periods, for repair and maintenance, and because of emergencies. A large number either permanently or temporarily exempted certain classes of employees, most usually supervisors, professionals, maintenance crews, office and clerical employees, watchmen, firemen, and outside salesmen. Finally, NRA was an administrative disaster and was noted for wretched enforcement. Thus, many employers violated their codes with impunity.

NRA was least successful in establishing rational uniformity on the minimum wage. Central to this failure was the complexity of the American wage structure, which overpowered the effort. Further, the regulatory system, broken down by industry and trade, was not adapted to the formulation of a national policy. Finally, administrative haste, imposed by the economic emergency, provided little time to resolve difficult policy questions.

The code minima ranged from 12½ cents per hour for needlework in Puerto Rico to 70 cents for the wrecking and salvage trade in New York City. Most of the male unskilled rates fell between 30 and 40 cents, the most popular being 35, 32½, and 37½ cents. Codes that covered 90 percent of the workers provided for differential minimum wages. They were based either solely or in combination upon region, size of community, or a time period. As the cotton-textile code demonstrated, the South received a lower wage. But there were ten different ways to define "the South" in order to meet the demands of particular industries and trades. In addition, many classes of workers were exempted entirely from coverage, most commonly the old and handicapped, office boys and girls, learners and apprentices, outside salesmen, and watchmen.

Widespread wage discrimination against women in American industry was too much for NRA. The Women's Bureau of the Department of Labor and the Labor Advisory Board urged policies of equal pay for equal work and the right of females to the same rates paid males whom they replaced, and a number of codes enunciated these principles. Nevertheless, industries and trades that employed significant numbers of women preserved wage discrimination, either in bald sex differentials, often 5 cents an hour, or for "light and repetitive work."

The experience with wages above the minimum was even more dismal. The Administration at the outset hoped to lift the entire wage structure, first, by raising the minimum for unskilled labor and, second, by maintaining existing differentials with semiskilled and skilled workers. Roosevelt amended the cotton-textile code to this end, but within a week the industry had lobbied an exemption. The President's Re-employment Agreement muddied the issue, and a stream of interpretations merely added to the confusion. Strong unions negotiated wage schedules that maintained differentials, but they covered only a fraction of the work force. For unorganized industries, lawyers devised rubbery code language to allow their clients to squeeze differentials. As a consequence, many firms raised the minimum without increasing rates for more skilled workers. Some, as the unions charged, made the minimum the maximum.

Probably the most successful of the NRA standards programs was that to eradicate child labor. The cotton-textile code, as noted above, flatly prohibited the employment of persons under sixteen. The President's Re-employment Agreement contained the same ban in manufacturing and mechanical industries, but permitted the working of fourteen- and fifteen-year-olds in other industries for periods of no more than three hours daily outside school schedules and only between 7:00 A.M. and 7:00 P.M. Of the first 455 approved codes, 423 established the sixteen-year barrier. In more hazardous industries the starting age was either seventeen or eighteen. Only 15 codes allowed the employment of children under sixteen, mainly the traditional employment of minors as newsboys, messengers, and office boys. Perhaps most significantly, the historical sweating garment trades were forbidden to employ children under sixteen.

These labor standards, of course, constituted only part of the NRA system. It also encouraged collective bargaining under Section 7(a), as well as providing control over prices, production, and trade practices in the codes. On May 27, 1935, the Supreme Court in the *Schechter* case unanimously ruled that Title I of the National Industrial Recovery Act was unconstitutional. The entire edifice, including the labor standards, collapsed.[2]

2

At this time the constitutionality of labor standards legislation, federal and state, was open to the gravest doubt. Moreover, this issue became central in the great constitutional conflict of the thirties, the struggle between Roosevelt's New Deal and a conservative Supreme Court majority.

Earlier federal regulation had dealt only with child labor. In 1916, Congress had passed the Owen-Keating bill. It prohibited the shipment in interstate commerce of goods produced in factories or canneries that employed children under fourteen or those between fourteen and sixteen who worked more than eight hours daily or six days weekly or after 7:00 P.M. or before 6:00 A.M. Mines that employed children under sixteen were forbidden to ship their products in commerce.

The Court struck down this statute by a vote of five to four in *Hammer v. Dagenhart* in 1918. The father of a child under fourteen and another between fourteen and sixteen, both employees of a North Carolina cotton mill, brought suit to set the law aside. The Court, with Justice Day speaking, did so. While Congress could regulate the shipment between states of lottery tickets, impure foods and drugs, and prostitutes, Day granted, this was only because these objects were in themselves "evil." But goods produced by children to which Owen-Keating denied the channels of commerce were "of themselves harmless." The power to regulate the hours of child labor, Day wrote, is "a purely state authority." If Congress abused the commerce power by invading the jurisdiction of the states, "our system of government [would] be practically destroyed." The main historical significance of the decision in *Hammer v. Dagenhart* is that it gave Justice Holmes the excuse to file a powerful dissent. Since Day's reasoning was tortured and absurd, Holmes was brief. The Constitution gave Congress alone the power to regulate interstate commerce. The Founding Fathers made no distinction between evil and harmless objects of commerce. If there is any "evil" about which "civilized countries have agreed," Holmes noted in passing, "it is the evil of premature and excessive child labor." Inasmuch as the authority to regulate commerce was reserved exclusively to Congress, "the act does not meddle with anything belonging to the states."

Congress reenacted the substantive provisions of Owen-Keating in 1918, this time tying enforcement to a 10 percent tax on the net profits of manufacturing or mining companies that violated the law. The Supreme Court set this statute aside in 1922 as an unconstitutional exercise of the taxing power. The sponsors of child-labor regulation now reluctantly turned to their last recourse, constitutional amendment. Congress passed the amendment in 1924 that would authorize it to regulate "the labor of persons under 18 years of age."

State regulation of minimum wages and maximum hours had fared almost as poorly in the courts as had federal statutes. Because of constitutional concern and the opposition of the AFL, no state tried to establish wage floors for men. But sixteen states and the Congress for the District of Columbia enacted laws between 1912 and the early twenties to guarantee "a living wage" for females. In the key case, *Adkins v. Children's Hospital,* in 1923 the Supreme Court struck them down by a vote of five to three.

The hospital employed women at less than the legal rate and the Minimum Wage Commission of the District of Columbia sought to enforce compliance. Children's Hospital appealed to the courts on the ground that the law was unconstitutional. Justice George Sutherland for the majority agreed.

His central argument was that the right to contract was a fundamental liberty of which no one could be deprived without due process of law. This right was protected against Congress by the Fifth Amendment and against the states by the Fourteenth Amendment. In contracts of employment "the parties have an equal right to obtain from each other the best terms they can as the result of private bargaining." Thus, Children's Hospital was free to hire a woman at a wage that, in the view of Congress, undermined her health and morals and she was correspondingly free to accept that rate. In Sutherland's view there was no difference between a contract to sell labor and one to sell goods. The minimum-wage law, therefore, was a price-fixing mechanism to determine a price for the labor of a female wage earner that was higher than one that she could bargain for herself. In a contract for employment "the amount to be paid and the service to be rendered shall bear to each other some relation of just equivalence." By exacting a tax upon the innocent employer, the law became "a naked, arbitrary exercise of power" prohibited by the Fifth Amendment.

This reasoning, both extreme and strained, gave Justice Holmes the opportunity to file another masterful dissent. He pointed to "the vague contours of the Fifth Amendment," in particular the meaning of the word "liberty." "That innocuous generality was expanded into the dogma, Liberty of Contract." The word "contract" was nowhere to be found in either the Fifth or Fourteenth Amendment. The courts had read it in, as Sutherland was doing here. Holmes then listed a series of restrictions upon freedom of contract that the Supreme Court had approved, including laws forbidding contracting on Sunday ("one-seventh of our whole life") and fixing the size of a loaf of bread. "Pretty much all law consists in forbidding men to do some things that they want to do, and contract is no more exempt from law than other acts."

The constitutionality of state laws restricting hours of work was mixed. Oregon enacted a statute in 1903 that forbade the working of women more than ten hours a day. On September 4, 1905, Curt Muller's Grand Laundry in Portland employed a female for more than ten hours and was fined $10. The conviction was upheld by the Oregon Supreme Court. The laundry then appealed to the Supreme Court of the United States, arguing that it had been deprived of freedom of contract under the Fourteenth Amendment. The state retained Louis D. Brandeis as counsel, and in *Muller v. Oregon* he submitted the first of his famous sociological briefs. It contained extensive evidence that long hours of work impaired the health, safety, and morals of working women. These were matters, he contended, that a state under its police power was free to regulate even if that infringed liberty of contract.

A unanimous Court through Justice David J. Brewer agreed, obviously impressed by the sociological evidence. Liberty of contract, Brewer argued, was not an absolute right under the Fourteenth Amendment. A state through its police power could restrict freedom to contract in order to protect citizens unable to take care of themselves. "Woman's physical structure and a proper discharge of her maternal functions . . . justify legislation to protect her from the greed as well as the passion of men."

The constitutionality of legislation that regulated hours of work of men was narrow and confused. Both the federal government and some of the states had eight-hour limits for work under public contracts. In 1903 the Court in *Adkin v. Kansas* had ruled that there was no freedom of contract where the government was a party. Both the federal government and the states limited hours of work in certain transportation industries in the interest of safety. The courts sustained their constitutionality, for federal law under the commerce clause and for state legislation under the police power. Several states, though not the leading coal producers, fixed an eight-hour limit for work in mines. The Court sustained their constitutionality in 1898 in *Holden v. Hardy.*

In industries other than transportation and mining the constitutionality of state restrictions on the hours men could work was in doubt. In *Lochner v. New York,* in 1905, the Supreme Court held that a New York law that fixed a ten-hour limit for bakeries violated the Fourteenth Amendment. But in 1917, the court sustained a ten-hour law in *Bunting v. Oregon.* It did so under the police power, without expressly overruling Lochner. No one knew which rule would prevail in the future.

The *Schechter* case, of course, involved a comprehensive federal regulatory scheme made pursuant to the National Industrial Recovery Act. On April 13, 1934, the President had approved the Live Poultry Code for the metropolitan New York City area, which applied to all firms engaged in the sale, handling, and slaughtering of live poultry. The code fixed maximum hours at forty weekly and a minimum hourly wage of 50 cents; it prohibited the employment of children under sixteen. It also forbade certain "unfair methods of competition," among them the sale of chickens in lots smaller than a half coop. The Schechter brothers operated two wholesale kosher markets in Brooklyn. The great majority of the live chickens they bought at the West Washington Market and the railroad terminals in

New York came from out of state. Kosher butchers (*shochetim*) in their employ slaughtered the chickens, which were then sold to retail dealers and butchers, all of whom operated within New York State.

The trial court convicted the Schechters of a number of code violations — working employees more than forty hours, paying them less than 50 cents an hour, and selling chickens individually, among others. The Schechters appealed on the ground that the statute was unconstitutional. The circuit court sustained most of the counts of code violations. The defendants then brought their challenge to the Supreme Court.

Chief Justice Hughes spoke for a unanimous Court, holding the law invalid on two grounds. The first was that the code-making power was inherently legislative, that the Constitution reserved that authority exclusively to the Congress, and that Congress could not transfer its power to the President. "We think," Hughes wrote, "that the code-making authority . . . is an unconstitutional delegation of legislative power."

The second consideration, the commerce clause, was to prove far more significant in the long run. The draftsmen of the Recovery Act had based its constitutionality on the authority of Congress, as Section 1 noted, "to remove obstructions to the free flow of interstate and foreign commerce." The question here was whether the Schechters, who bought live chickens raised mainly in other states but sold slaughtered poultry wholly within New York, were in a business Congress could regulate under the commerce power.

The government had argued that the chickens were in a "flow" or "current" of interstate commerce. The Court rejected this contention because the code did not cover the poultry until it reached New York. "The interstate transactions in relation to that poultry then ended." The chickens had come to "a permanent rest within the State." A related question was whether the actions of the Schechters "affected" commerce because the power of Congress extended both to the regulation of interstate transactions and to the protection of commerce from injury. Here the rule, Hughes noted, was to distinguish between direct and indirect effects, the former falling within the ambit of congressional power. "But where the effect of intrastate transactions upon interstate commerce is merely indirect, such transactions remain within the domain of State power." The government sought to show the indirect effects as related to the economic emergency, that hours and wages must be regulated in order to stimulate business recovery. "It is not the province of the Court," Hughes wrote, "to consider the economic advantages or disadvantages of such a centralized system. It is sufficient to say that the Federal Constitution does not provide for it."[3]

3

Frances Perkins, hardly surprised that the Supreme Court had thrown out the NRA, had mixed feelings about its value. The price-fixing and output restrictions in the program did not appeal to her, and she was all too aware of General Johnson's personal problems and the chaos that the system had become administratively. "I often thought that the NRA would blow up by internal combustion." On the other hand, she felt strongly that the minimum wages and maximum hours fixed by the codes had been very helpful, and she was eager to preserve them.

Anticipating the *Schechter* decision, Miss Perkins had the solicitor's office in the Labor Department draft two bills. The first dealt with public contracts and was based on Felix Frankfurter's advice, stemming from *Adkin v. Kansas,* that public instrumentalities had the authority to fix the labor conditions under which goods that the government itself purchased were produced. The other, resting on much shakier constitutional grounds, would regulate wages and hours in industry generally.

At a meeting with Roosevelt shortly before the *Schechter* decision came down, he had been gloomy about the prospect. "Never mind," Miss Perkins said, "I have something up my sleeve." He became curious and asked what it was. "I've got two bills which will do everything you and I think important under NRA. I have them locked up in the lower left-hand drawer of my desk against an emergency." Laughing, Roosevelt said, "There's New England caution for you." She reminded him of their meeting in New York when he asked her to become Secretary of Labor; they had agreed on an agenda of labor reforms, including wages and hours. She was determined not to give up.

The building trades unions, while unconcerned about protection of the wages and hours of workers generally, had long been interested in public contracts legislation for construction labor. They had pushed the Davis-Bacon Act through Congress in 1931 and had persuaded President Hoover to sign it. It required contractors who built, altered, or repaired federal public buildings or works to pay the prevailing wages in the locality as determined by the Secretary of Labor. The Secretary would fix these rates by craft on the basis of local union contracts. Under NRA, a code established wage-and-hour standards for all government contracts, not just those in the construction industry. The *Schechter* decision, of course, wiped out that code.

Immediately thereafter Miss Perkins had Thomas Eliot and Gerard Reilly, two attorneys in her solicitor's office, rework the public contracts bill in conjunction with the solicitor general's office in the Department of Justice. Senator David I. Walsh and Representative Arthur D. Healey, both of Massachusetts, introduced the measure. Walsh, who was chairman of the Committee on Education and Labor, held hearings immediately and reported the bill out on July 25. After brief debate, the Senate passed it on August 12, 1935.

This version was referred to the House Judiciary Committee, which conducted hearings late in August. Industry objected strenuously and Congress adjourned without a report. During the recess the bill was revised and then reintroduced by Healey. The Judiciary Committee resumed hearings in March 1936. The Administration and the AFL voiced strong support; industry was firmly opposed. Nothing happened. Hatton Sumners, the conservative Texan who was chairman of the Judiciary Committee, sat on the Healey bill.

Only forceful intervention by the President would pry it out of committee. On April 17, 1936, Miss Perkins asked Roosevelt to intervene. She stressed that since the *Schechter* decision over 30 percent of the government's contractors had reduced the old code standards. The federal government, she pointed out, was "in the paradoxical position of urging industry . . . to maintain fair labor conditions and yet placing vast orders for commodities with firms whose treatment of their own employees offends all decent standards." The President on May 16 instructed his staff to "push" the bill. Sumners remained unmoved. The AFL lobbied the Judiciary Committee vigorously but got nowhere. On May 29, William Green wired Roosevelt, "IN DESPERATION, I BESEECH YOU. . . . " The following day the President increased the pressure and Sumners gave way. The Judiciary Committee reported the bill on June 5 and the House passed it on June 18. The Senate adopted the lower chamber's version two days later.

The President signed the Walsh-Healey Public Contracts Act on June 30, 1936.

Like its predecessor, Davis-Bacon, Walsh-Healey was a prevailing-wage law. It required federal contractors to meet minimum labor standards in the production of the goods they sold the government. The wages must be no lower than those the Secretary of Labor determined to be "the prevailing minimum wages" for the industry or related work in the locality. The hours could not exceed eight daily and forty weekly. Child labor (males under sixteen and females under eighteen) and convict labor were forbidden. The working conditions were to be sanitary and not hazardous to the safety and health of the employees performing under the contract. The Labor Department would administer Walsh-Healey.

Miss Perkins was pleased with the law both substantively and administratively. Its basic provisions — flexible minimum wages, the forty-hour week, and the ban on child labor — bespoke her philosophy, and she insisted that enforcement should be lodged with the Labor Department. Since the more fundamental legislative task was to get a law covering industry broadly, in her mind Walsh-Healey was "an important forerunner of the Fair Labor Standards Act."

But the constitutional barrier seemed too high. While Charles E. Wyzanski, Jr., the solicitor of the Labor Department, and several other government lawyers thought a wage-and-hour bill might squeeze through the Supreme Court, Attorney General Homer S. Cummings and other authorities Roosevelt consulted were convinced that it would not. The President told Miss Perkins that she must wait. She used the time both to have the solicitor's office rework the bill and to consult constitutional lawyers herself, some of whom thought there was some hope.

But the Supreme Court erected a stone wall in two decisions in the spring of 1936. Almost everything about the first, *Carter v. Carter Coal Co.,* had an unreal quality. Many members of Congress, both those who voted for and those who voted against the Bituminous Coal Conservation Act of 1935, expected it to be nullified. Contemporary gossip said that the Department of Justice considered the bill unconstitutional and Cummings advised the House subcommittee to "leave the question to the courts." The big Wall Street law firm Cravath staged the lawsuit by having James W. Carter, the president and a leading stockholder of the coal firm, seek an injunction against his own company to prevent compliance with the law. The labor provisions of the statute, which became the crux of the Court's holding of unconstitutionality, were, in fact, inoperative because the Bituminous Coal Labor Board had neither a staff nor an appropriation.

With the collapse of the soft coal code following the *Schechter* decision, the United Mine Workers joined with some of the operators to push a little NRA through Congress. The Bituminous Coal Commission by code would fix prices and regulate marketing. The Labor Board would guarantee the right to bargain collectively and enforce wage-and-hour standards. Constitutionality rested upon the commerce clause; Carter sold over 97.5 percent of its coal interstate. The statute expressly provided for separability, that is, if one provision were held invalid, this would not taint the remainder.

The four conservatives on the Court were joined by Justice Roberts and, in a separate concurrence that reads like a dissent, by Chief Justice Hughes. Thus, on May 18, 1936, the Court by a vote of six to three spoke through Justice Sutherland. He preferred to make the *Schechter* decision dispositive of the coal law and, in fact, wrote that it was. But Sutherland did not believe himself. The logical difficulty was that the price-fixing system was probably constitutional even under his standards. Since the conservatives were determined to set his standards aside because they considered them bad policy, Sutherland hit on the device of attacking the more vulnerable labor provisions to throw out the entire law, thereby ignoring separability. The Chief Justice found this reasoning indigestible.

Interstate commerce, Sutherland wrote, is "intercourse for the purpose of trade." Economic activities that preceded or followed were not commerce. This excluded, among other industries, manufacturing, agriculture, and, pertinent here, mining. "Congress is powerless to regulate anything which is not commerce. . . ." Regulation of wages, hours, and collective bargaining "falls upon production and not upon commerce." While the proponents contended that strikes and lost production had an effect upon interstate commerce, they are "local evils over which the federal government has no legislative control." Since the labor provisions, Sutherland argued, were inextricably linked to the pricing system, the whole statute was repugnant to the commerce clause.

Justice Cardozo dissented for himself, Brandeis, and Stone with a simple argument: the price-fixing part of the law was valid; the labor provisions were not yet operative; and Congress had expressly provided for separability. Thus, the suits that launched the *Carter* case were "premature." "The proper course is to withhold an expression of opinion until expression becomes necessary. . . . What the code will provide as to wages and hours of labor, or whether it will provide anything, is still in the domain of prophecy."

Two weeks later, on June 1, 1936, the Supreme Court, five to four, set aside the New York minimum-wage law for women and children in *Morehead v. New York ex. rel. Tipaldo.* The Great Depression had revived sweatshops that exploited women and children and the Consumers' League, despite the *Adkins* decision, asked Felix Frankfurter and Benjamin V. Cohen to draft a model bill. Searching Sutherland's opinion for a small hole through which constitutionality might slip, they came up with the theory of "a fair wage" based on the value of the service performed. Seven states, including New York, enacted the bill. A laundry in New York refused to pay its female employees the legal minimum wage and the manager was sent to jail. The laundry challenged the constitutionality of the law.

Justice Butler spoke for the four conservatives and Roberts. He saw no difference between this case and *Adkins.* The only issue was freedom of contract under the due process clause of the Fifth and Fourteenth Amendments. "The State is without power by any form of legislation to prohibit, change or nullify contracts between employers and adult women workers as to the amount of wages to be paid."

Chief Justice Hughes dissented for himself, Brandeis, and Cardozo. The fair-wage theory, he stressed, had not been before the Court in *Adkins.* Since this was a constitutional issue of "grave importance" and "profound public interest," it should be faced on the merits, not swept away by an inapt precedent. If a state could regulate the hours women work, Hughes asked, why could it not regulate their wages? Liberty of contract is "a qualified and not an absolute right." The question under the Fourteenth Amendment is whether the regulation is arbitrary, whether there is a denial of due process. "In the statute before us, no unreasonableness appears. The end is legitimate and the means appropriate."

Justice Stone, who was outraged by both *Adkins* and the Butler opinion, could not restrain himself from filing a powerful and eloquent dissent. The regulation of women's wages, he noted, was hardly an exercise in novelty. The Congress, seventeen states, and twenty-one foreign nations had passed laws.

Stone dealt with freedom of contract as follows:

> There is a grim irony in speaking of the freedom of contract of those who, because of their economic necessities, give their services for less than is needful to keep body and soul together. But if this is freedom of contract, no one has ever denied that it is freedom which may be restrained, notwithstanding the Fourteenth Amendment, by a statute passed in the public interest.

Low wages in a period of mass unemployment and poverty, like the present, affect "profoundly the entire economic structure of society." What formerly had been individual problems had now become "public problems." They were "the burden of the nation," and legislatures had the right to respond to them.

Finally, Stone urged judicial restraint. Wage regulation "is not for the courts to decide." Authority in these areas should reside in legislatures, "where it seems to me the Constitution has left them." "The Fourteenth Amendment has no more embedded in the Constitution our preference for some particular set of economic beliefs than it has adopted, in the name of liberty, the system of theology which we may happen to approve."

The *Carter* and *Morehead* decisions slammed shut the doors of the commerce clause and the due-process clauses of the Fifth and Fourteenth Amendments. Miss Perkins could not get federal regulation of wages, hours, and child labor until the fundamental issue of the Supreme Court had been resolved.[4]

4

Roosevelt remained silent on the Court during the remainder of 1936, concentrating upon his own reelection and the ratification of his New Deal by the electorate on November 3, 1936. Election day was a triumph. He outpolled Alf M. Landon, the Republican challenger, by almost 11 million votes, won all the states except Maine and Vermont, and swept in with him huge Democratic majorities in both the Senate and the House.

Buoyed by his victory, Roosevelt sprang his Court plan on a startled nation on February 5, 1937. He did not attack the Supreme Court for nullifying New Deal laws. Rather, he asserted that the justices could not keep up with their cases and stressed their advanced age. The plan would give each justice who reached seventy the option to retire on full salary. If he left, the President, of course, would name a successor. If he elected to stay on, the President could name a new justice, up to a maximum of six. Roosevelt's Court "packing" plan aroused an enormous and angry debate in the Congress and in the country. It also affected the conduct of the Court itself.

On March 29, 1937, the Supreme Court, five to four, upheld the Washington minimum-wage law for women and children in *West Coast Hotel Co. v. Parrish*, reversing the *Adkins* and *Morehead* decisions. Justice Roberts had changed his mind, in fact, had done so prior to the announcement of the Court plan. The Washington law was more vulnerable than New York's because, dating back to 1913, it lacked the fair-wage theory based on the value of the service performed that Frankfurter and Cohen had written into the latter. The facts were routine. The Washington regulatory agency had fixed a minimum wage of $14.50 a week for 48 hours of work for chambermaids. The hotel paid Elsie Parrish, a chambermaid in the Cascadian Hotel in Wanatchee, less than this amount. She sued to recover the difference between her actual wages and the legal minimum, $216.19. The hotel challenged the constitutionality of the statute as a deprivation of freedom to contract under the Fourteenth Amendment. The Washington Supreme Court rejected this argument, sustaining the law as a reasonable exercise of the state's police power. West Coast Hotel appealed to the U.S. Supreme Court.

Hughes for the Court met *Adkins* head-on:

> The Constitution does not speak of freedom of contract. It speaks of liberty and prohibits the deprivation of liberty without due process of law. . . . But the liberty safeguarded is liberty in a social organization which requires the protection of a law against the evils which menace the health, safety, morals and welfare of the people. Liberty under the Constitution is thus necessarily subject to the restraints of due process, and regulation which is reasonable in relation to its subject and is adopted in the interests of the community is due process.

The Chief Justice then cited a long list of statutes that restricted freedom of contract that the Court had validated, noting particularly the maximum hours decision in *Muller v. Oregon.* "The protection of women is a legitimate end of the exercise of state power. . . ." The dissenting opinions of Taft and Holmes in *Adkins,* he observed, "are sound."

The Court made no effort to distinguish *Adkins.* "Our conclusion," Hughes wrote, "is that the case of *Adkins v. Children's Hospital* . . . should be, and it is, overruled."

Sutherland, who spoke for the minority, was outraged and commented acerbically about judges who did not honor their oaths of office. As the author of the *Adkins* decision, Sutherland was hardly ready to pronounce himself wrong. The Washington law, he wrote, "is in every substantial respect identical with the statute involved in the *Adkins* case." That decision was correct. Thus, the Washington statute was invalid on its face. The minimum-wage law was unconstitutional unless the Constitution was amended.

On April 12, 1937, the Supreme Court opened the master valve of the commerce clause for congressional regulation by sustaining the constitutionality of the National Labor Relations Act, again five to four. The constitutional theory of the Wagner Act rested entirely upon the commerce clause. The statute's purpose was to diminish labor disputes that were obstructions to "the free flow of commerce." It gave the NLRB jurisdiction over not only industries that were directly in interstate commerce, but also those that "affected" commerce. Over the preceding forty years the Court had swung back and forth between the "coming to rest" concept, which narrowed congressional power, and the "stream of commerce" theory, which broadened it. The omens were bad. In 1935 in *Schechter* and in 1936 in *Carter* the Court had opted for the narrow view.

The key case was *NLRB v. Jones & Laughlin Steel Corp.,* and it presented the issue squarely. J & L's basic steel manufacturing mills were concentrated at Aliquippa, Pennsylvania, and it was there that the labor dispute arose. But the company imported iron ore from Minnesota and limestone from West Virginia, carrying them on its own ships and railways. It operated a nationwide network of fabricating shops, warehouses, and sales offices, shipping three fourths of its products outside Pennsylvania. Was Jones & Laughlin in interstate commerce?

The Court, speaking through Hughes, held that it was:

> It is a familiar principle that acts which directly burden or obstruct interstate or foreign commerce, or its free flow, are within the reach of congressional power. Acts having that effect are not rendered immune because they grow out of labor disputes. It is the effect upon commerce, not the source of the injury, which is the criterion.

Congress, he wrote, had the power to "protect" commerce. Here Hughes cited regulation of the railroads along with the antitrust laws. "The fact that the employees here concerned were engaged in production is not determinative." He slid hastily around *Schechter* and *Carter.*

Justice McReynolds in his dissent restated the "coming to rest" theory. The flow of iron ore, coal, and limestone had stopped in Aliquippa. Manufacturing was not commerce. The *Schechter* and *Carter* decisions disposed of Jones & Laughlin. Congress had no authority under the commerce clause to regulate "local production."

Within two weeks the Supreme Court had fundamentally transformed the constitutional prospects for federal wage-and-hour legislation. In *Parrish* it had upheld state minimum-wage regulation for women and children. In *Jones & Laughlin* it had enormously extended the power of Congress to regulate under the commerce clause.

Roosevelt was exhilarated by the Court's action on April 12. "A Great Decision," he told the press the next day. "I have been having more fun." But he had not waited for this to start the legislative process. An incident during the 1936 presidential campaign in New Bedford, Massachusetts, had sharpened the issue. A girl in the large crowd tried to pass him an envelope. A policeman pushed her back. "Get the note from the girl," the President told Gus Gennerich, his bodyguard. It read:

> I wish you could do something to help us girls. . . . We have been working in a sewing factory . . . and up to a few months ago we were getting our minimum pay of $11 a week. . . . Today the 200 of us girls have been cut down to $4 and $5 and $6 a week.

Roosevelt recounted this event at his press conference on December 29, 1936. He added regretfully that he could do nothing because "I haven't any power to do it." A reporter asked whether he favored new legislation. "Absolutely." But he did not yet know its shape. "Say that something has to be done about the elimination of child labor and long hours and starvation wages. That is as far as I could go."

"What happened to that nice unconstitutional bill you had tucked away?" Roosevelt asked Miss Perkins. She produced it. At the end of 1936 and in the early months of 1937 he took soundings with labor and industry. The prospects were grim. The bitter split in the labor movement between the CIO and the AFL was disastrous. While Sidney Hillman, the president of the Amalgamated Clothing Workers and a CIO mainstay, was strongly supportive, John L. Lewis, the head of the CIO, was lukewarm at best. The AFL had opposed minimum-wage laws for men for years, holding that their wages should be determined in collective bargaining. The Executive Council at its meeting in Washington on February 12, 1937, unanimously reaffirmed its historic position. Though a handful of progressive employers would support a law, American industry overwhelmingly and vigorously opposed it. Perhaps most discouraging politically, the South as a region, with few exceptions, was almost hysterically against legislation. Its business and political promoters were busy seducing northern industry to relocate by offering low wages, long hours, and child labor. The prospective beneficiaries of such a law, the most exploited persons in the employed labor force, were unorganized and many, probably most, did not even vote. Since they did not speak, no one heard them.

In addition, there was a difficult strategic question relating to child labor. The 1924 child-labor amendment to the Constitution evoked formidable opposition, mainly from the southern textile industry, organized agriculture, the newspapers, and the Catholic Church. By 1932, only five states had ratified the amendment and thirty-five had rejected it.

The situation changed dramatically in 1933. Under NRA, the codes restricted the employment of children and the states began to ratify the child-labor amendment — fourteen in 1933, four in 1935, and four more in 1937, bringing the total to twenty-eight of the needed thirty-six. Roosevelt strongly supported the movement. In 1936, for example, he wrote the governors of nineteen states to urge ratification. But early in 1937 the momentum died. The Catholic hierarchy, fearful of federal intervention in their parochial schools, and newspaper publishers, eager to employ newsboys, joined to defeat ratification in Massachusetts and New York. Further, in Kansas and Kentucky, which had earlier voted against and now voted for ratification, suits were brought to set aside the later acts. The arguments were that a state could not reverse itself; that two thirds of the states had voted down ratification, thereby killing it; and that the amendment had expired of old age. During 1937, the Kansas Supreme Court rejected these arguments and the Kentucky Supreme Court accepted them. Clearly, the Supreme Court of the United States would have to resolve the issue in its good time. From the short-run legislative viewpoint, therefore, the amendment process seemed hopeless. In light of the Supreme Court's recent decisions, the congressional route was more promising, either in a separate statute or by linkage to wage-hour regulation.

The Children's Bureau and the National Child Labor Committee favored an exclusive law. Roosevelt overruled them, insisting that child labor be joined to wage-hour in a comprehensive bill. His soundings left no doubt that it would be extremely difficult, if not impossible, to push wage-and-hour legislation through Congress. Child-labor regulation, by contrast, was very popular. The President did not want to give members of Congress the luxury of voting against the former and for the latter. With a consolidated bill, those who voted it down would expose themselves to the charge that they favored oppressive child labor.

In addition, some authorities thought that linkage would enhance the prospects for constitutionality. This was based on the facts that *Hammer v. Dagenhart* was a five-to-four decision, had evoked a masterful dissent from Holmes, and was under strong and growing attack. Solicitor General Robert H. Jackson was eager to give the Court a chance to reverse the *Dagenhart* ruling. Moreover, Jackson argued, linkage would allow the justices to engage in one of their favorite pastimes — distinguishing. They would have the opportunity to distinguish a new fair labor standards law (including child labor) from the old Keating-Owen Act.

On May 24, 1937, the President sent the fair labor standards bill to Congress. He said that a "self-respecting democracy" could offer no justification for "the existence of child labor, no economic reason for chiseling workers' wages or stretching workers' hours." Goods produced under conditions that did not meet "rudimentary standards of decency" should be considered "contraband" and should not be permitted "to pollute the channels of interstate trade." Roosevelt insisted that Congress had the power to regulate in this area under the commerce clause. He cited the Holmes dissent in *Hammer v. Dagenhart* as expressive of his view. Hugo L. Black introduced the bill in the Senate. He had authored the earlier thirty-hour bill and, more important, was from Alabama. William P. Connery, Jr., was the sponsor in the House.

The bill was long and cumbersome and had several gaps. This resulted from the fact that it had been worked on by many draftsmen with differing views in the Labor Department, in the Department of Justice, and in the White House, the last by Cohen and Thomas Corcoran.

The core of the system would be a five-member Labor Standards Board with broad powers to fix minimum wages and maximum hours. While no numbers were written into the bill, the Administration made no secret of its intention — 40 cents and forty hours. But the board could fix a higher wage if it concluded that collective bargaining had been ineffective or that a larger amount was needed to provide a "fair" wage. In doing so, the board was to consider the cost of living, the reasonable value of the services rendered, rates paid for comparable work under collective agreements, and those paid for comparable work by employers who voluntarily maintained "fair wage standards." This was intended to reassure the unions that the board would intervene only when collective bargaining was "inadequate" or "ineffective." But, excepting overtime, night work, or shift differentials, the board could not fix a minimum wage exceeding 80 cents an hour or one that would yield an annual income of over $1200.

The board would have authority over maximum weekly hours, none over daily hours. Employers would be able to work their employees hours in excess of the weekly standard by paying a penalty of time and a half. The board could adjust the length of the maximum workweek for industries with seasonal peaks in employment.

The bill outlawed the labor of children under the age of sixteen. The Children's Bureau could raise the threshold age to eighteen in hazardous occupations and in those that endangered the "health or well-being" of youngsters.

The standards in all areas — wages, hours, and child labor — would be national. There was no provision for regional variances. Coverage would be spotty. Intrastate industries, of course, were exempt, and their precise definition, assuming constitutionality, would depend upon how the courts interpreted "affecting" commerce. The major industry groups covered would be manufacturing, mining, transportation, and public utilities. Agriculture would be excluded for wages and hours, but included for child labor. Executive, administrative, supervisory, and professional employees were explicitly uncovered. The board would have authority to exempt "small" employers, but the term was not defined.

Joint hearings opened before the Senate Education and Labor Committee and the House Labor Committee on June 2, 1937, with Senator Black in the chair. Administration spokesmen — Perkins for Labor, Jackson for Justice, and Leon Henderson for WPA — strongly endorsed the bill on both economic and constitutional grounds. Business generally, through the National Association of Manufacturers (NAM) and the Chamber of Commerce, was as vigorously opposed for the reverse reasons. The textile industry was divided. The northern sector hoped that national standards would help it overcome the southern advantage arising from lower labor costs. The southern branch of the industry, as Edgerton put it, was "mortally afraid" of precisely this result. The CIO was split. Hillman, heavily engaged in the textile organizing campaign, was eager for legislative support, particularly in the South. Lewis was ambivalent. He favored the "principles" of the bill, but wanted a number of changes. The board's authority over wages should be limited exclusively to the minimum, which he would fix at 40 cents. Wages above the floor, Lewis argued, should be left to collective bargaining. He wanted a thirty-five-hour weekly standard, with the board empowered to vary it between the outer limits of thirty and forty.

The AFL was a far more serious problem. Green, seeking to bridge a sharp cleavage within his Executive Council, endorsed the bill but only with significant amendments. The Federation supported the minimum wage for women and children, but opposed it for men. The AFL wanted a maximum workweek of forty hours, with the board empowered to vary it down to thirty. Green proposed six amendments that would insulate collectively bargained agreements, particularly those negotiated by craft unions, from regulation.

The Senate Committee's report on July 6, 1937, began the process of giving ground, particularly on coverage. The board could fix a wage of not more than 40 cents and a workweek of not less than forty hours. Vague language suggested that the agency would be empowered to establish southern differentials. The agricultural exemption was significantly broadened. In addition, seamen, fishermen, and railway employees were uncovered. Children employed in agriculture were exempted from the child-labor provisions and those under sixteen might work in other industries if such work did not impair their schooling or health.

When the bill moved to the floor of the Senate for debate, the division within the AFL became exacerbated. The railway unions had already gotten an exemption. Now the building trades and the metal trades asked the Senate to defer action for a year. Green disagreed, continuing his support for the measure with amendments. The Senate proceeded to emasculate the bill and then passed it on July 31, 1937, by a vote of 56 to 28. Trucking, airline, express, and a variety of agricultural processing employees were exempted from hours regulation. Many food-processing workers were also uncovered for the minimum wage. The prospect of a southern differential was enhanced. The regulation of child labor was virtually eliminated, and farmers, including those who raised sugar beets and tobacco, the worst abusers of youngsters, were made exempt.

The report on August 6 of the House Labor Committee on the Senate bill made the concessions that Green had asked for. The board would issue orders only for those trades that were not effectively represented by unions. Further, wages and hours fixed by collective bargaining agreements would be "prima-facie" evidence of the appropriate minimum wage and maximum workweek. The House Committee restored the child-labor provisions of the Senate Committee version. It also granted the feminist demand for equal pay for equal work without regard to sex.

There is no doubt that this bill would have easily passed the House. AFL opposition had been temporarily stilled and a Gallup poll showed that the public, including people in the South, strongly favored a fair labor standards law. But the Rules Committee refused to allow the bill to reach the floor. A coalition of five southern Democrats and four Republicans outvoted the five northern Democrats. A petition by eighty-eight New Dealers to force action through a party caucus failed on August 19 for lack of a quorum because the southern Democrats refused either to attend or to vote. Congress adjourned without House action.

Roosevelt was furious. His Court plan was dead and now there was the possibility that the wage-hour bill would be killed by a legislative maneuver. On October 12, 1937, he took his campaign for labor standards to the country in a fireside chat, and he called Congress into special session on November 15.

But AFL opposition to the bill mounted, particularly against the proposal for a Labor Standards Board. This was fueled by the bitter conflict with the CIO, especially between the latter's United Electrical, Radio and Machine Workers (UE) and the Federation's International Brotherhood of Electrical Workers (IBEW). In both the *National Electric Products* and *Consolidated Edison* cases the National Labor Relations Board set aside contracts the employers had made with the IBEW because the employees had not been given a choice between the two unions. The IBEW was outraged. The union was a pillar of the building trades, and its president, Dan Tracy, sat on the Executive Council. The Federation did not want another government "board" messing around in labor matters.

When Congress convened on November 15, 1937, the southern Democratic–Republican coalition in the House Rules Committee held fast. While John J. O'Connor of New York, the chairman, had written the members of his committee on October 13 ("As you well know I am for the Bill") asking for a rule, the Administration knew that he was dissembling. Further, southern opposition intensified. James A. Farley, the party chief, informed the President that Democrats in the South were solidly opposed. The NAM, the Chamber of Commerce, and the Southern Pine Association launched a big campaign to arouse southern farmers. The November issue of *Farm Journal* ran an advertisement exhorting, "FARMERS — TO ARMS!" The White House turned it over to the FBI.

The only parliamentary hope was the extraordinary device of a petition to discharge the Rules Committee from considering the bill, which required the signatures of 218 members of the House. Healey and Mary T. Norton of New Jersey, who had become chairman of the Labor Committee during the summer when Connery died, began circulating a petition on November 17, 1937. By early December they had the necessary number, the last batch, evidently, as the result of a deal with the farm bloc to trade urban votes for the agricultural bill.

On December 14, Mrs. Norton made a major concession to the AFL by eliminating the board and replacing it with an administrator in the Labor Department. It was too late. The Federation's Executive Council on December 3 had endorsed a flat minimum of 40 cents and a maximum of forty hours, with administration lodged in the

Justice Department. Green opposed the Norton bill and the AFL substitute was put before the House. It was defeated 162 to 131 on December 12. The Federation asked that the Norton bill be recommitted. The New Dealers thought they could squeeze it by, but they did not count on Mayor R. S. Maestri of New Orleans and Mayor Frank Hague of Jersey City. In the vote just prior to the Christmas recess, seven Louisiana and four New Jersey Democrats switched sides and the Norton bill went down to defeat 216 to 198.

This was the first time since March 4, 1933, that Roosevelt had been beaten on a major piece of legislation on the floor of the House. The general view was that the wage-hour bill was dead. Many, reading together the President's whippings on the Court plan and on fair labor standards, concluded that the New Deal was finished.

But Roosevelt refused to concede. He complained to Miss Perkins that the bill was too long and complex. She got her solicitor, Gerard Reilly, to boil it down from forty to ten pages. She also brought Rufus Poole over from Interior to track the bill closely in the Congress, a job he performed very effectively. In his message to the new Congress on January 3, 1938, Roosevelt asked for a law "to end starvation wages and intolerable hours." But his message was conciliatory to the South, to business, and to the AFL.

After a long and complicated struggle, Mrs. Norton got her Labor Committee to vote 14 to 4 for a "barebones" bill on April 28, 1938. It made significant concessions to the AFL. The minimum wage would start at 25 cents in the first year and move up a nickel a year to 40 cents in the fourth. The workweek would begin at 44 hours and drop by 2 annually for 2 years to 40. These would be national standards. The program would be run by an administrator in the Labor Department.

The political situation had begun to turn in the President's favor. On January 4, 1938, Lister Hill, a strong Roosevelt supporter, easily won the Alabama Democratic primary for the Senate over an anti–New Dealer. A Gallup poll in February showed a heavy majority in favor of a labor standards law, including the South. Nevertheless, the Rules Committee by a vote of 8 to 6 refused on April 29 to report out the Norton bill. With public backing from the President, Mrs. Norton announced that she would put up another discharge petition. The Democratic primary election for the Senate in Florida on May 3 was fought over the wage-hour issue. Claude Pepper, who strongly supported the bill, won overwhelmingly over the opponent, J. Mark Wilcox. This was the last blow politically. On May 6, when the Norton petition was placed on the Speaker's desk, 218 members of the House signed within little more than two hours and others were waiting in the aisles to do so.

The southerners put up a last-ditch fight on the floor for a wage differential and lost. The House passed the Norton bill by a vote of 314 to 97 on May 24, 1938. When the bill was in conference southern Senators threatened a filibuster unless they got lower wages, but nothing came of it. They did get limited wage flexibility through industry wage boards. The House passed the conference report on June 13 by a vote of 291 to 89, and the Senate accepted it the next day without a record vote. The President signed the Fair Labor Standards Act on June 25, and it became effective on October 24, 1938.

The law was a tissue of compromises made to appease a formidable coalition of opponents. It would be many years before its shortcomings were overcome by amendments. Since constitutionality depended on the commerce clause, intrastate industries, however the Supreme Court would define them, were automatically excluded. In addition, there were a large number of explicit exemptions from coverage: agriculture very broadly defined, fishermen, seamen, many transportation industries, executive, administrative, and professional employees, retail trade, a large number of service trades, most of the construction industry, and many newspapers. Paul H. Douglas and Joseph Hackman calculated for 1938 that fewer than 11 million workers were covered for wages and hours, less than one fourth of the employed labor force, including agriculture. The Wage and Hour Division estimated that about 300,000 covered workers earned less than 25 cents an hour and 1,380,000 were on a normal workweek of over 44 hours just prior to October 24, 1938.

The standard workweek was fixed at 44 hours in 1938, sliding down to 42 in 1939 and to 40 in 1940. Employers, of course, could work their people longer weekly hours but at the penalty of time and a half for the excess. The administrator was authorized to relax the standard in seasonal industries for no more than 14 weeks a year.

The minimum wage was set at 25 cents in 1938 and 30 cents in 1939. Between 1939 and 1945 the rate could vary by industry between 30 and 40 cents an hour. There was the anticipation, though not the guarantee, that the minimum wage would become 40 cents in 1945.

The child-labor section of the law fixed the age of entry into covered employment at sixteen. The Children's Bureau could raise the age to eighteen in hazardous and unhealthy industries, and it could lower the age to fourteen in industries other than manufacturing and mining where employment would not interfere with schooling or impair health. But the industries that were the largest employers of children were excluded from coverage — retailing, personal service, the street trades, and much of agriculture.

Except for child labor, administration of the statute was lodged in the Wage and Hour Division of the Department of Labor. The President would name the administrator and he would be confirmed by the Senate.

Roosevelt and Miss Perkins were delighted to have the Fair Labor Standards Act, despite its shortcomings. On the night before he signed it, the President said, "Except perhaps for the Social Security Act, it is the most far-reaching, and most far-sighted program for the benefit of the workers ever adopted." One can hardly argue with this judgment. Further, Roosevelt's political sense, despite the massive opposition, was unerring. The law was extremely popular. A Gallup poll published on January 1, 1939, showed 71 percent in favor of FLSA, including 59 percent in the South. Even 56 percent of the employers polled voted for it.[5]

5

Of the conflict between President and Supreme Court, many said that Roosevelt lost the battle and won the war, that is, the Court plan died but the Court rewrote the Constitution to accommodate the New Deal. By 1941, when the case testing the constitutionality of the Fair Labor Standards Act was before the high tribunal, its composition had changed radically. The old conservative bloc — Sutherland, Butler, Van Devanter, and McReynolds — had departed. In addition, Brandeis had retired. Since 1937, therefore, Roosevelt had named five new justices — Hugo L. Black, Stanley Reed, Felix Frankfurter, William O. Douglas, and Frank Murphy — all New Dealers. There could be no doubt over how *U.S. v. Darby Lumber Company* would turn out, and, in fact, the Court was unanimous.

Darby purchased timber, transported the raw material to its mill, and there manufactured it into finished lumber, all within the State of Georgia. But the company shipped much of the final product out of the state in interstate commerce. After the passage of the Fair Labor Standards Act, Darby paid its employees less than 25 cents an hour, worked them in excess of 44 hours a week without paying the time-and-a-half penalty, and failed to keep records of these actions. The Wage and Hour Division tried to bring the firm into compliance with the law. Darby answered that the statute was unconstitutional, at least insofar as Congress sought to regulate manufacturing under the commerce clause. The district court in Georgia agreed, relying heavily upon the precedent of *Hammer v. Dagenhart.* The government, of course, appealed.

Chief Justice Hughes asked Harlan Fiske Stone to write the opinion. Stone welcomed the assignment because Darby was a "great" case and because it offered him the opportunity to confront several constitutional issues over which he had been pondering for some time.

Stone's reasoning pivoted at two points. The first was to return the commerce power to Congress that John Marshall had bestowed upon it in *Gibbons v. Ogden* in 1824. Legislative authority over interstate commerce, Stone cited Marshall approvingly, "is complete in itself, may be exercised to its utmost extent, and acknowledges no limitations other than are prescribed by the Constitution." The states, Stone added, can neither enlarge nor diminish that power. Congress, Marshall had held, had the authority to prescribe the rules by which commerce is governed. "While manufacture is not itself commerce," Stone wrote, "the shipment of manufactured goods interstate is such commerce." Thus, under *Gibbons v. Ogden,* Congress could make rules for manufactured articles that found their way into the stream of commerce.

The other pivot of the opinion was, Stone wrote, "the powerful and now classic dissent of Mr. Justice Holmes" in *Hammer v. Dagenhart.* In that case "a bare majority" had undone a century of settled constitutional interpretation by denying to Congress the authority to regulate child labor. The power of the legislature under the commerce clause is "plenary." Thus, it need not be limited to articles that are themselves harmful. Stone wrote:

> The conclusion is inescapable that *Hammer v. Dagenhart* was a departure from the principles which have prevailed in the interpretation of the commerce clause both before and since the decision and that such vitality, as a precedent, as it then had has long since been exhausted. It should be and now is overruled.

The Fair Labor Standards Act, the Supreme Court held, was a valid expression of congressional power under the commerce clause. The Darby Lumber Company must pay the statutory minimum wage, observe the maximum weekly hours, and keep proper records.[6]

Six

Social Programs in Action

AFTER WPA was established Harry Hopkins kept the newspaperwoman Lorena Hickok on the road to report on the unemployed, the relief program, and labor conditions. She wrote a thoughtful letter from Baltimore on October 31, 1935:

> Let's take a look at our relief rolls. What have we got? I think they can be divided roughly into four classes.
>
> 1 — The permanently unemployable. Widows. The aged. The chronically ill, who will never be able to work again. They really aren't our problem any more. They belong to the states and to the Social Securities crowd. . . .
>
> 2 — Employables who stand some chance eventually of getting back into private industry. And I'm afraid their number is not so high as some of us would like to think it is. In any case, they'll be the last to be taken back. And it's up to us to see that they eat until they are taken back.
>
> 3 — Employables, rendered temporarily unemployable by physical disabilities, personality problems, loss of morale, and so on.
>
> 4 — Most of the relief clients of 40 and up, still able to work, but unacceptable to private industry because of their age. A "stranded generation." This group worries me more than any other, I think. Men between 40 and 55, with families growing up — children in grade school, children in high school. Children growing up in families whose father isn't ever going to get his job back. Children growing up "on relief." Getting all the bad habits that inevitably accompany relief. Oh, can't you see it? I can cite you industry after industry in which the age limit is 40 or 45. In some it's 35! From coal miners in West Virginia to former business executives in New York City. What ARE the children of these men going to be like when they grow up?

About the first group I don't think we need to worry so much. It's just a matter of getting our Social Security program to functioning and of getting the states to come through — and they'll do it, once they realize we mean business and once we prove that we'll carry out our end of the bargain. . . .

The second group you might call still emergency cases. But if all the dope I hear is true — if the advance of the machine is going to mean less employment instead of more — don't be too optimistic about their getting their jobs back right away. And in this group are your young people, the majority of them. They can work. All they need is JOBS. And perhaps some training, since there is so little employment that they are no longer able to learn on the job. It's going to be slow, I'm afraid, but the people in this group have at least got a chance — AFTER the unemployed NOT on relief, those borderline cases, are hired.

I think we ought to find out more about the third group — employables rendered temporarily unemployable because of physical disability or loss of morale. Lord only knows how large it is. Probably much larger than we think. Take the physical end of it. I was very much impressed with something Gay Shepperson told me last Spring. She had had all the workers in her Atlanta case load given a physical examination. FIFTY PER CENT of them, according to the doctors, were not in condition to work. They were not permanently disabled. But there were things like hernia and a host of evils rising out of insufficient food, lack of medical and dental care. Incipient tuberculosis, heart troubles that could be relieved if not cured, stomach troubles, nervous ailments, diabetes — probably in many cases simply toxic, arising out of neglected teeth and tonsils. . . . Here is a large group of people who must be rehabilitated before they've got even a slim chance of going back to work. They can't even work on PWA. What are we going to do with them?

The rest of that group interests me even more. The people who've "gone sour." The people who have lost their morale, have no ambition to work any more, have become "chiselers," have developed personality problems that right now would make it impossible for them to hold jobs if they had them. I think we ought to find out who these people are, too, how many of them there are, and make some plans for them. These are people who are going to have to be "case-worked." It's a tremendous job, of rehabilitation. I'm interested in these people because I think they are causing us most of our trouble, with the public. Lord only knows how many there are, but there are some in every community. And gradually they've managed to bring discredit on the whole idea of relief. They are the people we're getting letters about. . . . What about a vast group of them who won't take jobs in so-called private industry because relief, however inadequate, represents more than they ever earned working. Negresses who used to work ten hours a day in the truck gardens around Charleston, S.C., for 25 cents a day. Mexicans in Texas and Arizona who were perfectly happy on $8 a month relief, because they'd never earned that much in their lives. After all, can you blame a Mexican if he prefers relief to a contract in the beet fields so miserable that he's got to put his five- and six-year-old children out there pulling beets in order to get the barest necessities of life?[1]

The Roosevelt Administration, as the Hickok letter demonstrates, had learned by 1935 that dealing with those in need was exceptionally complex. The assumption, widely held at the outset of the New Deal, that people out of work were pretty much alike, had been discarded. By 1935 it was clear that there was a variety of discrete problems, each of which demanded a particular policy solution. They fell into five categories.

The first was relief for the unemployed. The basic program was work relief for jobless adults able to hold a job and administered by the Works Progress Administration. In addition, there were two special programs for young people. The Civilian Conservation Corps enrolled young men from relief families for training and work in the conservation of forests and other natural resources. The National Youth Administration provided needy young people of both sexes with part-time jobs to finance their education.

Second, the Social Security Act established three categorical public assistance programs: for the needy aged who did not qualify for old-age pensions (benefits were not scheduled to start until 1942); for families with dependent children; and for the blind.

The third basic policy was to provide employment for jobless construction workers on public works through the Public Works Administration.

Fourth, the Social Security Act created a system of unemployment insurance for workers who were laid off or lost their jobs. There was a parallel program for the railroad industry.

Finally, the Social Security Act established old-age pensions for retired workers. The Railroad Retirement Act created a similar system for the railroad labor force.

1

Under the Emergency Relief Appropriation Act of 1935, Roosevelt by executive order on May 6, 1935, established the Works Progress Administration to provide work relief for employable adults. Throughout its history, both the President and the Congress considered WPA a "temporary" if not an "emergency" agency, slated for oblivion as soon as severe unemployment disappeared. This assessment was reflected particularly in one-year appropriations, which made long-term planning by the agency impossible. Joblessness, of course, did not vanish, in fact, grew worse during the 1937–1938 recession. Thus, WPA became a semi-permanent program, surviving into World War II.

WPA in 1935 inherited the administrative apparatus of the Federal Emergency Relief Administration. Hopkins continued as Administrator and brought with him most of the old staff. The name became Work Projects Administration in 1937 without affecting the acronym. Hopkins left in December 1939 to become Secretary of Commerce. He was succeeded by Colonel F. C. Harrington of the Army Corps of Engineers, who died in October 1940. Howard O. Hunter then directed WPA until 1942. Since both joblessness and works projects were overwhelmingly local, WPA was highly decentralized, with a small Washington staff and 53 "state" organizations — the 48 states, New York City, half of California, the District of Columbia, Hawaii, and Puerto Rico. The arts programs — music, writing, art, theater, and historical records — were handled from Washington. Administrative costs, mainly for labor, were low. In March 1937, when there were 30,347 employees in administrative positions, 24,108 received less than $2000 a year and only 21 were paid more than $7000. WPA estimated that administrative costs during its first five years were about 4 percent of expenditures, though this excludes services provided by state and local agencies.

Sponsors, overwhelmingly local government agencies, proposed and helped plan WPA projects, met part of the costs, and furnished some of the supervision. The contributions were either in cash or in kind — labor, materials, building space, tools, equipment. The federal share of funding fell from about 90 percent in 1936 to 74 percent in 1940.

WPA operated on the force-account system, itself hiring and paying workers, securing materials and equipment, and supervising the work. This was in the face of constant complaints from the construction industry and the building trades unions, who urged contracting with private industry, as PWA operated. While the cost accounting is complex, there can be no doubt that some projects could have been performed more efficiently by contracting. But, as WPA insisted, its mission was to provide work for the jobless, which could not be guaranteed by letting contracts.

WPA set standards for the approval of projects: The proposal must be within the jurisdiction for which the sponsoring agency was legally authorized to function; the works must be publicly useful; there must be no substitution of WPA workers for regular employees; there must be an available supply of labor eligible for WPA employment; expenditures must go primarily into wages; the project must be completable within the fiscal year; and the work must be on public property. In addition, Congress over time imposed further restrictions: forbidding the production of armaments, of goods produced in prisons, of articles made in competition with private industry, of buildings costing more than a specified amount, and, after the Federal Theatre got into trouble, the staging of plays.

Nevertheless, there was much to be done. As Donald S. Howard has written:

> An enumeration of all the projects undertaken and completed by the WPA during its lifetime would include almost every type of work imaginable. These projects have ranged from the construction of highways to the extermination of rats; from the building of stadiums to the stuffing of birds; from the improvement of airplane landing fields to the making of Braille books; from the building of over a million of the now famous privies to the playing of the world's great symphonies.
>
> Projects have varied, too, from mosquito control to the serving of school lunches; from the beautification of cemeteries to beauty treatments to improve the morale of patients in hospitals for the mentally ill; from the repair of library books to the building of libraries; from the teaching of handicrafts to the teaching of Spanish to members of the country's armed forces; from the rendering of housekeeper service to needy families to mopping up the countryside after roaring, flooding rivers. One might further contrast sewing garments and rip-rapping levees; draining swamps and painting murals; repairing wharves and mending children's teeth; leadership in recreation and reconstruction of bridges; sealing abandoned mines and teaching illiterate adults to read and write; and planting trees and planting oysters.

In fact, WPA projects were highly concentrated in the construction, including repair, of sorely needed public facilities. Of $11.4 billion expended between 1935 and 1941, 78 percent financed building in the public sector. Over $4.4 billion was spent on highways, roads, and streets, adding 595,000 miles to the nation's system and repairing 32,000 more. The remaining construction expenditures spread broadly: bridges, culverts, irrigation systems, reservoirs, sewers, sewage treatment plants, landing fields, runways, playgrounds, swimming pools, parks, recreation buildings, schoolhouses, and administrative buildings. Examples: 75,000 new bridges and 45,000 repaired; 256 new airports and 385 repaired; 5898 new playgrounds and athletic fields and 11,849 repaired; 5584 new educational buildings and 31,629 repaired.

The remaining 22 percent of expenditures went into a category WPA called community service, covering a great variety of projects. Among them: over 300 million garments for the needy, 575 million school lunches, the renovation of 80 million library books, the operation of 1460 nursery schools, teaching 1.5 million adults to read and write, a training program for domestic servants, and publication of the WPA guides to the states. After the war broke out in Europe, WPA engaged in defense construction and trained skilled workers for defense industries.

WPA provided employment to a monthly average of more than 2 million people between 1936 and 1941. There was considerable fluctuation. The number rose sharply from 220,000 in August 1935 to 3,019,000 in February 1936. Thereafter, as the private sector picked up, the number on the WPA rolls fell steadily to 1,454,000 in September 1937. The recession that started in the fall of 1937 reversed this trend and the number of persons on WPA rose to a peak of 3,238,000 in November 1938. From that time on there was a fairly steady drop to 1,340,000 in June 1941. While the absence of reliable figures on joblessness makes precision impossible, between 20 and 30 percent of the unemployed seem to have found work on WPA projects.

Perhaps the most complex problem WPA faced was to establish a method of payment for its employees. The broad principle, which Roosevelt enunciated in January 1935, was that "security wages" should be higher than direct relief and lower than private employment. This would give the unemployed worker a double incentive: to prefer WPA employment over relief and to seek a private-sector job over one on WPA. At the level of broad national averages, the principle was effectuated. WPA earnings were, generally speaking, above relief payments and below private wages. But the averages concealed wide disparities in earnings, and there were a number of exceptions.

When Roosevelt used the term "security wages," this indicated an ambivalence within the Administration over whether the worker should be paid a wage rate, in which case he would have been paid by the hour for time actually worked, or should receive a guaranteed income sufficient to support him and his family, in which case he would be paid a monthly "salary" even if he was unable to work the prescribed hours for reasons beyond his control. This ambiguity was never resolved.

At the outset the President by executive order on May 20, 1935, established a schedule of "monthly earnings," based on three criteria: The first was the level of skill broken into four classes — unskilled, intermediate, skilled, and professional and technical. For example, in counties having a city with a population between 50,000 and 100,000 in the North the "monthly earnings" for the unskilled were $52, for the intermediate $60, for the skilled $75, and for professional and technical $83.

The second standard was by city size within the county. There were five classes — under 5000, 5000 to 25,000, 25,000 to 50,000, 50,000 to 100,000, and over 100,000. By way of illustration, intermediate rates in the North progressed by $5 steps from $45 monthly for the lowest population counties to $65 for the highest.

The third criterion was region, and four were established. Region I consisted of the Northeast, the Midwest, part of the Mountain area, and the Pacific Coast. Region II embraced the Plains states and part of the Border. Region III took in the rest of the Border and part of the Southwest. Region IV was the remainder of the Southwest and the Deep South. An example of the differentials for intermediate work in counties with a town with a population of 50,000 to 100,000 follows: I – $60, II – $54, III – $48, and IV – $43.

These monthly payments assumed a nominal 130-hour work month, or 30 hours a week. Another rule stated that actual hours worked would not normally exceed 8 daily and 40 weekly.

It proved impossible to effectuate this wage schedule. Early on, state administrators were empowered to modify the rates by no more than 10 percent and many did so. They advanced the full amount in

New York City, Cleveland, and Detroit. Some states were moved from one region to another. The number of county population classes was squeezed from five to four. Region IV was eliminated. A new low-wage class, "unskilled B," was established below the unskilled level. In some cases, differentials were fixed in the same county between urban and rural areas. In 1940, workers on defense projects were authorized to work 174 hours a month. Supervisors, who were hard to find, received extra pay. Household trainees got half the unskilled rate.

The most troublesome wage problem was in the South. Some in WPA favored flat national rates, but they did not prevail. In fact, the basic purpose of the regional criterion was to take account of very low wages paid by private employers in the South. Nevertheless, WPA earnings sometimes exceeded those in private jobs. It was said, for example, that the $21-a-month WPA rate for the unskilled was about twice as much as a farm laborer could earn in the rural South. Southern politicians in Congress, despite this presumed adverse effect on southern industries and their bitter fight for a regional differential under the Fair Labor Standards Act, pushed hard to eliminate differences in earnings under WPA. While they appeared inconsistent, they were not. They wanted a lower minimum wage to help southern industry and they wanted higher WPA rates to increase federal expenditures in the South. The effect of their efforts was to narrow, but not eliminate, the regional spread.

The WPA industrial relations policy, in the spirit of the Wagner Act, guaranteed its employees the right to organize unions without restraint. A union of WPA workers, the Workers Alliance, quickly emerged. Local grievance procedures were established, and in 1939 an appeals section was set up in Washington. But WPA signed no collective bargaining agreements. Further, both Roosevelt and Hopkins stressed that the agency's employees did not have the right to strike. This position was defended on the grounds that there could be no lawful strike against the government and that the "jobs" the workers held were really a form of relief. David Lasser, the president of the Alliance, seemed to accept this policy in principle but deviated from it in particular cases in which, he felt, the working conditions had become "intolerable." There were several strikes, notably in New York City and in Minneapolis.

WPA was almost unique among New Deal agencies in developing

a vigorous program to eliminate discrimination in the labor market. Roosevelt's executive order of May 1935 stated that workers "qualified by training or experience to be assigned to work projects shall not be discriminated against on any grounds whatsoever." The agency never imposed an upper age limit for hiring, and in 1939 Congress forbade it to bar employment to persons 65 years of age or older. Similarly, WPA policy prohibited discrimination against women. Most significantly, Hopkins strongly supported the employment of blacks.

There were serious impediments to the effectuation of these policies. Older people were sometimes denied jobs by other regulations, for example, the requirement that no one should be employed whose age or physical condition impaired safety or the acceptance of a state's eligibility standard that a worker over a certain age was unemployable. Nevertheless, the average age of the WPA work force was higher than that in private industry.

Women faced unusual difficulties in establishing eligibility for jobs because many lacked work experience, had not been in the labor market, were responsible for child care, or were not economic heads of families. Equally serious was the fact that there were very few "women's" jobs in the main area of activity, construction. WPA, therefore, devised special programs for female employment, notably the sewing projects, but also in the fields of health, education, recreation, library extension, research, clerical work, cooking, and the arts. Female employment ranged from 300,000 to 400,000, roughly 15 percent of the persons on the rolls.

Finding jobs for blacks was especially difficult, particularly in the South, because the states and localities determined eligibility standards and were the project sponsors. Despite these hurdles, WPA made a major breakthrough in providing work opportunities for blacks in the North and at least opened the door in the South. While there were no exact statistics on race, about 15 percent of the work force nationally was black, higher in northern states and lower in southern.

Conservative politicians and much of the press gave WPA a bad name, both for "boondoggling" projects and for employing Communists. While there was some merit to both charges, they fade in significance alongside the accomplishments: massive job creation, a lift in the morale of the jobless, a marked improvement in public facilities, and a big step forward in reducing discrimination in employment. A. W. MacMahon, J. D. Millett, and Gladys Ogden wrote:

> Five years of the works program left the nation better equipped, more richly endowed in the attributes that make for civilization, and better prepared to meet the requirements of building a strong and prosperous country than as if no effort had been made to utilize its wasting manpower and rusting skills.[2]

2

Franklin Roosevelt conceived the idea of the Civilian Conservation Corps (CCC) to meet two needs: conservation of natural resources and unemployment relief. He had developed a passion for trees as a child and had reforested both the family estate at Hyde Park and the abandoned farms he bought in the South. As governor of New York, Roosevelt had sponsored a reforestation program in which the jobless found work in tree nurseries and on planting crews. During the 1932 presidential campaign he promised to expand this into a national program.

He sent the bill to create the CCC to Congress on March 21, 1933, the first New Deal measure addressed to unemployment. In the brief hearings the American Federation of Labor voiced the most serious opposition. Green feared that free labor would be regimented and that wages would be depressed to the military level. He urged instead the contracting of conservation projects to private industry. Congress, ignoring the AFL, passed Roosevelt's bill on March 31. When the President established the CCC on April 5 by executive order, he mollified labor by naming Robert Fechner, vice president of the International Association of Machinists, as director. When Fechner died in 1940, another IAM official, James J. McEntee, succeeded him.

CCC was a bureaucratic labyrinth that worked. Fechner headed a kind of holding company that coordinated a variety of operating agencies. The Department of Labor was responsible for recruiting young men, though actual selection was performed by the state unemployment relief organizations. The Veterans' Administration named war veterans for enrollment. The superintendents of Indian reservations chose Indian enrollees. State foresters, the National Forest Service, and the National Park Service picked the experienced woodsmen. The Departments of Agriculture (mainly the Forest and

Soil Conservation Services) and Interior (largely the Park, Grazing, and Fish and Wildlife Services as well as the Bureau of Reclamation) chose work sites and planned and managed the projects. The Army, mainly with reserve officers, constructed, maintained, and administered the camps, including transportation, orientation, health, welfare, and discipline. The Office of Education was primarily responsible for education and training programs.

In March 1933 Roosevelt said that he hoped to have a quarter of a million men at work in the camps by early summer. Despite the formidable organizational problems, by July, 1520 camps were in operation with an enrollment of 293,582 men. The latter figure rose gradually to a peak of 519,623 in August 1935. Thereafter it declined to fewer than 400,000 in early 1936 and stabilized at about 300,000 until 1940. During the early war period enrollment dropped steadily to 108,487 in January 1942. The cost of keeping a man in camp for a year was about \$1000. Total expenditures for fiscal years 1933 through 1941 were less than \$3 billion, averaging around \$300 million annually.

The overwhelming majority of enrollees consisted of young men, called Juniors. Each state received a quota and its relief organization was expected to apply the following standards in their selection: men eighteen to twenty-five years of age (later dropped to seventeen to twenty-three and a half), out of work and from needy families, not in school, unmarried, citizens of the United States, physically and mentally fit, willing to allot a minimum of \$22 of the \$30 monthly wage to dependents and to enlist for at least six months. The VA picked the jobless war veterans, who were, of course, much older. The Indian program was administered separately.

The CCC, evidently, was the first federal program that sought to eliminate racial discrimination, and this proved both difficult and controversial. Representative Oscar DePriest of Illinois, the only black member of Congress, had inserted an amendment in the law in 1933 that said "that no discrimination shall be made on account of race, color, or creed." Southern states, particularly Georgia, ignored the provision by refusing to select blacks for the Corps. Since neither Fechner, who had been born in Tennessee and raised in Georgia, nor the Army, which itself practiced systematic racial discrimination, had any interest in enforcing the law, the burden fell upon the Labor Department, particularly W. Frank Persons, the head of the U.S.

Employment Service. He gradually succeeded in getting blacks admitted to the CCC.

By January 1937 about 9 percent of the enrollees were black, close to the black share of the population. As of 1941, about a fifth of the camps, 223, had minority men. But 152 of the camps were all black, 84 of them in the South. There were 71 integrated camps, 59 in New England. But the great majority of the officers, superintendents, and foremen in camps with black men were white. Both races received the same food, clothing, shelter, and other services. This represented a rise in the standard of living of most blacks, and they remained in the Corps twice as long as whites.

For three hundred years, as Kenneth Holland and Frank Ernest Hill wrote, Americans had

> cut, burned, wasted, and exhausted their land. Forests had once covered 800,000,000 acres of what is now the United States; in 1933 but 100,000,000 acres of virgin timber were left. Moreover, the growth of saw timber was only one-fifth of the amount being lumbered yearly. With the diminishing forests and the plowing up of grasslands receiving scanty rain, the soil had been exposed to wind and flood. American farmers had not yet learned to protect it by terracing and contour plowing; the states and the federal government had failed to guard it with adequate dams and levees. As a result an estimated three billion tons of earth were yearly being washed from the cultivated areas of the nation. In 1934 the new Soil Erosion Service . . . was to report that of 610,000,000 acres of land that were tilled or tillable in the United States, 50,000,000 acres had been "essentially ruined" by erosion, another 50,000,000 had been almost ruined, 100,000,000 acres had been seriously impoverished, and an equal area was being depleted at an alarming rate. A sixth of our heritage in fertile soil destroyed, and a third of it in danger of destruction.

The CCC was the first massive, systematic program designed to halt and, it was hoped, to reverse this devastation. A Library of Congress study published in 1942 sought to sum up the accomplishments. The CCC concentrated on renewable biotic resources — forest, grassland, wildlife, soil, and water — rather than on mineral resources, which were nonrenewable and largely privately owned.

Soil conservation was a major program. The Corps mapped areas to determine the character and magnitude of erosion and to develop techniques for its control. The men then built check dams; sodded channel outlets; plowed contour furrows; planted trees, shrubs, and grass; graded terraces; erected fences; and performed other work to encourage absorption of surface water. This was especially important in the two regions that suffered most from soil erosion — the South and the Great Plains. About 25 million acres received this protection.

Another significant program was water conservation. This was accomplished indirectly by improving watersheds and erosion control and directly by straightening stream courses. The latter involved the construction of several thousand impounding and diversion dams and the building of many levees, dikes, jetties, and groins.

The CCC's "most spectacular contribution" was reforestation. Two billion trees were planted. About four million acres of forest were thinned to allow stronger trees better access to soil and light. The Corps built roads, trails, lookout towers, and firebreaks to prevent forest fires and actively engaged in firefighting.

The CCC had a major program to improve recreation facilities in national, state, county, and metropolitan parks. This included the construction of campgrounds, picnic areas, roads, water and sanitary systems, and facilities for water sports.

A few statistics suggest the magnitude of these activities: over 300,000 permanent and more than 5.5 million temporary check dams, 66,000 miles of firebreaks, almost a billion fish stocked in streams and ponds, 45,000 bridges, 11,000 toilets, 115 radio stations, 72 airplane landing fields, 122,000 miles of minor roads, 4334 sewerage systems.

The CCC made an equally important contribution to the conservation of human resources. The selection standards forbade the recruitment of young men who were employed or who were in school or college. As a result, 80 percent of the enrollees had never held a steady job, 30 percent had not completed grade school and many were illiterate, and a large number had trouble adjusting, were undernourished, and were not in good health. Some local relief agencies tried to get rid of undesirables by fobbing them off on the CCC. It is hardly surprising that a substantial number of enrollees left camp within the first few weeks because of some variant of "homesickness."

Nevertheless, by June 30, 1941, over three million men had served in the CCC for periods of six months to two years. They performed productive work, their families received relief payments averaging about $25 a month, and the towns near the camps benefited economically. The program helped to sustain aggregate demand in the economic system. Further, these young men acquired both job skills and job discipline, thereby increasing their future employability in the labor market.

The Corps experience markedly improved the health of the enrollees. Outdoor life, toughening work, calisthenics, plentiful and nourishing food, regular medical and dental care, including immunization against epidemic diseases, and instruction in personal hygiene contributed to this result. Studies showed that the men grew in height, added an average of about twelve pounds, and had relatively low disease and death rates. Safety, however, was a continuing problem, because much of the work was dangerous. The accident rate was very high in the first year, and, while a safety program instituted thereafter brought it down significantly, the problem remained serious.

From the outset Fechner recognized that the CCC needed an education and training program. It was gradually developed with the assistance of the U.S. Office of Education, state departments of education, and schools and colleges near the camps. In 1937 the law was amended to make voluntary education a basic policy goal. By fiscal year 1940, classes were offered by 27,516 instructors, an average of 18 per camp. By that time the camps were fitted out with classrooms and libraries. The Library of Congress study concluded that the CCC "is now one of the important educational organizations in the country." Ninety percent of the enrollees, 2,700,895, participated, 36 percent in academic subjects, 45 percent in vocational classes, 72 percent in job training, and 14 percent in informal activities. By June 30, 1941, a total of 101,125 illiterates had learned to read and write, 25,223 had received eighth-grade diplomas, 5007 had graduated from high school, and 270 were awarded college degrees.

In the defense period, starting in the spring of 1940, the CCC program changed markedly. Enrollment, of course, dropped sharply as young men entered the armed services or took work in defense plants. The work projects shifted to the construction of military forts, reservations, and cantonments. The emphasis of the training program moved to skills useful in the armed forces, in defense manufacturing, and in agriculture. After Pearl Harbor, when unemployment dried up, the program was abandoned.

The CCC was exceptionally popular, almost certainly the least criticized of New Deal policies. While there was some carping over the structure and quality of education and over racial integration (from both sides), it proved impossible to mount a frontal attack on a program that conserved natural and human resources at low cost. This successful experience would be recalled later.[3]

3

When Hopkins and his colleagues had established the federal relief program in 1933, it was clear that they faced a special and acute problem with youth. While there were no precise statistics, the censuses of 1930 and 1940, the partial unemployment census of 1937, and a number of local surveys sketched the broad outlines. In a shrunken labor market many young people without employment experience and lacking skills could not find jobs. Poverty forced a large number to leave school early. The 1937 census showed that, among persons 15 to 24 years of age, 29 percent of the whites and 35 percent of the blacks were out of work. Numerous young people, including girls, took to the road. The European example was frightening. Heavy youth unemployment in Italy and Germany had provided massive support for the Fascist and Nazi movements. As the *Final Report of the National Youth Administration* put it, "The masses of unemployed youth were unmistakably social dynamite."

The CCC, of course, addressed part of the problem, but it left several important gaps. It gave work to only a fraction of the jobless young men, did nothing for young women, and failed to deal directly with the nexus between school and work. Between 1933 and 1935, FERA developed several experimental programs to meet these problems. Camps with training programs were set up for young women, but only 3000 enrolled. A college aid program, started at the University of Minnesota, gave part-time work to 75,000 students with an average income of $15 a month. FERA transient camps provided lodging for 54,000 young people. The President set up a federal-state apprenticeship-training program to develop skilled workers. But these actions did little more than acknowledge the existence of the problems.

No one was more sensitive to them than Eleanor Roosevelt. She was deeply concerned about the deprivation and the future of the generation coming of age during the Great Depression. From the outset of the New Deal, she urged her husband and Hopkins to develop a comprehensive program for youth. The passage by Congress of the large relief appropriation and the creation of WPA in 1935 paved the way. On June 26, 1935, Roosevelt by executive order established the National Youth Administration (NYA).

For four years NYA was a division of WPA. Aubrey Williams was both the Assistant Administrator of WPA and the Director of NYA, receiving no additional pay for the latter job. NYA got its funds from WPA. The executive reorganization of 1939 placed NYA in the new Federal Security Agency. Williams continued as Director, but now the agency had its own budget. In 1942, when it no longer had jobless young people to deal with, NYA became part of the War Manpower Commission. Williams resigned in 1943 and the agency was liquidated shortly thereafter.

The NYA student work program, which grew out of the successful Minnesota experiment, gave financial assistance to young people from needy families in order to continue their education. A study in May 1935 of 1,727,000 urban youth on relief between the ages of 16 and 25 showed that only 45 percent had progressed beyond grade school and less than 3 percent had entered college. A very large proportion, clearly, could not afford to stay in school. The NYA program had two objectives: to give these youngsters an income from work that would support their schooling and to keep them out of the overcrowded labor market.

NYA provided funds and set standards; school systems and colleges administered the programs at the local level. Each state and territory received an allocation based on its youth population, school enrollment, school facilities, and numbers on relief. This was divided into a dollar amount for each secondary school in the state. Colleges and universities got funds in relation to the number of students between 16 and 24 years of age who were regularly enrolled in day sessions. This number was multiplied by $15 to fix a monthly allocation. NYA, which was covered by the WPA antidiscrimination policy, went beyond it to add special grants to Negro colleges, which were in dire need, especially in the South. These were the student qualifying standards: need, age 16 through 24, acceptable academic standing, capacity to perform the work, regular attendance, citizenship, and an oath of allegiance. The rate of pay for high school students was no less than $3 and no more than $6 a month. The school fixed monthly hours of work, but they could not exceed four hours on school days and seven on other days. The pay for college students ranged from $10 to $20 monthly and for graduate students from $10 to $30. Hours could not exceed eight daily.

Between fiscal years 1936 and 1943 a total of 2,134,000 students worked on NYA projects, 1,514,000 in high schools and 620,000 in colleges, the overwhelming majority of the latter as undergraduates. The total cost of the program was about $170 million, somewhere between $20 and $25 million annually. Average monthly earnings of high school students were a little less than $5, of college students about $12, and of graduate students around $19. Females constituted a modest majority at the high school level, a narrow minority in the colleges, and about one fourth of the graduate enrollment. In 1939–1940 nonwhite high school students were 12.9 percent of the total and 6.3 percent of the college and graduate enrollees. In the academic year 1939–1940, 28,301 secondary schools and 1698 colleges and universities participated in the program.

NYA merely prescribed that the work performed should be "useful and practical." The institutions made the project assignments, which ranged from highly academic to menial. Job emphasis in the high schools was on construction and maintenance of buildings and equipment, machine and auto shop, landscaping, health and sanitation, home economics, and recreation. In the colleges, in addition to these activities, students became lab assistants, performed library services, and engaged in research.

The test of need was readily met. A study of the annual family income of 613,350 beneficiaries in 1939–1940 revealed an average of $645 per family, $526 for high school and $1124 for college and graduate student families. Over 20 percent had yearly incomes of less than $300. Among black families, 46 percent earned less than $300. In addition, the families of the recipients averaged five in number, one more than the national average. Finally, 23 percent of the parents of these students were unemployed. Without NYA support, many of these youngsters would have been forced to leave school.

Students assisted by NYA outperformed those who were not, at least at the post-secondary levels. A survey of the scholastic standing of 64,805 college and graduate beneficiaries during 1938–1939 showed that their grades were higher in 81 percent of the institutions and in all the states and territories.

The other major NYA activity was the out-of-school work program.

Prior to the war it closely resembled WPA. That is, young people worked under supervision on local public, school, hospital, and social agency projects. The primary areas of employment were construction and repair, conservation, sewing, woodworking, and hospital and school assistance. In rural and remote areas NYA established residential projects, mainly farms where the youth lived together and produced food, primarily for relief recipients.

The three standards of eligibility were: age 18 through 24, being out of work, and citizenship. There was a long waiting list for NYA jobs. From 1935 to the end of fiscal 1943, 2,677,000 young people worked in the out-of-school program, of whom 1,209,000 (45 percent) were young women. In February 1939, 12.1 percent of the workers were black and 1.5 percent were other nonwhite. Hours and wages at the outset were fixed at one third the WPA levels, including regional and other differentials. These short hours made scheduling difficult, and in 1939 they were increased. Average monthly earnings in 1940 were $15.15 for those not living in and $22.10 for residents. In fiscal 1940, this program cost a total of $67 million — $50 million in wages for young people, $11 million for supervisors, and $6 million for nonlabor costs. In addition to providing jobs for blacks, NYA had special programs for the handicapped and for refugees from Nazi Germany, mainly Jews.

As early as 1937, Williams, his eye on the gathering war clouds in Europe and the Far East, began to develop skill-training centers to prepare young people for work in the armed services and in defense industries. This became the dominant emphasis in 1940, and Congress appropriated substantial funds for this purpose. In that year, NYA shops began to fill production orders for the Army and Navy. NYA established machine, sheet metal, welding, foundry, forge, patternmaking, electrical, aviation mechanics, radio, industrial sewing, auto mechanics, and woodworking shops. They both trained workers and produced goods. Shortly after Pearl Harbor, NYA operated 3900 production units on two eight-hour shifts daily, mainly in machinery and metalworking.

In their 1938 book, Betty and Ernest K. Lindley wrote that NYA gave "less privileged youth . . . at least a measure of participation in the economic, social, and educational life of an era which frequently seems to have no place for them." Many were allowed to pursue an education that otherwise would have been denied them. A large proportion of the projects were economically and socially useful. Colonel F. C. Harrington directed a survey of the engineering on 108 projects in 1937 that concluded that "the National Youth Administration program as a whole is very good." This was recognized by Congress in 1940 when it gave NYA a large responsibility for defense training and production. The investment in NYA helped to sustain aggregate demand. The Lindleys were amazed at the agency's success in keeping costs down, largely by maximizing the use of state and local facilities and equipment. While the expense to CCC of keeping a youth in camp was hardly high, NYA kept a young person in high school for one thirtieth of that amount, in college for one tenth, on a work project for one fifth, and in a resident center for one fourth.[4]

4

Immediately after signing the Social Security Act on August 14, 1935, Roosevelt sent his nominees for the Social Security Board to the Senate and they were confirmed on August 23. The progressive Republican John G. Winant, former governor of New Hampshire, became chairman, and the other members were Arthur J. Altmeyer, who had been closely involved in drafting the legislation, and Vincent M. Miles, an Arkansas lawyer active in Democratic politics. The Board faced a gigantic task. It would be solely responsible for erecting the imposing administrative structure for the old-age insurance system, and it would have to take the lead in establishing nine federal-state social programs.

The Board's early life was beset with problems. The constitutionality of both old-age insurance and unemployment compensation was challenged at once, and the issue was not laid to rest until May 24, 1937, by the Supreme Court's decisions in *Helvering v. Davis* and *Steward Machine Co. v. Davis.* A Huey Long filibuster in the Senate in the closing days of the 1935 congressional session, for reasons unrelated to social security, denied the Board funds. Patchwork transfers from FERA and NRA floated the agency temporarily. Staffing, a critical early function, fell prey to politics. Members of Congress had patronage favorites, mostly incompetent, whom they pushed on the Board and who had to be turned away. More "ugly," as Altmeyer put it, both he and the President learned that the House Ways and Means Committee thought that the agency was hiring "too damn many New

York Jews." Fred M. Vinson, the Committee chairman, told Altmeyer gently that he had a high regard for "members of your race," but the Committee was concerned about the large number of Jews on the staff. Altmeyer informed a surprised Vinson that he was not Jewish and, in looking into the question, learned that the percentage of Jewish employees was "very small."

A number of governors sent Christmas letters to recipients, taking credit for their benefits. In two states, administration was so bad that the Board temporarily held back funds, but both straightened up soon enough so that no beneficiaries were penalized. Ohio was a special case. Governor Martin L. Davey made a big play to old-age assistance recipients by increasing their benefits $10 in 1936 and by 10 percent in December 1937 ("increased by order of Governor Davey"). In the primary election campaign in 1938, Davey ordered another $10 raise and sent a letter to each applicant for old-age assistance saying that a special investigator was working on his claim "day and night." The Board, after a hearing that Davey refused to attend, made a finding of improper administration and withheld the federal grant for October. Davey lost the election. In Altmeyer's view, the example helped to depoliticize the program.

The most important political controversy arose during the 1936 presidential campaign. The collection of the tax to finance old-age insurance was scheduled to start on January 1, 1937. In a speech in Milwaukee on September 27, 1936, Alf M. Landon, the Republican candidate, denounced social security as "unjust, unworkable, stupidly drafted and wastefully financed." He called it "a cruel hoax" and "a fraud on the workingman." Landon said that the system was "dangerous regimentation" and that the government would be "prying into the personal records of 26 million people." This was orchestrated with an attack from the conservative press, especially the Hearst papers, and by threatening notices employers gave their workers:

> PAY DEDUCTION. Effective January 1937, we are compelled by a "New Deal" law, to make a 1% deduction from your wages and turn it over to the government. Finally this may go as high as 4%. You might get this money back in future years . . . but only if Congress decides to make the appropriation for that purpose. There is NO guarantee. Decide, before November 3 — election day, whether or not you wish to take these chances.

Winant was outraged by the Landon speech and insisted, over Roosevelt's protest, on resigning as chairman so that he could be free to reply. Although Winant returned briefly after the election, Altmeyer became chairman in early 1937. This worked out well for the social security system because Altmeyer proved to be an extraordinary administrator. His mentor, John R. Commons, had taught that administration was critical, and Altmeyer heeded the precept.

The statute established three categorical public assistance programs — Old Age Assistance (OAA), Aid to Dependent Children (ADC), and Aid to the Blind (AB). All were federal-state in structure, and the Board administered them through its Bureau of Public Assistance.

The draftsmen of the statute viewed OAA as primarily a temporary system to tide the needy aged over the period until the old-age insurance program took effect. The latter would require a large accumulation of revenues in the trust fund and the construction of a formidable administrative apparatus before benefits could be paid. In 1935 the date for the first payout was fixed at 1942; by the 1939 amendments, it was moved forward to 1940. Meantime, OAA would fill the gap.

Prior to the passage of the statute, thirty-four states had old-age assistance laws, but they varied widely, met only a small fraction of the needs of the aged, and in many cases shifted the costs from the states to local governments. The new scheme established a grant-in-aid program under which the federal government paid a benefit of no more than $15 a month to match the contribution of the state and its subdivisions, plus a grant to defray the cost of administration. Thus, if the state fixed a payout of $20, it received $10 from the Board; if it fixed $40, it got $15. By the 1939 amendments, the federal contribution was raised to $20.

In order to qualify, the state law had to meet the following significant minimum standards: (1) Until 1940 the age for eligibility could not exceed 70 and thereafter 65. (2) The state could not shift the whole cost of its share to its subdivisions. (3) Benefits must be paid in cash to protect the autonomy of the recipient, and the federal program favored those in private homes over those who were institutionalized. (4) The state was restricted in imposing residence requirements. Most of the pre-1935 laws required ten or more years of residence. (5) No citizen of the United States could be excluded. This was intended to prevent states and localities from discriminating against blacks and other minorities.

These minimal standards allowed the states wide discretion in fixing benefits, in defining need, in establishing eligibility, in imposing obligations upon their subdivisions, and in administration. The result, of course, was great variation among states in all these areas. The states moved rapidly to enact or amend laws to meet the Board's criteria. By 1939 all forty-eight, plus the territories of Alaska and Hawaii and the District of Columbia, were in the system.

The number of recipients moved up steadily from 378,000 in 1935 to 2,234,000 in 1941. The outlay went from $65 million in 1935 to $542 million in 1941. The national average monthly benefit rose gradually from $18.79 in 1936 to $21.27 in 1941. But this was not very meaningful because of the great range. In 1941, for example, the highest state paid $36.51 and the lowest $7.95, the low end concentrated in the South.

There can be no doubt that OAA provided a vital means of support for the needy aged. It is certain that a large but undetermined number of people who could have used assistance did not receive it. No one was able to calculate precisely the adequacy of the benefits because some recipients had other sources of income in cash or in kind and because the states differed so sharply in their definitions of need. A single recipient, obviously, made out better than a family. As anticipated, the number of beneficiaries declined after 1941.

The Aid to Dependent Children program was similar. As of 1934, almost all the states had "mother's" or "widow's" pensions. The main purpose was to support a nonworking mother after the death of her husband. More recently, coverage was being extended gradually to cases in which the father had deserted, was in prison, was disabled, or in which the parents had divorced. Many of the state laws were optional, cast all or most of the financial burden upon localities, or provided meager benefits.

The Social Security Act gave federal support to the states on the grant-in-aid principle for "dependent" children. Dependency was defined as being "needy" (the criteria to be fixed by the state); as being under age 16 or, with the 1939 amendments, under age 18 if attending school; of being without parental support due to death, absence, or incapacity; and of living in the home of a close relative. In 1935 the federal subvention was one third of a benefit of $18 a month for the first child and $12 to succeeding children; in 1939 this rose to one half. To qualify for this support, the state must pass a mandatory law, must itself contribute in addition to its subdivisions, and must not restrict eligibility based on residence. Within a few years all the states came into the ADC program, again, as with OAA, with wide variations.

The number of children who received aid climbed from 286,000 (in 117,000 families) in 1935 to 941,000 (in 390,000 families) in 1941. The cost of the program rose from $42 million in 1935 to $153 million in 1941. The national average payment per family advanced from $29.83 a month in 1936 to $33.63 in 1941. Again, the spread from highest to lowest was very wide, in 1941 from $58.55 to $13.66. In most states, even with other sources of income, this was inadequate to maintain a minimally decent standard of living, but it helped.

Aid to the Blind was the smallest and least controversial of the assistance programs. In 1934, half the states had laws pertaining to the blind. The Social Security Act established a grant-in-aid system for persons who were both "blind" and "needy," leaving it to the states to define these terms. Inmates of public institutions were ineligible. The federal government paid half of a benefit that did not exceed $20 a month. The administrative and residence requirements were like those under OAA.

The number of beneficiaries rose from 35,000 in 1935 to 77,000 in 1941 and expenditures from $8 million to $23 million. The national average monthly benefit in 1941 was $25.81, ranging from $46.78 to $8.98.[5]

5

The Public Works Administration was responsible for the New Deal's heavy construction program. It started with funds provided by the National Industrial Recovery Act (NIRA) in 1933, received significant new money under the Emergency Relief Appropriation Act in 1935, and got supplemental funds in 1936, 1937, and 1938. In addition, PWA gained access to a Reconstruction Finance Corporation (RFC) revolving fund in 1935. As of March 1939, PWA had been involved in 34,508 projects (exclusive of public housing) whose combined cost was over $6 billion.

Harold L. Ickes, the Secretary of the Interior, was Public Works

Administrator from the inception of the program in June 1933 until the President's reorganization plan transferred PWA to the Federal Works Agency on July 1, 1939. While Roosevelt experimented with a variety of administrative arrangements, Ickes was always in complete command. On December 4, 1933, for example, he called in Colonel H. M. Waite, the Deputy Administrator, who was aggressive, and told him that "I would have to exercise the power that went with the responsibility." Waite resigned. While Ickes made several half-hearted efforts to decentralize administration, he never yielded final authority. Thus, Ickes imposed his style upon PWA. He was deeply devoted to the American landscape and to improving the welfare of common people. Government, in his mind, was the key instrument for reaching these goals. He knew no higher calling than public service, and it demanded efficiency and integrity.

Ickes was a ferocious worker. In 1935 his administrative assistant, E. K. Burlew, told him that he was putting in a full working day on public works alone, for which, incidentally, he received no additional pay. Ickes concluded that Burlew was right. His normal hours were from eight-fifteen to six-fifteen with a break for dinner and then from eight to ten-fifteen or ten-thirty. Since "I put in three-fourths of my actual working hours on PWA, I am doing what Burlew says I am doing." This regimen took a toll. He was irascible, dyspeptic, belligerent, demanding, and suffered from no lack of paranoia. He called himself a "curmudgeon." Ickes complained constantly of exhaustion, insomnia, and an upset stomach. While in office, he suffered a coronary thrombosis. As noted, his wife was killed in an automobile accident in New Mexico and he himself was in two car accidents. Working for Ickes, while rewarding, was hardly pleasant. As he wrote the President about the PWA staff in 1939, "I have bullied them and driven them to a degree that, at times, I have been ashamed of."

Ickes, having spent most of his professional life in legal and political affairs in Chicago, needed no lessons in the potentialities for corruption in public construction. He was determined to prevent it. In 1933 he lectured the Washington convention of the Associated General Contractors that "many contractors were crooks and chiselers and that we were not going to permit them to get away with that sort of thing in carrying out the PWA program." He required them to file comprehensive reports on their work for the agency. He set up an Interior Department Division of Investigation under the zealous Louis Glavis, who, reportedly, kept forty former FBI agents busy searching for fraud and waste. Ickes told Glavis that his job was to protect "the Government from being gypped by people on the outside." While the investigatory division was often in political hot water, Ickes insisted on keeping it. PWA won universal acclaim for its integrity and efficiency. Much to his annoyance, the press called Ickes "Honest Harold."

Keeping politics out of the program was extremely difficult. Members of Congress, governors, and mayors were hungry for a slice of the federal pie. Ickes was constantly at war with the likes of Senator Huey Long of Louisiana (over a New Orleans hospital) or Mayor Edward J. Kelly of Chicago (over a subway in the Loop). Moreover, the President insisted on personally approving the proposals, certainly those for major projects, and, when he had the time, spending long hours with Ickes on the lesser ones. As the latter wrote on August 11, 1937:

> It is slow work because the President is methodically going over every project, reading the memoranda and looking at the photographs. . . . I must say that the President is very fair in considering these projects. He approves projects even for Congressmen who have bitterly opposed him in the Court fight, . . . while he disapproves projects that he does not think qualify, although their proponents are Congressmen who have stood by him through thick and thin.

On rare occasions Roosevelt slipped, for example, raising the roads allocation for Mississippi in 1936 from $10 to $15 million as a favor to Senator Pat Harrison, chairman of the Senate Finance Committee.

Roosevelt, with his innate stubbornness, insisted on returning to pet projects that raised insurmountable problems. One was to harness the great tides in the Bay of Fundy to generate power at Passamaquoddy, Maine. Ickes finally persuaded him with the argument that the construction would be so expensive that steam power would be cheaper than tidal power. Another Roosevelt favorite was the Trans-Florida Canal. When the geologists pointed out that a sea-level canal could bring salt water into the state's underground water supply, Roosevelt grudgingly gave up.

PWA had three basic purposes: to revive the construction and building supply industries, to provide jobs, and to renew the nation's capital stock. The needs were obvious. Investment in new construction had declined from an annual average of $10.6 billion between 1925 and 1929 to $2.3 billion in 1933. The main disaster was in private building, which fell from an average of $8.3 billion to $1.1 billion over the same period, but state and local public construction suffered almost as severely. This collapse was equally evident in the industries that supplied building materials. The impact on employment was disastrous. From 1925 to 1929, annual average on-site employment was 2,265,000 — 1,780,000 private and 485,000 public. By 1933 the total had dropped to 1,501,000 — 348,000 private and 1,153,000 public. There was also a decline in hours worked. As a result of this massive contraction, existing public structures wore out and new needs were not met. By 1933 it was obvious that an economic recovery was impossible without a significant gain in building activity and employment.

PWA was a relatively small agency (11,000 employees at the peak in 1936) that confined itself to funding, planning, and approving projects and policing performance. It did no construction itself. That responsibility rested with the building departments of the federal, state, local, and special district governments and upon private contractors.

PWA had two basic programs (grants and loans) and two special programs (highways and public housing). Federal building projects were fully subsidized. Under NIRA, PWA was authorized to provide up to 30 percent of the cost of state and local projects as grants; this rose to 45 percent in 1935. The state or local instrumentality provided the balance either out of its revenues or by borrowing. PWA after 1935 made 15 to 25 percent of its grant in advance, 35 percent when the project was 70 percent completed, and 45 percent after it was finished.

PWA was authorized to lend the entire cost of the project less the grant, or, if there was no grant, the whole amount. In the early years certain nonpublic corporations, notably railroads, were eligible to borrow. Loans were usually secured by the borrower's bonds. The government charged private corporations between 4 and 5 percent interest and public instrumentalities 4 percent on their loans. As payments of principal and interest came in, PWA was able to utilize the RFC revolving fund for additional loans.

NIRA increased the federal highway fund for allotments to the states by $400 million in direct grants. Since several states were financially distressed, the earlier requirement for matching was waived. NIRA authorized PWA to enter directly into programs for slum clearance and low-cost public housing. A number of projects were built. While several administrative and financial arrangements were tried, none was wholly successful. PWA turned over the completed projects to the new U.S. Housing Authority in 1937.

PWA gave weight to several factors in its decisions to fund projects. Since heavy construction required a long lead time for engineering, site acquisition, and contract letting, the first consideration was the speed with which the project could be started and completed. The second, particularly with state and local applications, was the quality of the preparation and planning. The third was the financial and legal competence of the petitioning agency. Fourth was the usefulness or social justification for the project. Educational and hospital proposals, for example, received priority over recreational developments. Finally, PWA used a formula combining population and unemployment by state in making allotments. Nevertheless, by March 1, 1939, all but two of the nation's 3071 counties had received funds from PWA.

PWA significantly increased employment in the construction and related industries. The Bureau of Labor Statistics analyzed the records as of March 1, 1939. On the average, 35.8 percent of expenditures had been for on-site labor and 64.2 percent for materials. PWA projects had provided 1.7 billion man-hours of on-site work and 3.2 billion for the production of materials, equipment, and transportation. Over $1.2 billion had been paid in wages and almost $2.2 billion for materials. A BLS series showed that the maximum number of persons employed monthly on PWA projects rose sharply to 631,000 in July 1934, fell steadily to 282,000 in February 1935, increased slowly to 449,000 in July 1935, declined again to 201,000 in February 1936, climbed to over 300,000 for most of the rest of that year, and then dropped to about 200,000 in the first half of 1937, when the data ran out. In his study of the economic effects of the program, J. K. Galbraith pointed out that works expenditures had three employment results — primary (on-site), secondary (building materials), and tertiary (private investment). While the last was not measured, he cited several examples: a reclamation project leads to the formation of new farms; a highway brings in roadside enterprises and opens new areas for development; a metropolitan post office attracts satellite small businesses.

PWA projects with rare exceptions were performed under contract with private construction firms, many of which had collective-bargaining agreements with the building trades unions. Further, Ickes was convinced that the success of the program depended heavily on the full cooperation of organized labor. PWA policies reflected this view. In contrast with WPA, contractors were permitted to hire the majority of their workers without regard to relief status. In the later years, in fact, only a small minority of those hired were from the relief rolls. Yellow-dog contracts were prohibited. Contracts required workmen's compensation, accident insurance, and labor bonds. Generally speaking, the U.S. Employment Service supplied unskilled workmen "as far as practicable" and union hiring halls provided craftsmen.

In 1933 there was a strict 30-hour week. This was soon made flexible to take care of shutdowns caused by bad weather. The new rule allowed for no more than 130 hours in any month. An exception was made for sites at remote locations where the workday was 8 hours and the workweek 40. In 1935 the standard day was fixed at 8 hours and the month at 130 hours.

Wage policy proved troublesome. After extended debate and on the advice of Dr. Isador Lubin, Commissioner of Labor Statistics, PWA in 1933 established the following minimum regional rates:

	UNSKILLED	SKILLED
Southern	$ .40	$1.00
Central	.45	1.10
Northern	.50	1.20

While these were not unreasonable averages, they did not fit particular localities, they assumed a 30-hour workweek, they failed to recognize urban-rural differentials, and the zones were arbitrary (was California Central or Northern?). In unionized areas contractors ignored the minima and paid the "prevailing" — that is, the collectively bargained — rates. In 1935, as the result of a number of policy changes, union wage scales in the construction industry became the dominant wage standards on PWA projects, at least in the major cities. This, of course, was in line with the principle of the Davis-Bacon and Walsh-Healey Acts.

As of March 1, 1939, PWA had been involved in whole or in part in close to 35,000 construction projects. Among them were 44 conservation programs with hydroelectric features and 340 nonfederal power projects. There were 1527 sewerage systems, 2419 waterworks, and 762 hospitals. The transportation total came to 13,239 — 11,428 for streets and highways, 388 for bridges and viaducts, 384 for airports, 741 for water navigation aids, and 32 for railroads. Local and state public buildings totaled 1492, among them 206 town halls and 295 courthouses. PWA gave assistance to about 100 public housing projects. It also participated in the construction of 7282 educational buildings.

The major projects included the following: the Boulder and Parker dams on the Colorado River, the Grand Coulee and Bonneville dams on the Columbia River, the Fort Peck Dam on the upper Missouri, the Shasta Dam on the Sacramento River, the All-American Canal and the Imperial Irrigation District in Southern California, TVA, the Denver and Los Angeles water supply systems, the upper Mississippi River navigation project, the Hetch Hetchy Reservoir in California, the Cape Cod Canal in Massachusetts, the Triborough Bridge in New York City, the Lincoln Tunnel under the Hudson River, the Outer Drive Bridge in Chicago, the Skyline Drive in Virginia, and the Overseas Highway from Miami to Key West. Until Congress stopped it, PWA participated in naval construction, including the carrier *Yorktown* and the destroyer *Porter.* PWA provided the Coast Guard with seven large cruising cutters and five smaller ones, along with many patrol aircraft. The Pennsylvania Railroad electrified its route between New York and Washington. Among the major hospital programs were Kings County in New York City, Boston City, the Naval Hospital in Philadelphia, Allegheny General in Pittsburgh, the Jersey City Medical Center, Cook County in Chicago, Charity in New Orleans, and City-County in Houston. In Washington, D.C., PWA was involved in the reconstruction of the Mall and the Washington Monument and new buildings for the Interior Department, the Library of Congress, and the Federal Triangle.

Ickes, angered when Roosevelt took PWA away from him, wrote a sour letter to the President on June 26, 1939. "But," he closed, "instead of complaining, I ought to be thanking you for allowing me to be Public Works Administrator during the past six years. . . . I have loved this job." The nation was the beneficiary of this passion — in the revival of the construction and building materials industries, in increased employment, and in the replenishment of its capital stock.[6]

6

The establishment of the unemployment insurance system was unusually difficult. In part this stemmed from the general problems the Social Security Board confronted that have already been noted — constitutionality, budgetary constraint, political opposition, and staffing the new agency, here the Bureau of Unemployment Compensation. But there were two other specific problems. The first arose out of the fact that unemployment insurance was a federal-state scheme and that the Social Security Act laid down only minimal qualifying standards. Thus, it was necessary for all forty-eight states, along with the territories of Hawaii and Alaska and the District of Columbia, to enact comprehensive legislation. The second problem was that the first jobless benefits were paid out in January 1938. This was bad luck in timing because unemployment rose sharply during the 1937 recession and imposed a strain on the new system.

The act gave the Board two basic controls over the states. The first was the authority to approve the state law as a condition for participating in the system, but, as will be noted shortly, the criteria were narrow. In the area of administration, however, the Board read the law broadly, according to Altmeyer, to "require a state to establish a merit system." Public administration by the states was notoriously inefficient and politicized. Only nine states had civil service systems, several of which were inoperative. The Board, therefore, employed its approval power to push the states to adopt merit systems.

The second control was the tax offset. The Social Security Act imposed a federal tax upon the wages and salaries laid out by employers — 1 percent in 1936, 2 percent in 1937, and 3 percent thereafter. If a state enacted a mandatory unemployment insurance law, its employers would be credited with 90 percent of these contributions to the state system against the federal tax. The remaining 10 percent would be paid to the state to defray the cost of administration. The tax offset was designed both to assure the constitutionality of the statute and to bring the states into the system.

It was extraordinarily successful in achieving the latter aim. Led by Wisconsin, which had acted on January 29, 1932, only five states had passed unemployment insurance laws prior to the passage of the Social Security Act on August 14, 1935, the other four in early 1935. Three others moved later that year. On November 1, 1936, barely fifteen states had laws. Yet, only eight months later, by July 1, 1937, all the states and territories were in the system. Twenty-one passed laws in the last six weeks of 1936 for fear of losing that year's offset. Those whose legislatures did not meet in 1936 acted in the first half of 1937. The great majority of state legislatures worked from alternative model bills drafted by the Social Security Board, which guaranteed federal approval.

The limited substantive criteria used by the Board were essentially financial and protective of the rights of beneficiaries. All money received must be deposited to the state's account in the Unemployment Trust Fund in the U.S. Treasury; all money withdrawn must be used exclusively for jobless benefits; and all benefits must be paid at the public employment offices. The law guaranteed the eligible jobless worker a benefit even if he turned down a job offered under certain conditions — strikebreaking, wages and conditions less favorable than those prevailing in the locality, or signing a yellow-dog contract. Beyond these narrow restrictions, the states had control over the vital substantive features of the system — the type of fund, coverage (within limits), the waiting period for benefits, and the amount and duration of benefits.

The pioneer Wisconsin law raised a fundamental question over the nature and purpose of the system. Based on the teachings of John R. Commons, that statute established employer reserve accounts. The theory was that individual employers, offered the incentive of a lower tax rate, would stabilize employment. Most authorities were convinced that the theory was unsound, that the individual employer could control only seasonal unemployment in part and could do nothing about the far more serious forms of joblessness, cyclical and structural. Further, the individual reserve system was a windfall for industries with a steady demand for labor, like utilities, and appealed to employers simply as a means of reducing taxes. Thus, opponents of the Wisconsin idea urged a pooled fund in which, on the insurance principle, the contributions of all employers were commingled. There were several ways in which the two principles could be compromised, notably by merit rating, which had been widely used under workmen's compensation. Here the state pooled contributions and paid benefits from the combined fund, but the individual employer's tax rate varied with his experience with unemployment. That is, he contributed at a lower rate if he got a high "merit" rating.

Each state had to resolve this issue. The federal government was neutral. Neither the Social Security Act nor the Board favored or opposed merit rating: the latter, in fact, offered the states alternative model bills. But the American Federation of Labor, concerned that employer reserves might be used to support company unions, came out strongly for the pooled fund. Only two jurisdictions, Nebraska following Wisconsin, opted for a strict employer reserve account system. Forty-four chose the pooled fund, but thirty-three of them combined it with merit rating. Five states offered both employer reserves and pooled funds. Thus, pooling prevailed, but the Wisconsin idea had a significant impact on most of the systems.

The Social Security Act exempted certain broad categories of workers from coverage — agriculture, domestic service, public employment, nonprofit organizations, among others. While the federal law required only employers of eight or more employees to pay the federal tax, the states were free to broaden coverage and a significant minority did. The number of employees that triggered coverage was as follows:

8 or more	28 jurisdictions
6 or more	1 jurisdiction
5 or more	1 jurisdiction
4 or more	9 jurisdictions
3 or more	2 jurisdictions
1 or more	10 jurisdictions

Those states that extended coverage on grounds of equity to very small employers asked for administrative headaches. Little firms were hard to locate, kept poor records, and often went broke. These state agencies got into the collection business for delinquent accounts.

The states had to decide whether an otherwise eligible jobless worker must wait before receiving his benefit, and, if so, for how long. There were compelling reasons for imposing a delay. Many workers were laid off for short periods and it was both expensive and administratively burdensome to compensate them for no more than a week or two. Limited funds were better used to extend the benefits of the seriously unemployed rather than to assist the short-term jobless, many of whom could look after themselves. The administrative agency needed the time for paperwork, which was particularly important at the outset, when the personnel was green and the procedures were unformed. The states, therefore, opted for waiting periods.

The real question was how long. The states, concerned about solvency and administrative inexperience, were cautious and specified extended waiting periods. Thirty required a delay of two weeks from the date of filing the claim for the initial period of unemployment plus added weeks for subsequent spells. Five required three weeks. Fourteen imposed a three-week waiting period for the first claim and added weeks for later ones. Two states had four-week delays.

The most important decisions the states made were over the amount and duration of benefits, because they determined how much the jobless worker received and the solvency of the program, and they could have an effect on the tax rate. The Social Security Board, much concerned about the financial integrity of the system, urged caution and the states responded.

While the benefit level might have been based on need, as under the British system, this standard was ignored with one exception. The Committee on Economic Security, the President, Congress, and the Board had agreed unanimously that the standard should be 50 percent of prior earnings. The theory — perhaps *hope* is a better word — was that this would be enough to tide the worker and his family over a period of joblessness but not so much as to undermine his incentive to seek another job. The states, with insignificant exceptions, accepted this formula. They also fixed maximum and minimum levels, overwhelmingly a top of $15 and a bottom of $5 a week. The former, which conflicted with the 50 percent formula for high-paid workers, expressed the concern over solvency and the latter voiced the need theory. There was some variation among the states with regard to duration. The most common provision in the state laws was to limit the payment of the benefit to sixteen weeks, though some were lower.

A formidable administrative problem arose at once. If the formula to calculate the benefit was 50 percent of prior earnings, how were prior earnings to be reported? At the outset the Board urged and the states accepted a literal definition. Since the benefit was to be based on "full-time weekly wages," the employer must report monthly for

White Angel Breadline, San Francisco, 1933.
Dorothea Lange, Oakland Museum

Jobless workers on the New York City docks, 1934.
Lewis W. Hine, National Archives

Unemployed, South Street, New York City, 1932.
Walker Evans

Abandoned mining town, Zinc, Arkansas, October 1935.
Ben Shahn, Library of Congress

Raphael Soyer, *Transients,* 1936, oil on canvas.
James and Mari Michener Collection, Archer M. Huntington Art Gallery, University of Texas at Austin

Seattle Hooverville.
Historical Photography Collection, University of Washington Libraries

Migrant Mother, Nipomo, California, 1936. The woman, Florence Thompson, could not pick peas because they were frozen. This may be the most widely reproduced picture in the history of photography.
Dorothea Lange, Library of Congress

Breadline, New York City.
Franklin D. Roosevelt Library

Reginald Marsh, *Breadline, No One Has Starved,* 1932, etching.
William Benton Museum of Art, University of Connecticut

Christmas, 1938, for the unemployed, East 12th Street, New York City.
Russell Lee, Library of Congress

Migrants camped along U.S. 99 in Kern County, California, November 1938.
The billboard served as a windbreak.
Dorothea Lange, Library of Congress

Reginald Marsh, *East Tenth Street Jungle,* 1934, oil.
Yale University Art Gallery, Bequest of Charles Rosenbloom, B.A., 1920

LEFT: Federal Relief Administrator Harry L. Hopkins testifying before the House Ways and Means Committee, 1934.
Wide World Photos, Franklin D. Roosevelt Library Collection

BELOW: Hopkins, Harold L. Ickes, Secretary of the Interior and Public Works Administrator, and Frank Walker, head of the National Emergency Council, at the White House, May 8, 1935. A massive increase in the relief program led to sharp conflict between Hopkins and Ickes. Walker was supposed to keep the peace.
Thomas D. McAvoy, Franklin D. Roosevelt Library Collection

Civil Works Administration workers cleaning and painting the Capitol dome, Denver, 1934. CWA was a work-relief offshoot of the Federal Emergency Relief Administration to tide the country over the tough winter of 1933–1934.
National Archives photo

Relief workers laying track on the Seattle Municipal Street Railway, 1934.
Historical Photography Collection, University of Washington Libraries

CWA workers digging the Spokane Valley Canal, State of Washington, 1934.
Historical Photography Collection, University of Washington Libraries

Jobless city youths at work in the woods for the Civilian Conservation Corps.
Library of Congress

Reliefers at work on the Cedar River Bridge, Barneston, Washington, 1934.
Historical Photography Collection, University of Washington Libraries

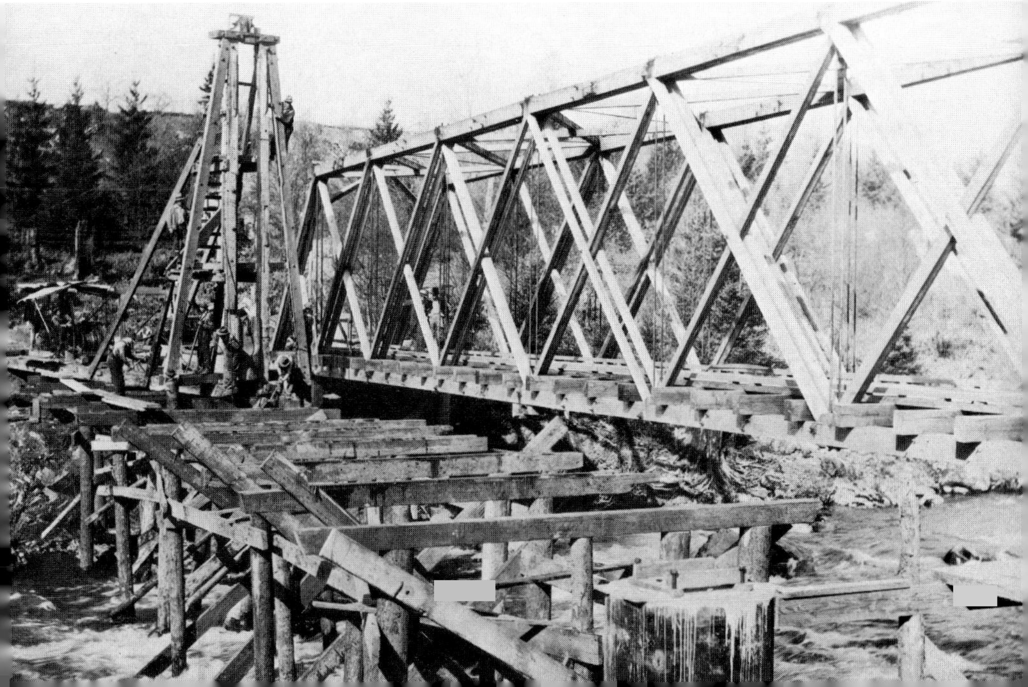

Grand Coulee Dam on the Columbia River, the largest concrete dam in the world, a Public Works Administration project built by the Bureau of Reclamation.
Historical Photography Collection, University of Washington Libraries

OPPOSITE: Payday for construction workers at Grand Coulee.
Public Works Administration

Sources of ideas

LEFT: John Maynard Keynes, the great English economist, whose *The General Theory of Employment, Interest and Money* (1936) offered the decisive analysis of joblessness during the Great Depression.
King's College Library, Cambridge University

BELOW: John R. Commons, the great University of Wisconsin institutional economist, was the intellectual source of much of the New Deal's social legislation. Witte and Altmeyer were his students.
State Historical Society of Wisconsin, M. E. Diemer, photographer

RIGHT: Edwin E. Witte, executive director of the Committee on Economic Security, which drafted the Social Security Act in 1934, and professor of economics at the University of Wisconsin.
State Historical Society of Wisconsin

BELOW: Arthur J. Altmeyer, chairman of the Social Security Board and the administrative architect of the social security system of the United States.
State Historical Society of Wisconsin

Old Age, near Washington, Pennsylvania, July 1936.
Dorothea Lange, Library of Congress

RIGHT: Dr. Francis E. Townsend. His popular old-age pension scheme built political pressure for social security. *United Press International*

BELOW: President Roosevelt signing the Social Security Act, August 14, 1935. First row, left to right: Senator Robert F. Wagner (D.–N.Y.); Senator Robert M. LaFollette, Jr. (Prog. – Wisc.); Secretary of Labor Frances Perkins; Senator William H. King (D. –Utah); Representative David J. Lewis (D.– Md.).
Wide World Photos

Jobless workers registering for unemployment insurance benefits at the California State Employment Service, San Francisco, January 1939.
Franklin D. Roosevelt Library

President Roosevelt campaigning at the Capitol grounds in Denver, October 12, 1936. During the 1936 presidential election, he drew enormous crowds and, with labor at its core, shaped the New Deal voting coalition, which would dominate American politics for a generation.
United Press International

RIGHT: Woody Guthrie, authentic Dust Bowl Okie, troubadour of the migrants, and extraordinary writer of folk songs.
Eric Schaal, Life © *Time Inc.*

BELOW: President Roosevelt, President David Dubinsky of the International Ladies' Garment Workers' Union, and the cast of the ILGWU's smash musical, *Pins and Needles,* at the "command performance" at the White House, February 3, 1938.
International Ladies' Garment Workers' Union

each covered employee the hourly rate, the hours worked, and the weekly earnings. Employers who were capable of supplying these data howled over the trouble and expense; little employers, some of whom kept no books at all, were unable to provide the figures; and the administrative agencies sagged under the load of paper and computations. In January 1937 the Board recommended and the states adopted a new definition of the full-time weekly wage: one thirteenth of the highest quarterly earnings in the base period, that is, the highest earnings in the first eight of nine completed quarters prior to the week in which the benefit was payable. Now the employer need report only quarterly earnings. Example: A worker became eligible for the benefit on April 2, 1939. The eight prior quarters for which his earnings were reported took place between January 1, 1937, and December 31, 1938. His highest earnings, $260, were for the quarter October 1–December 31, 1938. Dividing $260 by 13 gives $20 as the full-time weekly wage. The benefit, 50 percent, becomes $10 a week.

Wisconsin started paying benefits, though on a limited basis, in 1937. Twenty-three jurisdictions opened for business on January 1, 1938, eight later that year, and the remaining nineteen in 1939. As noted, the recession caused their offices to be swamped with claims, 2.1 million in January 1938 alone. During calendar 1938, the thirty-one states that paid benefits received almost 9.5 million claims (20.1 million workers were covered) and allowed 6.2 million. Over 38 million checks were issued for a total of almost $400 million. The average payout was $10.93 a week, ranging from a low of $5.89 in Mississippi to a high of $13.49 in Michigan. The problem, with a few temporary exceptions, was not that the states overdrew their balances. It was, rather, administrative — to train inexperienced personnel to handle the flood of claims and to finance the agencies. Rhode Island is an example. It had the heaviest ratio of claims to workers covered and never fell behind in paying benefits. But, because of a federal cut, the state ran out of money to pay for administration. Governor Robert E. Quinn, who strongly supported the system, implored the President on February 25, 1938, to restore the funds. Altmeyer agreed. In March the money for administration was supplied.

By 1939 the system was working quite smoothly. All the states were now paying benefits and the machinery functioned reasonably well. Even before the outbreak of war in Europe and despite the drain caused by the recession, it was clear that fiscal prudence was leading to a steady increase in the size of the Unemployment Trust Fund. If one anticipated in 1939 that the war would cause unemployment to shrink rapidly, hardly an unreasonable assumption, this trend would both continue and accelerate. The fiscal picture (in millions of dollars) was as follows:

	RECEIPTS	EXPENDITURES	ASSETS
1936	65	—	65
1937	575	2	638
1938	839	404	1072
1939	886	434	1525
1940	980	547	1958
1941	1143	357	2744

In fact, by 1945 assets would climb to $7.5 billion.

In 1939, both organized labor and organized employers tried to assert control over the growing surplus. The unions asked for higher benefits and management for lower taxes. The former fought their battles in the state legislatures and were successful in several. California and Idaho, for example, raised the weekly maximum to $18 in 1939. The employers had the more difficult task of amending the Social Security Act. Since the Administration itself offered significant amendments in 1939, dealing mainly with old-age pensions, Representative John McCormack of Massachusetts proposed an amendment to allow states with large reserves to reduce their employers' contribution rates. Altmeyer declined to take a position, merely saying that, if the Board had to choose between the McCormack amendment and an across-the-board cut in rates, it would prefer the former. The opposition of the state unemployment insurance agencies caused its defeat.

This was a signal that the states now had a vested interest in the federal-state unemployment insurance system. But between 1939 and 1941 the Social Security Board moved in the opposite direction. Altmeyer told the state agencies that the existing arrangement was little more than "a first line of defense." The Board was concerned because a very large proportion of beneficiaries (over half in 1940) were still out of work after exhausting their entitlements, because of the sharp disparities in benefits between the states, and because many state programs did not meet the Board's standards of administrative efficiency. Altmeyer had concluded that the only way to overcome these defects was by federalization of the system. In fact, he and the Board were moving beyond this in the direction of "a single comprehensive social insurance system" embracing old-age and survivors insurance, unemployment compensation, disability insurance, hospitalization, and public assistance. While the President had some sympathy for both federalization of unemployment insurance and a unified "cradle to grave" program, America's entry into the war made any action in either area impossible.[7]

7

The Social Security Board itself was responsible for the wholly federal old-age insurance program. It was popularly known as "the world's biggest insurance system" and its accounting processes as "the largest bookkeeping operation in history." Both clichés were true. The Board's Bureau of Old-Age Assistance ran this massive operation.

The provisions of the Social Security Act were relatively simple. The system was financed by a tax on both employers and employees, but only on the first $3000 of annual earnings. The tax started on January 1, 1937. The percentage rates were as follows:

	EMPLOYER	EMPLOYEE
1937–1939	1.0	1.0
1940–1942	1.5	1.5
1943–1945	2.0	2.0
1946–1948	2.5	2.5
1949 and after	3.0	3.0

The employer would make the contributions both for himself and for his employees (by payroll deduction) to the Bureau of Internal Revenue.

An employee for whom taxes were paid would become eligible for an old-age pension on reaching age sixty-five, provided he had worked for five years and had lifetime earnings of at least $2000. Thus, no one who was over sixty on January 1, 1937, qualified. Such a person for whom taxes had been paid would receive a lump sum of 3.5 percent of his total earnings, in effect, returning his contributions with interest. The estate of a person who died before reaching sixty-five would receive the same percentage, a death benefit. The annuities of those who qualified ranged from a minimum of $10 a month (for credited lifetime earnings of $2000) to $85 a month (for earnings of $129,000 or more). The returns were skewed to favor those at the low end of the earnings scale.

The 1935 law would cover hardly more than 50 percent of the employed work force. The main exclusions from coverage were farm labor, domestic service, casual labor, maritime employment, the self-employed, public employment, and nonprofit organizations.

While lump-sum payments started in 1937, no annuities would be paid until January 1, 1942. This would allow five years for the contributions and interest to build up a reserve. The anticipation was that it would reach $2 billion by 1940 and, since contributions and interest would exceed benefits, would grow to almost $47 billion by 1980.

The administrative problems in putting this system into operation were mind-boggling. John J. Corson, who took over after several others had run into trouble, called it "Leviathan." The Board at the outset favored the British stamp system, in which a worker carried a stamp book with him throughout his working life. The employer bought stamps at the post office, gave them to the worker, and the worker pasted them in the book as they were earned. When the employee reached the time for retirement, he presented the filled book to the Board for his pension. Internal Revenue refused to accept the stamp system because it did not want to share its authority to collect taxes with the post office.

The first mass problem was the assignment of social security numbers. The Board at Altmeyer's urging decided to defer this huge task until after the 1936 elections, which left little time. In the latter part of November, 45,000 post offices distributed 26 million application forms. By June 30, 1937, the Board had assigned over 30 million numbers and they were going out at the rate of half a million a month. There were also 2.6 million employer account numbers.

The most formidable task was to establish a central bookkeeping operation to maintain the individual accounts. Quarterly earnings reports would have to be posted to each account. The system had to be both readily accessible and accurate. By 1937, there were 294,000 accounts for people named Smith, 227,000 for Johnson, 164,000 for Brown, plus large numbers for Williams, Jones, Miller, Davis, et cetera. The records were housed in an old warehouse on the Baltimore waterfront. "Employees," Altmeyer wrote, "were obliged to work at unfinished wooden tables whose rough lumber made slivers run into hands and arms."

The Board, eager for help, turned to the big insurance companies for advice in setting up centralized record keeping. Although their systems were no guide, they did recommend an expert in office management and the Board engaged him. After several months of study he reported that the job could not be done and recommended that Congress break the system up into manageable units. The Board had no choice but to do the job itself. A master index was set up and a punch card, which could be processed on the latest mechanical sorters, was assigned to each account. There were problems at the outset; for example, a large number of earnings reports without social security numbers. By the spring of 1938, according to Corson, the record-keeping function had been fully mechanized and was running smoothly. He estimated the cost of maintaining an account at less than 25 cents a year.

The Board established field offices around the country to deal directly with employers and employees. Altmeyer was appalled to receive a recommendation for 2000 offices. He calculated that Wisconsin, which he knew well, could be adequately served by 12 or 13 and he multiplied that number by 40 to come up with a total of 500. This proved about right. By 1941 there were 12 regional offices and 477 field offices in operation. At that time the Social Security Board had a total of 12,682 employees, 9353 in the Bureau of Old-Age and Survivors Insurance.

In 1937 the private insurance industry, which was ambivalent about the public program in general, did become agitated over "the full reserve system," that is, the growing surplus in the trust fund and, particularly, the projection of a $47 billion balance by 1980. The industry feared that this huge accumulation of cash would tempt legislators to expand the program. By an irony of history, the insurance industry attack led to the 1939 amendments to the Social Security Act, which provided exactly the result the industry sought to avoid.

At the insistence of Republican Senator Arthur H. Vandenberg of Michigan, the political spokesman for the insurance industry, the Senate Finance Committee held hearings on this issue in 1937, which seem to have lacked focus. At their conclusion, however, Vandenberg asked Altmeyer whether he would object to an inquiry by a congressional commission into the reserve issue. Altmeyer countered by proposing that the investigation be made by an advisory committee named jointly by the Board and the Finance Committee. After complications with the overlooked House Ways and Means Committee were straightened out, this led to the formation of the Advisory Council on Social Security.

As Altmeyer and his colleagues at the Board mulled over this rather confusing situation, he became convinced that the Advisory Council could be used to deflect the industry attack by amending the Social Security Act "to advance a socially desirable program." In essence: if the industry complains about our not spending the money, let's spend it usefully. On September 11, 1937, he sent a memorandum to the President dealing with this question and, more briefly, with unemployment insurance.

The full reserve feature, Altmeyer wrote, "may be essentially sound, but is under considerable attack." The opposition came both from Republicans and from liberals. From a political standpoint, therefore, it might be necessary to abandon the full reserve. There were two options: "increasing and extending both the size and character of the benefits provided" or "reducing the present tax rates." The latter, he pointed out, were already "relatively low." Altmeyer strongly urged the former. He wanted to "convert our old-age insurance system into an old age, *permanent* invalidity and survivors' insurance system." He would

(a) start benefit payments no later than January 1, 1939, rather than January 1, 1942, and raise benefits in the early years;
(b) provide an extra benefit for the wife of a recipient;
(c) provide benefits for widows and orphans; and
(d) provide benefits for permanent total disability.

Altmeyer also recommended an extension of coverage, particularly to agricultural workers, domestic servants, and the self-employed. This was the inception of the shift in emphasis under social security from individual equity to social adequacy, from the worker to his family.

Altmeyer then met with Roosevelt, who endorsed both the Advisory Council and the proposals for changing the law, the latter in general terms. The twenty-five-member Council began meeting late in 1937. While Altmeyer was wary, he need not have been. In its final report on December 10, 1938, the Council, including its industry members, recommended starting liberalized payments on January 1, 1940, and the payment of benefits to wives and survivors. But it urged that the financing of this enlarged system not exceed costs under the present law. While the Council supported permanent and total disability insurance in principle, it did not recommend immediate legislation. It urged extension of coverage to farm and domestic workers and to employees of nonprofit organizations. Anticipating rising costs, the Council proposed that financing in the future be split into three, rather than two, equal contributions — from the employer, the employee, and the government. This much larger program, obviously, would reduce the surplus in the reserve account.

The Social Security Board submitted its own legislative recommendations to the President on December 30, 1938. They were essentially those of the Advisory Council. The differences were as follows: The government should not contribute until disbursements for benefits exceeded payroll tax collections plus interest; federal employees should be covered; and state and local government workers should be covered if constitutional problems could be overcome. On January 16, 1939, Roosevelt warmly endorsed the Board's proposals and submitted them to the Congress.

The legislative process was complex, at times tortured, and its details are of little historical interest. Roosevelt signed the amendments to the Social Security Act on August 10, 1939. There were modest alterations in the public assistance and unemployment compensation programs, but the old-age insurance system was changed fundamentally. Lyle L. Schmitter and Betti C. Goldwasser put it this way:

> The revision of the benefit formula reflects the change in the emphasis of the program. The original provisions offered primarily a plan for systematic savings for old age. The amendments, on the other hand, are designed to provide a minimum subsistence income for the retired worker and his dependents or for certain of his survivors, relating the amount of the benefit to his family responsibilities and, roughly, to the level of his former earnings as well as to the extent of his participation in the system.

The 1939 law had the following major features: Benefits became payable on January 1, 1940, rather than on January 1, 1942. Lump-sum payments were abolished. The contribution rates for employer and employee were reduced modestly by continuing the 1 percent rate from 1940 to 1942 rather than by raising it to 1.5 percent during these years. Coverage was unchanged except for slight extensions to some national bank and maritime workers. The eligibility formula now became wages of at least $50 per quarter in each of 40 quarters with a minimum qualification in 6 quarters. The age for payment was 65 for all old-age annuitants — the worker, his wife, a widow, dependent parents. There was no age limit for a widow with dependent children. The latter were eligible if under 16 or, if still in school, under 18.

The fundamental change introduced by the 1939 amendments was the distinction between primary and supplemental benefits. The eligible retired worker still received a primary benefit between a minimum of $10 and a maximum of $85 a month. But now his wife and dependent child qualified for supplemental benefits of 50 percent of his primary benefit. If the covered worker died, his family would receive a lump-sum death benefit, usually six times the monthly primary benefit. His widow would be paid 75 percent of the primary benefit, a dependent child or dependent parent 50 percent. The Social Security Board quite properly changed the name of the Bureau of Old-Age Insurance to the Bureau of Old-Age and Survivors Insurance.

The payment under the 1935 law of lump-sum 3.5 percent refunds to workers who reached age 65 stopped on August 10, 1939. As of that date, 89,682 claims had been paid for a total of almost $8 million. Lump-sum death benefits were payable under the 1939 amendments and in 1941 they averaged $144.58.

By June 27, 1941, the Social Security Board was maintaining 55,922,710 employee accounts. For the April–June 1941 quarter it received reports on taxable wages of $10.4 billion for 33.4 million workers. For the fiscal year ending June 30, 1941, the general financial operations were as follows:

Contributions	$ 688 million
Interest	143 million
Benefit payments	100 million
Assets in trust fund	2398 million

Between January 1940 and June 1941, the Board awarded 531,869 claims. As of June 30, 1941, there were 372,339 beneficiaries on the rolls — 184,541 primary and the others supplemental. The average age of a retiring worker in 1941 was 69.1 years. In 1940, the average monthly primary benefit was $22.60 — $23.17 for men and $18.37 for women. In that year, the average monthly survivors' benefits were $20.30 for an aged widow, $33.90 for a widow with one dependent child, $47.10 for a widow with two, and $51.30 for a widow with three or more dependent children.

By 1941, the Old-Age and Survivors Insurance program was in full operation under highly favorable circumstances. Employers and employees were in compliance with the contribution and reporting requirements. The claims of beneficiaries were being processed and paid promptly. The complex bookkeeping machinery was working smoothly and at low cost. Further, the system benefited from the defense program. Rising employment automatically increased contributions, and many older workers preferred working to retirement, thereby reducing the payout. The trust fund, therefore, was growing rapidly.[8]

8

Davis, a stockholder in the Edison Electric Illuminating Company of Boston, sought to enjoin the corporation from paying the tax to support old-age insurance under Title VIII of the Social Security Act on the grounds of unconstitutionality. The District Court denied the injunction. Davis appealed and the Circuit Court agreed with him. Helvering, the Commissioner of Internal Revenue, brought the case to the Supreme Court of the United States. On May 24, 1937, that Court upheld the validity of the tax with Justices McReynolds and Butler dissenting.

Justice Benjamin N. Cardozo wrote the opinion for the Court. While the tax issue was neither especially challenging nor interesting, Cardozo's general comments were illuminating:

> The purge of nation-wide calamity that began in 1929 has taught us many lessons. Not the least is the solidarity of interests that may once have seemed to be divided. Unemployment spreads from State to State, the hinterland now settled that in pioneer days gave an avenue of escape. Spreading from State to State, unemployment is an ill not par-

ticular but general, which may be checked, if Congress so determines, by the resources of the Nation. . . . But the ill is all one, or at least not greatly different, whether men are thrown out of work because there is no longer work to do or because the disabilities of age make them incapable of doing it. Rescue becomes necessary irrespective of the cause. The hope behind this statute is to save men and women from the rigors of the poor house as well as from the haunting fear that such a lot awaits them when journey's end is near.[9]

Seven

Images of the Worker

His friends did not like to call him a liar. They preferred to say that he was prone to exaggerate, that he was a reincarnated Baron Munchausen, that he told "an endless labyrinth of fables." Sometimes he said that he was descended from a Spanish marquis, that he had been baptized Diego María de la Concepción Juan Nepomuceno Estanislao de la Rivera y Barrientos Acosta y Rodríguez. At other times he said that his ancestry was mixed Spanish, Dutch, Portuguese, Italian, Russian, and Jewish; occasionally he added Chinese. The civil register for December 1886 in Guanajuato records the birth of Diego María Rivera. After his father's death he was simply Diego Rivera, destined to become a great painter of the twentieth century.

Rivera was a man of Gargantuan appetites — for food and drink (he weighed in at 325), for women (no reliable statistics), and, most important, for work. He was tireless on the scaffold and was indifferent to the clock. His feet were also in the gigantic mold and he had to have his shoes made to order.

Rivera's genius in drawing became evident when he was a child and Mexico's resources in art education hardly matched his talent. He went to Europe to study and paint in 1907 and did not return to Mexico for twelve years. His style was shaped by El Greco and Goya, by Cézanne, and, in one sense, most by Giotto. The medieval Florentine master had told the story of Christ to audiences of illiterates in frescoes on church walls in Assisi, Padua, and Florence. The pre-Columbian Indians of Mexico had also painted murals. Rivera reckoned that the uneducated workers and peasants of modern Mexico could be reached this way. But now the message would be political.

In Europe, Rivera, fired by the Russian Revolution, had become politicized and a revolutionary. Bertram Wolfe, who was an expert in these matters, wrote that Rivera's politics were "an undigested mixture of Spanish anarchism, Russian terrorism, Soviet Marxism, Mexican agrarianism, and Paris studio revolutions." He joined the Communist Party of Mexico in 1922, with which he maintained an uneasy relationship until he was expelled for heresy in 1929, evidently because of Stalinist machinations in Moscow. Later, he shifted his allegiance to Stalin's enemy and persuaded President Cárdenas in 1936 to allow Leon Trotsky to live in Mexico as Rivera's personal guest. Unsure of sectarian labels, Rivera called himself a "Worker." At the minimum he knew what he was against: capitalism, clericalism, and militarism.

In the twenties Rivera and José Clemente Orozco were the luminaries in the Mexican renaissance in art. Rivera blanketed the walls of public buildings with his paintings, notably the 124 frescoes, covering over 17,000 square feet, in the Ministry of Public Education in Mexico City. They brought him world renown. Rich Americans, including the Rockefellers, began to buy Riveras. One of the Ministry panels was a caricature of capitalists, including John D. Rockefeller, Sr., J. P. Morgan, and Henry Ford, dining on ticker tape. Mrs. John D. Rockefeller liked it so much that she asked the painter for a copy.

Rivera began to receive commissions in the United States, almost all politically absurd. In 1930 he did the murals for the new San Francisco Stock Exchange, which aroused a storm of protest. In 1931 he painted the frescoes at the Detroit Institute of Arts. Edsel Ford, the chairman of the Art Commission, engaged Rivera and personally paid the $25,000 fee. Rivera also painted a sympathetic portrait of Ford. In 1932, Nelson Rockefeller, who was in charge of the development of Rockefeller Center in Manhattan, invited Rivera to paint the fresco on the wall facing the entrance to the RCA Building.

But the negotiations were complicated. The theme, perhaps because of the Depression, was to be "Man at the Crossroads Looking with Hope and High Vision to the Choosing of a New and Better Future." Rockefeller aspired to stage a competition between Matisse, Picasso, and Rivera. Matisse said the project simply was not his style. Picasso refused to receive the Rockefeller representative. Rivera announced that he was too famous to stoop to a competition. Since Rivera was the only one of the three who had not categorically refused, Rockefeller had no choice but to award him the commission, more or less on Rivera's terms. The painter sketched out his ideas both in monochrome and verbally and they were approved. There can be no doubt that Rivera at the outset intended to paint a Communist mural; it is equally clear that he did not propose to depict Lenin.

In March 1933 Rivera and his crew set to work at the RCA Building. He painted at furious speed in hope of completing the fresco by May Day. He grabbed spectators as models. The man standing at the crossroads of civilization was the night watchman. The dedicated female student was an onlooker who had flunked out of Hunter College. As the painting emerged, its revolutionary theme became increasingly evident: police breaking up an unemployment demonstration; a gory battlefield representing the evils of the existing order; a May Day demonstration, evidently in Red Square, of marching, singing workers; a bourgeois bridge game somehow linked to venereal disease with a matchbox on the table showing the hammer and sickle; great splashes of red. The architect, the contractor, and the rental agent grew uneasy. But Nelson Rockefeller appeared to remain steady ("Everybody is most enthusiastic about the work which you are doing"). On April 24, the *World-Telegram* ran a story headlined, "Rivera Paints Scenes of Communist Activity and John D. Jr. Foots Bill." Rivera saved the best for last. The dominant figure turned out to be none other than Nicolai Lenin!

This was too much for Rockefeller. He wrote Rivera that the fresco was "thrilling" and "beautifully painted," but the portrait of Lenin "might very easily seriously offend a great many people." It would be all right in a private house, but not in a public building. "As much as I dislike to do so I am afraid we must ask you to substitute the face of some unknown man where Lenin's face now appears."

Rivera was outraged and called a council of war. Wolfe advised him to yield on Lenin in order to save the rest of the fresco. His young assistants urged him to stand fast. He wrote Rockefeller that Lenin must remain. But he offered to remove the bridge game and replace it with a Civil War theme, perhaps Lincoln freeing the slaves. Rockefeller had had enough of both Lenin and Rivera. On the evening of May 9, 1933, Hugh Robertson, the contractor, came on the scene with his assistants and uniformed guards. He told Rivera to come down from the scaffold, gave him the final payment of $14,000, and fired him. Robertson's workmen then covered the wall with canvas.

The incident stirred up a small tempest. Liberal and radical artists and writers defended the freedom of the artist. Conservative artists opined that Lenin's face was "unsuitable" in America. Archibald MacLeish wrote a sympathetic poem, "Frescoes for Mr. Rockefeller's City." General Motors, which had commissioned Rivera to do the mural for its building at the Chicago World's Fair, promptly sacked him. The Communist Party, which admired neither Rockefeller nor Rivera, maintained a discreet silence. The painter went on the radio with a logic-defying analogy. Suppose, Rivera asked, an American millionaire bought the Sistine Chapel along with the Michelangelo frescoes from the Vatican. "Would the millionaire have the right to destroy the Sistine Chapel?" The Rockefellers, evidently, promised not to destroy the Rivera. But at midnight on February 9, 1934, the fresco was ground to dust.[1]

1

The Great Depression transformed American literature. Many writers became, in the phrase of the time, "socially conscious." They were shocked and outraged by mass unemployment, poverty, and the suppression of labor unions. Their writings depicted, often from direct experience and usually with care, the problems of the worker and his family, the conditions of the workplace, the terrors of joblessness and poverty, and the struggles, usually involving strikes, to form unions. Farm labor, particularly tenancy in the South and the terrifying tragedy in the Dust Bowl, gave rise to a special literature of its own.

One must note, though with marginal interest in the present context, that many American writers, particularly in the early years of the Great Depression, veered sharply leftward politically as they lost faith in America and gained hope in the Soviet Union. A number joined the Communist Party and many others followed its line with varying degrees of intensity and duration. The party systematically cultivated these writers by publishing their works, especially in *The New Masses,* by obtaining their public support for Communist causes and manifestoes, by organizing them into John Reed Clubs, and by holding American Writers' Congresses in 1935, 1937, 1939, and 1941. The inherent conflict between a party with tight discipline and an individualistic and obstreperous group of writers produced endless controversy. Except for party hacks and a handful of writers of modest stature, it seems fair to conclude that the party had only a slight impact on the mainstream of American writing during the Depression. "The strongest writers of the thirties," Daniel Aaron has written, "used politics and were not used by it. The party could not have dictated to a Dos Passos, a Hemingway, a Lewis, a Dreiser, a Steinbeck, a Wolfe even if it had tried to do so." The same can be said of many lesser figures.

A basic theme of the fiction of the Great Depression is ethnic division within the American work force. Sometimes it is merely descriptive. Elliot Paul's *The Stars and Stripes Forever* (1939) is set in a New England mill town. The boss of the Starrett-Loring factory is a baseball nut and organizes a company league that plays on Saturday afternoons. The members of the office team have Anglo-Saxon names like Loring and Bascomb. Among the players on the plant team are Pip Mangini, Hunjak Wojciechowski, Ham Callahan, and Izzy Feldstein. Jack Conroy recalled that the workers at the Monkey Nest coal mine in Missouri were "a miniature United Nations." Mostly they were English, Welsh, and Irish, but there were many Italians, Frenchmen, and Germans. In Albert Halper's *The Foundry* (1934), Duffy, one of the workers, is annoyed when a young Pole has been hired because his name, Ladislas Jareszewski, is a jawbreaker. He exclaims, can't they hire "a Scandinavian or an African or something!"

But often national origin becomes the basis for position in the pecking order and, thus, for prejudice. In Robert Cantwell's *The Land of Plenty* (1934), Walt hates his job in the lumber mill because he has to work too hard. "The Polack I work with, he gives me the heavy end of every truck." But Walt does not hesitate to make time with the Turner sisters (real name: Dombroski) who have a reputation for saying yes. A sling slips as a ship is unloaded in Walter Havighurst's *Pier 17* (1935), and a heavy load of hemp drops and kills the Russian, Urbik. Harry feels guilty. "I never killed a man before." The mate tells him to forget it, Urbik was standing in the wrong place. "That wop didn't belong in America." In Louis Colman's *Lumber* (1931), Jimmie is about to lose his job in the mill. The foreman tells him to stick around. "I'll find you something else to do to-night. . . . I think I'll can a Filipino. I never hired any of the black bastards." The Chicago shanty Irish in James T. Farrell's trilogy, *Studs Lonigan* (1935), know that "Americans" don't perform menial work. Studs leaves home right after breakfast to avoid his mother's nagging to do "janitor's" work — beating rugs or cleaning the basement. "Janitor's jobs were for jiggs, and Hunkies, and Polacks, anyway." Benny Taite lectures the gang in the poolroom:

> You guys complaining that there's nothing to do ought to just stop and think about all the poor chumps who got to work on a day like this. Think of some goddam Hunkie swinging a pickaxe, chopping up the street with his fanny dragging to the ground, swinging away with that goddam pickaxe, thirsty, his underwear dripping, wishing it was all over and he was sitting in the shade of the old apple tree.

The edge cuts sharper during a strike. In Wellington Roe's *Begin No Day* (1938), the CIO is organizing a New England hat town, including the fur factory that supplies the mills, and a strike looms. Dominic Yaccarino, an immigrant from the Fucino and now a foreman in the fur company, tells his friend Frank Sacco, the grocer, "We Americans aren't going to be quiet while they steal our Government." The union buster in Upton Sinclair's *Little Steel* (1938) warns the steelmaster that the Steel Workers Organizing Committee is run by Communists and preaches class war. "That is the war which is going to bring your hunkies and wops swarming up to this mansion, to loot the wine cellar and the safe where the jewels are kept."

As the Depression deepened, "Americans" explained its causes and proposed a remedy. Cass and Clay, two white hoboes in Nelson Algren's *Somebody in Boots* (1935), drop off a freight train in New Orleans and walk through a black neighborhood. "Goddam," Cass says, "ah never did see so many jigs in mah life befo'." Clay agrees. "Yep, niggers got all the jobs, everywhere, an' that's why you'n me is on the road. Up north they's six dings for every telygraph pole. A white man don't stand a chance no more, anywhere." Old man Lonigan explains the situation to Studs: If the U.S. had not loaned money to Europe, there would have been no Depression. If we kept "undesirable aliens" out, there would be jobs for "Americans" and no hard times. "America was a fine country. And all these foreigners came here to take jobs away from Americans." He would put all the foreigners in boats and send them back where they belong. This would also get rid of the Reds who were down South "exciting the niggers . . . , telling them they're as good as white men and they can have white women." Studs thought the old man was right for a change. "America," he said, "should be for Americans."

In this context a unique work is Pietro DiDonato's haunting *Christ in Concrete* (1937). The whole novel is intensely Italian, relevantly here in that the workers are brickmasons and stonecutters, traditional Italian crafts. Geremio prays that "all my children must be boys so that they someday will be big American builders." Italians work harder. Geremio's "American" boss complains about a slack member of his crew and orders Geremio to "put a young wop in his place." Geremio is killed when the building collapses. His son, Paul, still a child, assumes responsibility for feeding the family and goes to work as a brickmason. He has a remarkable innate mastery of the craft. A race is staged to see who can lay the most bricks properly — Paul against Dave, the Jew, Frank the Scotchman, Barney the Irishman, Tommy the Englishman, Hans the German, and Grogan, a "real" American. Paul wins and the mayor presents him with the certificate of victory.

The decisive ethnic factor in this literature is race, that is, the status of blacks in the American labor market. It is a harrowing and brutal catalogue of discrimination. Fielding Burke's *A Stone Came Rolling* (1935) is set in a southern mill town. Ishma asks an old black woman, "Somebody must be working, Auntie?" "No, we's jest perishin'. . . . Our belly buttons air jest hangin' loose." If the mill cuts white folks' wages, "Lawd, help us!" In Charles B. Givens's *The Devil Takes a Hill Town* (1939), the union organizer comes to a Tennessee community and talks to the blacks. Hattie, the cook, tells the white preacher that the union man says wages are too low. "Hattie," growled Brother Alf, "are you workin' for the Good Lord? Or, ain't you?" "Sho is Rev'un, but when you talks wid de Good Lawd ergin kindly tell Him He's er payin' a heap less wages dan de union man say He orter." The black stable buck, Crooks, in John Steinbeck's *Of Mice and Men* (1937), is not allowed in the California ranch bunkhouse even to play cards. He sleeps in a segregated room. He is particularly enraged because he is not from the South, having been born in California on his father's chicken ranch. Crooks: "They say I stink. Well, I tell you, you all of you stink to me." In Jack Conroy's *The Disinherited* (1934),

Larry becomes desperately thirsty working in the broiling sun on the road gang. The water boy brings a pail of very warm water with two rusty cups. Larry grabs one, fills it, and pours the hot liquid down his throat. " 'Hey!' shouted the horrified water boy, '*That's* the niggers' cup.' "

Conroy also recounts an incident early in the Depression in a midwestern Hooverville. Ed, just arriving, asks, "Don't suppose a man could *buy* a job around here, could he?" The old man cackles, "Jobs went out o' style, son, two years ago." Then he adds that one white man had found work sandhogging underwater on the riverbed. "It's a nigger's job, but times has got so hard the white man is chasin' the niggers away and takin' the job theirselves." Ed goes to the riverbank and stands in a group of overalled white men. The foreman tells them,

> "Get me right. I ain't no nigger lover, I come from Peachtree, Georgia, where niggers step off the sidewalk and take off their hats when they see a white man comin'. I tried my best t' use white men, but they play out on me. So I gotta use the niggers. I'm sorry as hell."

In *A Stone Came Rolling* the union man works with the blacks. The mayor of the southern town warns him, "If you keep on helpin' niggers organize, you are going to run against something that will put a rope around your neck." Edwin Lanham's *The Stricklands* (1937) is a blending of Oklahoma tenant farming and southwestern outlawry. Jay Strickland is an organizer for the Southern Tenant Farmers Union and tries to recruit whites, blacks, and Indians equally because all share the same economic woes. He confronts a stone wall on race. A poor white tenant says, "I ain't joining up with no nigger union. . . . Anytime I join a union it will be a union of white men like me." In the climax Jay's brother Pat, who has robbed a bank and killed several men, and Rocky, the black union organizer, are shot down together by a posse.

William Attaway's *Blood on the Forge* (1941) is wholly devoted to the race issue. Big Mat, a powerful Kentucky sharecropper, kills a white riding boss who humiliates him because he is black. Mat and his brothers, Chinatown and Melody, are recruited by a jackleg as strikebreakers for the Pennsylvania steel mills and are shipped north in a sealed boxcar. The unionized white steelworkers, especially the Slavs, hate the blacks. "When white folks git mad," Chinatown says, "all niggers look alike." Work in the mill is hot, filthy, noisy, and dangerous. Outside the air is so thick with smoke that one can hardly breathe and the sun is hidden. "A nigger needs sun so's he kin keep black." Big Mat is such a good worker that the boss Irish claim him: "He's got some Irish in him somewhere." Mat, they say, is "a whole lot better than a hunky or a ginny." During the strike Mat is deputized and is paid $4 a day extra. He is told, "You're the boss in this here town. Anythin' you do is all right, 'cause you're the law." Mat is intoxicated with pride. He is no longer a "nigger," the "badge signifying poverty and filth." "He is a boss, a boss over whites." Big Mat joins the mounted troops in assaulting white strikers. A crazed Slavic striker splits Mat's head open with a pickaxe handle. The sheriff says, "Sure is a shame that big nigger had to go and git himself killed. . . . That's the thing 'bout nigger deputies — they're fightin' the race war 'stead of a labor strike."

Richard Wright's autobiographical *Black Boy* (1945) is a harrowing account of a young black's struggle to find identity and to make a living in the Deep South. When he is a child, his mother takes him and his brother to the white folks' kitchen where she cooks. If the whites do not finish their plates, the black boys eat well. Otherwise, bread and tea. As Richard grows older, he learns from other blacks that they must steal from whites. "How in hell you gonna git ahead?" When he asks for a job doing chores for a white woman, she asks, "Now, boy, I want to ask you one question and I want you to tell me the truth." "Yes, ma'am." "Do you steal?" Richard thinks the question ridiculous and laughs. He realizes immediately that he has erred in being "a sassy nigger." One summer he cannot hold a job and asks a friend to explain his trouble. "Dick, look, you're black, *black,* see?" White folks watch Negroes. "You act around white people as if you didn't know that they were white. And they *see* it." The other black boys act out the roles whites expect of them.

Richard finds a job learning the optical trade. The owner, a Yankee from Illinois, wants to train a black. But the two southern whites who grind and polish lenses refuse to teach him. They order him to sweep out the shop. Later they grab him, slap him, and threaten him with a steel bar until he promises to leave.

Finally, desperate to get money to leave the South, Richard finds a job as a ticket-taker in a black movie house. A street-smart Negro lets him in on the racket. Richard withholds tickets from the box, returns them to the black girl at the ticket booth, she sells them again, and they split the take. After two weeks he has enough money to pay for the trip to the North.

Many of these writers stress the insularity of the American working class. In their eyes it is blue collar, poorly educated, and predominantly male.

For Conroy, the divide between manual and white-collar work is virtually unbridgeable. In *A World to Win* (1935) Robert, who is writing a novel, holds a clerical job in an auto plant. After the crash he often enters the virtually empty shop to ask the handful of remaining workers how much work they are getting. They always say, "plenty," an obvious untruth. He gradually realizes that his collar makes him a spy in their eyes, "a natural enemy." Leo goes one step further: "I don't want t' be no clerk. I ain't afraid o' work." In *The Disinherited,* Larry, finishing a course in accounting, is walking with a friend in Cadillac Square in Detroit. Ed tells him to stay away from white-collar jobs. The pay is lower and they "keep you there till you dry up and blow away." But where, Larry asks, will a factory job lead? Ed says,

> "You might get t' be a foreman. That pays higher than most white-collar jobs. . . . It'll only be an accident if you ever get out of your class. You might as well make up your mind that you're a workin' stiff and that you'll stay one unless lightning happens to strike you — some kind of luck that hits only one out of a million workin' men. You'll work a while, maybe raise a mess of kids, get too old t' work in the factories and hafta sponge offen your kids the rest of your life. It's in the cards, kid."

During the Little Steel strike in Upton Sinclair's novel, the town of Valleyville is split into two camps — the white-collar people against "the sweaty-shirted toilers."

In these novels, there is ambivalence about higher education. On the one hand, "college guys" are the natural enemies of the working class. On the other, the university is the roadway to upward mobility and self-fulfillment. The former view is expressed by the crotchety old apple-picker about the checker in Steinbeck's *In Dubious Battle* (1936): "They go to them colleges and they don't learn a God-damn thing. That smart guy with the little book couldn't keep his ass dry in a barn." Young Johnny, who works in the lumber mill in Cantwell's *The Land of Plenty,* takes the other side. He dreamed of

> ivy-covered walls, the long slopes of green lawn, the beautiful coeds, each with her own sports roadster, giving herself as gaily and passionately with a true F. Scott Fitzgerald abandon; yes, and long canoe rides on the lake, with the water lapping the frail sides of the fragile craft, and the long bull-fests, blue with tobacco smoke, before the open fire of the country-club fraternity house, and fellows smoking pipes sitting up all night chewing the fat about philosophy and sex! What a life!

Johnny knew that his friends were going to college and that 99 percent of the successful men in *Who's Who* were graduates. But his family was broke and could not afford to send him. What would he do? "Work in the factory all his life? The thought of it made his blood run cold."

Albert Halper poses the same dilemma in *The Chute* (1937), a novel about a Chicago mail-order house. Early in the summer a handsome, strapping young man comes to work. The other employees, especially the girls, most of whom barely finished grade school, buzz over the fact that "a university man, a collegiate, [is] picking orders." They ask Craig if he intends to return to college in the fall. He says he plans to stay in the business. But he leaves at the end of summer and they learn from the sports pages that he is a famous football player who took the summer job only to keep in shape. More pointedly, Halper raised this issue in the context of the Jewish family. Paul is eager to go to architecture school, but, because his family has nothing, gets a job in the mail-order "madhouse." His older sister, Rae, who was forced to leave high school after one year for work in a sweatshop, is anxious to further Paul's education. But the family cannot get the money together and rich Uncle Julius refuses to help. Paul is fated to remain in the mail-order business.

Conroy is torn by this ambivalence. In *A World to Win,* the college men who work in the auto plant are "finks." But a major theme of *The Disinherited* is that education is the route out of the working class. Larry's father, who digs coal in the Monkey Nest, tells him, "I want you to study hard; I don't want you to be a coal miner like me." The father takes the dangerous job of shot firer for the wage premium in order to keep Larry in school. This leads to his death underground. Conroy himself, who worked in the mines, in auto plants, in railroad shops, and on road gangs, liked to say that he studied at the University of Hard Knocks in boxcars, doubtless studying the graffiti. But he wrote novels and when he was back home he spent weekends "gawking about the campus of the University of Missouri in Columbia."

While there is only limited consideration of the place of women in the American labor market, the novels that deal with it are predominantly negative. In Halper's *The Chute,* Florina Puccini, who works in the mail-order house, invites Paul to Christmas dinner with her family. Her father, an anarchist, questions him about labor troubles on the job. His wife yells from the kitchen, "Today ees Christmas, no politics!" Puccini shouts back, "Woman, you cook! We man's have to talk; you cook!" In Algren's *Somebody in Boots,* when Nancy, who is overworked, asks her brother, Bryan, to help with the household chores, he answers that he has no time for "women's tasks." Steinbeck in *To a God Unknown* (1933) has the Marxian philosopher in Monterey, McGreggor, expound to his daughter, Elizabeth, on the time "when women will earn their own bread" and learn trades. But he is shocked when she decides to become a schoolteacher. In Conroy's *A World to Win* the workers are "real men." In Edward Dahlberg's *Bottom Dogs* (1930) girls are described as undependable workers. The dissenting voice is that of the radical feminist author, Meridel LeSueur. Her stories, written during the Depression, are about women at the bottom — those in the most degrading jobs or those out of work. They are filled with tears and rage.

That work that the characters in these novels perform is brutally hard. In DiDonato's *Christ in Concrete,* Old Nick says, "Master Geremio, the Devil himself could not break his tail any harder than we here. . . . America beautiful will eat you and spit your bones into the earth's hole! Work!" At the end of the day Geremio's crew of "calloused and bruised bodies sighed, and numb legs shuffled" home. "Home where my broken back will not ache so." After Geremio is killed and his son gets a job, Paul works for hours on his knees filling beams. Each time he bends there is "a lightning-like splitting of his back," his trowel wrist hangs "helpless," and the brick dust and mortar bruise his fingers and eat away the skin of his hands. "O God how it hurts!" Nazone shows him how to protect himself. "You will pee on your hands." At the end of the day Paul is so exhausted that he cannot sleep.

Backbreaking labor is a central theme of Conroy's work. In *The Disinherited,* the miners come home from the Monkey Nest "dog-tired," gulp down supper, and fall asleep. "On the Judgement Day

Gabriel would not be able to arouse them with his trumpet." In the railroad shop Larry finds that the hours limp along at "the speed of a rheumatic turtle." Each day is "an ordeal to be dreaded." At night he crawls into bed with "muscles numb" and in the morning they ache like "a sore tooth." The work breaks men early. The senior workers have "bleary, leaden eyes . . . humped backs and gnarled hands." The railroad soon lets them go as "unfit for further service." In *A World to Win,* when the migrant family finds work picking beets for the Mormon bishop in the West, they say, as is said of most kinds of work, "All you need is a weak mind and a strong back." In a story Conroy has a father tell his son, "Ye don't know, me bye, how many times in the spring of an airly morning I ha' felt like throwin' me lunch pail far as I c'd and niver goin' back t' that hell-hole of a mill."

Halper's chute is insatiable. "The chute began to call, calling to be fed." The order pickers must work furiously to answer its demands. Paul is so exhausted by the end of the day that he cannot eat his supper. In Dahlberg's *Bottom Dogs,* Lorry gets a job as a drover in the Kansas City stockyards, pushing cattle into the slaughterhouse for twelve hours a day. When he comes home at night he is "all in and not fit for anything else." Later, when Lorry is out of work, he applies for a job on a Union Pacific road gang in Wyoming. The hiring agent demands "a look at them hands, bo." After Lorry shows them, the agent says, "Them cornflake mitts won't do."

In *Studs Lonigan,* Farrell uses hard work as a bone for intergenerational conflict. Old man Lonigan says that he had "nearly killed himself working." His wife agrees. They had "worked like niggers in those days back of the yards before their children were born." They expect the same of Studs. But he and his pals are not "chumps." When Studs refuses to go to work for his father, the old man slaps him.

In Attaway's *Blood on the Forge,* the men who shovel hot slag in the steel mill are quickly exhausted and "the needles started all over your back." Chinatown and Melody stagger at the lunch break and Melody is too tired to eat. When he thinks of the afternoon task, "he got sick in his belly." At night they tumble into bed and are "asleep before their heads touched the bunks." In order to face the prospect of work, the hot-metal men must "keep liquored up." They are checked at the gate to make sure they do not bring booze into the mill.

James Agee wrote a strange and notable book, *Let Us Now Praise*

Famous Men (1941), with photographs by Walker Evans, that describes the lives of three tenant farmer families in Alabama. "Dull and heartless" work absorbs "their minds, their spirits, and their strength." Cotton demands unremitting labor and provides no reward beyond bare subsistence. In late August, when the plants ripen, the entire family turns to picking in the brutal heat. The picker drags a sack, which holds 100 pounds, from plant to plant and must stoop to reach the ripe cotton. "A strong back is a godsend, but not even the strongest back was built for that treatment." The pain starts in the kidneys and radiates down the thighs and up the spine to the shoulders. As the saying went, "Picking goes on each day from can to can't." Agee hears of families that take no rest at midday, but these three have a simple meal and a brief respite from the high sun. In the afternoon they return to picking "hour after hour . . . speechless, silent, serious, ceaseless and lonely work along the great silence of the unshaded land."

For these writers American industry is an armory of risks to life and limb. Several of the books, in fact, center on the theme of death on the job, particularly the death of the father.

To some of the novelists the industrial accident is merely an everyday occurrence. In his story "Johnny Bear," Steinbeck writes:

> The next morning one of those accidents so common in construction landed on us. One of the new wires parted on the in-swing and dropped the bucket on one of the pontoons, sinking it and the works in eight feet of ditch water. When we sunk a dead man and got a line out of it to pull us from the water, the line parted and clipped the legs off one of the deck hands. We bound the stumps and rushed him to Salinas. And then little accidents happened. A leverman developed blood poisoning from a wire scratch.

Many writers treat injury on the job in the same matter-of-fact manner. In Steinbeck's *In Dubious Battle* the old apple-picker, Dan, is working on a shoddy ladder and two rungs snap. He falls to the ground and breaks his hip. Tim says, in Roe's *Begin No Day,* that hatting is "a tough man-killin' job." Those who walk off on their own legs are "shakin' like November leaves." The sizing room is the most hazardous because of the heat, the boiling water, and the acid. "Every day somebody gets scalded." The men work naked above the waist with only a rubber apron and rubber boots beneath. "Clothes wouldn't help anyway. If they get splashed, clothes'd just stick to 'em an' make the burn worse." Halper's *The Foundry* recounts a series of accidents — an apprentice getting his arm caught in a machine when someone mistakenly throws the switch, a trimmer losing the tip of his left index finger to the knife, and a bad day with eight small and three "not so minor" accidents. When the ship is dropping anchor in Puget Sound in Havighurst's *Pier 17*, the chain wraps itself around the boy Adrian, and, later, as already noted, Urbik is killed by a falling sling. Pete Schultz in Josephine Herbst's *The Executioner Waits* (1934) loses his job at Ford's when the Depression strikes. On learning the news, his wife says, "Thank God for it. . . . I'd rather have you home alive than dead."

The novelists who write about the notoriously dangerous industries treat the accident with much greater intensity. In Cantwell's *The Land of Plenty,* almost every sawyer has lost a few fingers and the logging camps are said to kill a man "every week." But the major event occurs in the lumber mill when a huge log rolls onto the hoist man. The other workers have great difficulty raising it in order to move him to the hospital, where "the poor son of a bitch" dies. When the accident takes place, everyone in the mill falls silent and all are "touched and influenced, even those who did not know that the hoist man was hurt, who had never seen him, who did not even know who he was." Winters, who had worked furiously to lift the log, is drained and sick. He muses bitterly:

> Now his memory would give him nothing but images of horror and terror, until it seemed he had lived all his life on the scene of some vast wreck that had strewn the world with its victims; now he remembered the "accidents" in the logging camps and in the mills where he had worked, the ruined bodies of cripples, the loggers whose intestines were ruptured and torn from the weights they pulled and the mad pace of their labors, the old men who had worked in the mills and now had no hands on their arms or no fingers on their hands; he remembered the times in his childhood when, in the little lumber camp in the mountains, the heart of the town stopped beating while the accident siren screamed at the mill.

Colman's *Lumber* is structured around the death of the father. Jimmie's father has lost his job in the mill and finds work in the woods. On his first day he does not hear the warning cry of "Timber!" and a tree falls on him, breaking his back. He dies within twenty-four hours. The lumberjack informs Jimmie's mother, "He said he didn't want us to bring him home — said he wanted to die in camp." Later, when Jimmie is grown and married, he works in the mill. Both of his children die and his wife is pregnant. One day Jimmie gets into a fight with Anders in the mill. Anders pushes Jimmie away, he staggers backwards, stumbles on a log, and is cut in two by the saw. His wife is left alone with an unborn child.

Attaway's *Blood on the Forge* is an extremely violent novel and stresses the danger of working in the steel industry. Smothers, who is severely crippled, warns the new men, "Any time you foolin' round fast metal it liable to blow up. It always blow for no reason at all, 'ceptin' it want to." The faces of the hot-metal men are "scorched, spark-pitted." With the drinking over the weekend, Monday is always "trouble," like a test block falling and crushing a worker's toe. Melody's right hand is accidentally smashed by Bo's rod and he worries that he will not be able to pick his guitar. One night, as Smothers had predicted, a blast furnace blows its top. There is "a blinding flash" that lights the far side of the Monongahela and "a mushroom cloud streaked with whirling red fire." The smell of burning flesh is pervasive. Fourteen men lie dead, including Smothers. Chinatown loses both eyes.

The novelists who write of coal mining must confront the underground disaster. Ruth McKenney's *Jake Home* (1943) opens dramatically at 10:46 A.M. on February 25, 1912, in Luyskill, Pennsylvania. Jake is studying an elementary botany book. Miss Farrell is reading to her pupils, "And then the little fox said. . . ." Mrs. O'Neill is relating stale gossip to Mrs. Raymond. A tremor shakes the mining town "like a distant blast of thunder," and there is a single scream from the whistle — "Doomsday." Everyone knows what has happened and moves silently to the mouth of the shaft, where the children find their mothers. The company had cheated on the timbers and had bribed the inspector. The night-shift men organize the rescue. Eighteen miners are found dead. Mrs. Home does not stay outdoors during the cold, damp night because she is pregnant. Frank Rickert, a night man, comes to the house. "It's all over, Martha." Pete Home, age 36, is dead. At first Jake refuses to believe that his father has died, but, when he looks into Rickert's eyes, "He knew, too, that it was all over."

In Conroy's *The Disinherited,* the Monkey Nest takes a frightful toll of miners' lives. Many people are afraid to stand near the open shaft for fear of becoming "obsessed by an insane desire to leap into such a pit." In Larry's family his brother Danny, who is fourteen, is the first to die in a mine accident. Shortly afterward his father and another miner set off a blast from the underground room. The wall is so thin that it "leaped toward them with a terrific detonation." His father is found "buried under a huge lump of coal with another chunk embedded in his side."

DiDonato's *Christ in Concrete* focuses on the dangers of working in the construction industry and, given the unity of the Italian family, the tragedy of the death of the father. At the outset, Paul's father, Geremio, is working on the sixth floor of a building. The structure shudders and lurches, the supports burst, and the "floor vomited upward." Geremio catapults to the ground and is impaled on steel reinforcing bars. Later, Paul's Uncle Luigi is working in the deep pit of a building foundation. A huge boulder is dislodged from the wall of the pit and rolls down on him. Luigi loses a leg. At the end, Paul's godfather, Nazone, is working on the twentieth floor of a skyscraper. In a ridiculous altercation with the foreman, Nazone loses his footing and hurtles to his death.

In these novels, workers' wages are low, their hours are long, and their working conditions are oppressive. An important theme is that the Depression induces cutthroat competition that forces employers to reduce wages. In Roe's *Begin No Day*, Chick, who is just taking over the hat factory, contracts with a New York chain to deliver 500 dozen top grade felt hats at $13.85 a dozen. Tim explodes because they never before sold below $17.50. To make the new price, Chick must cut his workers' piece rates nearly 20 percent. This leads to accidents, a strike, and violence. Last year, in Cantwell's *Land of Plenty*, Winters worked in a crew of five in the lumber mill and received $4.25 a day. This year, three men do the same work and he gets $3. "I can't live on it." The owner of the southern cotton mill in Burke's *A Stone Came Rolling* is an expert on the stretch-out, squeezing a few minutes of extra work daily from each of his 800 workers. When the boss in Halper's *The Foundry* demands that Franck, the wax caster, work faster, Franck goes berserk and almost kills him. Paul in DiDonato's *Christ in Concrete* does a man's work and receives a child's pay — $5 a week. "What could Annunziata and the children do with five dollars?"

The steel mill in Attaway's *Blood on the Forge* is on the twelve-hour shift. The night-turn men seldom see the sun and, when the shifts rotate, they work twenty-four consecutive hours. "Sometimes men went crazy." The Slavs want a union to win the eight-hour day. But Big Mat does not complain. "Only reason a nigger in the mill is cause o' trouble." In Halper's *The Chute* an increase in business leads the mail-order house to impose mandatory overtime. The shift ends at 5:30; there is a half hour for supper; and the people work from 6:00 to 8:00 without pay. Big Bill, the Dutchman, says, "We are joost slaves here, slaves!" There is no choice because there are long lines of the unemployed eager to take their jobs.

Workplaces affront the senses. In Conroy's *The Disinherited,* Larry has a job in a rubber-heel factory. The air is "thick enough to cut with a knife." Lungs are soon "clogged" and a piercing odor penetrates the workers' clothing. In the shaping mill in Attaway's novel the saws emit "awful screams" as they bite into hot metal and the open hearth is "full of agony." The men work at the Bessemer furnaces in intense heat and air so thin that they can barely breathe. Chinatown can kill somebody for water. In Thomas Bell's *Out of This Furnace* (1941), the Depression shuts the steel mills down. They "lay silent month after month, under a sky that had never been so clean and blue before." It became hard to remember "the smoke and the dust, the glare in the sky at night."

The workers in these books are highly ambivalent toward the work they do. On the one hand, they must have jobs, particularly during a time of mass unemployment. DiDonato in the Italian world of *Christ in Concrete* carries this further. When Louis, Paul's intellectual Jewish friend, tells him to stop working, to study in order to nurture his "fine brain," Paul gives the only answer he knows: the job is "food" and "freedom." Moreover, working with stone and brick is poetry, the "meter of soul's sentence to stone." Even when the scaffolds are unsafe, the men "prefer death or injury to loss of work." The nurse who tends Luigi in the hospital after he loses his leg is "a good woman. She is a worker." Luigi, no longer able to work in construction, must remain at home with Annunziata and the children. He is consumed with "boiling restlessness" and his "muscles strain for Job." Cola, who has lost her husband and does home work on textile goods to support herself, asks him to help with the embroidery. Luigi, with his great, clumsy fingers, learns to steer the little scissors through the rolls of embroidery material.

With Agee's Alabama farm tenant families in *Let Us Now Praise Famous Men,* work is the axle around which life turns:

> It is for the clothing, and for the food, and for the shelter, by these to sustain their lives, that they work. Into this work and need, their minds, their spirits, and their strength are so steadily drawn that during such time as they are not at work, life exists for them scarcely more clearly or in more variance and seizure and appetite than it does for the more simply organized among the animals and for the plants. This arduous physical work, to which a consciousness beyond that of the simplest child would only be a useless and painful encumbrance, is undertaken without choice or the thought of chance of choice, taught forward from father to son and from mother to daughter.

But, on the other hand, most of the workers in these novels detest their work, are bored by it, cannot escape from it, see no future in it, and are depressed by the dreariness of industrial life. In Burke's *A Stone Came Rolling,* Ishma hates her job in the textile mill. Paul in Halper's *The Chute* suffers constant misery. The working women in Dahlberg's *Those Who Perish* and LeSueur's stories find their jobs insufferable. In Attaway's *Blood on the Forge,* Chinatown shudders at the thought of going back into the steel mill. Melody tells him, "Mill your home now." Chinatown replies, "Mill never be my home." Conroy's novels and stories are peopled with workers who despise their work. The faces in Walker Evans's photographs of the tenant families in *Let Us Now Praise Famous Men* tell the same dismal story. A smart boss, like Duffy in Halper's Chicago-based *The Foundry,* assumes that no one likes his job. He announces to a long line of applicants from whom one will be selected: "The last shipping clerk was canned because his grandmother died too often when the Cubs were playing their last home games of the season."

Cantwell in *The Land of Plenty* deals with boredom at work. The girl's job on night shift in the lumber mill is to grade veneer as the pieces float by her work station, an exceedingly simple task.

> While she worked she made up long and complicated bets with herself, forgetting whether she won or lost. A part of her would say that an hour had passed, a part would say that only five minutes had gone by since she had looked at her watch. Then she would bet with herself — that she could wait for half an hour before looking to see what time it was, that she could count to a thousand before looking around. Sometimes she would count the dead pieces of wood that floated so gravely under the lights, giving them quick names and numbers as they passed with their eyes closed and their hands folded beside them. . . .
>
> All night long she made up games and bets with herself, trying to

> spur the slow hands of the watch. She began to hate the priggish little hand that barely moved, then held back so stubbornly from one figure to the next, her heart warming to the minute hand that tried to hurry.

A shallow defense against boredom is daydreaming. Many of these fictional workers fantasize about the beautiful world away from the job, usually about sex. But there are risks. When Leo in Conroy's *A World to Win* daydreams about his girl, he nods off into sleep and his finger is nicked by the saw. Smart old Willie tells him that you have to work steadily "at nothing when there was nothing to do, to deceive the eyes of the foreman or stool pigeons." Later Leo passes on the wisdom to his brother, Robert. "One of the first things you've gotta learn when you're f——n' the dog is t' look like you're workin' hard enough t' make yer butt blossom like a rose."

Another form fantasy takes is the return to the land. Britt in Burke's *A Stone Came Rolling* hates his job in the furniture factory because the only work he likes is farming. This, of course, is a central theme in Steinbeck, nowhere more poignantly expressed than in *Of Mice and Men.* Crooks tells Lennie that he has met hundreds of bindlestiffs with the same dream of owning their own farms. "Nobody gets no land. It's just in their head." But Lennie must have the dream. As he and George heat their canned beans, George tells him once again about how some day they will have a little house, a couple of acres, a cow, and some pigs. Lennie breaks in with *"An' live off the fatta the lan'."*

Unemployment casts a heavy shadow over this entire literature. In the final volume of Farrell's *Studs Lonigan*, the Great Depression overpowers Chicago and Studs trudges its streets looking for work. His failure to find a job is the prelude to his death in defeat. In the conclusion of Halper's *The Chute*, with hard times the mail-order house goes broke, the boss falls into the chute, and the employees lose their jobs. DiDonato begins the climax of *Christ in Concrete*, "NINETEEN TWENTY-NINE!" The building boom collapses. "The active world of Job shrunk and overnight men were wandering the street trowel on hip and lunch beneath arm in futile search of a wall." Conroy, who in retrospect considered himself "a witness of the times rather than a novelist," lost his job at the Willys Overland plant in Toledo after the crash. He literally thought that he would starve to death. *A World to Win*, which is autobiographical, is the harrowing account of the efforts of Leo and his family to stay alive, in spite of being out of work for four years. Leo's wife does not succeed.

Bell, in *Out of This Furnace*, summarizes the impact of the catastrophe on workers in the context of steel:

> Outside the walls idle men lingered like ghosts staring at the quiet buildings, the vacant roadways, the weeds showing green against a pile of metal rusting in the yard.
>
> The wire mill shut down and when some of its men were transferred to other mills the word went around that it would never run again. Nor did it. Bad times finished what the construction of new automatic mills, like the one in Donora in which John worked, had begun. The chain mill shut down. The Eighth Street foundry shut down. The Westinghouse laid off all five-year men, all ten-year men, and shortly thereafter Frank and Alice were evicted for nonpayment of rent. Their furniture was sold by the sheriff; Dobie saw his mother's bedroom set and sewing machine, all that he recognized as once here, go for a few dollars. "I was born in that bed," he thought. "We all were. Made and born." He felt that it should have seemed more important than it did. Chuck went to stay with his girl's family; they had been waiting to marry for two years. Alice went to Homestead, where her daughter was living with a man separated from his wife; he was a former automobile salesman but people had stopped buying cars and he had turned to writing numbers, the daily lottery brought to the steel towns by the Negroes and become almost a mania with the coming of bad times. Frank disappeared into the First Ward. Frankie, the younger son, was somewhere on his way to California.
>
> In Donora John was, like Dobie, getting two days' work a month; the rest of the time he and the boys — they hadn't had steady work since they'd graduated from high school — sat around at home while Alice reverted to the past and did housework by the day, competing with Negro women whose menfolk the company had imported as strikebreakers in 1919. Agnes was working in a chain store, but her wages had been cut to the vanishing point.
>
> An air of listlessness and decay settled over the steel towns; along their ever-shabbier Main Streets empty stores multiplied. People lost their businesses, their cars, their houses, their furniture. Families broke up, young men took to the roads. Tax receipts dropped, and the town sent its men around shutting off water until the danger of disease penetrated even their stupidity and compelled them to be generous. When the public utilities cut off their services people found ways of getting what they needed for nothing; gas and electric lines were tapped and the illegal wires and pipes replaced as fast as they were torn out. Dobie fed and smoked for weeks on his skill at by-passing electric

> meters and constructing long, wired poles to be hooked over the nearest power line. Movies cost him nothing; Helen Dobrejcak let him in free. Depression gardens scratched the hillsides; underneath men picked at long-exhausted coal veins. Here and there, in Pittsburgh, in McKeesport, Homestead, Turtle Creek, groups of people organized Unemployed Councils and marched on borough halls, shocking the newspapers and the well-fed not merely with their bad manners but with their fantastic demands for adequate relief, unemployment insurance, old age pensions and what not. They were instantly identified as Communists and dealt with accordingly. The utterly defeated gathered with unconscious symbolism on wastelands and garbage dumps, and ramshackle "Hoovervilles" immortalized a President who refused to undermine American self-reliance by feeding the hungry and clothing the naked. The mill began distributing food boxes, forbidding its employees to seek relief from charitable organizations. People starved slowly.

The feature of joblessness that stirred these writers most deeply was transiency, the often aimless movement of people out of work across the face of the land. Several of the novelists revived the older figures of the hobo and the Wobbly.

There was a hobo jungle near the Monkey Nest mine in Missouri where Conroy was raised. The men came to his house often because they knew that his mother would feed them. The theme of the hobo and the flivver tramp run through *A World to Win.* Steinbeck's *Of Mice and Men* is the story of George and Lennie, two hoboes who are only casually attached to farm labor. His *In Dubious Battle* deals with similar people in the context of an agricultural workers' strike. Dahlberg's *Bottom Dogs,* evidently autobiographical, is mainly an acccount of the life of Lorry as a hobo bumming his way around the West. Davey Cohen, a vagabond, is a shadowy figure in Farrell's *Studs Lonigan.* Algren's *Somebody in Boots* is appropriately dedicated to "The Homeless Boys of America" and is the account of the Depression transient, Cass McKay. Algren poses two Americas — "We" (the bums) and "Them" (regular folks). The nation of the transient is hungry, filthy, disease-ridden, dangerous, violent, unforgiving. "Bummin' takes everythin' out of a feller."

The novels set in the Pacific Northwest deal with the Industrial Workers of the World. The Wobbly theme is secondary in Cantwell's *The Land of Plenty*, but it comes to the fore in Colman's *Lumber.* Jimmie joins the IWW as soon as he starts work and he participates in the big lumber strike after World War I. The employers and the established community ruthlessly destroy the IWW by shipping Wobblies into the desert in sealed cars, by blowing up their homes, and by murder. Jimmie is fired because he is a member. Later he resigns and is killed in the mill.

In his masterful trilogy, *U.S.A.* (1937), John Dos Passos joins the hobo and the Wobbly. In the prologue a "young man walks by himself searching through the crowd with greedy eyes, greedy ears taut to hear, by himself, alone. . . . No job, no woman, no house, no city." He becomes Mac, a radical Irish kid from Chicago who takes to the road. He rides the rods to Duluth, the Canadian West, Vancouver, Seattle, Salem, San Francisco, where he joins the IWW. He goes to Goldfield, Nevada, to help in a Wobbly strike and to Mexico to join Zapata's revolution. Dos Passos inserts profiles of Big Bill Haywood, the founder of the IWW, Joe Hill, the minstrel of the "Wobblies hoboes bindlestiffs," and Wesley Everest, the Wobbly logger who was lynched by "patriots" in Centralia, Washington, in 1919.

The epilogue to the trilogy is titled "Vag."

> The young man waits at the edge of the concrete, with one hand he grips a rubbed suitcase of phony leather, the other hand almost making a fist, thumb up. . . .
>
> Head swims, hunger has twisted the belly tight,
>
> he has skinned a heel through the torn sock, feet ache in the broken shoes, under the threadbare suit carefully brushed off with the hand, the torn drawers have . . . the feel of having slept in your clothes; in the nostrils lingers the staleness of discouraged carcasses crowded into a transient camp, the carbolic stench of the jail, on the taut cheeks the shamed flush from the boring eyes of cops and deputies, railroadbulls. . . . Git the hell out, scram. . . .
>
> The punch in the jaw, the slam on the head with the nightstick, the wrist grabbed and twisted behind the back, the big knee brought up sharp into the crotch,
>
> the walk out of town with sore feet to stand and wait at the edge of the hissing speeding string of cars where the reek of ether and lead and gas melts into the silent grassy smell of the earth.

Overhead an airplane flashes across the sky. It is filled with "big men with bankaccounts, highlypaid jobs, who are saluted by doormen." They are thinking "contracts, profits, vacationtrips." They have "silver in the pocket, greenbacks in the wallet."

> The young man waits at the side of the road; the plane has gone. . . . went to school, books said opportunity, ads promised speed, own

your home, shine bigger than your neighbor, the radiocrooner whispered girls. . . .
waits with swimming head, needs knot the belly, idle hands numb, beside the speeding traffic.
A hundred miles down the road.

People on the move needed a place to stop temporarily on their journey. Such an encampment, an extension of the traditional hobo "jungle," became the Depression "Hooverville."

Conroy lived in the St. Louis Hooverville, "a colony of the dispossessed." A sign read: "WELCOME TO HOOVER CITY. TWO CAR GARAGES. A CHICKEN IN EVERY POT." Some people arrived with a few possessions from their wrecked homes; others came empty-handed. The "houses" were made of "packing crates, bits of tar paper, tin advertising signs, discarded automobile bodies, ancient delivery wagons." The inhabitants made daily foraging expeditions to the commission houses and garbage cans to salvage "overripe bananas, half-rotten potatoes, stale bread, wilted lettuce and cabbage." They worked feverishly to put something together that might be sold, but there were no buyers. Conroy assumed they were fighting the despair that went with inactivity. Nearby the city's sewage was dumped into the river and the men panned the muck in hope of finding treasure. "No one had found a five-hundred-dollar diamond ring like the legendary one everybody had heard of but nobody had seen."

In their trek from the Dust Bowl to California the Okie families in Steinbeck's *The Grapes of Wrath* (1939) huddled together near water in tent camps. "In the evening a strange thing happened: the twenty families became one family, the children were the children of all." Leaders emerged and unwritten laws of conduct were observed or, if they were violated, the culprits were punished. A man pulled out a guitar and sang "Ten-cent cotton and forty-cent meat." Social status was transformed. "They were not farm men any more, but migrant men." In the morning the camp was folded up and stuffed into the jalopies. The next camp was only a short distance from the last, always to the West. "Along the highway the cars of the migrant people crawled out like bugs." When they got to California they went straight to Hoovervilles, for there was one at the edge of every town. The houses were "tents, and weed-patched enclosures, paper houses, a great junk pile." The paper structures washed away in the rain.

The Grapes of Wrath is the Homeric epic of the Great Depression. This is partly because it is a literary masterpiece, became a notable motion picture, and Steinbeck won the Nobel Prize for literature. Certainly as important is the fact that it deals with rural poverty and transiency. A society not long removed from the land was haunted by the collapse of the Jeffersonian dream of a democracy built on stalwart yeoman farmers. Steinbeck was hardly alone in addressing this problem. Among others, three teams of writers and photographers produced moving and memorable books about farm workers: Erskine Caldwell and Margaret Bourke-White, *You Have Seen Their Faces* (1937), Paul S. Taylor and Dorothea Lange, *An American Exodus* (1939), and the aforementioned Agee and Evans, *Let Us Now Praise Famous Men.*

Steinbeck's novel is the saga of the Joads, tenant farmers from Oklahoma. In the summer the wind rises and the dust blows. "The dust hung like fog, and the sun was as red as ripe new blood." The corn and the cotton wither and die. "A man didn't get enough crop to plug up an ant's ass." The landowners decide that the tenant system "won't work any more. One man on a tractor can take the place of twelve or fourteen families." The Joads and many others are evicted. A tractor rips their house off its foundation. They have been dusted out and tractored out.

The Joads buy a beat-up Hudson Super-Six sedan, rip the top off with a cold chisel, and convert it into a truck. Three generations of Joads, a dog, and all they own pile on. "The truck crawled slowly through the dust to the highway." All the roads lead to Oklahoma City — 64 from Clarksville, Ozark, Van Buren, and Fort Smith, 66 from Tulsa, 270 from McAlester, 81 from Wichita Falls, Enid, Edmund, McLoud, and Purcell. At Oklahoma City they converge on U.S. 66, "the mother road, the road of flight." They cross Oklahoma through Clinton, Elk City, and Texola, then over the Texas Panhandle through Shamrock and Amarillo, on to Tucumcari, Albuquerque, and Gallup in New Mexico, then into Holbrook, Winslow, Flagstaff, and Kingman in Arizona, and finally enter California at Needles and cross the terrible Mojave Desert to Barstow. "Then suddenly a pass, and below the beautiful valley, below orchards and vineyards and little houses, and in the distance a city. And, oh, my God, it's over."

California may be the land of milk and honey, but not for Okies.

The border patrol and the Los Angeles police turn the state line into an armed frontier. Tom Joad doesn't know that he is an "Okie." "It means you're a dirty son-of-a-bitch," he is told. "Okie means you're scum." The landowners hate them because they are strong and hungry; the storekeepers and bankers hate them because they have no money; the laboring people hate them because they are hungry and work for lower wages. A deputy tells Ma, "You're in California, an' we don't want you goddam Okies settlin' down." There is no work and epidemics sweep through the camps. Casy the Preacher and Tom are murdered and Rose of Sharon's baby is born dead. At the end, Rose of Sharon gives her breast milk to a starving man.

Perhaps the most common theme in these novels is that of the union combined with the strike. The books fall into three categories. In the first, labor strife is no more than a topical background for a plot devoted to another purpose. The works of Attaway, Givens, Johnson, Lanham, Paul, Roe, and Sandoz fall into this group. A few illustrations will suffice.

Paul's *The Stars and Stripes Forever* is basically about the Loring family, and the strike in their factory is only the backdrop. Mark Loring is tyrannical and violently antiunion. His brother-in-law, Ned, gets out of college in 1929 and cannot find a job. Mark makes him assistant superintendent in the factory, but Ned has almost nothing to do. The workers form a union and strike. Ned is vaguely liberal and falls for Anne, who is good-looking and works for the CIO. Ned switches sides in the class struggle and joins the strikers. *Capital City* (1939) by Mari Sandoz is a panoramic novel about the main town in a fictional midwestern state during the Great Depression. Occasional strikes are incidents typical of the times. Lanham's *The Stricklands* is the story of an Oklahoma family, one of whose members, Pat, is a bank robber, killer, and outlaw on the order of John Dillinger or Pretty Boy Floyd. The fact that his brother Jay is an organizer for the Southern Tenant Farmers Union is only a sidelight. Attaway's *Blood on the Forge* is basically about the lives of black steelworkers who have been hired as strikebreakers. It is heated by racial violence, in part between white unionists, mainly Slavs, and the blacks.

The second group consists of novels in which the central theme is the effort of workers to organize a union and win a strike. Two deal with the unionization of steel. Bell's *Out of This Furnace* is the saga of the family of a Slovak immigrant of 1881 who becomes a Pennsylvania steelworker, culminating in the involvement of his descendant Dobie in the CIO drive of the 1930s. Sinclair's *Little Steel* focuses more narrowly on the struggle to unionize the mill in a small town in the thirties. A number of the novels are built around organizational strikes: Burke's *A Stone Came Rolling* in a southern hosiery mill, Havighurst's *Pier 17* in the Seattle maritime industry, Cantwell's *The Land of Plenty* in a northwestern lumber mill, Leane Zugsmith's *A Time to Remember* (1936) in a New York City store, and Steinbeck's *In Dubious Battle* in California agriculture. Halper's *The Foundry* is unusual in that it deals with the actual conduct of collective bargaining in a Chicago printing shop.

The third category consists of Marxist novels based on the class struggle. Here the primary concern is the political rather than the labor issue. Thus, few deserve consideration in the present context. The most impressive is Ruth McKenney's *Jake Home*, which is a kind of Communist epic.

Jake is from a Pennsylvania coal-mining family, and his father, as noted already, is killed in a mine accident when Jake is a child. He grows up a hero — huge, powerful, courageous, brilliant, with flaming red hair. He goes down into the mine, joins the union, and leads the local in the 1919 strike. When the operators break the union, Jake is blacklisted. He goes to work for the Pennsylvania Railroad in Altoona, rises rapidly into management, and marries Margaret, who wants a new house, a car, and children. When the shopmen strike in 1922, Jake quits his job, joins the strikers, is beaten by the cops, and Margaret leaves him.

When he recovers, Jake moves to New York, joins the Communist Party, and becomes an organizer on the docks for the Trade Union Educational League. He becomes involved in the Sacco-Vanzetti case and gets a job on the *Daily Worker*. Jake takes up with Kate, a banker's daughter, who is a casual Communist. They fall out over politics and Kate leaves him. When the Depression strikes, Jake organizes the unemployed in Cleveland and Youngstown. Kate returns. They join a hunger march across Ohio and Pennsylvania. Jake then works furiously to stage an immense demonstration of the unemployed on October 20, 1932, in New York City. Kate notifies him the day before the demonstration that she is sailing for Europe on the twentieth. Two hundred and fifty thousand people gather in Union Square. Jake proudly lifts the red flag of the working class. He addresses the huge crowd: "We march today. . . . This is the beginning of a new life." The cops try to break up the demonstration and Jake is injured. But he steadfastly marches to City Hall singing "The Internationale."[2]

2

Modern theater emerged in Europe at the end of the nineteenth century and flowered just before World War I. It was founded on the works of a masterful group of playwrights — Ibsen, Shaw, Chekhov, Strindberg, Hauptmann, Maeterlinck, and Schnitzler. Their plays compelled a restructuring of the art of dramatic presentation by imaginative new directors, set designers, and actors. Stanislavsky was a co-founder of the Moscow Art Theatre in 1897, and there worked out his system for acting. The director Meyerhold started with the Moscow Art at the turn of the century. In 1899, William Butler Yeats, Lady Gregory, and others formed the Irish Literary Theatre, which in 1902 became the Abbey Theatre. Max Reinhardt opened the Kleines Theater in Berlin in 1902. Gordon Craig publicly exhibited his drawings of set designs that same year.

The American commercial theater ignored these changes, but universities and little theaters responded. George Pierce Baker's English 47 course at Harvard in playwriting and the 47 Workshop for dramatic presentation led the way. Baker's students would later be among the leading dramatists, producers, directors, and set designers of the American stage. Columbia, Pennsylvania, Wisconsin, Carnegie Tech, North Dakota, and North Carolina soon followed. Several universities and community groups established little theaters, in New York and Chicago associated with settlement houses.

The modern American theater is said to have been born in New York in February 1915 when the Washington Square Players opened at the Bandbox Theatre at 57th Street and Third Avenue. In the summer of 1916 a new drama group staged plays on the wharf at Provincetown on Cape Cod. In the fall they set up the Provincetown Theater in a converted stable on MacDougal Street in Greenwich Village. The first bill was a one-acter, *Bound East for Cardiff.* The author, Eugene O'Neill, played a role. The Washington Square Players disbanded in May 1918, but in September several members of the company formed the Theatre Guild, which put its first production on the boards of the Garrick Theatre in April 1919.

This ferment presaged the "golden age" of the American theater, the twenties. The Guild was at its center. A new group of brilliant playwrights emerged — O'Neill, Maxwell Anderson, S. N. Behrman, Marc Connelly, Paul Green, Sidney Howard, George S. Kaufman, Elmer Rice, and Robert E. Sherwood. One may note that O'Neill's early work dealt largely with labor, the short plays, *Anna Christie* and *The Hairy Ape*, with seamen, and *The Emperor Jones* and *All God's Chillun Got Wings*, with blacks.

The prewar Russian theater, now led by Meyerhold, also flowered in the decade following the October Revolution. At the same time, the Soviet government, under the slogan "Drama is a weapon," developed a variety of propaganda forms to bring the uneducated masses under its wing — the staging of political issues, the propagandistic trial, "living" reports and debates, animated posters, literary montage, the living newspaper, and mass spectacles. Playlets with a simple political message, known as agitprops, as the name suggested, combined agitation and propaganda. In 1927, Stalin moved to undermine and ultimately destroy the pre-Revolutionary theater in the Soviet Union. In the late twenties, the agitprop was exported, particularly to the German, Czech, and American Communist parties. In 1930, the German-language Prolet-Buehne and the Workers' Laboratory Theatre were presenting agitprop skits on the streets of New York.

In the twenties, the American theater both bloomed and boomed. At its peak during the 1927–1928 season, over 80 theaters were running on Broadway and 280 new plays opened. This activity, of course, provided a great deal of employment. The end of the decade, however, brought economic disaster. The first reason for this was growing competition for audience from the new media — radio and sound films. The other was the onset of the Great Depression. During the thirties the number of theaters with their lights on shrank steadily, and new productions fell to 80 annually. This was accompanied by severe unemployment.

While hard times did not affect the style of the American theater, they transformed its mood. Robert Ardrey lived through and captured that change. At the University of Chicago his decisive experience was Thornton Wilder's course in creative writing. "By

December, 1930, when I took my degree, the Great Depression was revealing itself in all dark magnificence as a force, quite outside my control, which would guarantee for years to come that I should have nothing to do but write." Ardrey scratched for a living — playing piano in a speakeasy, lecturing on anthropology at the Chicago World's Fair, making a door-to-door survey in a West Side slum, composing fake medieval plainsongs with square notes for the University chapel. "As if such dividends were not enough, the Great Depression capped its payments by giving me something to write about."

Ardrey wrote for the stage because playwriting was the most challenging literary form. Before the war "even the best of our plays had been vehicles designed by a producer to exhibit a star." With "the clustering of talents," particularly O'Neill, in the twenties "the playwright became the alpha fish." The Depression transformed the context in which dramatists viewed the world. Ardrey wrote,

> An *avant garde* theatre occurs when enough skeptical artists raise their voice in a common tune. . . . We had no real name for our kind of play in America. Sometimes it was called the Theatre of Social Protest, a phrase which scarcely did the plays justice. On the Continent it was called the *théâtre engagé* — the theatre engaged with its times — and that is the term I prefer. We sought to discover in the materials of the contemporary scene moods and themes of enduring value.

The social drama of the thirties fell into two broad categories, plays concerned with domestic hard times — social disintegration, poverty, slums, unions, strikes — and those that dealt with war. In the earlier part of the period, when public attention concentrated on internal problems, the former predominated. Later, with Hitler running loose in Europe and the Japanese war machine rampant in the Far East, the latter became more important. Here the concern will be limited to domestic issues.

The Communists, who had predicted the collapse of capitalism, were hardly surprised when it appeared to occur. Further, their agitprop groups were already in place. Thus, they led the way into the new social drama.

The Workers Laboratory Theatre (WLT) and Prolet-Buehne were active in New York and similar groups sprang up in cities across the country. In early 1931, WLT began to publish a monthly, *Workers Theatre,* which printed the skits. In the spring of 1932 the journal held a national conference, a "Spartakiade," in New York to which fifty-three troupes sent delegates. They voted to form the League for Workers Theaters. Since the characters in agitprop playlets were one-dimensional (capitalist with top hat and dollar sign over his heart shouting, "Prosperity is just around the corner!"), it was not necessary to use professional actors. The skits had such titles as *Vote Communist!*, *15 Minute Red Revue, Unemployed, Scottsboro, Fat Fiorello.* In 1933, the Shock Troupe, a company of full-time actors who studied both drama and dialectical materialism, presented agitprop on the streets, at factory gates, and on the docks of New York.

Whether this primitive form was "theater" was debatable and was debated. A number of professionals became interested in it as a variety of dramatic expressionism. In 1931, Hallie Flanagan, the director of Vassar College's Experimental Theatre, staged three agitprops in Poughkeepsie. Two were standard items from the New York repertory, *Miners Are Striking* and *We Demand.* Flanagan and Margaret Ellen Clifford, the director of the Barnard College Theatre, wrote the third, *Can You Hear Their Voices?* It was based on a short story by Whittaker Chambers on the plight of Arkansas tenant farmers that had been published in *New Masses.* But there was no political message.

The serious Communist theater people were dissatisfied with the crude propaganda and amateurism of agitprop. WLT formed Theatre Collective in 1932 to stage full-length plays indoors. Over the next several years it presented three off-Broadway productions. A revival of *1931* — by Paul and Clare Sifton, which dealt with unemployment and had run for twelve performances when produced by The Group Theatre, received a more "revolutionary line" and the audience sang "The Internationale" when the curtain fell. It closed after four performances. *Marion Models,* an agitprop full-lengther about the needle trades, lasted for three showings. *The Klein-Ohrbach Strike* dealt with a labor dispute in the low-price stores in New York. Before it expired in 1936, the Collective produced two other revivals — *Till the Day I Die* by Clifford Odets and *Private Hicks* by Albert Maltz.

WLT renamed itself the Theatre of Action in 1934 and announced that it would operate on a "full professional basis" in presenting realistic plays indoors. It managed three productions over the next two years: A one-acter by Peter Martin, *Daughter,* was based on an Erskine Caldwell story about an impoverished father who shoots his daughter because she is starving. *The Young Go First,* by Martin, George Scudder, and Charles Friedman, was a full-length play that attacked the Civilian Conservation Corps. It ran for a month. Michael Blankfort's *The Crime* dealt with a meatpacking strike and was put on at the Civic Repertory Theatre on 14th Street on a few Sunday nights. The Theatre of Action died in 1936.

In 1935, reflecting the new Stalinist Popular Front line, the League of Workers Theatres changed its name to the New Theater League and the Communists invited "progressives" to participate. Aside from producing Archibald MacLeish's *Panic,* a disappointing verse drama, it accomplished little. But it was party to a sensation. In 1934, it rented the Civic Repertory on Sunday nights to stage one-acters. During the fall Odets presented the League with the script of *Waiting for Lefty.* He was an actor with The Group Theatre who had turned his hand to playwriting. His first drama, *Awake and Sing!,* was produced by The Group in 1935. *Lefty,* written later but staged earlier, was about the revolt of taxi drivers against their corrupt union leaders by going on strike. Played by actors from The Group, it became a minor classic of the American theater overnight. Those who attended the opening on Sunday night, January 6, 1935, were electrified and stormed the stage. Odets brought the agitprop to its ultimate development. He became an instant celebrity. The Group in March took *Lefty* uptown, where it ran for seventy-eight performances. By June it had been staged in fifty cities, benefiting from the efforts of several to ban its presentation.

In 1932, Charles R. Walker, a scholar in the labor field as well as a novelist, had the idea of a theater to produce prolabor plays for workers and the general public. The Theater Union opened shop in 1933. The executive board consisted of left-leaning professionals, Communists, Socialists, and liberals. The board announced that it would present drama that dealt with "deep-going social conflicts, the economic, emotional and cultural problems that confront the majority of the people." In order to bring workers to the theater, it fixed very low ticket prices — 30 cents to a top of $1.50. Walker rented the Civic Repertory.

Over the four years of its life, 1933 to 1937, the Theater Union concentrated on labor plays. *Peace on Earth,* by George Sklar and Albert Maltz, dealt with the conversion of a mild college professor into a militant supporter of workers who were striking to protest the sale of munitions to foreign powers. It ran for 125 performances. *Stevedore,* by Paul Peters and Sklar, was a melodrama about the unionization of black longshoremen in New Orleans that also raised the issue of race. The latter was bold for 1934, as was the employment of black actors. It was shown 111 times. *Black Pit,* by Maltz, is about the betrayal of a coal miners' strike by a former union activist who desperately needs work to provide medical care for his wife. It made 85 performances. Theater Union took over Albert Bein's *Let Freedom Ring,* which had failed on Broadway. A dramatization of Grace Lumpkin's novel, *To Make My Bread,* it was about the strike of textile workers in Gastonia, North Carolina, in 1929. It was shown 108 times. In 1936 the owner of the Civic Repertory razed the building for a parking lot and Theater Union was forced to move uptown for its last production, John Howard Lawson's *Marching Song.* Lawson, who was a zealous Communist and had written a turgid book on Marxian dramaturgy, rang the changes on an automobile strike. It ran for 61 performances. Theater Union went out of business in 1937. While its plays had attracted fair audiences and it had employed distinguished writers, directors, scene designers, and actors, its low ticket prices and limited sales proved disastrous financially.

In 1928 a "group" of young theater people had begun meeting informally to discuss the state of the American stage, which, they agreed, was deplorable. The leaders were Harold Clurman, the Theatre Guild's play reader, Cheryl Crawford, the Guild's casting director, and Lee Strasberg, an actor dedicated to his version of Stanislavsky's system. Others, mainly actors, but also playwrights and designers, joined their meetings. By 1931 their thinking had crystallized into the concept of a self-contained theater with a permanent acting company (no stars), with its own hard-hitting style, that would stage serious plays about contemporary social problems. At the outset the young actors included Franchot Tone, Morris Carnovsky, Sanford Meisner, J. Edward Bromberg, Odets, Stella Adler, Phoebe Brand, and Margaret Barker. The designer Mordecai Gorelik joined, and Paul Green supplied the script of *The House of Connelly.* They spent the summer in the Connecticut countryside rehearsing Green's play. For want of anything better, they called themselves The Group Theatre. On September 23, 1931, *The House of Connelly* opened at the Martin Beck Theatre on West 45th Street.

As measured by accomplishment, The Group was the most impressive theater of the decade. Under Strasberg's whip, the level of acting was exceptionally high and many of the players later became stars on Broadway and in films. Its designers — Gorelik, Boris Aronson, Donald Oenslager, Cleon Throckmorton — were outstanding. It discovered a number of fine new playwrights, notably Odets, but also Sidney Kingsley, William Saroyan, Irwin Shaw, and Ardrey. The Group sometimes erred, passing up Maxwell Anderson's *Winterset* and Saroyan's *The Time of Your Life.* The Group engaged in an endless struggle. The directors constantly begged for money and the entire company was underpaid, except for psychic income. Because they were so talented, many, especially the actors, were lured away by Hollywood and Broadway. As all the theater organizations discovered to their dismay, there was a severe shortage of good new plays. For a while there was a Communist cell within the organization. Personality clashes erupted constantly. Clurman, exhausted and about to leave for directing in films, allowed The Group to die quietly in 1941.

In a general sense, almost everything The Group produced has relevance here. Gorelik liked to say ironically that the standard theme was, "What shall it profit a man if he gain the whole world and lose his own soul?" More specifically, The Group produced: The Siftons' *1931* — (1931) was the first Depression play about joblessness, which flopped. *Awake and Sing!* (1935) by Odets dealt with the disintegration of a Bronx Jewish family under the hammer blows of hard times. It was a literary hit but fared modestly at the box office. As already noted, The Group picked up *Waiting for Lefty* in 1935. *Weep for the Virgins* (1936), by Nellise Childs, was about a San Diego waterfront family in which the daughters worked in a fish cannery and fantasized about escape. It lasted only nine performances. In 1936 Odets submitted *Silent Partner,* which dealt with the effort to establish a union in a violently antilabor company with a subplot of two brothers, both union leaders, who loved the same girl. Clurman thought it potentially exciting but much in need of reworking. Odets delayed the revision and it was not produced. Ardrey's *Casey Jones* (1938) was about the washup of a locomotive engineer at fifty and played only twenty-three performances.

The International Ladies' Garment Workers' Union (ILGWU) began staging pro-union amateur playlets in 1933, established a Dramatics Department in 1934 in the vain hope of founding a trade-union theater, and incorporated Labor Stage in 1935. Louis Schaffer, an ILGWU official, was in charge and he rented the small Princess Theatre. He thought Labor Stage should do a musical revue that combined entertainment with a point of view. Schaffer recruited Harold Rome, a young songwriter who had worked in the borscht belt, along with Arthur Arent, Charles Friedman, and Marc Blitzstein, among others. They put together a series of funny, sexy, and biting sketches, called *Pins and Needles,* that were played and sung by workers from the shops — cutters, pressers, dressmakers, embroiderers, and neckwear makers. The show opened at the tiny Princess on November 27, 1937, played only weekends, and attracted no press notice. But word-of-mouth soon made it a smash hit. It went on a regular schedule and moved to the much larger Windsor Theatre. The skits were often changed in response to political developments. *Pins and Needles* had the second-longest run of any show of the decade, 1108 performances, and closed on June 22, 1940. It did a "command performance" at the White House, which Roosevelt loved, and a road company toured the country. After *Pins and Needles,* Labor Stage shut down; anything else had to be an anticlimax.

The Theatre Guild and independent Broadway producers, while primarily involved with diverting plays and musicals that appealed to upper middle-class audiences, presented a few social dramas. The Guild's productions were the following: John Wexley's *They Shall Not Die* (1934) was based on the Scottsboro case and both depicted black misery in the South and offered a Marxist analysis of the trial. It ran for 62 performances. The musical review *Parade* (1935), by Paul Peters and George Sklar, was a heavy-handed series of sketches satirizing topical themes (two of the songs were of love blighted by hard times), which was shown only 40 times. Leopold Atlas's *But for the Grace of God* (1937), dealing with a slum boy who committed robbery and murder to provide for his family, quickly failed. Saroyan's *The Time of Your Life* (1939), a brilliant depiction of the author's antic view of the times, had 181 performances in its first season, won the Pulitzer Prize and Drama Critics' Award, and became a staple of the American theater.

Independent producers were somewhat more active in social drama. Wexley's *Steel* (1931), a melodramatic plea for Red Unionism, made only 14 presentations. Jack Kirkland's adaptation of Erskine Caldwell's novel of a destitute Georgia sharecropper family, *Tobacco*

Road (1933), was a sensation that ran for 3184 performances. Audiences came more for its sex and obscenity than for its exposure of rural poverty. Gilbert Miller, Leslie Howard, and Arthur Hopkins produced Robert E. Sherwood's *The Petrified Forest* (1935), a haunting view of Depression transiency and outlawry, set in the Arizona desert, which was a hit. Norman Bel Geddes offered Kingsley's *Dead End* (1935), a dramatic contrast of rich and poor along New York's East River, especially of the children, including the famous "Dead End Kids," which ran for 687 performances. Guthrie McClintic's production of Anderson's formidable *Winterset* (1935), also set in Manhattan along the East River, was concerned with the aftermath of the Sacco and Vanzetti case, was shown 195 times, and won the Drama Critics' Award. Herman Shumlin presented Lillian Hellman's *Days to Come* (1936), set in the context of a strike in an Ohio brush factory, which was this dramatist's worst failure, lasting only 7 performances. James Hagan's *Mid-West* (1936), which dealt with farm labor conflict and, in a switch, favored the farmers over their workers, quickly folded. Richard Aldridge and Richard Myers presented George Brewer, Jr.'s, *Tide Rising* (1937), which was concerned with a violent strike and condemned the greed of both labor and management. It lasted for 32 performances. One of the most successful social dramas of the era was Steinbeck's *Of Mice and Men* (1937), which won the Drama Critics' Award. D. A. Doran's production of F. E. Faragoh's *Sunup to Sundown* (1938) was about an uprising of tobacco plantation workers and survived only 7 performances. Sherwood's *Abe Lincoln in Illinois* (1938), presented by the Playwright's Company, ran for 472 performances and won the Pulitzer Prize. It had Lincoln's famous speech in favor of labor unions. The same producers put on Elmer Rice's *Two on an Island* (1940), a love story about a young couple struggling to survive during the Depression, which missed being a hit. Herman Shumlin's production of Emlyn Williams's *The Corn Is Green* (1940) dealt with the oppression of workers in the Welsh coal mines and was performed 477 times.

The most exciting development of the decade was the emergence of the Federal Theatre (FT), which, in its four short years, 1935–1939, combined remarkable dramatic achievement, work relief for unemployed stage people, administrative chaos, and strangulation by censorship, bureaucracy, and politics.

FT started with that many-talented dreamer, Harry Hopkins. In the early Depression years, when he was at the New York Tuberculosis Association, Hopkins had been touched by the suffering of jobless musicians and actors. Neither as head of the New York relief program nor with FERA had he been able to help them because both were direct-relief programs. But the Civil Works Administration provided an opening, and in early 1934 CWA put to work modest numbers of artists painting murals in public buildings, opera singers touring the Ozarks, and actors presenting vaudeville, marionette, and dramatic performances in New York's schools and hospitals. With WPA in 1935, Hopkins finally had what he wanted. The Arts Project, Federal One, headquartered in the McLean Mansion on Dupont Circle in Washington, covered writing, painting and sculpture, music, and theater.

Hopkins invited Hallie Flanagan to head the Federal Theatre. They were old friends, having attended grade school, high school, and Grinnell College together (Mrs. Flanagan graduated in 1911, Hopkins in 1912). Widowed in 1919, she started the theater at Grinnell to support her children and parents. She caught the eye of George Pierce Baker, who in 1923 invited her to the 47 Workshop at Harvard. This was followed by the formation of the Grinnell Experimental Theatre and a Guggenheim Fellowship, the first won by a woman, which provided a year to study European theater in 1926–1927. Flanagan then established the Vassar Experimental Theatre, from which Hopkins, with the help of Mrs. Roosevelt, plucked her.

Hopkins instructed Flanagan that she would have to learn to spend money to put people to work, that he wanted "a noncommercial theatre," and that the plays should be about "American life," not just "a New York job." Hopkins wanted no financial bar for the public. The ticket prices must not exceed $1; admissions were usually 10, 25, or 50 cents; and the needy came in free. Flanagan only vaguely grasped the size of the undertaking. Equity said there were 5000 jobless actors in New York alone and WPA estimated 20–30,000 unemployed stage people in the country. Flanagan concluded that a national theater on the European model would not work because the country was too big and the traditions were so different. Rather, she visualized five regional theaters, one each, certainly, in New York, Chicago, and Los Angeles, and others, perhaps, in Boston and New Orleans. But that was not the way it worked out.

FT mushroomed in odd and, sometimes, wonderful ways. It presented an enormous variety of productions: classical revivals (Shakespeare, Marlowe, Molière), perhaps a hundred modern dramas, often first productions, a score of dance dramas, about forty plays for children, theater in German, Spanish, and Yiddish, living newspapers, many musicals, a large number of plays with black casts, pageants and spectacles, puppet shows, and radio programs. An adaptation of Sinclair Lewis's anti-Fascist novel, *It Can't Happen Here,* opened more or less simultaneously in twenty-eight theaters around the country, including black, Spanish, and Yiddish versions. There were cycles of fourteen O'Neill and nine Shaw plays. O'Neill marveled when Flanagan told him that *The Emperor Jones* was in marionettes, that *Anna Christie* was showing in Atlanta, San Diego, Denver, Hartford, and Detroit, that the sea plays were on the boards in Chicago, New Orleans, New York, and Philadelphia, that *Ah Wilderness!* was in production in Los Angeles, San Diego, Miami, New Orleans, Cincinnati, Seattle, Newark, Salem, Peoria, and twenty other towns on tour. Communities that seldom, if ever, saw theater, now had it. Indianapolis witnessed stage versions of local novels, including Booth Tarkington's *Clarence,* Edward Eggleston's *The Hoosier Schoolmaster,* and Meredith Nicholson's *The Campbells Are Coming.* The University of North Carolina, which had a vigorous theater led by Frederick Koch and Paul Green, got the state humming — a touring production of *Jefferson Davis,* children's theaters in Charlotte and Greensboro, a marionette theater in Raleigh, black theaters in Durham, Raleigh, and Greensboro, and a historical pageant at Roanoke Island. Twelve thousand high school students in Omaha saw live actors for the first time. Valley, Nebraska, population 1000, witnessed the first play in its history.

A number of FT productions were notable. T. S. Eliot's *Murder in the Cathedral* received its world premiere. The Chicago Negro *Swing Mikado* opened to rave reviews in September 1938, had audiences dancing in the aisles, ran for sixty-two weeks, and private producers clamored to take it over. Yasha Frank's *Pinocchio* enchanted children in a Los Angeles run of more than a year and then moved to New York for six months. Shaw's *Androcles and the Lion* was a smash with a black company in Harlem. The most impressive living newspaper, Arthur Arent's *One-third of a Nation,* dealing with housing, ran for almost a year in New York and then moved to ten other cities. The musical *Sing for Your Supper* contributed several popular Depression songs — "Papa's Got a Job" (on the WPA) and "Leaning on a Shovel" — as well as "Ballad for Americans," the theme of the 1940 Republican National Convention.

Chance brought FT some exceptional talent. John Houseman had been an international grain dealer who went broke in the crash. He gradually drifted into the theater and in 1934 staged the Gertrude Stein–Virgil Thomson opera *Four Saints in Three Acts,* with a largely black cast. At the end of the year he was at the opening of Guthrie McClintic's *Romeo and Juliet,* starring Katharine Cornell. Houseman was overpowered by a "monstrous boy," then nineteen, who played Tybalt, with a voice that "tore like a high wind." In 1935 Houseman was asked to direct MacLeish's *Panic,* which he felt had "insurmountable production problems," but which evoked a certain empathy because its leading figure, McGafferty, was a tycoon who lost his fortune in the Depression. To MacLeish's astonishment, Houseman persuaded Orson Welles to drop Tybalt in order to play McGafferty. *Panic* lasted for only three performances, but it established a remarkable collaboration.

In the latter part of 1935 the WPA Negro Theatre Project started up in Harlem. The black actress Rose McLendon was asked to head the program. Already terminally ill, she insisted on a white co-director and, because of his experience with *Four Saints,* she suggested Houseman.

He opened with two routine black plays — *Walk Together Chillun!* and *Conjur Man Dies* — but he yearned for black Shakespeare, particularly *Macbeth.* He co-opted Welles, who was employing his mellifluous vocal chords on radio as "The Shadow," as the voice of chocolate pudding, and in impersonations of Haile Selassie, Hindenburg, and Emperor Hirohito on "The March of Time." The *Voodoo Macbeth,* as Welles staged it at the old Lafayette Theatre in Harlem, was a sensation. Everything thereafter was anticlimax, such as *Turpentine,* which Houseman described as "a naive play of protest, full of leftist clichés." It is remembered only for the review in the *Naval Stores Review and Journal,* which described the play as a malicious libel on a fine southern industry, as Senator Richard Russell of Georgia reminded Congress when he helped destroy FT.

After *Turpentine,* Houseman left Harlem and persuaded Flanagan to establish a "classical theater," housed in the Maxine Elliott at 39th Street and Broadway, where Welles joined him. Since it was an official WPA project, they called it Project #891. The first production was a revival of Labiche's nineteenth-century comedy, which Edwin Denby and Welles converted into a frenzied farce, *Horse Eats Hat.* They followed with a powerful and ingenious presentation of Marlowe's *Tragical History of Doctor Faustus,* with Welles in the leading role, which ran for five months in 1937.

Project #891's next production, Marc Blitzstein's *The Cradle Will Rock,* made theatrical history. Everyone, Blitzstein included, considered him a revolutionary Marxist, and his "play with music," as he described it, or "labor opera" or "marching song," as others saw it, was viewed as a proletarian epic. In fact, Blitzstein's father was a Philadelphia banker, though a Socialist. Marc had studied at the Curtis Institute and with Schoenberg and Nadia Boulanger, and he had married the daughter of a Viennese operetta star. While honeymooning on the beach at Majorca in 1934, Blitzstein decided that he ought to go home to do his bit. He wrote *The Cradle* in a white heat in five weeks. Blitzstein dedicated it to Berthold Brecht, and it owed much to Brecht and Weill's *Three-penny Opera.* Blitzstein had trouble finding a producer and showed it to Welles, who was enthusiastic. Houseman, anticipating political trouble, wanted Hallie Flanagan to hear the audition. Blitzstein played the piano, sang, and recited the opera at the apartment Houseman shared with Virgil Thomson on a Sunday evening in March 1937. Flanagan was enchanted. While she would be severely criticized for authorizing so controversial a work, Houseman thought "she knew exactly what she was doing." Knowing that FT was already in deep political trouble, she felt that "there was no safety in prudence and no virtue in caution."

The setting for *The Cradle* was Steeltown, U.S.A., in the midst of a violent steel strike. The opera, Jane DeHart Mathews wrote, was "complete with bloated capitalists, sadistic 'cops,' heroic union organizers, and the proverbial prostitute with a heart of gold." Welles and Houseman had it ready to open in June. Depending upon one's point of view, the time could not have been worse, or better. Nineteen thirty-seven was one of the gravest strike years in American labor history. The great General Motors sitdown had just ended. More relevant, the Little Steel strike now dominated the headlines and the Memorial Day Massacre had just taken place at the Republic Steel plant in South Chicago. The WPA budget, under attack in Congress, was due to expire on June 30 and 1700 FT workers had already been dismissed. On June 12, WPA notified all FT directors that no new plays would be allowed to open prior to July 1, 1937. Appeals to headquarters and the White House were unavailing.

The public preview was scheduled for June 16 with the opening night two weeks later. On June 15, WPA guards, the "Cossacks," seized the Maxine Elliott and locked up the scenery, props, and costumes. Houseman, Welles, Blitzstein, the cast, and the musicians decided to stage *The Cradle* in defiance. On the afternoon of June 16, Equity ruled that its members, including the most important actors in the cast, could not appear "on the stage" for any management except FT. Houseman and Welles opted to put Blitzstein "on the stage" and the players in the audience. Late in the afternoon a decrepit upright piano, rented for $5, was on a truck circling the theater district for want of a destination. In the early evening the Venice Theatre on Seventh Avenue near 59th Street was rented for $100 and the piano was unloaded. At 8:00, the scheduled opening, the audience, which had gathered outside the Maxine Elliott, started the twenty-one-block trek to the Venice. By 8:50 the house was jammed.

After brief speeches, Welles boomed: "We have the honor to present — with the composer at the piano — *The Cradle Will Rock*!" Blitzstein, alone on the stage, had no idea whether the cast would participate and was prepared to do the entire opera himself. He broke into Moll's opening lyrics. Houseman heard "a faint, wavering soprano" and the spotlight caught Olive Stanton, "a thin girl in a green dress with dyed red hair . . . only half-audible at first in the huge theatre but gathering strength with every note." She did it — actors, singers, chorus, musicians played their parts. The evening was a triumph. "As the curtain fell and the actors started to go back to their seats," Houseman wrote, "there was a second's silence — then all hell broke loose." The press reported the preview, not in drama sections, but in headlines on the front pages.

The producers somehow managed a two-week run at the Venice. Houseman and Welles then left the WPA to establish the Mercury Theatre.

As the experience with *The Cradle* emphasizes, FT constantly skirted administrative and political disaster. Censorship, attempted and realized, was a continual problem. The living newspaper production of *Model Tenement* was closed at the insistence of the mayor of Chicago, and the White House demanded that its New York show,

Ethiopia, include no impersonations of foreign dignitaries. Elmer Rice, FT director in New York, resigned. The quality of personnel was extremely uneven. Many areas had no talent. Some unemployed "actors" turned out to be aged vaudevillians who had staged animal acts. Many WPA officials had no understanding of the arts. Colonel Connolly, who headed WPA in Los Angeles, warned Flanagan that "he had been trained in the army and believed in military discipline." He wanted complete control or would wash his hands of the project. Communists and their sympathizers invaded FT, which imposed no political test. The class struggle theme recurred, not only in such productions as *The Cradle* and *Turpentine,* but also in the sophisticated children's play *Revolt of the Beavers.* The *New York Times* wrote that Mother Goose had been studying Marx. The anti–New Deal press, led by the Hearst papers, the *Chicago Tribune,* and the *New York Herald Tribune,* had a field day. A sober doctoral dissertation concluded that eleven of eighty-eight FT plays "sanction Communism or Communistic activities." The Dies Committee (House Committee on Un-American Activities) "investigated" FT in 1938–1939, thereby putting itself in the headlines and making Flanagan's life miserable. By this time the New Deal was in political retreat, Hopkins was gone, and no one in power would protect the WPA. Congress killed the Federal Theatre effective June 30, 1939. At the Adelphi Theatre in New York, after the song "Papa's Got a Job" in *Sing for Your Supper,* the producer announced that Papa would lose his job at midnight. At the Ritz Theatre the stagehands knocked down the sets in view of the audience and the cast proclaimed, "Thus passed Pinocchio. Born December 23, 1938, died June 30, 1939. Killed by Act of Congress."

The social drama of the Great Depression had two dominant themes: institutional disintegration and the strike, often edging over into the class struggle. It is a remarkable fact that the social drama almost totally ignored the nation's primary domestic problem — unemployment. While joblessness was an incident in a number of plays, it seems to have been central to only one, the Siftons' *1931 —*. That play was a flop and received dreadful reviews. According to Malcolm Goldstein, the little vitality it had was in its "plotless agitprop." Even the Federal Theatre's Living Newspapers, which had productions on the labor injunction, housing, electric power, agriculture, and syphilis, did not deal with unemployment.

A central theme was disintegration, a society and its institutions torn loose from their traditional moorings. Saroyan, in his airy way, put this succinctly in *The Time of Your Life* in the most notable line of the decade. The scene is Nick's Pacific Street Saloon, Restaurant, and Entertainment Palace at the foot of the Embarcadero in San Francisco. The time is October 1939, a month after the guns of World War II have opened fire. Nick is at the bar studying *The Racing Form.* Arab, "an Eastern philosopher and harmonica-player," is at the end of the bar. Joe, "a young loafer with money and a good heart," is seated at a table. A newsboy enters and inquires whether anybody wants a paper. Joe asks, "How many you got?" Newsboy: "Five." Joe buys them all, glances at the headlines, and, with irritation, throws them away. Arab picks up a paper, reads the headline, and shakes his head. He says, "No foundation. All the way down the line."

MacLeish's verse drama, *Panic,* symbolizes the collapse of the business system through the figure of McGafferty, "the leading industrialist and financier of his time." The setting is his office on an evening in late February 1933. An old man recites:

> Slowly the thing comes.
> There are many signs: there are furnaces
> Dead now that were burning
> Thirty years in a town —
> Never dark: there are foundries —
> Fires drawn: trestles
> Silent. The swifts nest in
> Stacks that for generations
> Flowed smoke.

Immelman, the president of McGafferty's bank, tolls a litany of failures:

> Atlanta . . . Seamen's National . . . branch closed.
> Indianapolis . . . People's and Guaranty . . . closes.
> Frankfort . . . Farm Mortgage . . . forced closing.
> Memphis . . . Mechanics closed . . . National closing.
> Louisville . . . Lincoln Title & Loan . . . closed —
> Yes and twenty more. And why? What's done it?
> Who's behind it?

The bankers are baffled, cannot answer.

> No one against you . . . Boat in a fog . . . Motionless . . .
> How can you fight fog? . . .

Nothing to fight against . . .
No one!
The dead stacks: the black dust: the
Rust on the tracks and there's no one.

Gloating unemployed bums, McGafferty tells Immelman, have come to stare at him before he dies, "broke and his pockets full of sand to sink with." He says to his mistress:

Done for.
Dead and done for. My time's done. I'm finished.
Destiny's got me. History's through with me. . . .
End of a world: end of a man: end of
Everything! Washed up! Done for!

Kingsley's *Dead End,* a sentimental play, contrasts wealth and poverty and links poverty and crime. It is set where a crosstown Manhattan street deadends at the East River. The garden of East River Terrace, where the rich live, stands next to a crumbling tenement, inhabited by the poor. From the pilings of a wharf the kids dive into the fetid river. Philip Griswald, a delicate rich boy, intermittently protected by a French governess and the Terrace doorman, is bedeviled by the tough street gang. These kids don't go to school; they fight, steal, play cards, and "cockalize" boys they dislike. Tommy's older sister, Drina, has gone on strike from her job for an extra $2.50 a week "so's Tommy and I can live in a decent neighborhood." Gimpty, an unemployed architect, tells Drina, "The place you live in is awfully important. It can give you a chance to grow, or it can twist you." Gimpty, who has a withered leg from rickets, cannot find work because there is no building. Gimpty sits on the piling designing an imaginary slum clearance project to clean up the neighborhood.

Babyface Martin, who grew up in this dead end, is a notorious gangster and killer who has had his face lifted so the police will not recognize him. But Gimpty does. Martin returns to dead end to see Francey, his first love, "my goil when we were kids," and his mother. Francey, now a streetwalker with venereal disease, turns Martin's nostalgic dream to dust. His mother rejects Babyface as a "butcher." "Don't call me Mom! Yuh ain't no son of mine." She slaps his face and rejects his offer of "blood money." Gimpty points out Martin with his cane and the G-Men kill him.

The gang beats up Philip, and Tommy steals his watch. Philip's father catches Tommy in order to turn him in to the cops. Tommy slashes Griswald's wrist with his knife and breaks free. The police look for Tommy. They grab Spit, who, in return for a promise to be let loose, rats on Tommy. Tommy learns of the betrayal, puts Spit down, and takes out his knife to mark his face as a squealer. Drina pulls Tommy off, and Tommy turns himself in. Gimpty pleads with Griswald to drop the charge. If Tommy is sent to the reformatory, Gimpty argues, he will come out another Babyface Martin. Griswald refuses. The police take Tommy, Drina cries, and Gimpty says he will hire "the best lawyer in this city, and we'll get Tommy free." Since Gimpty has been turned down by Kay, the mistress of a rich guy who lives in the Terrace, because she has already had a "lifetime" of poverty, Gimpty walks off with his arm around Drina. The kids sing — "If I had duh wings of a Angel. Ovuh dese prison walls I wud fly. Straight tuh dee yahms a my muddah . . . " — as the curtain falls.

Kirkland's adaptation of Caldwell's novel *Tobacco Road* reached the lowest depth of social disintegration. It is difficult to imagine more than 3000 Broadway audiences voluntarily subjecting themselves to such squalor at any time other than the era of the Great Depression.

The setting is back-country Georgia, "a famished, desolate land," the soil mined out by tobacco and cotton. The Lesters lost their farm to Captain John three generations back and have cropped on shares since. But Jeeter has not farmed for seven years because "we just ain't been able to get credit down here on the Tobacco Road." The house is a "squalid shack," ready to collapse. They eat only when Jeeter steals food. He and Ada have raised seventeen children, but have lost touch with most. When Jeeter is desperate he sends to his son Tom for money and Tom returns the message "to tell you to go to hell." Only two children are still at home. No one will marry Ellie May, eighteen, because she has a harelip. Dude, sixteen, is a scrawny, dirty, vicious adolescent.

Pearl, who is lovely with beautiful yellow hair, was married at twelve to Lov Bensey. But she refused to talk to him or sleep in his bed and runs away to her mother. Jeeter looks her over lecherously. Ada protects Pearl and informs Jeeter, "You ain't her Pa. . . . Do you think a lazy old fool like you could be the Daddy of a gal like Pearl?" Lov longs to have her back.

Sister Bessie, about forty, an itinerant lady preacher with a direct line to God, has her eye and her hands on Dude, ostensibly because she plans to make him a preacher. She is eager to marry him but Dude has no interest. Bessie offers to use the $800 she got in insurance from her husband's death to buy him a new car. Dude cannot resist.

Jeeter hears that Captain Tim, Captain John's boy, is coming and thinks he will loan him money to make a crop. But Captain Tim arrives with a banker from Augusta. Captain Tim says that he had to borrow on all the farms he owns and, since he cannot pay, the bank is foreclosing. The banker tells Jeeter: "We're going to try putting this whole section under scientific cultivation and there wouldn't be any use for you." Jeeter is crushed. "If you mean go off and work in the mills, I say, by God and by Jesus, no!"

But Jeeter fails to get money to save the farm. Dude backs the car wildly and runs over his mother. Ada dies. Pearl flees from Jeeter and Lov, presumably to town to look for work in the cotton mill. Jeeter sends Ellie May to Lov's house. "Be nice to him and maybe he'll let you stay." Jeeter picks up a pinch of earth and slowly rubs it with his fingers as the curtain falls.

The most incisive of the plays of social decay, Chekhovian in quality, was *Awake and Sing!* Odets chronicled the disintegration, under the Depression sledgehammer, of the Bergers, a lower middle-class Jewish family in the Bronx. The setting is the Bergers' apartment.

Bessie is the boss, as she says, both the mother and the father. She desperately fears poverty. "Without the dollar who sleeps at night?" She worries when families are dispossessed, their furniture on the sidewalk. She wants her daughter to marry a man with a steady job and her son to be a successful businessman. "I should only live to see the day when he rides up to the door in a big car with a chauffeur and a radio. I could die happy." But Bessie insists on appearances; everyone in the family must look respectable.

Myron, her husband, has failed Bessie. When they got married she worked in the factory to put him through law school, but he did not finish. For thirty years he has been a clerk in a haberdashery on Fourth Avenue and now he is on short time. He buys raffle and sweepstake tickets in the vain hope of getting rich overnight. "The moment I began losing my hair I just knew I was destined to be a failure in life . . . and when I grew bald I was." Hennie, the daughter, is attractive and lonely. She is pursued by Moe Axelrod, who gets a government pension for the leg he lost in the war and who lusts after her, and by Sam Feinschreiber, a recent immigrant who has a job and wants to marry her. Ralph, the son, is ardent and bitter. "I never in my life even had a birthday party. Every time I went and cried in the toilet when my birthday came." Ralph hates his job and Bessie takes most of his pay. "I can't even save for shoe laces." Jacob, Bessie's father, dotes on Ralph and tries to cheer him up. "Boychick, wake up! Be something! . . . Go out and fight so life shouldn't be printed on dollar bills." Jacob has a library of Marxist books that he does not read and emits Marxist homilies that no one hears. Basically he loves to listen to his records of Caruso singing.

Odets provides no winners. Hennie becomes pregnant, and Bessie, to preserve the family's reputation, forces her to marry an unsuspecting Sam. After the birth of the baby Hennie tells him "like a lightning from the sky. The baby ain't mine." Hennie leaves Sam. Moe is still interested. "Get your coat and hat and kiss the house good-bye." To escape Bessie, Hennie goes off with Moe. Bessie will not allow Ralph to pursue Blanche because she is an orphan and Bessie needs his income. Ralph is outraged by the way Bessie has treated Sam. "You trapped that guy." She refuses to listen to him. "I'm boiling over ten times inside." In a rage she breaks Jacob's Caruso recordings. Jacob then walks Tootsie, the poodle, in the snow on the roof, falls off, and is killed. He leaves the insurance, $3000, to Ralph. They worry because "sometimes you don't collect on suicides." Bessie says, "It belongs for the whole family." Odets took his title from Isaiah 26:19, "Awake and sing ye that dwell in dust." Perhaps he should have selected the latter phrase.

The strike plays fell into three categories: rousing one-acters that preached a Marxist message; longer, more complex dramas with a class-struggle theme; and a miscellany of plays that looked at the world from other viewpoints.

The strike appealed to Marxists because it could be made to show the militancy of the working class against its exploiters and, if effective theater, could also enhance class consciousness. *Waiting for Lefty* and *The Cradle Will Rock* were notable examples. Odets wrote *Lefty* during the brief period in which he was a member of the Communist Party and Blitzstein composed *The Cradle* while he was a Marxist. Ben Bengal, who shared their political outlook, wrote a pale imitation of *Lefty*, *Plant in the Sun,* which is of little interest. Aside from their political message and excitement, the Odets and Blitzstein plays had two basic features, both stemming from agitprop: a primitive plot and cartoon characterizations. The authors emphasized the latter in naming their characters. In *Lefty* Fatt is the corrupt union boss and Agate is the radical hackie with a glass eye. Blitzstein went further: Mr. Mister is the steelmaster, Reverend Salvation is the preacher, Moll is the prostitute, and so on.

In *Lefty* the whole theater becomes the union hall so that the audience and the cast intermingle. The question is whether the taxi drivers shall call a strike. Fatt, "of porcine appearance," opposes a walkout because he is in the pay of the bosses, but he says because "the times ain't ripe." He denounces the militants as "Reds" and has a gunman on duty to intimidate them. Before they vote, the members are waiting to hear from Lefty Costello, the chairman of the strike committee, but he has not showed up yet.

Odets uses flashbacks for background. Joe, discouraged because he can't make a living for his family by hacking, fears that a strike will fail. Edna, his wife, is disgusted with him. "Who's the man in the family, you or me?" She threatens to sell herself to her old boy friend for money. That stiffens Joe's back and he becomes a militant. Sid and Flor have been engaged for three years, but Sid doesn't make enough as a cab driver to afford marriage. Flor's family depends on her and they push her to leave Sid. He says, "We got the blues, Babe — the 1935 blues."

At the meeting Fatt produces "Clayton" to recount how the drivers lost the strike in Philadelphia. A militant, Clancy, denounces "Clayton" as a notorious labor spy. "Boys, do you know who this sonovabitch is?" Clancy asks. "HE'S MY OWN LOUSY BROTHER!!"

Agate rises to speak and is called "cockeye." He says he lost his eye in an unguarded machine when he was working in the factory at age eleven. He wears a glass eye "like a medal 'cause it tells the world where I belong — deep down in the working class!" Agate denounces "walkin' delegates" for sitting "on their fat little ass." He is so ashamed of Fatt that his "union button just blushed itself to death." Fatt and the gunman try to handle him, but he breaks away and is protected by other militants. Agate poses the choice: "Slow death or fight. It's war!" Why wait? he asks. "Don't wait for Lefty. He might never come." A man bursts into the theater, dashes up the center aisle, and mounts the stage. "Boys," he shouts, "they just found Lefty! . . . Behind the car barns with a bullet in his head!"

Agate cries, "HELLO AMERICA! HELLO. WE'RE STORMBIRDS OF THE WORKING-CLASS. WORKERS OF THE WORLD. . . . OUR BONES AND BLOOD!" He asks everyone, "Well, what's the answer?" Actors and audience scream, "STRIKE!" He demands, "LOUDER!" All: "STRIKE, STRIKE, STRIKE!!!"

The Cradle Will Rock is set in Steeltown, U.S.A. Mr. Mister owns almost everything — the mills, the courts, the newspaper, the college, the doctor, the arts. Only his workers resist his will; they are meeting in the square to call a strike. Mr. Mister is determined to smash their union.

According to Blitzstein, whoring is a widely practiced profession and there are good whores and bad whores. Moll is an honest prostitute with a big heart. Life, Moll sings, is tough:

> I work two days a week;
> The other five my efforts ain't required.
>
> * * *
>
> So I'm just searchin' along the street
> For on those five days it's nice to eat.

The Liberty Committee, formed by Mr. Mister to fight the union, is made up of crooked "prostitutes," that is, the town's leading citizens who have sold out. "We don't want a union in Steeltown!" Reverend Salvation preaches what Mr. Mister tells him to preach. Dr. Specialist knows that Hammer, the machinist and union activist, never drank and was pushed into the ladle, but tells the reporter that "he was obviously intoxicated." Editor Daily prints "for whichever side will pay the best." The painter, Dauber, and the violinist, Yasha, depend on the largesse of Mrs. Mister and they say what she likes to hear. Dauber: "She asked me to bring El Greco to tea this summer!"

Mr. Mister orders the police to clear the street and both Moll and the Liberty Committee are rounded up. So is Larry Foreman, the union leader. The police take them to night court.

Mr. Mister comes to court to spring the Liberty Committee. "Release them at once. I told the Judge to go on home. I have his authority." To Foreman he offers both freedom and a wad of money if he will sell out the union. But now thousands of steelworkers are gathered outside the courthouse. Larry sings:

> That's thunder, that's lightning,
> And it's going to surround you!

No wonder those stormbirds
Seem to circle around you. . . .
Well, you can't climb down, and you can't sit still;
That's a storm that's going to last until
The final wind blows . . . and when the wind blows . . .
The cradle will rock! [Music, bugles, drums, and fifes.]

The longer Marxist plays offered more complex plots and a measure of character development. In *Private Hicks*, which he based on the violent Toledo auto parts walkout in 1934, Albert Maltz viewed the strike from the perspective of the National Guard, which had been called out to break it. The Guard unit is quartered in the storeroom of the Boller Stamping Mill.

Offstage there has been a deadly confrontation between Guardsmen and strikers and the former have used both vomit gas and rifle fire. A number of strikers lie dead in the streets. Hicks had been in the squad that had been ordered to shoot and had thrown his gun down. He then yelled at the other soldiers, "Stop it! Goddamit, don't shoot!" Hicks did so because "I don't think the National Guard oughta shoot at unarmed strikers." His father, a hand molder in an iron foundry, struck for higher wages. A striker had given Hicks a leaflet that urged the Guardsmen not to fire on the workers.

For failure to obey orders, Corporal Cavanaugh had struck Hicks a vicious blow on the head with his revolver butt and had reported him to Major Eccles. The major suspects Red infiltration of the Guard and demands to know where Hicks got the leaflet. Hicks tells him and says, "There's no law against readin'." Eccles leaves and Nurse Thompson, who sleeps with him, enters, ostensibly to dress the wound but really to find out about the leaflet. She butters him up and begins her probe. Hicks sees through her at once and kicks her out.

Eccles returns and threatens Hicks with a court-martial leading to three to five years in the federal penitentiary. He will forget the incident if Hicks repents before the squad. Hicks agrees. The men are called in and Hicks repeats after Eccles: "I'm sorry for what I did. For this disgrace to my squad, my officers, and the National Guard. I am grateful for this opportunity to get back my standing. I will go back to the line of duty immediately, ready to carry out all orders. If I'm ordered to shoot — " Major: "I will obey." Hicks whispers, "I will obey." Then he cries, "No, I won't do it. I won't shoot!" Eccles dismisses the squad and orders Hicks to a court-martial the next day.

In *Let Freedom Ring,* a hackneyed play, Bein deals with the southern textile strikes of 1929. The McClures, a mountain family, lose their land to the lumber company. Grandpap is a Confederate captain who fought with General Lee to preserve slavery in the South. The three brothers are symbolic figures. Kirk leaves the mountains for the mills, is outraged by the exploitation of the workers, and becomes an organizer for the Textile Workers Union. Basil is a fundamentalist preacher who sells out to the millowner. John, deft with machinery, installs machines in the mill and becomes a foreman.

An itinerant peddler tells the McClures that the mill in Leesburg is "goin' full blast an' they're shorthanded." He says the "rivers flow with milk and honey, and money grows on trees." They leave the mountains to work in the mill. Like others, they are ruthlessly plundered. Wages are low and frequently cut. Hours are from six to six. Accidents are frequent. The children cannot attend school because their quick hands are needed to run machines. Company housing is deplorable. Grandpap is too aged for the mill, and he and another old man become garbage collectors. The company then hires a young Negro to replace both. John's new machines displace workers.

At the end of the twenties another wage cut enrages the millhands and they strike spontaneously, as workers are doing elsewhere in the southern textile mills. Kirk comes to Leesburg to lead the strike. Basil denounces him. John is torn. But when the boss tells him to become a stool pigeon, he angrily joins Kirk to stand by his own people. Kirk persuades the white millhands to allow the blacks in the packing room to join the strike. " 'Cause they kin be used against folk as scabs." Even Grandpap comes around. "Ye shore got me a-goin', boy."

Basil appeals to the family to abandon the strike. The millowner, he says, is "a fine, honest and church goin' man." "The whole family," Basil says, "hit's pizened by the Serpent's tongue o' that agitator with a devil twisted smirk on his face." Kirk laughs. "Shore I'm an agitator. . . . What else kin a body be that longs fer toilin' humans every whar t' burst the chains that the rich have forged t' hold 'em enbondaged in."

The sheriff threatens that his deputies will murder the "furriner," Kirk. They blackjack him, slowing him only momentarily. When they start to lynch a black striker, Kirk rushes to help. The deputies kill him. John carries in his "limp, bleeding body." At the funeral in the union hall strikers from other mills pay tribute to Kirk's memory.

John says, "Kirk kem an' give his life t' sweep us out in t' the world o' workers that are every whar on the march now a-strugglin' like ourselves fer freedom. . . . We're a-goin' on buildin' this here Textile Workers Union."

Peace on Earth, by Sklar and Maltz, is superficial and propagandistic, owes much to agitprop, and fires from two barrels — against war and for the strike. In the setting of a New England university, Peter Owens, a professor of psychology, is drawn into a free-speech fight by students. He is arrested for reciting from the Declaration of Independence at a public meeting. John Andrews is an industrialist and the head of the university's trustees. His mill produces guncotton for sale in Europe, where World War II is about to break out. The longshoremen strike to stop the shipment of munitions and the National Guard is called out.

Owens supports the strike and protests the granting of an honorary degree to Andrews at the commencement. He is arrested. War breaks out. In the hysteria, Owens is falsely charged with killing a superpatriot. When he is convicted, he says that he did not commit murder. "If my crime was opposition to war, if my crime was association with workers fighting against war, then I am guilty." At the curtain he walks from his cell to be hung. Workers demonstrate outside the jail. "Fight with us. Fight against war."

Stevedore, by Peters and Sklar, is a taut melodrama that also uses two themes — race and the strike. The setting is the New Orleans waterfront. A white woman falsely reports that she has been raped by "a nigger." Lonnie Thompson, an "uppity" black longshoreman who is active in the union, is picked up by the police. A lynch mob screams for his blood. At the bridge Lonnie jumps into the river and escapes. He makes his way to Binnie's Lunchroom in the black section of the city. The mob, led by the stevedoring company's strong-arm man, comes after Lonnie.

The question, as the authors pose it, is whether the first loyalty is to class or to race. Lem Morris, the white leader of the longshoremen, stands by Lonnie because he is convinced that the black man has been framed "to keep him from organizing the Stuyvesant Dock." But some unionists refuse to support "a rape nigger." "The only way we can tie up this river front," Lem says, "is by organizing these black boys. . . . There are three of them to every white man on these docks." At Binnie's, the black longshoremen, learning that the mob is coming, confront the same question. Jim says to Lonnie: "You de boy dat gwine organize de black race and unite wid de whites. . . . You gwine organize yo'self right in de 'lectric chair." Lonnie keeps his faith in Lem and the union.

The armed mob approaches. Some of the blacks want to run. "Nobody leaving hyar now," Lonnie says. "We stay hyar and defend ourselves. . . . The lowest animal in the field will fight fo' its home." Jim says, "White man own this country. . . . You can't fight against him." "De black man got to walk humble in de eyes of de Lawd," the preacher adds. The black man, Lonnie argues, will never find peace "till he fight for it." "We can't wait fo' de judgment day. . . . We got to fight fo' de right to live. Now — now — right now."

The blacks arm themselves, mainly with brickbats. The mob attacks with rifle fire and Lonnie is killed. Lem and his white longshoremen join in a pitched battle in which the workers, black and white, fight side-by-side against the white mob. Then the blacks shout, "They're running!" The united longshoremen stand in silence over Lonnie's body.

Several strike plays, not Marxist in ideology, express a wide range of views. Lillian Hellman's *Days to Come*, while a box-office flop and melodramatic, is the best of these dramas by far. She uses the strike as an instrument for provoking a crisis within the employer's family.

For three generations the Rodmans have run a high-quality brush factory in a small Ohio town and have had close relations with their employees. To the extent that they still control the firm, it is now owned by Andrew, whose executive style is bewilderment, and his shrewish sister, Cora, who holds him accountable for all mistakes. Andrew's wife, Julie, is attractive and bored and takes long walks. She has had a desultory affair with Ellicott, their lawyer, who lends money to Andrew and takes increasing control over the company.

The Depression has ruined the brush business, and the company must cut prices to survive. Andrew, therefore, slashes wages. His workers think the reduction too deep, form a union, and call a strike. Needing money, Andrew negotiates a loan with a Cleveland bank. The bank and Ellicott insist that he agree to break the strike. With a heavy heart, Andrew asks the lawyer to hire professional union-busters. Whelan, "attractive in a simple, clean, undistinguished way," comes to town to lead the strike, and Julie falls for him.

Wilkie, the strikebreaker, arrives with 192 goons. Cora is

frightened by the strikers and insists on protection. Wilkie assigns Dowell and Easter to guard the Rodmans' house. Since there is no need for protection, they play two-handed poker. Dowell marks the backs of the cards with his fingernails and Easter catches him. Easter demands back the money he lost. Dowell refuses. Easter kills him with his spring knife. Wilkie is enraged by the murder of Dowell and orders Easter to "dump him in the right place."

Julie walks to strike headquarters to see Whelan. He tells her the story of his life. She describes herself as "a silly, rich woman" who is searching for "somebody to show me the way." There is the sound of a car in the alley; Whelan rushes out and finds Dowell's body. Whelan dismisses Julie and phones Firth, a strike captain, to tell him that he will soon be in jail, that Wilkie will attack, and that the strikers must be told: *"Don't fight with him."*

Whelan is arrested and the goons make war on the strikers and gun down Firth's daughter. Enraged, he and the other strikers join the battle. Andrew is sickened by the violence and orders Wilkie to leave town. Wilkie refuses because "I can't let people get the idea they can slice up my folks. . . . I'm the police here, Mr. Rodman." Ellicott backs him up. The gunfire resounds all night.

Julie tells Andrew that Whelan should be released from jail because he had nothing to do with Dowell's murder. "I was with him last night when it happened." Andrew phones the judge to let Whelan go. Firth says to his old friend Andrew, "You must have been bad all along."

Andrew demands to know why Julie was in Whelan's office. She says, "I wanted to go away with him." But Whelan has left without her. Cora tells Andrew that Julie has been cheating on him for years and points to Ellicott. Julie tells Andrew that she did not love him when they were married but loves him now. Cora informs Andrew that Ellicott loaned him money to support Julie's whims. Andrew pulls off the curtain of gentility because "there's no need to be polite any more." Cora and Ellicott always held him in contempt. Everyone knows that Cora is "slightly ill." Ellicott is a manipulator with "his money and his wife." Andrew's presumed best friend, Ellicott, has been sleeping with his wife. Ellicott, Cora, and he himself made Andrew "a murderer." It is no longer safe for him to go into town. Cora hates Andrew and Andrew hates both Cora and Ellicott. Julie asks Andrew if he wants a divorce. He gives no direct answer but mentions Firth's child. "Murder is worse than lost love." Cora, finally contrite, says, "Things went entirely too far." At the curtain Andrew orders Cora: "Get out."

All that can be said for *Altars of Steel*, by Thomas Hall-Rogers, is that it was one of the few plays to fulfill Hallie Flanagan's goal of having the Federal Theatre foster regional drama. The author was from Birmingham and his play was presented in Atlanta and Miami. It refought the Civil War in the dress of a modern strike.

United Steel, a northern octopus, gobbles up a small southern firm. Jung, the head of United, is brutal and scheming; he worships profits and ignores human values. Worth, the southern businessman, believes that workers and employers in the South must stand together to protect their "freedom." The welfare of society comes before profits. Somehow this embraces the right of workers to engage in collective bargaining.

Jung completely changes the conditions in the southern mill. The workers must double output at the same wages; safety regulations are abandoned; worker committees are abolished; and the mayor is bribed to provide police protection. The workers protest by forming a union. Their leader, Draper, is a Communist who preaches the class struggle. But the workers are unpersuaded and remain loyal to the South and its businessmen.

Jung orders an unsafe furnace into operation and its explosion kills sixteen men. An enraged crowd of workers comes to the plant to murder Jung. Worth intercedes both to denounce northern greed and to urge southern workers not to behave like "wild beasts." The guards fire into their ranks. The play ends without resolution.

While *Tide Rising*, by George Brewer, Jr., is barely a footnote in the history of the American theater, it is interesting ideologically. The New Theatre League tried to ban its production in 1937 and the Communist press denounced it as "Fascist propaganda," a charge that was ridiculous. The play, in fact, is an essay in nostalgic pre–World War I Americanism. The original title was "Small Town America"; the setting is a drugstore and customers keep coming in for ice cream; the hero is the public-spirited druggist who much prefers following baseball to settling labor disputes; most of the characters have Yankee names like Cogswell, Peabody, Hay, Perkins, Lawrence, and Choate; the radical labor leader, Ruth, is vaguely "foreign," and is described as either "Jewish" or "Slavic" and of mixing with Poles and Greeks on the other side of the tracks. Most important, Brewer's message is that "Americans," here capital and labor, must stand together rather than cut each other up.

The setting is a decaying New England textile town. Because of the Depression, Jim Cogswell is having a rough time at the drugstore, but he bites his lip and carries on. He serves the community — dispensing remedies to the sick, sitting on the town's finance committee, passing out commonsense advice. Jim befriends the town idiot, Galoot Wilson. When Jane, Jim's daughter, refuses to go out with Spike Webb, the town bully, Spike beats up Joe, Jane's boyfriend, who is studying to be a licensed pharmacist. Jim prefers charges and Spike is put in jail. Spike never forgets.

Graham Hay, the textile magnate, keeps his mill running by paying very low wages. His workers are restless. David, Jim's son, brings Ruth, his new wife, home. The Cogswells accept her as their daughter and give the newlyweds Jane's room. But Ruth is a radical, joins the textile workers, and calls for a strike. Hay imports strikebreakers from South Boston and asks for police protection. Violence breaks out.

Jim is disturbed but hesitates. "I'm a small town druggist. . . . I can't tell you how to solve the problems of industrial democracy . . . but I know it don't consist of burning down the house." Judge Choate and the chief of police tell Jim that he alone is "the man to do it" because "you got common sense." Jim gets Hay and Ruth into the drugstore and cajoles them into bargaining. The workers now get $2 and Ruth demands $4. Jim asks Hay "the highest wage you can possibly pay and break even?" Hay reluctantly goes to $2.75 and Ruth, with as little enthusiasm, accepts. Jim proposes arbitration of the other issues and Ruth agrees. But Hay refuses to arbitrate the closed shop; his strikebreakers have arrived and the sheriff has promised protection.

Jim will not give up. Judge Choate suspends the sheriff for failing to preserve order and names Jim to succeed him. Jim takes the badges off the deputies, padlocks the mill, and drives the scabs out of town. But the workers are now rioting. Jim asks Ruth to tell them to stop. Spike appears suddenly and threatens to kill Jim. Galoot sneaks into the lab at the rear of the drugstore. Spike pulls out his revolver, but Galoot fires first and kills Spike. When Ruth learns that David has been wounded, she is shocked and announces that she is leaving town. "You can still make this town your home," Jim says.

"Please don't be kind," she says. "There's no place for me here." Ruth departs.

What with the killing and the mediation, the drugstore is a mess. "Well," Jim says at the curtain, "we open at seven. Lots of work to be done. Let's get goin'."

Pins and Needles is unique among the labor plays of the thirties. Most of the others were box-office flops, or, at best, marginally successful. The ILGWU revue was a smash hit. The mood of the others is dour, violent, scolding, and dogmatic. Its spirit, despite an underlying seriousness, is gay, irreverent, satirical, funny, and sexy. There had to be a connection between success and mood.

As a revue, *Pins and Needles* is a series of unconnected sketches that deal with topical issues, which necessarily change with the times. It depends critically upon Harold Rome's songs. There are three major themes: the international situation, the left theater, and domestic issues, both political and labor. Among the popular international numbers is "Four Little Angels of Peace," based on the *Mikado* song, which satirizes Hitler, Mussolini, Chamberlain, and a Japanese general, and, after the Hitler-Stalin Pact, adds Stalin to make "Five." Another is an attack on British appeasement, "Britannia Waives the Rules." There are several in jokes about the radical theater — a satire of Brecht's *Mother* called "Mother, Let Freedom Wring," a denunciation of the Federal Theatre for suppressing *The Cradle Will Rock,* and a parody of the Odets flop, *Paradise Lost,* called "Paradise Mislaid."

The memorable numbers from the show deal with internal American problems starting with love. In "Why Sing of Stars Above!" a chorus of working girls demands that boys turn to a new kind of love song: "Sing us a song of social significance." Another hit was "One Big Union for Two," in which the boy woos the girl with the promise that he will picket her until she says yes and pledges that they add a "union made" member who "looks like me and like you." In "Nobody Makes a Pass at Me" a working girl laments that she has failed to win a man despite buying all the products supposed to guarantee sex appeal. "Vassar Girl Finds Job" satirizes the department store policy of hiring only college graduates as lowly clerks. In a notable line, the Vassar alumna who works the brassiere and girdle counter at Macy's sings sadly that she was once on the daisy chain but is now only "a chain-store daisy." The split in the labor movement between CIO and AFL is satirized in "Papa Lewis, Mama Green."[3]

3

An uninformed George Biddle returned to the United States in 1932. He had spent the preceding fifteen months painting in an Italian village on the edge of the Abruzzi many miles from either a telephone or a public bath. His discovery of the ravages of the American Depression shocked Biddle, especially the condition of his fellow painters, who had not even had jobs to lose. He thought back to his visit to Mexico in the twenties, when he had lived with Diego Rivera. He was much taken with the murals that Rivera, Orozco, and Siqueiros had painted under the sponsorship of President Alvaro Obregón. The mural, Biddle reckoned, was the answer to the painter's plight, particularly the "wealth of young, anonymous talent." Public buildings in the United States were full of blank walls. Mural painting was cheap; only the supervisor need be a fine artist. Obregón, Rivera complained, had bought great art at "plumbers' wages."

Biddle, who was from a distinguished Philadelphia family, had known Franklin Roosevelt at Groton and Harvard. On May 9, 1933, he wrote a "Dear Franklin" letter, suggesting that the government launch a mural program. Recognizing that the President had more pressing problems, he suggested that they chat at Hyde Park during the summer. Roosevelt did not wait. On May 19 he wrote Biddle that he was "interested in your suggestion" and proposed that the painter talk with Assistant Secretary of the Treasury L. W. Robert, who was in charge of federal public buildings, including those nearing completion in the new Federal Triangle.

Biddle wrote later, "My heart beat with excitement. Here was an entering wedge." He gathered a group of notable painters — Henry Varnum Poor, Thomas Hart Benton, Reginald Marsh, Boardman Robinson, Maurice Sterne, among others — and they drafted a three-point program, "A Revival of Mural Painting." A handful of "social-minded, creative artists, representing the modern movement, and experienced in mural painting" would constitute the nucleus. The government would assign the wall space. The painters would be given "as complete freedom as possible."

Biddle sent "A Revival" to the White House and Roosevelt passed it on to the National Commission of Fine Arts. The Commission was dominated by classicists who zealously guarded L'Enfant's conception of Washington against assaults from modern art. The Commission denounced Biddle and his friends as "painters of easel pictures of an incidental nature" who were noted for "chaotic composition." They urged the President to ignore the proposal. Roosevelt, who hardly needed a quarrel over painting, forwarded the report to Biddle, observing that "it does not sound very encouraging for the mural paintings."

Biddle was undaunted. Robert was interested in murals for the new Department of Justice Building and both the Treasury and the building architects agreed. More important, Robert brought Edward Bruce into the discussions. A lawyer and a businessman and publisher in the Far East, Bruce had quit work at forty-four to study painting with Sterne in Italy for six years and then to paint for a decade. He was now a monetary authority at the Treasury and had been the silver expert with the American delegation at the London Economic Conference in June 1933. Bruce was wildly enthusiastic about Biddle's proposal and they joined forces. On November 8 they descended upon Ickes, who, as head of PWA, had $400 million to disburse. He liked the idea and instructed Hopkins, who was setting up CWA with PWA funds, to give $1,039,000 to the Treasury for art. On December 3, 1933, the Public Works of Art Project (PWAP) opened shop in the Treasury under Bruce and his technical director, Forbes Watson, an art critic.

Bruce had the program humming in short order. By February 7, 1934, he had 2294 artists and 168 laborers at work in all 48 states. In hiring, PWAP had trouble defining "artist." The first applicant in Los Angeles, for example, was an unemployed plumber who did a little painting on the side. The wages followed the PWA scale: $42.50 a week for artists, $26.50 for assistants, and $15 for laborers. At its peak PWAP employed 3600 people.

But CWA funds ran out in the spring of 1934 and Bruce had to drop most of these employees. He then negotiated for funds from FERA, which continued the Treasury program from April 1934 through June 1935. But now it was much smaller, with no more than 1000 employees. With the establishment of WPA in the summer of 1935, Bruce received $530,000, which allowed him to set up the Treasury Relief Art Project (TRAP). But Hopkins insisted that three fourths of the artists come from relief rolls and that the work be confined to federal buildings. TRAP never had more than 356 artists on its payroll, and it ceased to exist on June 30, 1938.

Bruce had also set up the Treasury's Section of Fine Arts, which continued on a small scale between 1938 and 1943, conducting competitions for murals and sculpture for public buildings. It held 190 contests and awarded 1371 commissions. The Section was constantly embroiled in controversy. Painters and sculptors hated the competitions and local juries made quixotic choices. Its most notable event was the 48-States Competition to place a mural in the post office of one small town in each of the states.

The Treasury programs reflected Bruce's philosophy rather than Biddle's proposal. Since the rich would no longer finance art privately, the government must replace them. Social commitment was of little moment, in fact, was sometimes an embarrassment. Bruce was a skilled political operator who reached into high places and exploited public relations to promote art and to enhance his program. He had no special interest in mural painting and was wholly concerned with output as distinguished from art education.

The production statistics were impressive: Artists on PWAP completed 15,663 items, including 3821 oils, 2938 watercolors, 1518 prints, 647 sculptures, and 400 murals. The Treasury operation provided murals and sculptures for federal buildings in 1101 cities. Even the small TRAP program produced 10,215 easels, 85 murals, and 39 sculptures. The structures in the Federal Triangle were decorated with these works, and Biddle was one of the painters on the Justice Building. After viewing a smash show at the Corcoran Gallery in Washington in the spring of 1934, Miss Perkins took 130 oils for the new Labor Department. The House Office Building got 451 pictures and the White House took 42. There was a large art program in the CCC camps. Murals graced the walls at West Point and Annapolis. A special program for Indians in the Southwest and the Plains stressed traditional crafts, which embellished schools, hospitals, and community centers.

For Bruce and Watson the Treasury programs were intended to procure art of high quality to decorate public buildings and thereby to reach a wide public. The relief of artists in need was incidental. While they were concerned to safeguard the artist's freedom of expression, there were inevitable pressures for conformity. Modern nonrepresentational works evoked either public indifference or hostility and were rarely done. Nudes were out.

The Navy was a special problem. Bruce and Watson chose a wonderful work by Paul Cadmus, "The Fleet's In," for the Corcoran show. It depicted a group of drunken sailors, as Richard D. McKinzie put it, "engaged in highly informal interchanges with curvaceous damsels of obviously insecure reputations." Admiral Hugh L. Rodman found the picture "disgraceful, sordid, disreputable." One would have to search hard to find a sailor "who would stoop to such a disgraceful orgy." Secretary of the Navy Claude A. Swanson admired the work artistically, but said that it was "not true of the Navy." The Cadmus was withdrawn. The artists who worked on the mural "The Battle of Santiago" for hallowed Memorial Hall at Annapolis had to confront the Superintendent of the Naval Academy. Rear Admiral Thomas C. Hart insisted on precise representation. He arranged to send the destroyer *MacFarland* and the painters to Santiago so that they could make sketches of the ship and the harbor. But he refused to install the mural in Memorial Hall because the battleship *Brooklyn* was too prominent. It was later placed in a lesser building.

Roosevelt, mindful of the Rivera controversy at Rockefeller Center, said that he wanted no Communism. The painters who were doing the murals for San Francisco's new Coit Tower did not hear him. Clifford Wight painted three panels — "Rugged Individualism," "The New Deal," and "Communism." The Park Commission, outraged by the last, locked the doors. Bruce told them to "wipe the damn painting out of the Tower."

The Treasury's 48-States Competition in 1939 turned into a nationwide conflict over taste. Perhaps the most ferocious battle took place in the Coeur d'Alene lead mining district at Kellogg, Idaho. Fletcher Martin, a noted painter, did a mural, "Mine Rescue," depicting two burly miners carrying a third out of the shaft on a stretcher. The Section was wildly enthusiastic and compared Martin's work to the great religious paintings of the Renaissance. The local culture barons, including the union, but not its Ladies Auxiliary, considered it "sordid" and an insult to "our leading industry." "Mine Rescue" went into the Treasury vault and Martin painted another mural showing two smiling miners and their burro discovering the mine at Kellogg in 1885.

The preponderant, almost exclusive, style of Treasury art was realism, depicting life exactly as it was. The subject matter was overwhelmingly America. Thus, the program reflected the resurgence of cultural nationalism that was broadly evident in the thirties. The

Corcoran show stressed machinery, locomotives, ships, workers, and common items of village and farm life. A reporter calculated that 192 of the 498 subjects dealt with labor and industry. The President found the exhibit "robust and American." Mrs. Roosevelt thought the "Unemployed Boy" painting "almost the swellest thing in the exhibit."

The much larger federal program was based on relief. Its origins went back to New York City in December 1932. Hopkins, as head of the state relief administration, financed art education, which proved very successful. A private arrangement with only $20,000 sponsored both art education and works of art, and it, too, had impressive results. Between 1933 and 1935, FERA did little for artists, relying upon PWAP.

In 1935, WPA established Federal One, of which the Federal Art Project (FAP) was a basic component. Holger Cahill, the director, had been a novelist and biographer, had worked at the Newark Museum on American art, had written a study of American folk art, and had been director of exhibitions at the Museum of Modern Art. Cahill was an excellent choice and was the administrative star of Federal One.

FAP's basic objective was to assist artists in need, and no fewer than 90 percent of its employees came off relief rolls. There were several programs: production of contemporary art, art teaching, applied art, and research. Cahill moved swiftly. By early 1936 he had 6000 employees, mainly concentrated in major cities, particularly New York. Even as late as 1939 there were no activities in ten southern and western states. Cahill's field staff worked closely with community leaders, adapting programs to their needs through local sponsorship.

The accomplishments of FAP were formidable. By 1938, artists had produced 42,000 easel paintings and watercolors. FAP confined its mural paintings to nonfederal public buildings, and by the end of 1938 its artists were working on 1150 projects. It employed between 400 and 500 sculptors who worked in both monumental and smaller modes. Print and poster making was an important activity, especially at the Graphic Arts Workshop in New York. Daniel Defenbacher established three community art centers in North Carolina in late 1935. Their success led FAP to launch a national program, particularly in the South and West. A chain of galleries, many built with WPA labor, extended the length of Florida and there were over 100 centers in Arizona. "The glory of the centers," William F. McDonald wrote, "lay in their children's classes." In New York art therapy was used with the emotionally disturbed. FAP's monumental research project, the Index of American Design, involved the preparation of 23,000 plates tracing the history of design from colonial origins to the close of the nineteenth century.

Since most of FAP's employees were on relief, the aesthetic quality of their work was uneven, that is, much was mediocre. Cahill worried about this. Nevertheless, there were notable accomplishments. FAP artists won a large number of awards. Several established artists made contributions, for example, Stuart Davis, Raphael and Moses Soyer, Joe Jones, Ben Shahn, and William Gropper. A number of younger artists who would later achieve success received the opportunity to paint during the Depression, among them, Jackson Pollock, Willem de Kooning, Philip Guston, Edward Laning, Philip Evergood, Jack Levine, Mark Rothko, Arshile Gorky, and Anton Refrigier.

There were many notable exhibitions. The Museum of Modern Art held a dramatic showing, "New Horizons in American Art," in 1936. A number of established museums in the United States and abroad had exhibits. The world's fairs in San Francisco and New York in 1939 and 1940 provided important showcases for WPA art. National Art Week in 1940 and 1941 constituted the largest mass display of art in the nation's history. The 1940 shows attracted 5 million visitors.

FAP sponsored significant advances in technique in the graphic arts. Printmakers in Philadelphia developed the carborundum process, which yielded rich tones and sparkling luminosity. There were gains in carborundum color etching, in color lithography, and in color wood-block printing. Postermakers dramatically improved the silk-screen process. Meticulous photographic fidelity was achieved in the design index plates.

Cahill was committed to freedom of expression for his painters and sculptors, and many later testified that they had never worked with so few restrictions. While Cahill, because of his own preferences and the prevailing cultural nationalism, encouraged depiction of the American scene, there was no such requirement. "To most project artists," McDonald wrote, "America meant the working man, on the farm or in the city, the factory, the street scene, the tenement, the proletarian beach, and other aspects of industrial culture." Yet, there were many traditional portraits of local celebrities, and five monumental sculptures of Civil War generals were installed at Grant's Tomb. Nudes were discouraged. While Cahill imposed no strictures on style, realism was the dominant FAP school. Erica Beckh Rubenstein's study of the murals, however, uncovered Mexican, Italian Renaissance, French academic, and abstractionist influences.

FAP, of course, could hardly avoid controversy. Beniamino Benevenuto Bufano's proposal for a gigantic statue of St. Francis of Assisi in San Francisco (the Statue of Liberty West) evoked a storm of opposition. The Protestant Defense League demanded a companion statue of Martin Luther. Bufano's dream faded. Some thought they saw a hammer and sickle in Abraham Lishinsky's mural at Samuel Tilden High School in New York and a Soviet star in Gorky's "Aviation" at the Newark Airport. The conservative press — the Hearst papers, the *Chicago Tribune*, and the columnist Westbrook Pegler — maintained a steady drumbeat. While the Dies Committee concentrated on the theater and writing sections of Federal One, it did not ignore FAP.

Unemployment was the central labor theme of the art of the thirties. Reginald Marsh and Raphael Soyer dealt with it most imaginatively. In Marsh's case this raised some eyebrows because his father had inherited a packinghouse fortune and had worked at his leisure as a muralist. His mother painted miniatures. Marsh was born in Paris and educated at Lawrenceville and Yale. A masterful draftsman, he began to draw at three and sketched constantly thereafter. His line, Edward Laning noted, was "nervous and jittery." His work in every medium projected restless human figures. He crowded his canvases with people, and the energy passed from one figure to the next. His architectural forms, by contrast, were placid. Thus, he surrounded restless people with tranquil structures.

Marsh settled in New York shortly after World War I, adored the city, and refused to leave even during the oppressive summers. In the twenties he freelanced for newspapers and fashion magazines, designed sets for the theater, and drew cartoons for *The New Yorker*. But his passion was the life of the city. "No painter knew the city more completely," Lloyd Goodrich wrote. "He walked its streets continually, he frequented every kind of neighborhood, he observed and drew the city in all aspects." In 1929 he moved to Fourteenth Street, and in 1937 his address became No. 1 Union Square. In the twenties

Marsh had begun to record the town and its people, particularly, as Goodrich put it, its "less fashionable aspects." He concentrated on the Bowery, Fourteenth Street, the Lower East Side, the waterfront, and the railroad tracks on Tenth Avenue. His vision was a direct, fresh realism, without sentiment or glamour.

The Depression did not change Marsh; he merely continued what he had already begun. But now there were many more derelicts, breadlines, flophouses, and jungles to paint. His work — paintings, prints, and murals — is a searing record of the human cost of the Great Depression.

Several of his masterful works deserve note. In "The Bowery" (1930), a group of derelicts are standing under the El in an area of cheap hotels and second-hand clothing stores. While the people seem to be at rest, the painting teems with life. "Chatham Square" (1931) has similar subject matter. There is an air of idleness and decay, enhanced by deep browns and reds. "Holy Name Mission" (1931) depicts a long line of the jobless standing in front of a Chinese laundry and a barbershop waiting patiently for a handout. "Tattoo and Haircut" (1932) has a smaller group of the jobless standing by a tattoo-barbershop. A cripple in the foreground sets the mood. The etching "Breadline — No One Has Starved" (1932) is a lineup of nineteen men, each individualized by face, headgear, and feet, waiting for free food. There is a feeling of total defeat. "East Tenth Street Jungle" (1934) is Marsh's greatest Depression work. The background is composed of a factory, a gas works, and a partially demolished building; the foreground of the last has become a Hooverville. The people seem burned out, and there is an aura of desperation and decay. But most of the derelicts are busy with the basic chores of survival. They exude vitality.

Like Marsh, Soyer was a dedicated New Yorker, paced the city's streets, painted its people, and, during the thirties, focused on the jobless. He and his twin, Moses, also an artist, were born Shoar in 1899 to the wife of a Hebrew teacher in Borisoglebsk, Russia, a dreary town. They arrived in Philadelphia in 1912 and soon after moved to New York. The family was poor and Soyer sold newspapers, tended a soda fountain, and was an errand boy. He took free drawing lessons at night at Cooper Union and then moved to the free school of the National Academy of Design. To an important extent, Soyer was self-taught. His early paintings are considered "primitives," and he did not develop a distinctive style until around 1929. In that year he joined the new John Reed Club and developed vaguely Marxist politics. But Soyer was so individualistic and his art was so personal that only two of his paintings, about which he was later apologetic, were "political."

Soyer, physically tiny, was, Lloyd Goodrich wrote, "introspective, intensely shy, inarticulate, with a low, barely audible voice." As a boy, he had sketched people on the streets, particularly on the Lower East Side. About 1933, he began to concentrate on the Bowery and Fourteenth Street, painting, Goodrich noted, "men existing without hope, begging, sleeping in parks and under bridges, dependent on missions for food and shelter." Soyer saw them everywhere. He discovered Walter Broe, whose haggard face, watchful eyes, and worried forehead made him the ultimate Depression model. The painter found him fishing for coins through a subway grating with a pole tipped with chewing gum. Broe posed for several painters, including Marsh. Soyer, Jerome Klein wrote, became "the sympathetic painter of the unemployed, the painter of those shaken loose from their moorings, their faces clouded with uncertainty of every day's existence." Given Soyer's temperament and sensitivity, this was "inescapable reality."

Soyer recorded the victims of the Depression in both paint and prints. "How Long Since You Wrote to Mother?" (c. 1934) depicts five derelicts, including Broe, drinking coffee from tin cups and eating bread at the mission. Signs on the wall include the title and "God's Your Friend." The somber mood is enhanced by heavy blacks and browns flecked with small points of dull red, green, and yellow.

"In the City Park" (1934) portrays a group of idle men seated on a park bench. One is deep in sleep, and several, including Broe, seem worried. There is a contrast with strollers and an equestrian statue in the background.

"Transients" (1936) is excruciatingly sad. The men, with sharply differentiated faces, have morose, puzzled expressions. One holds crutches. The painting is in somber blues, browns, and blacks.

"Reading from Left to Right" (c. 1936) pictures three derelicts with marvelously delineated faces and headgear. A chalkboard in the background advertises coffee, crullers-buns-rolls 5¢, pie 8¢. Dark greens, browns, and blacks add to the mood.

Several of Soyer's prints were reworkings of "How Long . . ."— notably "The Mission" (c. 1935) and "Men Eating" (1937). But most of the prints, several done for the WPA, were of a single figure, sometimes Broe, and other times some man Soyer found in the streets who posed for a quarter or a half-dollar. They evoke a mood of sadness and defeat — "Old Laborer" (1935), "Old Laborer Warming His Hands" (1937), "Old Man" (1937), "A Transient" (1937). "Furnished Room" (1937) pictures a worried Broe and a cheerless woman seated in a bare room, facing away from each other. The mood is of intense loneliness.

Several other notable artists dealt with joblessness, but with less passion. Ben Shahn, who was both a graphic artist and a photographer, produced two important Depression works: "Seward Park" (1938), a colored lithograph, pictures four defeated unemployed men, as Shahn put it, "little people," seated on a park bench. Their bulbous, sharply differentiated faces have vacant expressions. His "Unemployed" (1938) shows six standing jobless men, their faces drawn and eyes angry. They seem to be waiting . . . for work. Rockwell Kent's "Drifter" (1933), a wood engraving, is a stylized man alone in a skiff, oar in the boat, drifting under the stars. His "And Now Where?" (1938), a lithograph on stone, pictures a man standing and a woman seated, staring morosely into space. The question they seem to ask poignantly is that of the title. Even Jackson Pollock during his WPA period painted a representational "Abandoned Mill," which is quite undistinguished and is said to have been sold by a second-hand dealer in New York in 1943 for $5.

Government art, both the Treasury and the WPA programs, was centrally preoccupied with labor, but treated it in a special way. Works that would be seen by large numbers of people, murals and large sculptures, usually sought to divert attention from the miserable present with its massive joblessness by glorifying the past and the future. Post offices and other public buildings were bathed in lakes of paint that romantically recounted their town's history: Americans working hard together to build the steel mill, the railroad, the gas works, the cheese factory, the plow mill, or, commonly, sorting and delivering the mail. Often work became heroized and was performed by gigantic, heavily muscled workers. This was evident in Philip Guston's exterior mural on the WPA Building at the New York World's Fair in 1939, in Cesare Stea's heroic pipefitters in the relief on the Bowery Bay Sewage Disposal Plant in New York, in Chaim Gross's burly riveters in the relief on the Federal Trade Commission Building in Washington, and in Michael Lantz's monumental sculpture at the convergence of Pennsylvania and Constitution Avenues in the nation's capital.

But several distinguished artists broke out of this mold. Edward Laning's murals for the dining room at Ellis Island in New York harbor portrayed the immigrant contribution to the building of America. He showed Chinese and Irish laborers at work on the construction of the Union and Central Pacific railroads. So successful were these works that Laning was invited to do "The Story of the Printed Word" murals for the New York Public Library. George Biddle, after a prolonged wrestling match with both Bruce and the Commission of Fine Arts, was allowed to paint a mural of a sweatshop in the Department of Justice Building. To thumb his nose at the authorities, Biddle put himself at a sewing machine and had Frances Perkins nearby. Some thought they recognized other celebrities, as well as the third girl from the end of the chorus line at the Gayety Burlesque.

Reginald Marsh was one of several painters who worked on the Post Office Building in Washington. He did two dramatic murals showing the transfer of mail from an ocean liner to a mail boat and the sorting of mail sacks in a central post office. His workers are straining at their jobs. In 1937 Marsh was invited to do the most important and complex murals of the time — eight large, concave, trapezoidal spaces alternating with eight smaller concave spaces in the dome of the rotunda of the New York Custom House. The undertaking was immense, presented formidable problems of perspective, and required fresco. He was assigned eight assistants, but did virtually all the painting himself in little more than three months. The eight large scenes picture the successive stages in the arrival of a great liner in New York harbor (the *Queen Mary,* the *Normandie,* and the *Washington* were the models) from passing Ambrose lightship to discharging cargo at the pier. The painter placed figures of the great maritime explorers in the smaller spaces. Given his love for New York harbor and for the workers who made it function, Marsh was the ideal choice for this undertaking. The painter was so eager to get the commission that he agreed to work for "any price." The government could not resist the bargain. He started at $30 a month and, because of a budget cut, ended at 90 cents an hour (his assistants got $1.60).

He probably was out of pocket on the project. But Marsh did not complain. Goodrich wrote,

> The style of the Custom House murals was strong, vigorous realism, without the stylization that seemed inescapable in much mural painting of the time. By the nature of their subject matter the murals were less exuberantly crowded than Marsh's city paintings; the elements were large and simplified, and there was a greater sense of space. The forms throughout were realized with a solidity and power that made academic mural painting seem anemic. Marsh had achieved something akin to Renaissance mural painting: he had embodied living content in monumental form. The Custom House murals remain not only an outstanding success of the federal art projects, but one of the most impressive creations in the history of American mural art.[4]

4

Documentary photography, though seeded earlier, burst into flower during the Great Depression. Mathew Brady during the Civil War, Jacob Riis on New York tenement life at the turn of the century, and Lewis W. Hine on immigration and labor conditions in the following generation had produced notable documentary photographs. But each had worked alone and against odds.

By the thirties everything was in place. The equipment was now very good — a range of fine cameras from the large 8-by-10-inch to the new 35-mm. machines, faster and sharper lenses, flash lighting, and fast, fine-grained black-and-white films. Distinguished photographers — Alfred Stieglitz, Edward Steichen, Paul Strand, Edward Weston, Ansel Adams — had set high standards. The newspapers and press associations employed photojournalists who roamed the streets. Picture magazines were highly successful. *Life* began publication in November 1936, *Look* in January 1937. Perhaps most important, the anguish of the American people during hard times demanded a pictorial record.

The documentation poured out of the darkrooms. Press and magazine photographers took enormous numbers of shots of workers — breadlines, Hoovervilles, dispossessions, strikes, riots — which dramatically visualized the times. But more important in the long run was the work of the Farm Security Administration photographers, a collection characterized by its historians as "overwhelming" and "a national treasure." One must marvel at the result because the program developed in a casual, even absent-minded, way and operated against formidable odds.

Roy E. Stryker was the engine. He had been born on a farm in Kansas in 1893, and his father, an ardent Populist, later scratched a living from the soil west of Montrose, Colorado. Stryker attended the Colorado School of Mines, homesteaded, and served in the infantry during World War I. He moved to New York in 1922 to study economics at Columbia, where he became friendly with Rexford G. Tugwell, one of his instructors. An institutionalist, Tugwell insisted that his students "see" the economic institutions of their society. When Stryker became a teaching assistant in 1924, he took his students to union meetings and strikes.

Tugwell and Thomas Munro put together a text on American economic life for the Columbia freshman course in contemporary civilization and asked Stryker to work up the illustrations. He began what would become a lifetime obsession, the collection and evaluation of photographs. Of the 215 illustrations in the first edition, more than 70 were by Lewis Hine. Stryker then spent five years on the photographs for the second edition. In 1929 he became an instructor in economics. In the early thirties, Tugwell demanded to know whether Stryker intended to take a Ph.D. He said that he did not, that he just loved to teach and look at photographs. Arthur Rothstein was one of his bright students.

Tugwell became a member of Franklin Roosevelt's Brain Trust and was named Assistant Secretary of Agriculture in 1933. The next year Stryker went to Washington as a photo expert in the Information Division of the Agricultural Adjustment Administration. In 1935, Tugwell became head of the Resettlement Administration (RA), which assisted poor farmers, and installed Stryker as chief of the "Historical Section." He told Stryker that RA would stir up a storm of political protest and wanted a photographic record of rural poverty as a reply.

This was a rather vague mandate, but Stryker was never at a loss for ideas. Rather, his problems were mundane. During the eight years of its life (Resettlement became the Farm Security Administration [FSA] in 1937), money was always extremely short and, at times, virtually nonexistent. Stryker worked out of what he called "a grubby little government office." His staff had to wait until he could afford a darkroom. No photographer received more than $3000 a year. He hired Dorothea Lange for $2300 (quite a bargain) and fired her whenever the budget was tight. The Department of Agriculture often preempted the FSA photographers because they made such nice pictures of farmers' wives canning fruit or of farmers building pens for their pigs.

Stryker recruited an almost totally nonprofessional staff. He refused to hire Hine, the nation's top documentary photographer who desperately needed the work, because he was "too old" at sixty. Among the FSA luminaries, only Lange had really made a living out of photography. Walker Evans had been an unsuccessful painter who taught himself photography in the late twenties. Ben Shahn was a painter who took up 35-mm. photography to make visual records for his paintings. He seems to have picked up the little he knew technically by sharing a studio with Evans. Russell Lee had studied painting but made a living as a chemical engineer. He was self-taught in photography. Stryker hired John Vachon as an assistant messenger and slowly promoted him to junior file clerk, unofficial photographer, and junior photographer. Carl Mydans was a reporter for *The American Banker* who learned to use a 35-mm. camera to supplement his stories. Arthur Rothstein was also self-taught.

Dorothea Lange, characteristically, was a special case. Born in Hoboken, New Jersey, in 1895, she was the oldest star in the FSA galaxy. While in her teens, she decided to become a photographer and found work in darkrooms in New York portrait studios. Lange moved to San Francisco in 1918 and opened her own studio the next year. In the twenties, aside from a stormy marriage to the western painter Maynard Dixon, she specialized in portraits of the families of rich Californians. The Depression, however, hit San Francisco like a sledgehammer, and her business dried up.

Lange began to observe the jobless from her studio window on Montgomery Street. By 1932 she could no longer bear the contradiction between her portraits of the rich and "what was going on in the street." Feeling insecure (her brother came along as bodyguard), she ventured out and made twelve exposures in a Graflex. Of one she said later, "There are moments such as these when time stands still and all you can do is hold your breath and hope it will wait for you." It waited. She called the photograph "White Angel Bread Line," and it has become, Milton Meltzer wrote, "one of the great images of the

Depression era, of people in trouble." An obscure portrait photographer had now become a great documentary photographer.

In the summer of 1934, Willard Van Dyke exhibited the street Langes at his gallery in Oakland. Among the impressed viewers was Paul S. Taylor, professor of economics at the University of California in Berkeley, who was much interested in agriculture and farm labor. He used Lange's photographs to illustrate his articles, and they started to work together. In the winter of 1934–1935, the California Emergency Relief Administration became concerned about a sharp increase in the rural migrant families entering the state in search of farm work. CERA hired Taylor to study the problem, and he brought Lange along to do the photographs. They discovered the "Okies." The report and the pictures reached Washington and made a big impression. Stryker hired Lange immediately. In December 1935, after both obtained divorces, Lange married Taylor.

The FSA photographers, armed with Stryker's formidable shooting scripts, covered virtually the entire nation and made 270,000 photographs. While they inevitably concentrated on the rural, they did not ignore urban America. At the outset, Stryker, sitting at his desk in Washington, did not know what to expect. Soon, "every day was for me an education and a revelation. I could hardly wait to get to the mail in the morning. . . . We introduced Americans to America." No such record has ever been made, before or since. A few highlights deserve note.

Evans, the most exacting artist in the group, produced a striking gallery of needle-sharp images of the small-town and rural East and South. Rothstein recorded the Dust Bowl in the Great Plains. His cow's skull on eroded soil was a media sensation. Rothstein's "Dust Storm, Cimarron County, Oklahoma," shot in 1936, is the masterpiece that sums up the entire disaster. Mydans and Lee recorded the Midwest. Shahn, with his painter's eye, made a set of brilliant images in the South.

Lange was in a class by herself. Her ability to "see" in a flash was unrivaled, and she became the visual historian of the transiency of the thirties. Curiously, she was ill at ease in the darkroom. While she knew this better than anyone, she fought with Stryker against having her work processed in Washington and won. The developing and enlarging was done in her own darkroom in Berkeley. But she needed help, usually from Ron Partridge, a young photographer, and occasionally from Ansel Adams, which was surely overkill and a tribute to her powers of persuasion. Adams complained to Stryker that his people were "not photographers. They're a bunch of sociologists with cameras."

The Lange masterpiece, perhaps the most famous and widely reproduced photograph ever made, is "Migrant Mother." When Stryker left FSA in 1943, he took along 1300 of his favorite prints. Many years later, in his retirement in Grand Junction, Colorado, he kept all but one in desk drawers. He had a superb enlargement of "Migrant Mother" on display in a special place. "When Dorothea shot that picture," Stryker said, "that was the ultimate." It has an interesting history.

In February 1936, Stryker gave Lange an assignment to photograph "slums" (did California have slums?), pea pickers in San Luis Obispo County, a housing project in El Monte, soil erosion, and migrants in the Los Angeles area. She drove down alone in the station wagon in terrible weather. Nothing worked in the pea camps because of the heavy rain. She had better luck in Southern California. After a month in the field, she was exhausted and eager to return to Berkeley. Rain fell as she drove up U.S. 101. As she sped through San Luis Obispo County, a crude sign caught her eye: "PEA-PICKERS CAMP." For the next twenty miles she convinced herself that there was no need to stop. "Just one more of the same. Besides, if you take the camera out in this rain. . . ." To her surprise, the car made a U-turn and she soon reached the soggy camp like "a homing pigeon." Now, in her own words:

> I saw and approached the hungry and desperate mother, as if drawn by a magnet. I do not remember how I explained my presence or my camera to her, but I do remember she asked me no questions. I made five exposures, working closer and closer from the same direction. I did not ask her name or her history. She told me her age, that she was 32. She said that they had been living on frozen vegetables from the surrounding fields, and birds that the children killed. She had just sold the tires from her car to buy food. There she sat in that lean-to tent with her children huddled around her, and she seemed to know that my pictures might help her, and so she helped me. . . .
>
> The pea crop at Nipomo had frozen and there was no work for anybody. But I did not approach the tents and shelters of other stranded pea-pickers. It was not necessary; I knew I had recorded the essence of my assignment.

The work of the FSA photographers won almost immediate acclaim. The *U.S. Camera* show in 1936 featured Lange and Rothstein. The press and the magazines published many FSA photographs. The International Photographic Exhibition in Grand Central Palace in New York in 1938 had seventy FSA enlargements. Viewers, including Steichen, were much impressed. The Museum of Modern Art in 1938 published a book of Evans's works and put a show, including many FSA photographs, on the road. There was a small flood of picture books either based upon or aping the FSA work: Erskine Caldwell and Margaret Bourke-White, *You Have Seen Their Faces* (1937); Archibald MacLeish, *Land of the Free* (1938), poem and Lange photographs; Sherwood Anderson, *Home Town* (1940); Agee and Evans, *Let Us Now Praise Famous Men* (1941); Arthur Raper, *Sharecroppers All* (1941); Edwin Rosskam, Richard Wright, Russell Lee, *Twelve Million Black Voices* (1941). In writing *The Grapes of Wrath,* Steinbeck studied the FSA files diligently, particularly the Langes, and her influence is evident in the novel. When John Ford made the film for Twentieth Century–Fox, he used the Langes as a primary source. With the passage of time, a number of the FSA photographers became famous, and their works were published and shown in many museums around the world.[5]

5

From the beginning of settlement in North America, immigrants from the British Isles — the English, Scots, Welsh, and Irish — brought over a tradition of folk song, including the tunes and words of their old ballads. With industrialism and urbanization, folk singing gradually retreated to the South and Southwest, to rural areas, to isolated industries and communities — to workers in textile mill towns and coal camps in Appalachia, and to seamen, cowboys, and migratory farm workers. In the twentieth century, folklorists, both amateur buffs and academic scholars, busily gathered and published folk songs, depending increasingly on the advancing technology of recording equipment. By the nineteen thirties a huge collection of music was at hand. While this tradition had always contained a significant labor theme — work songs, union songs, songs of protest — the Great Depression honed it to a sharp cutting edge. This was most evident among textile workers, coal miners, and migrants.

The textile industry, which launched the factory system, recruited children, especially farm girls, to work in the mills and ruthlessly exploited them. They sang in protest, particularly "The Lowell Factory Girl," which seems to have been written in the 1830s. It survived in various forms, and John Lomax heard it in Fort Worth in the early twentieth century. The singer said she had learned it in Florida. Still another variant, "No More Shall I Work in the Factory," was sung in North Carolina in the thirties.

The bitter textile strikes of 1929–1930 in the southern Piedmont were singing events. The millhands, called by the owners "cotton mill trash," had been tenant farmers and mountaineers with a strong folk-singing tradition. Music was central in their intensely emotional religion. Liston Pope wrote that this sacred music appealed to "the hands and feet more than to the head." A favorite hymn went:

> While some live in splendid mansions,
> 	And have wealth at their command,
> I'm a stranger and a pilgrim
> 	Passing through this barren land.

Tom Tippett noted that the strikes became "a folk movement" and the strikers sang. The favorite song in the Danville strike was "Cotton Mill Colic":

> I'm a-going to starve.
> 	Everybody will.
> 'Cause you can't make a living
> 	In a cotton mill.

The singing presented problems for the Communist National Textile Workers Union (NTWU). Fred Beal, who led the Loray strike, thought he would teach his pickets Ralph Chaplin's great Wobbly song, "Solidarity Forever," until he realized that the tune, hardly appropriate in the South, was "John Brown's Body."

The Marion, North Carolina, strike was violent. Deputies shot more than a score of unarmed workers, six of whom died, all shot in the back. Two songs were written about the event. "The Marion Strike" was a straightforward ballad to the tune of "Wreck of the Altoona," which recounts the tragedy. The workers struck against the stretchout —

They put us on two men's jobs,
And just gave us half enough pay.

The millowner called for the sheriff, who "brought all his men along." He and the workers argued over who was right.

So one word just brought on another,
And the bullets they started to flying,
And after the battle was over,
Six men lay on the ground a-dying.

"The Marion Massacre" described the same event, but ended on a high note:

But some day they'll meet them
On that bright shore so fair,
And live in peace forever,
There'll be no sorrow there.
    There'll be no sorrow there,
    There'll be no sorrow there,
    In heaven above
    Where all is love,
    There'll be no sorrow there.

The Loray strike in Gastonia, North Carolina, produced an authentic troubadour, Ella May Wiggins. She came from mountaineer stock in the Great Smokies, married at sixteen, and bore nine children before she was thirty, four of whom died of whooping cough. She had slaved ten years in the mill, sixty hours a week, never earning more than $9 a week. Ella May supported the NTWU strike passionately. She had a good voice, an innate sense of rhythm, and a talent for composing "song ballets." During the walkout a truckload of union members set out for the "speakin' ground." Vigilantes intercepted them, and Ella May was shot through the heart.

Ella May's most popular song was "Chief Aderholt," named for the police chief who had been murdered. The tune was "The Death of Floyd Collins." "Come all you good people, and listen while I tell. . . ." Ella May recounted Aderholt's sins — locking up the leaders, denying them bail. The closing refrain was militant.

We're going to have a union all over the South,
Where we can wear good clothes, and live in a better house.

After her funeral in the rain Ella May's friends sang her most haunting song, "The Mill Mother's Lament":

We leave our homes in the morning,
We kiss our children goodbye,
While we slave for the bosses
Our children scream and cry.

* * *

But understand, all workers,
Our union they do fear,
Let's stand together, workers,
And have a union here.

Along with the miners, they appropriated the Negro blues. In Tennessee they sang "Shirt Factory Blues" — "Lawd, Lawd, got them shirt factory blues." A verse of "The Winnsboro Cotton Mill Blues" went:

When I die, don't bury me at all,
Just hang me up on the spool-room wall;
Place a knotter in my hand,
So I can spool in the Promised Land.

The strongest labor folk-song tradition persisted in coal mining. The British heritage, the concentration of the industry in Appalachia, the isolation of the coal camps, the extreme hazards and loneliness of underground mining, and the importance of booze joined in making song a staff of life.

Coal music was marked by several significant themes. One was to lament the miner's fate. The exemplar was "Only a Miner," which Archie Green has called "the American miner's national anthem." The tune may be a revival hymn or a variant of a Scottish migratory farm workers' song dating from the Napoleonic Wars. In 1877, the Indian fighter "Captain Jack" Crawford wrote a poem entitled "Only a Miner Killed," about the death of a silver miner in the Comstock Lode in Nevada. A variation was sung in coal as early as 1888. It also appeared in gold, silver, copper, and lead. In time an "Only . . ." family emerged — "Only a Cowboy," "Only a Brakeman," "Only a Tramp," "Only a Miner." The last was recorded by the Kentucky Thorobreds in 1927. One of the Thorobreds had learned it from his father, a Methodist preacher who had served miners in Laurel and Harlan counties, Kentucky. The song had religious overtones — "God pity miners, protect them as well." It was very popular in Appalachia during the thirties.

Variants appeared. Aunt Molly Jackson, the Kentucky minstrel of the Communist National Miners Union (NMU), altered it to "Poor Miner's Farewell" in 1932, and it was printed in the *Red Song Book.* Aunt Molly eliminated the mood of resignation and the invocation of the Lord: "I will help you to get bread." A hymn-like version, "The Hard-working Miner," was much like "Only a Miner" and was widely sung in Kentucky, West Virginia, and Virginia. Some metal miners in the West sang their own variant, "Only a Miner Killed in the Mine," or "Only a Miner Killed in the Breast," evidently transported to hard-rock mining by coal miners.

As recorded by the Thorobreds, the first stanza and chorus of "Only a Miner" went:

> The hard-working miners, their dangers are great,
> Many while mining have met their sad fate,
> While doing their duties as miners all do,
> Shut out from daylight and their darling ones, too.
> He's only a miner been killed in the ground,
> Only a miner and no more is found,
> Killed by an accident, no one can tell,
> His mining's all over, poor miner farewell.

The second theme, one of several lamented in "Only a Miner," was disaster, the danger of death or dismemberment in underground mining. Disaster songs, bespeaking their British origins, were ballads, which "Only a Miner" was not. There was a large demand for these songs. In the three years following April 14, 1912, when the *Titanic* sank, 106 songs chronicling that calamity were sent to the copyright office, all to the tune of "Nearer My God to Thee." American miners began to memorialize their tragedies with "Avondale Mine Disaster" in 1867 and have never stopped. In the twenties and thirties the hillbilly ballad "The Dream of a Miner's Child" was the favorite. According to sleuth Archie Green, it had an unusual history.

There had been a great mine disaster at St. Genaed in South Wales in 1907. Two English songwriters composed "Don't Go Down in the Mine, Dad," which was published in 1910 and became popular in Britain. It quickly crossed the Atlantic and was picked up by American miners, both coal and hard-rock. As a boy in the twenties, Woody Guthrie heard it around the mines in eastern Oklahoma. But now the title had become "The Dream of a Miner's Child," and the lyrics had been altered. The "author" was Andrew Jenkins, a blind Georgia preacher, who with his stepdaughters made up the Jenkins Family, a gospel group on an Atlanta radio station. In 1925 he wrote "The Death of Floyd Collins" about the spelunker who died in a Kentucky cave he had discovered. Jenkins reworked "Don't" into "Dream," and Vernon Dalhart, a popular country singer, recorded it in 1925. "Dream" became a hillbilly hit and a popular folk song at the same time. The first verse and chorus of "The Dream of a Miner's Child," as sung by Dalhart, went:

> A miner was leaving his home for his work,
> He heard his little child scream,
> He went to the side of the little girl's bed —
> "Oh! Daddy, I've had such a dream.
> "Oh! Daddy, don't work in the mines today,
> For dreams have so often come true,
> Oh! Daddy, my Daddy, please don't go away,
> I never could live without you."

The third important theme of coal folk music was of the union and the strike. There were a great number of these songs in the thirties. One of the most popular and interesting was "The Death of Mother Jones." This feisty Irish lady became a fiery union organizer in 1876, participated in a great many strikes for half a century, adopted the miners as her "children," died at 100 in 1930, and was buried in the Union Miners' Cemetery in Mt. Olive, Illinois. According to Green, an unknown miner probably wrote a memorial poem in late 1930. Not knowing its origin, the singing cowboy Gene Autry recorded the song in 1931 and the record, which was pressed on at least seven labels, became very popular. Miners sang it during the coal strikes of the thirties. In the Autry version the first stanza ran:

> The world today's in mourning
> O'er the death of Mother Jones;
> Gloom and sorrow hover
> Around the miners' homes.
> This grand old champion of labor
> Was known in every land;
> She fought for right and justice,
> She took a noble stand.

Many new coal songs emerged during the turbulent decade. Aunt Molly Jackson reworked traditional tunes, lyrics, and lines into militant left-wing protest songs, as in "Poor Miner's Farewell." She wrote strike songs, a dirge for Harry Simms, a murdered NMU organizer, and the mournful "Dreadful Memories," about the starving children of blacklisted miners. George Korson collected a number of more conventional songs that supported John L. Lewis and the United Mine Workers or President Roosevelt and the New Deal. He also picked up "A Coal Miner's Goodbye," written by Archie Conway, a preacher and miner whose back was broken by falling slate in a West Virginia mine in 1938:

> For years I have been a coal miner,
> I worked day by day in the mine,
> But no longer am I a coal miner,
> I have come to the end of the line.

The most notable strike song was "Which Side Are You On?" written by Mrs. Sam Reece, the wife of an organizer in Harlan County, to the tune of the Baptist hymn "Lay the Lily Low."

The blues form adapted readily to coal song. Black miners, starting with convict laborers in the nineteenth century, had sung the blues and Trixie Smith's "Mining Camp Blues" was a popular race record in the twenties. Black miners in Alabama sang the blues as work songs. Korson collected a great many, of which six were sung by white miners in Kentucky and West Virginia. "Harlan County Blues" went:

> "You don't have to be drunk," they said,
> "To be throwed in the can;
> The only thing you needed be,
> Was just a union man."

The Carter Family, a celebrated country group, picked up "Coal Miner's Blues" ("that coal black blues") from miners in Wise County, Virginia, and made a popular recording in 1938.

The greatest of the coal songs, reflecting the professionalism of their author, were "Dark as a Dungeon" and "Sixteen Tons" by Merle Travis. He was raised in Ebenezer, Kentucky, and his father worked in the mine. The entire family was musical and Merle was the most gifted. After working in the CCC, Travis left Ebenezer in 1935 to become a country singer in radio, particularly over WLW in Cincinnati. He was with the Marine Corps during World War II and then settled in Hollywood. In 1946 Travis recorded nine *Folk Songs of the Hills,* including three he had written, two of which were his masterpieces. They are in his father's speech and reflect the miner's outlook in Ebenezer in the thirties.

Travis asked an old miner why he never tried another line of work. "If you ever get this old coal dust in your blood, you're just gonna be a plain old coal miner as long as you live. It's a habit, sorta like chewin tobaccer." The first stanza and chorus of "Dark as a Dungeon" ran:

> Come and listen you fellows, so young and so fine,
> And seek not your fortune in the dark dreary mines.
> It will form as a habit and seep in your soul,
> 'Till the stream of your blood is as black as the coal.
> It's dark as a dungeon and damp as the dew,
> Where the danger is double and pleasures are few,
> Where the rain never falls and sun never shines,
> It's dark as a dungeon way down in the mine.

"Sixteen Tons" embodied a common miner's figure of speech — being so far in debt that he owed his soul to the company store. The title referred to the initiation of a new man. Experienced miners loaded eight to ten tons a day. When a youngster came on, they slacked off so that he could "make sixteen" on his first day to show his manhood. The first stanza and chorus went:

> Now, some people say a man's made out of mud,
> But a poor man's made out of muscle and blood,
> Muscle and blood, skin and bones,
> A mind that's weak and a back that's strong.
> You load sixteen tons and what do you get?
> Another day older and deeper in debt.
> Saint Peter, don't you call me 'cause I can't go,
> I owe my soul to the company store.

Migratory workers, hoboes, and tramps had sung almost instinctively. This was both because they had time and because they had relied on the railroad, which was the source of so much folk song. The IWW, composed in large part of hoboes and migratory farmhands, inherited this tradition. The Wobblies also produced several notable songwriters — Mac McClintock, Joe Hill, and Ralph Chaplin. Their lyrics were laced with irony and protest. *The Little Red Song Book* became the IWW Bible. Several of their songs passed into the mainstream of folk song — "Halleluyah, I'm a Bum," "The Big Rock Candy Mountains," "Solidarity Forever," and "The Preacher and the Slave."

The migrants of the thirties, particularly those from the Dust Bowl, were primarily of British stock, came from rural and isolated areas, and were fundamentalist in religion. They sang naturally. When John Ford was filming *The Grapes of Wrath,* he asked the migrants he had hired as extras to sing something every Okie, Arkie, and Mizoo knew. They immediately broke into "Goin' Down the Road Feelin' Bad."

This migration produced an authentic voice, the troubadour Alan Lomax has called "the best folk ballad composer whose identity has ever been known" — Woody Guthrie. That Woody produced anything enduring is a tribute to his genius, at bottom a wildly imaginative command of language. He was no more than a passing guitarist and his raspy voice was not well designed for singing. Otherwise, the whole world, including Woody himself, conspired against him.

He was born on July 14, 1912, to Charley and Nora Guthrie in the raw frontier town of Okemah, Oklahoma. Because Charley was an aspiring Democratic politician, he named the baby after the candidate his party had just nominated for President — Woodrow Wilson. Only Nora ever called him Woodrow. She also sang him the sad mountain ballads her mother had brought from Tennessee.

The Guthrie family was plagued by disaster. A fine house Charley's father had built for them burned down a month after it was completed and there was little insurance. Nora became obsessed by the loss. Charley, who had been a hustler as a young man, proved a loser and spun out his life aimlessly. Clara, Woody's sister, after an argument with her mother, poured oil on her dress, set herself afire, and burned to death. Nora went mad. Worst of all, Nora came down with Huntington's chorea, an incurable disease that attacked the central nervous system and was transmitted from mother to son to daughter and so on. Woody's childhood was wretched. He had no home and received very little formal education.

Woody had a bad itch about traveling and never learned to settle down. He married three times and there were other women. Only his second wife, Marjorie, understood him. He drank heavily, kept weird hours, and constantly disappeared. Woody was so extraordinarily talented — at drawing, painting, songwriting, singing — that he could always find work, even at the bottom of the Depression. But he refused to hold a job. When he began making big money on network radio in 1940, he found he hated the commercial straight-jacket and walked out.

Woody's politics brought him grief. He and Mary, his first wife, lived in Pampa, in the Texas Panhandle. On April 14, 1935, the sky turned black, the wind blew 70 m.p.h., and the temperature dropped 50 degrees. He watched the migrants go through town on their way west. In 1936 he joined them and moved to California. Thus, Woody was an authentic Dust Bowl Okie. But he did not realize it until the bigots in California badmouthed his people because they were poor and dirty. He then remembered riding in boxcars with old Wobblies who had told him that it was the system, the rich against the poor, you had to take sides. Woody got real mad and became a Communist, remained one for most of the rest of his life. The Stalinist line made him look foolish during and after the war and right-wingers were always gunning for him.

In 1952 Huntington's disease got to Woody. It tortured him horribly for fifteen years and, finally, on October 3, 1967, killed him. Shortly thereafter his daughters by Mary, Gwen and Sue, learned that they too had Huntington's chorea.

Even Woody's "funeral" did not work. When Marjorie received the ashes from the crematorium in a drab olive canister, she insisted, over her children's opposition, on a minimal ceremony. They would go to Woody's favorite beach between Coney Island and Sea Gate and spread the ashes on the Atlantic. They walked out on the jetty where the wind was blowing and then could not figure out how to open the can. Finally, Marjorie got a beer-can opener and pried holes in the top. She handed the can to Arlo. He shook it, but no ashes came out. "What should I do?" Arlo asked. Nobody knew. He tossed the canister out to sea and the family watched it go under. Marjorie tried to think of what Woody would want them to do next. "Why don't we go to Nathan's," she said, "and have a hot dog?"

Woody began writing Okie songs while he was still in Pampa. He got serious about songwriting in 1937 when he was singing on station KFVD in Los Angeles on "The Oklahoma and Woody Show," at first with his brother Jack and later with Maxine Crissman ("Lefty Lou from Old Mizzoo"). He both adapted old tunes and verses and wrote new songs. They poured out.

Woody loved the old Negro spiritual "This Train," and the phrase

"Bound for Glory" became the title of his autobiography. But he removed the religion and made it a migrant's song. "This train is a-leaving town, hitting the road and heading down." "So Long, It's Been Good to Know You" is a straight Okie song. "This dusty old dust is a-getting my home, and I got to be drifting along." "Talking Dust Bowl" is a farmer's story in talking blues. The man had "a little farm and I called that heaven." But "the rain quit," the wind rose, and a "black old dust storm filled the sky." He traded his farm for "a Ford machine" and set out, "rockin' and a-rollin' " for California. The trip was big trouble, but the family made it "dad gum broke." He bummed some spuds that the wife made into "tater stew" that was "so damn thin" that you could read a "mag-i-zine" through it. "Goin' Down This Old Dusty Road," an adaptation, tells the same story, but with protest. The narrator has "lost my farm down in old Oklahoma" and sets out for the promised land where "the water tastes like wine." He wants a job at "honest pay" and three square meals a day for his kids. But they call him "a Dust Bowl refugee." "I ain'ta gonna be treated this-a-way." "Hard Travellin' " was the transient's lament. He could have been a hammer driller in a hard-rock tunnel, a steel-worker from Pittsburgh, a farm laborer. But now he was out of work and was "hittin' that Lincoln Highway," "that sixty-six." "I been a-havin' some hard travellin'."

Woody vented his anger against the people on the Coast who wanted to ban the Okies. In "Do-Re-Mi," California was all right if you could afford to buy a home or a farm or take a vacation by the sea. But it was no Garden of Eden "if you ain't got the Do-Re-Mi." In "Pastures of Plenty," the migrant has "travelled a hot dusty road." He came from the Dust Bowl to work the crops in California, Arizona, and Oregon. He would defend his right to move and work with his life " 'cause my pastures of plenty must always be free."

Woody wrote several ballads in the traditional form. "The Ballad of Pretty Boy Floyd" was about the famous outlaw who came from his part of Oklahoma. While Pretty Boy committed "every crime," he only stole from the rich to give to the poor. He saved the homes of poor farmers by paying off their mortgages. When someone provided a stranger with a meal, there would later be a $1000 bill under the napkin. Pretty Boy gave Christmas dinners for families on relief. Woody also told the story of *The Grapes of Wrath* in seventeen stanzas in "The Ballad of Tom Joad." He said this was so that the folks back in Oklahoma who could not afford either the book or the movie would be able to hear the story. Actually, Victor Records, hoping to capitalize on the popularity of Ford's film, talked Woody into doing it. He wrote it in one night with the help of half a gallon of wine.

The great Dust Bowl migration to California excited the artistic imagination as did no other event of its time. It produced Steinbeck's novel, Dorothea Lange's photographs, and Woody Guthrie's folk songs. They almost justified the suffering.[6]

6

The winter of 1939–1940 was a bad time for Woody. He had gone back to Pampa with Mary and the kids, and everything tasted sour. He hated the town, and his marriage was on the rocks. An old friend refused to invite Woody to his wedding. He could hardly wait to get out of Pampa. He left for New York just after the first of the year and had a miserable time hitching rides in the wind and snow. That was bad enough. Even worse, every time he stopped at a diner or a bar the jukebox blared out Irving Berlin's "God Bless America." Woody grew to hate that song for its mawkish sentimentality, for its assurance that everything was going to be O.K. because God was in charge.

As he moved east, Woody began to write a parody in his head. When he got to a fleabag near Times Square, he wrote down "God Blessed America" on foolscap. The tune was the old Baptist hymn "Oh My Lovin' Brother," which the Carter Family had used for "Little Darlin', Pal of Mine." It started soberly enough — "This land is your land, this land is my land." There were lines of Woody at his best —

> As I went walking that ribbon of highway
> And saw above me the endless skyway

But the song closed in irony —

> Was a big high wall there that tried to stop me
> A sign was painted said: Private Property.
> But on the back side, it didn't say nothing —
> God Blessed America for me.

* * *

One bright sunny morning in the shadow of the steeple
By the relief office I saw my people —
As they stood there hungry,
I stood there wondering if
God Blessed America for me.

In April 1944, when Woody and Cisco Houston were between hazardous wartime voyages in the merchant marine, Woody, Cisco, Bess Lomax, and Sonny Terry went down to Moses Asch's studio in New York and recorded 132 songs. At the last session Woody trotted out a new song. The parody was gone and he now called it "This Land Is My Land." Moe Asch later claimed that he knew immediately that something very important had happened in his studio.

At the end of 1944 Woody briefly had a Sunday afternoon radio show on WNEW in New York and used "This Land" as his theme. But it would take a while to catch on.

On March 17, 1956, when Woody was already in the grasp of Huntington's disease, his old friends gave him a benefit concert at Pythian Hall in New York. It was a memorable occasion. The singers closed with "This Land." The spotlight then turned on the little guy in the balcony who struggled to his feet and saluted with a clenched fist. Pete Seeger, his banjo pounding and tears streaming down his cheeks, led the audience through "This Land." Pete and most everybody else there later said it was the birth of the folk-song revival. It was also, Joe Klein wrote, "the beginning of Woody Guthrie's canonization." Finally, America had a magnificent patriotic song that everyone could sing and that many people thought should be the national anthem.[7]

Eight

Watershed

THE ERA OF THE GREAT DEPRESSION was a watershed in the history of American labor. Economic collapse ravaged employment and undermined wages. Social disorganization, the erosion of basic institutions, followed inevitably. Unions lost membership, income, and power, the last both economic and political. These profound changes generated massive unrest, which manifested itself in both the economic and political spheres.

Franklin Roosevelt and his New Deal sought solutions to these problems with a caring society, a welfare state that preserved many features of capitalism while assisting those too weak to help themselves. This included relief for the unemployed, attacks on several fronts against unemployment, particular programs for the aged, those who had lost their jobs, and the young, and the fixing of labor standards. Equally important, the New Deal encouraged workers to form unions by legal protection of the right to organize and to engage in collective bargaining.

The Depression and the New Deal transformed the distribution of power in American society both in politics and on the shop floor. The Democratic Party, with massive labor support, supplanted the Republican Party as the dominant political force. Economic power, formerly concentrated in business and banking, was now shared with the government and with the trade union. Roosevelt, by preempting the center and most of the left, undermined both native populist demagogues and the Marxist parties.

1

Prior to 1929, American labor had known hard times. In the late nineteenth century there had been deep depressions with severe and persistent unemployment. But in the first quarter of the twentieth century the cyclical declines had been modest and of limited duration. By 1929, few remembered the nineties and almost no one anticipated a recurrence, to say nothing of a much worse slump. The "Great Depression" was unique and earned its name. No decline had been so deep, so long lasting, or so international in scope. While it ravaged every feature of the American economy — business, banking, agriculture — its most visible impact was on labor, particularly in joblessness.

Despite the absence of reliable statistics prior to 1940, one may chart the broad course of unemployment during the Great Depression with reasonable accuracy. The table, based upon the Bureau of Labor Statistics retrospective annual estimates, shows the civilian labor force, employment, and unemployment for the period 1929 through 1941. If one adds to this the monthly estimates of unemployment by Robert R. Nathan, the movements become quite clear.

The civilian labor force grew steadily throughout the Depression. The increment approximated 600,000 annually between 1929 and 1939 and then dropped to about 300,000 in the last two years. Several reasons for this increase in the size of the labor force are clear: entry by young people of both sexes, increased longevity in some occupations, and a higher female participation rate. There was a controversy among experts over whether joblessness among male breadwinners forced wives and children to seek jobs or whether unemployment so discouraged workers as to drive them out of the labor market. Clarence D. Long, the leading authority, much preferred the latter explanation. Employment, the table shows, dropped precipitously between 1929 and 1933, rose steadily until 1937, fell off in 1938, and then climbed again between 1939 and 1941.

The extraordinary feature of the first three and a half years of the Depression was the unrelieved disaster. The economy dropped straight down, like a block of concrete in the water. This is evident in the monthly data. According to Nathan, about a million Americans were out of work in October 1929. In January 1930 the number

UNEMPLOYMENT, 1929–1941
(add 000)

	CIVILIAN LABOR FORCE	EMPLOYED	UNEMPLOYED	PERCENT UNEMPLOYED
1929	49,180	47,630	1,550	3.2
1930	49,820	45,480	4,340	8.7
1931	50,420	42,400	8,020	15.9
1932	51,000	38,940	12,060	23.6
1933	51,590	38,760	12,830	24.9
1934	52,230	40,890	11,340	21.7
1935	52,870	42,260	10,610	20.1
1936	53,440	44,410	9,030	16.9
1937	54,000	46,300	7,700	14.3
1938	54,610	44,220	10,390	19.0
1939	55,230	45,750	9,480	17.2
1940	55,640	47,520	8,120	14.6
1941	55,910	50,350	5,560	9.9

passed 4 million and reached 5 million in September. By January 1931 the figure went to 8 million. The winter of 1931–1932 was dreadful. By March 1932 there were 12 million jobless. In January 1933 the number out of work was 14.5 million and in March, the most desperate month in history, more than 15 million people were jobless, about 30 percent of the labor force.

One of the New Deal's greatest accomplishments was stopping the slide and reversing its direction. By October 1933 the figure for unemployment was down to a little more than 11 million. For the next two years it held around that number. According to Nathan, a sustained recovery began in the summer of 1935 that continued until October 1937. The BLS annual unemployment estimate for 1937 was 7.7 million, suggesting about 7 million at the top of the boomlet. Nonagricultural unemployment, Nathan calculated, dropped to 6.3 million in September 1937. During the late summer and fall of 1937 the recovery collapsed. The annual estimate of joblessness in 1938 climbed to 10.4 million. Improvement began, slowly at first, in the summer of 1938. Thereafter the impact of the war in Europe and the Far East significantly reduced unemployment in the United States. When America entered the war in December 1941 (reliable monthly data were now available), the number of persons unemployed was down to 3.8 million.

Economic decline during the Depression had a formidable impact upon the incomes of those workers fortunate enough to have jobs. Annual earnings of full-time employees in all industries fell from $1405 in 1929 to $1048 in 1933. In manufacturing the drop was from $1543 to $1086, in mining from $1526 to $990, and in construction from $1674 to $869. Average weekly earnings of production workers in manufacturing peaked in May 1929 at $25.51. Then they slid down, at first slowly and later accelerating, to a bottom of $14.86 in March 1933. In bituminous coal weekly earnings averaged $25.11 in 1929. The trough was reached in April 1933 – $10.37. As distressing as these data are, they conceal the scandalously low wages paid to marginal workers, such as young women, blacks, children, and farm laborers. They earned as little as a nickel or a dime an hour.

Wages started to move up in 1933. Average annual earnings for full-time employees advanced every year from 1933 to 1941, but they did not surpass the 1929 top until 1941, when they were $1443. Weekly earnings in manufacturing followed the same pattern with occasional dips. They exceeded the 1929 peak in September 1940 and reached $32.01 in December 1941. Weekly earnings in coal passed those of 1929 in December 1940 and were $32.33 in the month of Pearl Harbor. These wage gains were attributable to rising employment, the NRA and the Fair Labor Standards Act, and growing union power.

Economic disaster ineluctably produced social disorganization. The Lynds returned to Middletown (Muncie, Indiana) in 1935, a decade after their original field work. "The City," they wrote, "had been shaken for nearly six years by catastrophe. . . . The great knife of the depression had cut down impartially through the entire population." This was evident in that basic institution, the family.

A large number of young people either did not marry at all or deferred wedlock because of hard times. In the nation the number of marriages dropped from 1,233,000 in 1929 to 982,000 in 1932, the lowest level ever recorded. Recovery began in 1933, and the figure rose steadily thereafter except in 1938, the recession year. In Middletown's county the number of marriages declined from 753 in 1929 to 478 in 1932. Samuel A. Stouffer and Lyle M. Spencer reckoned that 794,000 marriages had been "lost" nationally by 1933.

The decline in marriage, along with other factors, led to a marked falloff in the birthrate. The number of live births per 1000 of population was 21.3 in 1930. It declined to between 18 and 19 during the decade and did not surpass the 1929 rate until 1942. In Middletown the birthrate fell from 21.9 in 1929 to 18.4 in 1933. This was the era of the "Depression generation," that exceptionally small cohort born during the thirties.

The housing crisis struck many families a heavy blow. The number of housing starts in urban areas plummeted from 400,000 in 1929 to 45,000 in 1933 and did not recover fully until 1941. A larger population, therefore, had to squeeze into a smaller stock of eroding housing. In Middletown, the total number of houses built during the six years 1930–1935 was one third of those constructed in 1928 alone. Over 40 percent of the dwellings in town were more than 40 years old, while 35 percent were 20 to 40 years of age. A large proportion had no hot water (13 percent had no running water), bathtub, inside toilet, or central heating. The number of foreclosures increased more than tenfold, and renters were constantly being evicted. The people who took to the road slept under bridges or lived in Hoovervilles. Quite a few families in Middletown moved back to the farm. Many doubled up. "Light housekeeping" increased sharply. That is, a family that wanted to keep the sheriff away rented part of its house to another family. These options both degraded the quality of housing and increased crowding.

The impact of sharply lower income upon the family as an institution, contemporary studies show, was complex. Families that were integrated and adaptable made the adjustments to hard times and in some cases came through strengthened. Families that were internally weak and inflexible suffered in many ways. Worry, irritation, and discouragement were widespread. Families that treasured their self-reliance felt disgraced by accepting relief. In many cases anxiety turned into depression as manifested by "nervous breakdowns," alcoholism, and threatened or actual suicides. Dishonesty was widespread; sometimes rational — stealing food, refusing to pay rent, or tapping into utility lines — and sometimes irrational — mindless shoplifting. When the pressures became too heavy, families disintegrated.

In a society with sharply defined sex roles, particularly in the working class, mass unemployment undermined the husband-father. No longer the provider, he lost authority and face with his wife and children, particularly if his spouse or daughter supplied the income. Remaining at home increased family disillusionment and conflict. Most men bitterly resented the loss of authority and manifested their feelings in irritability, alcoholism, unfaithfulness, and child abuse.

Loss of income and family disintegration led to that extraordinary Depression expression of social disorganization — transiency. Historically, the American hobo had been a single man. He was now joined by single women and by families, some headed by women. An enormous number of people took to the road. While no one knew how many, the Tolan Committee, using the first social security data, estimated that there were 4 million transients in 1937. The flow tended to move south and west, because one could better weather a winter in the open in a mild climate and because the Far West, particularly California, retained the image of the land of golden opportunity.

Generally speaking, there were four categories of transients: traditional single men, new single men, families, and the special case — Okies. In 1933 the Federal Emergency Relief Administration made grants to the states for shelters and camps. By February 1934, 44 states and the District of Columbia were assisting 300,000 homeless persons. This program allowed for study of the first three categories of transients. Information about the Okies came from many sources, including the Farm Security Administration that assisted them.

Edwin H. Sutherland and Harvey J. Locke studied traditional homeless men in the Chicago shelters in 1934–1935. There was a minority core of historical residents of Hobohemia — bums, home guard casuals (men who had worked at odd jobs in the city), and migratory laborers (who had worked casually in agriculture, on the railroads, and in lumber). The majority had been reasonably steady workers who had lost their jobs and could find no others. The blacks, who fitted into all these categories, nevertheless formed a special group.

All of these men entered the shelters because they were destitute and had no families. The great majority had been unskilled workers, had very little education, scored low on intelligence tests, had separated from their parents at an early age, had not married, and lacked social contacts. The average age was forty-five, which meant that about half of them had virtually no prospect of employment. Half were immigrants, particularly from Poland. Excepting the blacks, most of whom had migrated from the South, the majority had lived in Chicago before entering the shelter. These were lonely men without hope.

John N. Webb analyzed a quarter of a million persons who were assisted by the FERA transient program in 13 cities in 1934–1935, 80 percent of whom were homeless individuals. Unemployment was the primary reason they had taken to the road. Two thirds of the unattached persons were between ages sixteen and thirty-five. Only 2 percent were female. The overwhelming majority were native whites, with sprinklings of blacks and foreign-born. Two thirds had completed at least grade school. Almost all were physically capable of working and were eager to find jobs. The great majority came from urban areas, only a small number from farms. For these homeless people migration was frustrating both because they rarely knew their destination and because few located work.

Webb concluded that they differed little from the jobless who stayed home. The main distinction was that they were younger, which suggested that they were more energetic and restless and needed an escape from idleness.

Webb and Malcolm Brown studied 5489 interstate migrant families in transient shelters in 85 cities in September 1935. Again, unemployment was the main reason for moving. Most of them traveled by automobile and headed for a predetermined destination, usually a short distance, where they knew someone. The places of both origin and destination were predominantly urban. Very few of these families were chronic wanderers.

The heads of the migrant families were relatively young, half of them under thirty-five. The families were small, an average of 3.1 persons. They were overwhelmingly native-born whites. Slightly over half of the individuals were female and 14 percent of the heads of families were women. Three fifths of the family heads had completed at least grade school. Two thirds were employable and wanted work. The others had physical handicaps (usually a chronic disease), were too old, or were mothers of small children. An unusually large proportion had been semi-skilled laborers, skilled workmen, or white-collar workers.

The Okies were farm people from the semi-arid Great Plains who had been pushed out by drought and the mechanization of agriculture and who trekked overwhelmingly to California. They had raised cotton back home and headed for the cotton ranches in the San Joaquin Valley. Between 300,000 and 400,000 Okies came to California. Like the Joads, they traveled by automobile and in families. Of native white stock, they were farm people who moved from one rural area to another. They were eager to work and many did so, at first in agriculture and later in defense plants. Their migration stirred up a storm of protest.

Throughout the decade, settled communities found the transients extremely unsettling. This was evident in Middletown. In the early Depression years housewives became upset when "tramps" begged for or stole food. The city, therefore, welcomed the FERA shelter on the outskirts of town, which housed and fed 300 homeless men. But, when federal funds ran out in 1935, the city promptly shut the camp down. Middletown would take care of "our own," but would not pay for someone else's needy. Panhandlers now roamed the streets and slept in City Hall. Most people said that was a police problem.

In California, hatred of the Okies bordered on hysteria. Walter J. Stein wrote, "The malnourished physique of the migrants, the deplorable settlements along the ditch banks, even the slightly nasal drawl . . . were the touchstones for a stereotype of the Okie as a naturally slovenly, degraded, primitive subspecies of white American." The police hounded them, the churches ignored them, public health officials warned of epidemics along the ditches, school systems groaned under the load of their laggard children. In 1936, Police Chief Davis of Los Angeles converted 150 of his officers into a frontier legion that established an unconstitutional "bum blockade" at the points of entry along the California border. Here they rousted, searched, and evicted those migrants they considered undesirable.

Transiency was a form of social unrest, silent protests by individuals and families who could no longer maintain settled lives. But it was atomized and inchoate, an admission of defeat. Far more serious forms of protest emerged during the Great Depression, particularly between the stock market crash of 1929 and the presidential election of 1936. This unrest crested in three waves of mounting size and intensity.

The first ran for two years, from the onset of the Depression until the fall of 1931. While unemployment was serious and steadily worsened, it was not yet disastrous, and the society, including the economy, functioned. Further, President Hoover, high officials of his administration, and leading bankers and industrialists issued a stream of cheerful prognoses. If one believed them, and many did, the system would soon correct itself. The jobless, on the other hand, were melancholy and defeated. They blamed themselves for their troubles. They merely stole food and occasionally threatened storekeepers if it was not given to them.

Only Marxists, who, of course, rejected the system, tried to galvanize and organize unrest. The Socialist Party established urban unemployed councils, starting in 1929, to agitate for relief and public works. But the party's appeal under Norman Thomas was to middle-class intellectuals rather than to jobless workers. Its only success, an extremely modest one, was in Chicago. The Communists were more effective. They staged unemployment demonstrations in 1930 in Cleveland, Philadelphia, Chicago, Los Angeles, and New York. Several involved confrontations with the police, got wide press coverage, and helped make joblessness a national issue.

The second wave of unrest began during the winter of 1931–1932 and continued until the New Deal took office on March 4, 1933. Now a "severe recession" became the Great Depression. Unemployment rose to astronomical heights and the economy, including the banking system, came unstuck. People in high places, themselves frightened, no longer forecast a quick turnaround. Desperate workers began to take matters into their own hands.

By 1932, the Unemployed Citizens' League in the State of Washington was said to have 80,000 members. It stressed self-help, relief, and jobs and was important in the 1932 Seattle mayoralty election. The Unemployed Cooperative Relief Association established self-help cooperatives in Southern California. By the end of 1932 there were 330 self-help organizations in 37 states, with an asserted membership of over 300,000. They relied mainly on bartering work for food.

In the summer of 1932, unorganized hosiery and furniture workers in over 100 mills around High Point, North Carolina, struck spontaneously against wage cuts and turned to violence. By that time jobless workers were stealing food almost everywhere. The chain stores did not call the police because they feared the publicity. In northeastern Pennsylvania anthracite coal bootlegging became an important industry. Though it was a form of stealing, it was approved by both the constituted authorities and the public. At its peak the bootlegging employed 15,000 to 20,000 men.

There were four large demonstrations. The Communists staged a national Hunger March on Washington on December 7, 1931. While the advance ballyhoo promised a huge crowd, only 1570 "marchers" rode into town in trucks singing "The Internationale." Father James R. Cox, a Pittsburgh radio priest, led 12,000 Pennsylvanians to Washington on January 7, 1932, demanding federal relief. The most important Communist demonstration was the Ford Hunger March in Dearborn, Michigan, on March 7, 1932. A crowd of 3000, mainly unemployed, walked from downtown Detroit to Dearborn to present demands to the Ford Motor Company. The Dearborn police tried to halt them at the Detroit line. The marchers defiantly moved into the town, and the police responded with tear gas and, that failing, with gunfire. Four marchers were killed and at least fifty were seriously wounded.

The greatest of the second-wave demonstrations was the Bonus Army march on Washington in the summer of 1932. Under a congressional compromise, ex-servicemen would receive a deferred bonus in 1945. Since great numbers of veterans were out of work, a bill was introduced for immediate payment. Veterans from across the nation spontaneously descended upon Washington, riding the rods, hitchhiking, or driving jalopies. The Bonus Army probably came to 22,000 men. They intended to stay in town until the bill was enacted and, with the assistance of the Washington police, settled into encampments. The House passed the measure on June 15. But the Senate overwhelmingly rejected it two days later, sparing Hoover the odium of a veto. Nevertheless, the veterans refused to leave town and more joined them. Hoover's patience wore out. On July 28, 1932, he sent in the Army, commanded by General Douglas MacArthur, to burn the encampments and to drive the Bonus Army out of the District of Columbia. A handful of people died, and more than 1000 were gassed. The incident exposed the bankruptcy of the federal government in the face of massive unemployment.

Unrest in the third wave differed markedly. Now employment was rising and the government had emerged as a friend of the jobless. Defeatism gave way to hope and millions of aggrieved people voiced a primal scream. The trade union became a basic means of expressing unrest.

The labor movement during the first four years of the Depression had suffered losses in membership, income, and power in virtual silence. In 1933, as jobs increased and wages rose and with the encouragement of Section 7(a) of the National Industrial Recovery Act, workers streamed into the unions. Many employers, particularly large manufacturing corporations, both refused to bargain with the unions and tried to smash them. Nineteen thirty-four was a year of confrontation. There were 1856 work stoppages, involving almost a million and a half workers, largely over the issue of union recognition. Equally important, there were four big and violent strikes of historic significance — auto parts workers in Toledo, truck drivers in Minneapolis, longshoremen and then virtually the whole labor movement around San Francisco Bay, and cotton-textile workers in New England and the South.

Labor unrest continued into the next year. But 1935 was particularly noted for the passage of the Wagner Act, intended to protect the right of workers to organize and bargain collectively, and for the formation by John L. Lewis of the Committee for Industrial Organization, which vigorously organized in the mass-production industries. But again there was confrontation. Many employers refused to comply with the new law on the ground that it was unconstitutional. Until the Supreme Court struck down this theory in 1937, labor had no option but to strike for recognition. The number of work stoppages rose to 2014 in 1935, 2176 in 1936, and 4740 in 1937.

Labor unrest in the third wave was accompanied by political ferment outside the historic two-party system. Many deeply troubled Americans searched for easy solutions.

Embryonic fascists, who amounted to little, and populist demagogues, who won wide followings, preyed upon public fears and hopes. The Detroit radio priest, Father Charles E. Coughlin, attracted enormous audiences and contributions for his broadcasts. His preachings were a goulash of anti-Communism, anticapitalism, remonetization of silver, opposition to international bankers, anti-Semitism, and, after a grace period, anti–New Dealism. Dr. Francis E. Townsend of Long Beach, California, gained a huge following for his nostrum of giving each old person $200 a month on condition that he spend it within 30 days. Senator Huey P. Long, Jr., "the Kingfish," who had established one-man rule in Louisiana, now moved on to take over the nation. His Share-Our-Wealth scheme would guarantee every family a $5000 allowance, an annual income of $2000, and an "adequate" pension for the aged. He hired Gerald L. K. Smith, a fundamentalist preacher with a bull voice, to run the plan. By 1935 Smith claimed 7 million followers. Almost everyone, Roosevelt included, assumed that Long was running for President when he was cut down by an assassin's bullet in Baton Rouge on September 8, 1935.

A group of native radicals rose to prominence. Governor Floyd B. Olson of Minnesota, who said he was "radical as hell," was the darling of the Farmer-Labor movement. He detested American capitalism and thought the Depression had finished it off. Olson spoke vaguely about "the ultimate cooperative commonwealth." In nearby Wisconsin, the La Follettes, Senator Bob and Governor Phil, ran the Progressive Party. Their rhetoric was less inflamed than Olson's and their methods were more pragmatic. Phil said they wanted "a cooperative society based on American traditions." Upton Sinclair, the prominent novelist and a lifelong Socialist, captured the Democratic nomination for governor of California in 1934. Only a formidable opposition prevented Sinclair from winning with his EPIC plan (End Poverty in California).

The Marxist parties were beset with problems. The Socialists had no mass base and the New Deal drew off much of the small intellectual and trade-union following that remained. The Communists disillusioned American radicals by jerking with every jump in Stalin's line. Their main success was within the CIO, for which Lewis deliberately recruited them as zealous organizers. They established strongholds in a handful of unions, mainly small ones.[1]

2

The caring society erected by the New Deal consisted of many elements: unemployment relief, a variety of attacks on joblessness, unemployment insurance, old-age pensions, welfare programs, wage, hour, and child-labor standards, and protection of the right of workers to organize and bargain collectively. Two important groups in the

American labor force, women and blacks, went uncared for except insofar as they were covered by the broad programs.

Politically considered, the Roosevelt Administration's labor legislation was crowded into two years, 1933 and 1935, the so-called First and Second New Deals. During the Hundred Days in 1933, Roosevelt got whatever he wanted from Congress. The longer-term statutes — the Social Security Act, the National Labor Relations Act, and WPA — were enacted in 1935 by the overwhelmingly Democratic Congress elected in the landslide of 1934. After 1936, the country and the Congress moved to the right, and further changes became almost impossible. The passage of the Fair Labor Standards Act in 1938 was the exception, but its enactment was an ordeal and exacted a heavy price in a weakened law.

Perhaps the most urgent task facing the federal government in 1933 was relief for the destitute jobless. Roosevelt signed the Federal Emergency Relief Act on May 12 and named Harry Hopkins as Administrator. He had $500 million for grants to the states for unemployment relief, sums that they would match. FERA provided both direct and work relief. By October, 3 million families, 12.5 million persons, were receiving assistance. Despite bitter local resistance, Hopkins insisted upon relief for blacks in the South.

When the revival of employment topped out in the fall of 1933, Hopkins persuaded Roosevelt of the need for a work-relief program to get through the winter. An executive order on November 8 established the Civil Works Administration, funded jointly by FERA and the Public Works Administration. In general, CWA built short-term and PWA long-term projects. Hopkins had 4 million people on the rolls by December 15, 1933. CWA got the country through a rugged winter with virtually no unrest and closed down in the spring of 1934. In fact, CWA was an extraordinary administrative feat. The success persuaded Roosevelt and Hopkins to convert FERA into a predominantly work-relief program.

This was accomplished in the Emergency Relief Appropriation Act of May 6, 1935, which provided $4.88 billion, mostly for the Works Progress Administration headed by Hopkins. With the cooperation of local government agencies, WPA completed an enormous number of projects between 1935 and 1942, mostly involving the construction and repair of public facilities. There were, in addition, a number of community service programs. Finally, WPA assisted the arts and scholarship — music, writing, painting and sculpture, theater, and historical records. The administrative costs were extremely low, allowing the beneficiaries to receive almost all of the funds spent. While the number of jobless workers on the rolls varied in relation to the volume of unemployment, WPA hired about one fourth of those persons who were out of work. The wages were lower than those paid in the private sector and higher than direct relief payments. WPA had an antidiscrimination policy for the aged, women, and blacks, which was moderately successful.

The Civilian Conservation Corps, established on March 21, 1933, provided work relief for unemployed young men in the conservation of natural resources. CCC projects were designed to preserve renewable resources — forest, grassland, wildlife, soil, and water. Employment peaked at more than half a million in 1935 and stabilized around 300,000 for the latter part of the decade. Administrative costs were low and the price of keeping a man in the woods for a year was about $1000. CCC sought with limited success to eliminate racial discrimination against blacks. The program was extremely popular, both because it conserved resources and because it improved the health, job skills, and education of the enrollees. The National Youth Administration, established on June 26, 1935, supplemented CCC by providing assistance to young people of both sexes in order to complete their education.

The problem of unemployment that Roosevelt confronted was massive, complex, and intractable. By disposition eclectic, he experimented with a number of policies. During the Hundred Days the New Deal launched three programs — NRA to raise prices and wages, devaluation of the dollar, and the pumping up of federal investment with public works (PWA) and jobless relief (FERA and CCC). Along with a restoration of public confidence, they succeeded in halting the economic slide and in adding several million jobs. But the boomlet flattened out in the fall of 1933 and little else was tried for two years.

A second and more sustained recovery began in 1935, caused both by increased federal expenditures under the Emergency Relief Appropriation Act and payment of the soldiers' bonus and by a sharp rise in consumer spending. This advance broke two years later in the severe recession that struck in the fall of 1937. Roosevelt, who had cut back on federal spending as the economy gained, now seemed at sea over policy. Although Keynes had published *The General Theory* in 1936 and many of the President's advisers urged Keynesian fiscal policies, Roosevelt held back. By the spring of 1938 the dismal economy forced him to launch a two-pronged program. One was a Keynesian appropriation of $3.75 billion for work relief, public works, and government loans. The other was a sharp step-up in antitrust enforcement to stimulate competition and lower prices, the opposite of the earlier NRA program.

War broke out in Europe in 1939. Orders from Britain and France and American rearmament, of course, stimulated the economy and put the United States on the road to wartime full employment.

The Social Security Act of 1935 introduced fundamental structural changes in order to limit the hazards of American society — unemployment insurance, old-age pensions, and permanent welfare programs. Unemployment compensation was set up as a joint federal-state program, with the United States retaining general supervisory controls and the states gaining authority over administration and the amount and duration of benefits. By 1937, all of the states had joined the system. At the outset, a substantial number of categories of workers was excluded from coverage. On the theory that joblessness was a cost of doing business, the system was financed by a tax on employers, with the revenues going into the Unemployment Trust Fund in the U.S. Treasury. Between 1937 and 1939 all of the states began to pay benefits, and by the latter year the system was working quite effectively.

The old-age insurance system was wholly federal. It was financed by a tax on both the employer and the employee, but only on the first $3000 of annual earnings. The money was deposited in the Old-Age Insurance Fund in the Treasury. An employee would qualify for a pension at age sixty-five provided that he had worked for at least five years and had lifetime earnings of $2000. Under the 1935 law the benefits would be modest and would not start until 1942. Little more than half the employed labor force was covered. Setting the system up was a gigantic administrative task that was accomplished with great speed and efficiency. Because of a rapid build-up in reserves, Congress significantly amended the law in 1939. The payment of benefits would begin in 1940. In addition to the retired worker, who alone had qualified under the original scheme, coverage was now extended to his dependents and survivors.

The Social Security Act also established three categorical public assistance programs that began payments in 1936. Large numbers of jobless old people in dire need could not qualify under the pension program. They were provided with old-age assistance. There was a relatively small number of families without a male breadwinner in which the mother was unable to support her dependent children. They were given "mothers' pensions," a program later known as Aid to Families with Dependent Children. Finally, a small program assisted the blind.

The Fair Labor Standards Act of 1938 established labor standards for industries in interstate commerce, but with severely restricted coverage. The minimum wage was fixed at 25 cents in 1938, rising to 30 cents the next year, and with the prospect of 40 cents in 1945. The standard workweek was 44 hours in 1938, 42 in 1939, and 40 in 1940. Employers were free to work their employees longer hours, but they were required to pay a penalty of time and a half for the excess. The employment of children under age sixteen was prohibited.

The New Deal's collective-bargaining policy emerged in Section 7(a) of the National Industrial Recovery Act of 1933, was refined in the 1934 amendments to the Railway Labor Act, and took final shape in the National Labor Relations Act of 1935. This policy embraced the following basic principles: Workers shall be free to associate and to select representatives for collective bargaining; employers shall not interfere in the exercise of these rights; employees may elect their own representatives and the choice of the majority shall govern all; and employers shall recognize and bargain with representatives so selected. Since many employers refused to comply with the rules and procedures of the National Labor Relations Board because, they argued, the law was unconstitutional, the system did not start to operate until the Supreme Court sustained the validity of the Wagner Act in 1937. Thereafter, the law and the Board provided the underpinning for a rapid increase in union membership and the widespread acceptance of collective bargaining.

As stated earlier, the New Deal did relatively little to assist two groups in the labor force, women and blacks, who suffered the most from both historic discrimination and the impact of the Depression. Working women entered the troubled decade under heavy disabilities. According to the 1930 census, their employment was highly concentrated in "women's jobs" — clerical, domestic service, other personal service, and sales. The same was true in the professions — teaching, nursing, social work, and librarianship. Female earnings were much lower than male. Average hourly earnings of women production workers in selected manufacturing industries in 1929 were 39.8 cents compared to 62.5 cents for men. Average weekly female earnings were $17.61 in contrast with $30.64 for males.

While there are no data on unemployment rates for the sexes, there can be no doubt that the Depression severely eroded female job opportunities. It is a certainty that women sustained a devastating loss of income. Average hourly earnings in manufacturing fell to 32.5 cents and weekly earnings to $11.73 by 1932. Some of the wage rates defy belief. Here are a few collected by Lois Scharf: Early in 1933 a skilled garment operator was netting 58 cents for a nine-hour day. In Texas many domestic servants received $1 a week. Black girls sold their labor on street-corner "slave markets" in the Bronx for 9 cents to 15 cents a day. Industrial homework revived. Women, often with their children, worked on knit goods for 5 cents an hour, 70 hours a week.

Women's earnings were lower than men's both because they were segregated into lower-paying jobs and because they earned less than men for performing the same work. Women's organizations were shocked to learn that many NRA codes signed by the President approved sex differentials. Almost a fourth of the 465 codes established rates 14 to 30 percent lower for women.

The New Deal jobless relief programs had the effect, though not the intent, of discriminating against females. PWA, FERA, CWA, and WPA concentrated on construction projects that employed men overwhelmingly. For example, only 7 percent of CWA employment was female. The CCC program was for young men. At the insistence of Mrs. Roosevelt, 86 camps were established for young women, but only 6400 persons were enrolled.

Perversely, the most important public-policy issue of the decade was the movement to deny jobs to married women. For many Americans of both sexes, kicking women out of the labor force was the solution to unemployment. Opposition to jobs for married women was extremely popular. George Gallup said he had never seen people "so solidly united in opposition as on any subject imaginable including sin and hay fever." In the Economy Act of 1932 Congress, after extolling the virtues of the American home looked after by a wife, required that in reductions in force in federal employment the spouse of a government employee must be the first to be fired. After a year 1505 women had lost their jobs and 186 others had resigned to protect their husbands. In 1939 there were "married persons clauses" bills in twenty-six state legislatures, though only Louisiana passed one. Married female teachers, whose position had always been precarious, came under sharp attack. Many school districts refused to hire them and required women to terminate employment upon marriage.

The fundamental problem during the thirties was that equal rights for women was simply not a significant political issue. The women's organizations — the Women's Trade Union League, the General Federation of Women's Clubs, the National Consumers' League, the YWCA, and the Women's Bureau of the Department of Labor — had no clout and were safely ignored. In a society in which traditional roles were almost universally accepted by both sexes, discrimination was assumed. The Equal Rights Amendment, which had originated in the early twenties, split the supporters of women's rights, many favoring protective legislation over a constitutional assertion of equality. In the thirties ERA was a nonissue. Though, as Susan Ware has pointed out, women occupied higher positions in the New Deal than in any prior administration and constituted a "women's network," they accomplished little for their sex except as role models, particularly Eleanor Roosevelt and Frances Perkins.

The position of blacks was far worse because it rested on virtually universal discrimination. Gunnar Myrdal, in his decisive study *An American Dilemma,* summed it up:

> The economic situation of the Negroes in America is pathological. Except for a small minority enjoying upper or middle class status, the masses of American Negroes in the rural South and in the segregated slum quarters in Southern and Northern cities, are destitute. They own little property; even their household goods are mostly inadequate and dilapidated. Their incomes are not only low but irregular. They thus live from day to day and have scant security for the future.

Most blacks lived in the South, the most backward section of the nation, and were heavily concentrated in cotton agriculture, which was extremely depressed. Few owned their own land; rather, they were in "the lowest occupations as sharecroppers or wage laborers." There were virtually no northern black farmers. Myrdal continued:

> Nonagricultural Negro workers are, for the most part, either in low-paid service occupations or have menial tasks in industry. Few are skilled workers. Most of the handicrafts and industries in the South where they have a traditional foothold are declining. The majority of manufacturing industries do not give jobs to Negroes. Neither in the South nor in the North are Negroes in professional, business, or clerical positions except in rare instances and except when serving exclusively the Negro-public — and even in this they are far from having a monopoly.

The American labor market was racially stratified. The upper tier consisted of white jobs and white industries, the lower of black jobs and black industries. The latter were, as Myrdal put it, "undesirable from one or several viewpoints." Many carried a "social stigma" because they were at the bottom of the occupational ladder and because they were historically "Negro jobs." Wages were very low, especially in the South. Men's jobs were largely outdoors and subject to frequent layoffs due to bad weather. They were also unstable because of linkage to the business cycle. Many were physically strenuous, repetitive, dangerous, and unpleasant. Since black incomes were so inadequate, more black than white women entered the labor market. They were heavily concentrated in domestic and other personal service jobs, particularly in the South, where wages were very low.

While there are no statistics, it is clear that the black unemployment rate exceeded the white prior to the Depression. That calamity must have widened the differential markedly. At the end of 1932 a black sociologist estimated that a third of his race was jobless and another third was underemployed. At that time the unemployment rate for blacks in Harlem was said to be 40 to 50 percent, over 56 percent in Philadelphia, more than 40 for males and 55 percent for females in Chicago and Detroit, and, evidently, much higher in Gary. In the urban South frightened jobless whites fought for traditional "Negro jobs" as street cleaners, garbage collectors, hotel and restaurant employees, elevator operators, and domestic servants. In Atlanta, racists chanted, "No Jobs for Niggers until Every White Man Has a Job!" In Mississippi, white railroad workers terrorized black firemen to drive them off locomotives. The collapse of cotton devastated black workers in southern agriculture.

In a real though not a political sense the condition of the black worker, urban and rural, was the New Deal's most intractable problem. Roosevelt's government committed itself to the exercise of federal power in order to help those in need, and no other group had such great need. Strong voices within the Administration — notably Eleanor Roosevelt and Harold Ickes and, with time, Harry Hopkins and Aubrey Williams — made this argument eloquently. But the opposition was formidable. Roosevelt was the leader of the Democratic Party, and the old Confederacy was a basic constituency. With a house in Warm Springs, he passed himself off as a "Georgian." Until 1936, the Democratic convention required a two-thirds vote to nominate a candidate for President, giving the South a veto. Under the seniority system, Senators and Representatives from the South dominated the committees of both houses of Congress, whose support Roosevelt needed. American industry almost universally and systematically discriminated against black workers. Most of the labor movement, especially the craft unions, took the same hard line. At the outset of the New Deal the civil rights organizations — the National Association for the Advancement of Colored People (NAACP), the Urban League, and the Brotherhood of Sleeping Car Porters — were weak and ineffective. Finally, black voters, that minority who went to the polls, historically supported the party of Lincoln.

Nonetheless, the era of the Great Depression, Harvard Sitkoff has written, was a fateful and painful "turning point in race relations." It was a time of "rising black expectations and decreasing Negro powerlessness, an age of diminishing white indifference to the plight of Afro-Americans." While the tangible gains were modest, they constituted the first significant reversal in the status of blacks in American society since Reconstruction.

At the outset, the New Deal made only one major commitment to destitute blacks: relief. Legally, jobless black workers became entitled to the same benefits as white workers under FERA, CWA, CCC, PWA, and WPA. In fact, however, there was discrimination, particularly in the South. Blacks had more trouble getting onto the rolls and often received lesser benefits. Governor Eugene Talmadge of Georgia, for example, flatly rejected equal treatment of the races as laid down in Washington, and white families in Atlanta received almost twice the relief payments as black. In the Deep South, young black men found it hard to get into the CCC, and when they succeeded, most were put into segregated camps. Even Ickes was forced to discriminate on PWA projects in the South.

Despite these failings, black people regarded the New Deal as a great stride forward. Federal relief, Samuel Lubell has written, was "almost like manna from God." In 1933 there were 2 million blacks on the rolls and their number rose to 3.5 million by 1935. WPA became "an economic floor for the whole Negro community," lifting the bargaining power of the entire race.

For the rest, the early New Deal substantially ignored blacks. While the NRA codes did not fix racial wage differentials, regional differentials had much the same effect. When employers were required to pay white and black workers the same wage, they gave the jobs to whites. There were no NRA codes for agriculture and domestic service, which constituted 70 percent of black employment. Under the Agricultural Adjustment Administration's cotton program, white landlords received the lion's share of government payments, leaving little for black tenants. The acreage-reduction program forced eviction on many blacks. The National Labor Relations Act conferred exclusive representation upon certified unions. During the legislative history, the NAACP and the Urban League urged that only unions which did not discriminate racially should have this right. Strong AFL opposition killed this proposal.

As the decade advanced, Roosevelt gradually moved toward a more caring position. In part this was because he became better informed about the plight of the black race and also because he found the opposing view morally repugnant. One could hardly ignore the rising number of lynchings during the early Depression years. In 1934, the President merely let it be known that he supported the Costigan-Wagner Anti-lynching bill without bringing pressure on the southern leadership in the Senate to enact it. By 1938, in contrast, he committed himself to the legislation. In addition, Roosevelt appointed more blacks to positions in the federal government, some at quite high levels, than any of his predecessors. There was, in fact, an informal "Black Cabinet." Further, there was a shift in political power. In the 1934 and 1936 elections the Democrats won resounding victories in the North, making the President less dependent upon the southern bloc. The 1936 Democratic convention repealed the two-thirds rule for nominations. In the election that November the black vote swung heavily to Roosevelt and the New Deal. Finally, the civil rights organizations became stronger and a vigorous leadership emerged, particularly Walter White of the NAACP and A. Philip Randolph of the Sleeping Car Porters.

A showdown was inevitable and it came in 1941, as both the military forces and defense plants sharply increased recruitment while either excluding or discriminating against blacks. At a civil rights meeting in Chicago in January the concept of the March-on-Washington Movement emerged, and Randolph promptly took over as leader. The idea was to bring 5000 people to the city to protest. The movement raged like a fire storm through the black communities. By June, Randolph was talking of 100,000 marchers and a "monster" demonstration at the Lincoln Memorial. Everyone, including the President, became convinced that Randolph could deliver.

In June, Roosevelt moved to head off a confrontation. Mrs. Roosevelt and Mayor La Guardia met with Randolph and White in New York to try to persuade them to call off the march. The black leaders flatly refused. On June 18, Roosevelt conferred with Randolph and White at the White House to determine their price. They demanded four executive orders: to forbid government contracts to employers who refused to hire blacks; to end discrimination in the civilian sector of the federal government; to root out discrimination and segregation in the armed forces; and to deny discriminatory unions the benefits of the Wagner Act. This led to six days of hard bargaining between the black leadership and the top military and civilian officials of the government.

A much reduced compromise was reached on June 24 — to forbid discrimination in civilian federal employment and in defense industries. The next day the President issued Executive Order 8802, which established the Committee on Fair Employment Practices to administer this policy. As a condition for the order, the black leaders called off the March-on-Washington. While Roosevelt bought time for the war crisis, which was his main concern, and the FEPC would have only limited effectiveness, for blacks the executive order was a triumph and a portent for the future. They had compelled the federal government to begin to care.[2]

3

During the 1936 presidential campaign the Roosevelt Administration was concerned about Michigan. Historically the state had gone heavily Republican. In 1928, for example, Herbert Hoover had defeated

Al Smith almost three to one. In 1932, even with political "help" from the Depression, Roosevelt had outpolled Hoover by little more than 100,000 votes.

The big question now was how the automobile workers would vote. Harry Hopkins sent Lorena Hickok to Michigan for ten days to find out, and she wrote him a long report on September 19, 1936. The auto workers would go for Roosevelt "anywhere from 75 to 90 percent." He would carry Detroit and the automobile belt in the eastern part of the state by "a thumping big majority." With the Upper Peninsula, that should outweigh Alf Landon's strength in the small towns and rural areas of western Michigan.

A tool-and-die maker at Ford told her that "somewhere around 80 percent of the workmen would vote for the President." A Democratic poll of 200 assembly-line workers in Lansing showed that 180 favored Roosevelt. The pollster could not believe the result and checked 129 homes in a working-class district in the town. One hundred and sixteen were for FDR. In Saginaw, a Republican newspaper publisher told Hickok that Roosevelt would carry the auto towns by "large majorities." At the Buick and Fisher Body plants in Flint the sentiment was "almost solidly Roosevelt." Republican polls among workers in a variety of industries showed FDR out in front, usually by 70–30, in one case by 98–2.

Hickok's sources were reliable. Roosevelt carried Michigan over Landon in November 1936 by 1,016,794 to 699,733. He won in Wayne County (Detroit) 404,055 to 190,732, in Saginaw County 22,592 to 15,527, in Genesee County (Flint) 49,891 to 21,097, in Ingham County (Lansing) 27,086 to 19,434, in Oakland County (Pontiac) 40,329 to 30,071.

While Lorena Hickok probably did not realize it when she wrote her report, she was a witness to a profound transformation in microcosm in the American political system, a peaceful revolution. V. O. Key, Jr., has postulated a theory of "critical elections" in which

> voters are, at least from impressionistic evidence, unusually deeply concerned, in which the extent of electoral involvement is relatively quite high, and in which the decisive results of the voting reveal a sharp alteration in the pre-existing cleavage within the electorate. Moreover, and perhaps this is the truly differentiating characteristic of this sort of election, the realignment made manifest in the voting in such elections seems to persist for several succeeding elections.

Nineteen thirty-six fits Key's criteria precisely. Here Roosevelt forged the New Deal electoral coalition with labor at its core. For the first time since the Civil War the Democratic Party became dominant, and the coalition would persist for at least a generation.

The election results, James MacGregor Burns wrote, "were a tidal wave, an earthquake, a landslide, the blizzard of '36." Roosevelt received 27,478,945 votes, 60.2 percent of the 45,643,297 cast. Landon polled 16,674,665, or 36.5 percent. The minor parties combined got 1,489,687, or 3.3 percent. William Lemke of the Union Party (a coalition of Father Coughlin, Dr. Townsend, and the heirs of Huey Long, held together only by hatred of Roosevelt and a faith in cheap money) received fewer than 900,000 votes. Norman Thomas, the Socialist candidate, polled only 187,572, the party's poorest showing since 1900. Roosevelt carried 46 states, with 523 electoral votes. Landon won only in Maine and Vermont, with 8 electors. Democrats in Congress and in the states rode into office on FDR's coattails. The huge Democratic majorities in the legislature mounted. The margin in the House moved to 334 Democrats to 89 Republicans from 321–104. The Senate ratio became 75 to 17 compared to the former 70–23.

This great victory was won in the northern cities. In all probability no national election in American history was so class-based as that of 1936. The Republicans gained solid backing from the bankers, the industrialists, and the newspaper publishers; the Democrats received the votes of the urban working class.

The pattern of voting shown in the Michigan auto towns appeared in every important northern urban center. FDR, anticipating this result, campaigned vigorously in the cities of the Northeast and Midwest.

Pennsylvania had not voted for a Democrat since James Buchanan in 1856, and even Hoover had defeated Roosevelt by 150,000 votes in 1932. The 1936 Democratic convention was held in Philadelphia, and more than 100,000 wildly enthusiastic people cheered the President's acceptance speech in Franklin Field. Later he drew huge crowds of steelworkers and coal miners in the Pittsburgh district. The streets in Chicago's Loop were jam-packed and there were said to be 150,000 marchers. Cadillac Square in Detroit was a mass of humanity. There were 30,000 people outside the capitol in Providence, and the trip north to Boston brought out huge crowds in every industrial town. The Boston Common was packed with 150,000 people. The return trip through Connecticut was frenzied, and the President had trouble getting back into his vehicle in Stamford. The closing thirty-mile drive in an open car through New York City was greeted by jammed crowds on every block and was capped by the final speech in Madison Square Garden before a roaring, standing, stamping audience. The campaign, Roosevelt said, brought out "the most amazing tidal wave of humanity" he had ever seen.

The presidential vote for Roosevelt and Landon in the twelve largest cities, including FDR's percentage of the two-party ballot, was as follows:

CITY	ROOSEVELT	LANDON	ROOSEVELT PERCENTAGE
New York	1,802,502	665,951	73.0
Chicago	1,253,164	701,206	64.1
Los Angeles	757,351	357,401	67.9
Philadelphia	539,757	329,881	62.1
Detroit	404,055	190,732	67.9
Pittsburgh	366,593	176,224	67.5
Cleveland	311,117	128,947	70.1
St. Louis	260,063	127,887	67.0
Boston	223,732	96,418	69.9
Milwaukee	221,512	54,811	80.2
Baltimore	210,668	97,667	68.3
San Francisco	196,197	65,436	75.0

As Roosevelt amassed these huge majorities in the northern cities, he piled up even larger margins in the important cities of the South — Atlanta, Birmingham, New Orleans, and Houston.

The Republican Party had dominated the northern cities between the 1890s and the 1920s. The shift to the Democrats became evident in the 1928 presidential election. Smith, a lower-class Irish Catholic associated with the Tammany Hall political machine in New York City, carried New York, Cleveland, St. Louis, Milwaukee, and San Francisco and barely lost Pittsburgh and Baltimore. Smith's appeal, Carl N. Degler noted, "was not simply that he was of urban origin but that his Catholicism and Irish background stamped him as a champion of immigrants and the children of immigrants." The flood of newcomers from southern and eastern Europe who entered the United States between the 1890s and 1914 and their offspring, mainly Catholic and Jewish, began to participate politically in large numbers in 1928, and they voted overwhelmingly Democratic. By now these peoples constituted the bulk of the northern urban working class, and many, including women, were casting ballots for the first time. They bore the brunt of the joblessness of the Great Depression; they poured into the unions, especially those in the mass-production industries, in the thirties; they supported the New Deal; and they voted for Roosevelt.

Chicago, according to Kristi Andersen, was a good illustration. The 1930 census showed that only 28 percent of the population was native white of native parentage, and many of them were Irish Catholics. There were large numbers of Germans, Poles, Jews, Italians, Russians, Swedes, Czechs, and blacks. In 1936 there were 505,000 Protestants in contrast with 927,000 Catholics and 363,000 Jews. During the twenties the Republicans had controlled the city under Mayor "Big Bill" Thompson. The issue on which the "ethnics" united was opposition to Prohibition. Anton Cermak, a Czech and a Democrat, took over the anti-Prohibition organization, the United Societies for Local Self-Government. In 1928 the immigrant wards swung heavily to Smith. In 1931 Cermak was elected mayor. (He would be killed by an assassin's bullet aimed at Roosevelt while talking to the President-elect at his motorcade in Miami on February 15, 1933.) In 1936 Roosevelt received 81 percent of the vote in Chicago's immigrant wards.

Blacks were a special case. The majority remained in the South, where they were disfranchised. But the great migration to the northern cities, which began during World War I, had by 1936 brought significant numbers to New York, Chicago, Philadelphia, Detroit, Cleveland, Pittsburgh, St. Louis, Cincinnati, Kansas City, Indianapolis, and Newark. The old black vote had been solidly Republican for "the party of Lincoln." But the 1936 election, Nancy J. Weiss has written, "brought black Americans decisively into the Roosevelt coalition." Both parties, but especially the Democrats, recognized that blacks would vote in substantial numbers and for the first time campaigned for their support. Roosevelt made enormous gains among black voters in all the northern cities and won big majorities in every one but Chicago (his 21 percent share in 1932 rose to 48.8 percent in 1936). "The key to black electoral behavior," Weiss observed, "lay in economics rather than race." Black voters, of course, knew that they were the victims of discrimination, including that in some of the New

Deal programs. "But the point was that they got something, and that kept many families from starving."

Samuel Lubell uncovered another internal migrant stock, native white Americans who had come from Appalachia and the Ozarks to the rubber and auto towns of the Midwest, notably to Akron, Detroit, and Flint. Akron had so many hillbillies that it was called "the capital of West Virginia" and Flint had "little Missouri" and "little Arkansas" neighborhoods. These people signed up in the CIO unions in auto and rubber and were among those who sat down during the great strikes. They joined the European immigrants and the blacks in voting overwhelmingly for Roosevelt in 1936.

The CIO committed itself totally to Roosevelt's reelection. The United Mine Workers gave the Democratic Party almost half a million dollars and other CIO unions matched that amount. John L. Lewis created Labor's Nonpartisan League to support the President and installed George L. Berry of the AFL Printing Pressmen as its chairman. In New York the League established the American Labor Party so that old Socialists could vote for Roosevelt while keeping their distance from Tammany Hall. The CIO, often with help from AFL unions at the local level, campaigned vigorously to get out the labor vote in the cities.

The 1936 election was also significant in that Roosevelt, by preempting the liberal center, shattered both the radical right and the radical left. Even during the campaign the "union" in the Union Party's name came unstuck. Lemke, virtually unknown and colorless, drew little attention. Townsend seemed bewildered and, in any case, was interested only in his Plan, which had been torpedoed by the Social Security Act. Gerald L. K. Smith, campaigning on "the blood memory of Huey Long," stirred audiences by teaching " 'em how to hate." Father Coughlin was frightened by Smith and kept his distance. As the campaign disintegrated, the priest became increasingly shrill and launched vitriolic attacks on Roosevelt and the Jews, which evoked Church disapproval. The Union Party vanished on election day.

The Socialist Party was ravaged by the 1936 election, though the signs of decay had become evident earlier. In 1933, there had been a large defection to Fiorello La Guardia's successful Fusion-Republican campaign for mayor of New York City. Upton Sinclair, a lifelong Socialist, left in 1933 and the next year ran unsuccessfully for governor of California as a Democrat, taking most members of the party with him. Over the succeeding two years the Socialists tore themselves to pieces with internal factionalism, a process in no way eased by an infusion of Trotskyites. In 1936 the unions that had traditionally backed the Socialists, particularly those in the needle trades, deserted the party en masse. This cost far more than votes because these organizations had largely financed the party. Thoroughly discouraged, Norman Thomas was convinced that another presidential campaign would invite disaster. Nevertheless, he allowed himself to be persuaded to run, made a disheartened campaign, and, as he had foreseen, received a miserably small vote. Later, when asked the cause of the Socialist Party's downfall, Thomas said, "It was Roosevelt in a word."

The Communists did not expose themselves to this calamity. In 1935 the Comintern had made a 180-degree turn in its line by proclaiming a "Popular Front" with bourgeois parliamentarians and Socialists against fascism. Under Soviet pressure, the American party, led by Earl Browder, swung behind the new policy with the slogan "Communism Is Twentieth-Century Americanism." While Browder was an ostensible candidate for President in 1936, the party apparatus covertly supported Roosevelt.[3]

4

In 1941, William Temple, Archbishop of York, published a pamphlet entitled "Citizen and Churchman." On the basis of "Christian presuppositions," he rejected "the power state," that is, tyrannical rule by one group of citizens over other groups. Rather, the Archbishop opted for what he called "the welfare state." The term caught on quickly in Britain and shortly after the war spread round the world, including the United States, where it gained general currency by 1949.

No one has ever defined the welfare state in a universally acceptable way. This is to be expected since, by the midtwentieth century, all the democratic industrialized nations had become welfare states, but each with its own unique history and style. Despite these variations, there is, clearly, a two-part core of central ideas that provides a workable definition. The first consists of two preconditions — a democratic society and the preservation of capitalism. Both fenced out the Communist nations, which, though they had some welfare-state features, were totalitarian and anticapitalist. The capitalism that is preserved, however, is not laissez-faire. Rather, the welfare state maintains private property, the profit motive, and free markets where they work effectively. Elsewhere the welfare state asserts social control. Drawing the line is not neat. Piet Thoenes, the Dutch sociologist, has observed:

> A remarkable feature of the Welfare State is that nobody has the courage to propagate it properly and completely. To the socialist it is nothing but semi-socialism, to the liberals only semi-liberalism. To each and all it is an inevitable half-way house; to nobody is it a noble and inspiring ideal.

The second part is the definition itself. While many have been offered, Asa Briggs, the British historian, has been most precise:

> A welfare state is a state in which organized power is deliberately used (through politics and administration) in an effort to modify the play of market forces in at least three directions — first, by guaranteeing individuals and families a minimum income irrespective of the market value of their work or their property; second, by narrowing the extent of insecurity by enabling individuals and families to meet certain "social contingencies" (for example, sickness, old age and unemployment) which lead otherwise to individual and family crises; and third, by ensuring that all citizens without distinction of status or class are offered the best standards available in relation to a certain agreed range of social services.
>
> The first and second of these objects may be accomplished, in part at least, by what used to be called a "social service state," a state in which communal resources are employed to abate poverty and to assist those in distress. The third objective, however, goes beyond the aims of a "social service state." . . . It is concerned . . . with equality of treatment.

In the era of the Great Depression three nations made dramatic advances along the road to the welfare state — Sweden, New Zealand, and the United States. In the case of the two small countries, led by the Social Democrats in Sweden and the Labour Party in New Zealand, this entailed an expansion of programs already in place. In America, where there was little more than a patchwork of state policies mainly devoted to workmen's compensation, Roosevelt's New Deal broke sharply with the past. The caring society was a giant step in the direction of the Briggs definition of the welfare state.

First, individuals and families received a minimum income without regard to the market value of their labor in the relief programs — FERA, CWA, WPA, CCC, and NYA. This was in part the case with public works under PWA. The establishment of a minimum wage, a standard workweek, and the abolition of child labor by NRA and the Fair Labor Standards Act fell under the same rubric. Finally, the encouragement of collective bargaining by the National Labor Relations and Railway Labor Acts indirectly served the same end. Second, individuals and families gained a measure of security against "social contingencies" by the Social Security Act — old-age pensions, unemployment insurance, and the categorical programs to assist the aged, families with dependent children, and the blind. Finally, a movement was begun to afford equality of treatment to all citizens, especially important to blacks, women, and the aged, in the relief programs and, more important for the future, with the creation of the Fair Employment Practices Commission in 1941.

The welfare state emerged in the developed world, including the United States, because it was, as Richard M. Titmuss has noted, "an integral part of industrialization." Modern societies expose individuals and their dependents to hazards — joblessness, old age, poor health, industrial injury and disease, low wages, and so on. At the same time they erode the primary groups that formerly provided protective services — the nuclear family, the parish, the local community. "Within this context," Charles Frankel wrote, "the welfare state . . . cushions the shocks of industrialism." The greatest of these traumas, of course, is unemployment, and "it is unemployment," Briggs observed, "more than any other contingency which has determined the shape and timing of modern welfare legislation." During the thirties, the United States was the world's most industrialized nation, and it suffered from an extremely high unemployment rate.

The ideas that lie behind the welfare state are not new. William A. Robson, writing out of the British experience, pointed to the French Revolution for liberty, equality, and fraternity, to Bentham for the greatest happiness of the greatest number, to Bismarck and Beveridge for social insurance, to the Fabians for public ownership, to Tawney for a renewed emphasis on equality, to Keynes for controlling the trade cycle, to the Webbs for attacking the cause of poverty, among many others. Sidney Fine, in tracing the ideological conflict between laissez-faire and "the general-welfare state" between 1865 and 1901 in the United States, pointed for the latter to spokesmen of the social gospel, to unorthodox economists like Richard T. Ely, John R. Commons, and Simon N. Patten, to the sociologist Lester F. Ward, to the political scientist Woodrow Wilson, along with William James and John Dewey. Their ideas lay behind the Progressive movement, which shaped the thought of Franklin Roosevelt. Frances Perkins studied with Patten. Commons, of course, profoundly influenced the New Deal.

"In no country," Gunnar Myrdal has pointed out, was the welfare state "originally planned in advance." While Myrdal is certainly correct in general, Britain is a semi-exception. The origins of its welfare state go back to the nineteenth century and the additions by the Lloyd George government on the eve of World War I. But the modern British welfare state flows from the "Beveridge Revolution," which occurred during World War II, particularly his reports, *Social Insurance and Allied Services* (1942) and *Full Employment in a Free Society* (1944). At the outset of the first, Beveridge noted that Britain's system had grown "piece-meal." The time had come, he urged, to assert "a comprehensive policy of social progress." The war had cleared the decks for action. "A revolutionary moment in the world's history is a time for revolutions, not for patching." After the war the Labour government acted as Beveridge had recommended.

But there was no American Beveridge. "In Roosevelt's America," Briggs wrote, the welfare state was "the child of improvisation." Frankel called the American welfare state "a postscript to emergency." The programs were adopted "under the spur of necessity, and some at the spur of the moment." This was simply another example of the American predilection for reacting to rather than anticipating crisis. And it certainly was Franklin Roosevelt's style.

In 1908 Sidney Webb's paper "The Necessary Basis of Society" prefigured a central feature of the welfare state as it emerged later in the century. The role of government, Webb argued, was to provide the basis for a civilized society by establishing national *minimum* standards of life. This would create a foundation upon which a capitalist superstructure could be erected. While it is unlikely in the extreme that Roosevelt read Webb's paper, his innate parsimony and congressional recalcitrance made that unnecessary. The New Deal programs were without exception minimal with regard to costs, to benefits paid, and to coverage. This was even the case with the National Labor Relations Act. Except for a certain ambiguity over the duty to bargain, it sought merely to bring the parties to the negotiating table, with the bargaining itself left to them. The inevitable consequence was that in the future there would be constant demands, often successful, to increase benefits, to extend coverage, and to add new programs, all leading to rising costs.

Thus, as Myrdal wrote in 1960, the welfare state was "the end product of a long process of piecemeal, gradually induced changes." Over time it was built into the way Western democratic societies conducted their daily business. The social services, Titmuss observed, are not "phenomena of marginal interest, like looking out of the window on a train journey." Rather, they are "part of the journey itself."

While some differ, many argue that the welfare state is an indispensable precondition to the survival of both democracy and capitalism. Marquis Childs reached this conclusion about Sweden. There, capitalism throve under the "bell-jar" of the welfare state. For Thoenes, who studied a number of European nations, democracy, capitalism, and the welfare state were locked into one piece. Roosevelt consciously undertook the creation of his caring society in order to preserve both American democracy and American capitalism. The welfare state, Frankel wrote, "is a profoundly conservative institution."[4]

5

Lorena Hickok was in Pennsylvania in August 1933 and wrote to Hopkins:

> From the labor standpoint, and among the unemployed, the Federal government is hugely important. . . . You seldom hear the average man say, "I'm a Republican," or "I'm a Democrat." What they say is: "I'm for the President." . . . It is the tremendous popularity of the President that undoubtedly brings the Federal government so prominently into the picture. The soft coal miners, for instance, seem to have no faith at all in anyone save the President. . . . The people on relief generally seem to have the same feeling about him. . . . They look to the Federal government for aid.

The novelist Martha Gellhorn, who also sent in field reports to Hopkins, wrote in November 1934, when she was in the Carolinas:

> Gaston County is my idea of a place to go to acquire melancholia. The only ray of hope is the grand work our own office is doing; it's a kind of desperate job like getting the wounded off the battlefield so that they can die quietly at a base hospital.
>
> But with all this, the employed and the unemployed go on hoping. The President stands between them and despair, and all the violence which desperation can produce.
>
> I am astonished by the good humor, or faith or apathy (or even good sense) of the unemployed; and the still (but not very happily) employed. There are no protest groups. There are no "dangerous reds." If anything, these people are a sad grey; waiting, hoping, trusting. They talk of the President very much as if he were Moses, and they are simply waiting to be led into the promised land.
>
> * * *
>
> Every house I visited — mill worker or unemployed — had a picture of the President. These ranged from newspaper clippings (in destitute homes) to large coloured prints, framed in gilt cardboard. The portrait holds the place of honour over the mantel; I can only compare this to the Italian peasant's Madonna. And the feeling of these people for the President is one of the most remarkable phenomena I have ever met. He is at once God and their intimate friend; he knows them all by name, knows their little town and mill, their little lives and problems. And though everything else fails, he is there, and will not let them down.

Ordinary people with no power and lots of trouble believed that someone in Washington with power cared.[5]

Notes

THE NOTES are grouped by chapter and numbered section here at the back of the volume.

Several manuscript collections are cited. The Franklin D. Roosevelt Library at Hyde Park, New York, has the Roosevelt papers (including his press conferences), the Harry Hopkins papers (including the field reports by Lorena Hickok and Martha Gellhorn), and papers relating to the National Emergency Council, the Federal Emergency Relief Administration, and the Committee on Economic Security. The Harold L. Ickes papers are in the Manuscript Division of the Library of Congress. The papers of Robert F. Wagner are at Georgetown University. A microfilm of the William Green correspondence is at the School of Industrial and Labor Relations at Cornell University. Arthur Krock's reminiscences are in the Oral History Collection at Columbia University.

*

The following short references are used to conserve space:

Irving Bernstein, *The Lean Years* (Boston: Houghton Mifflin, 1960), cited as Bernstein, *Lean Years.*

Irving Bernstein, *The New Deal Collective Bargaining Policy* (Berkeley: University of California Press, 1950), cited as Bernstein, *New Deal Collective Bargaining.*

Irving Bernstein, *Turbulent Years* (Boston: Houghton Mifflin, 1970), cited as Bernstein, *Turbulent Years.*

Bureau of the Census, *Historical Statistics of the United States, Colonial Times to 1957* (Washington: 1960), cited as *Historical Statistics.*

James MacGregor Burns, *Roosevelt: The Lion and the Fox* (New York: Harcourt, Brace, 1956), cited as Burns, *Lion and Fox.*

Interstate Migration, Hearings before or Report of the Select Committee to

Investigate the Interstate Migration of Destitute Citizens, H. R., 76 Cong., 3 sess. (1940), cited as *Tolan Committee Hearings* or *Report.*

Frances Perkins, *The Roosevelt I Knew* (New York: Viking, 1946), cited as Perkins, *Roosevelt.*

Franklin D. Roosevelt, *Public Papers and Addresses,* S. I. Rosenman, comp. (New York: Random House, 1938–1950), cited as Roosevelt, *Public Papers.*

Arthur M. Schlesinger, Jr., *The Coming of the New Deal* (Boston: Houghton Mifflin, 1959), cited as Schlesinger, *Coming of the New Deal.*

Arthur M. Schlesinger, Jr., *The Politics of Upheaval* (Boston: Houghton Mifflin, 1960), cited as Schlesinger, *Politics of Upheaval.*

Robert E. Sherwood, *Roosevelt and Hopkins: An Intimate History* (New York: Harper, 1948), cited as Sherwood, *Roosevelt and Hopkins.*

Studs Terkel, *Hard Times, An Oral History of the Great Depression* (New York: Pantheon, 1970), cited as Terkel, *Hard Times.*

Prologue

1. Thomas Wolfe, *Look Homeward, Angel* (New York: Modern Library, n.d.), 513; Woody Guthrie, *Bound for Glory* (New York: Dutton, 1943), 1.
2. *Tolan Committee Hearings,* pt. 8, 3245–46.
3. *Tolan Committee Report,* 467, 468, 554–82, *Hearings,* pt. 1, 45; pt. 6, 2403, 2404; pt. 9, 3745; pt. 10, 4086, 4087; Leonard Leader, "Los Angeles in the Great Depression" (unpublished Ph.D. dissertation, UCLA, 1972), ch. 10.
4. *Tolan Committee Hearings,* pt. 7, 2902–11; pt. 9, 3608–12; pt. 6, 2394–2402; pt. 3, 906–12; pt. 9, 3733–42; pt. 1, 293–98; pt. 4, 1377–84; pt. 7, 2811–24.
5. Terkel, *Hard Times,* 146.

One

1. Minutes of the National Emergency Council, Jan. 28, 1936.
2. Robert R. Nathan, "Estimates of Unemployment in the United States, 1929–1935," *International Labour Review* 63 (Jan. 1936), 49–73; *Historical Statistics,* 70; United States Steel Corporation memorandum, n.d., Roosevelt Papers; Terkel, *Hard Times,* 34, 36, 42, 45, 47, 50, 51, 82–83, 85–86, 93, 96–97, 98, 104, 106–7, 122, 145, 196, 278, 381, 389, 390, 404, 407, 413, 444, 458, 461; Alfred Kazin, *On Native Grounds* (New York: Reynal & Hitchcock, 1942), 363–64; Martha Gellhorn to Harry Hopkins, Dec. 10, 1934, Hopkins Papers. The Committee on Economic Security considered Nathan's estimates of unemployment too high and did not accept them as "official." Edwin E. Witte, *The Development of the Social Security Act* (Madison: University of Wisconsin Press, 1962), 34.
3. *Federal Aid for Unemployment Relief,* Hearings on S. 5125, Senate Subcommittee on Manufactures, 72 Cong., 2 sess. (1933), pt. 1, pp. 79–80, 124,

347; Sherwood, *Roosevelt and Hopkins,* 31–32; Josephine C. Brown, *Public Relief, 1929–1939* (New York: Holt, 1940), chs. 5–6; Perkins, *Roosevelt,* 183–84; Schlesinger, *Coming of the New Deal,* 263–65; Roosevelt to Lehman, May 19, Lehman to Roosevelt, May 19, 1933, Roosevelt Papers.

4. Sherwood, *Roosevelt and Hopkins,* chs. 1–2; "Harry Hopkins," *Fortune* XII (July 1935), 59; Searle F. Charles, *Minister of Relief, Harry Hopkins and the Depression* (Syracuse: Syracuse University Press, 1963), 25; Arthur Krock, "Reminiscences" (Oral History Research Office, 1950), 64.
5. Brown, *Public Relief,* chs. 7–12; Sherwood, *Roosevelt and Hopkins,* 48; Harry L. Hopkins, *Spending to Save* (New York: Norton, 1936), ch. 4; Harry L. Hopkins, "The Developing National Program of Relief," in *Proceedings of the National Conference of Social Work* (Chicago: University of Chicago Press, 1933), 65–71; Edith Abbott, *Public Assistance, Volume One, American Principles and Policies* (Chicago: University of Chicago Press, 1940), 675–87; Charles, *Minister of Relief,* 28–32; the Ickes quote is from Eric F. Goldman, *Rendezvous with Destiny* (New York: Knopf, 1952), 331; Corrington Gill, "A Study of the Three Million Families on Relief in October 1933," *Annals* 176 (Nov. 1934), 26–33; Lorena A. Hickok to Harry Hopkins, Oct. 2–12, 1933, Hopkins Papers.
6. Sherwood, *Roosevelt and Hopkins,* 50–57; Charles, *Minister of Relief,* ch. 3; *The Secret Diary of Harold L. Ickes, The First Thousand Days, 1933–1936* (New York: Simon and Schuster, 1953), 99–100, 116–17, 119; Hopkins, *Spending to Save,* ch. 5; Winfield Riefler reports, Aug. 22, Sept. 12, Oct. 3, 1933, National Emergency Council Papers; Marriner S. Eccles, *Beckoning Frontiers* (New York: Knopf, 1951), 127; Aubrey Williams to Harry Hopkins, Dec. 11, 1933, FERA Papers; Lt. Col. J.C.H. Lee, "The Federal Civil Works Administration: A Study Covering Its Organization in November 1933 and Its Operations until 31 March 1934," Hopkins Papers. Eccles, at the citation above, recounts a 1938 remark by Mrs. Roosevelt to the President that the then-current economic downturn was the "2d Roosevelt Depression," following that of the fall of 1933. Eccles, of course, agreed.
7. Charles, *Minister of Relief,* ch. 4; Brown, *Public Relief,* 160–63.
8. Witte, *Development of the Social Security Act,* 3–8; Schlesinger, *Coming of the New Deal,* 301–4.

Two

1. Charles McCarthy, *The Wisconsin Idea* (New York: Macmillan, 1912); for an analysis of the thought of John R. Commons, see the essay by Neil W. Chamberlain in *Institutional Economics: Veblen, Commons, and Mitchell Reconsidered* (Berkeley: University of California Press, 1963); Arthur J. Altmeyer, *The Formative Years of Social Security* (Madison: University of Wisconsin Press, 1966), vi–x; Edwin E. Witte, *The Development of the Social Security Act* (Madison: University of Wisconsin Press, 1962), 3–14. It is worth noting that Witte brought one of his students at Wisconsin, Wilbur J. Cohen, to Washington with him in 1934 and that Cohen thereafter was

to be continuously involved with social security until his term as Secretary of Health, Education, and Welfare terminated on January 20, 1969. Senator Paul H. Douglas of Illinois, who had himself been an authority on this subject when he was at the University of Chicago, would say that an expert on social security was anyone with Wilbur Cohen's phone number. The book by Witte deserves explanation. He was much interested in American history and recognized that he was playing a historic role. He, therefore, kept a daily diary. In 1936 he transformed this journal into an organized account at the request of the Committee on Public Administration of the Social Science Research Council. He referred to it as a "memorandum" and did not plan for its publication, though interested persons, myself among them, were allowed to see the manuscript. After his death in 1960, Altmeyer, Cohen, and Professor Robert J. Lampman of the University of Wisconsin arranged for its publication with a foreword by Miss Perkins. This Witte "memorandum," written with his hallmarks — precision and inclusiveness — removes all mystery from the legislative history of the Social Security Act.

2. Roy Lubove, *The Struggle for Social Security, 1900–1935* (Cambridge: Harvard University Press, 1968); Abraham Epstein, *Insecurity: A Challenge to America* (New York: Smith and Haas, 1933); Paul H. Douglas, *Social Security in the United States* (New York: Whittlesey House, 1936), ch. 1; Bernstein, *Lean Years,* ch. 15.
3. Perkins, *Roosevelt,* ch. 23; Schlesinger, *Coming of the New Deal,* 304–9; Roosevelt, *Public Papers,* vol. 3, pp. 287–92; William Graebner, *A History of Retirement* (New Haven: Yale University Press, 1980). The President's stress in the June 8 message upon federal responsibility for economic security caused concern in an influential quarter. Paul Raushenbush, who had written the Wisconsin unemployment insurance law, was the husband of Elizabeth Brandeis, the daughter of Supreme Court Justice Louis D. Brandeis. The Justice was a firm believer in the idea that the states should be encouraged to experiment with social legislation. Before leaving Washington for the Court's summer recess, Brandeis met with Roosevelt to urge him strongly to allow the states to play an important role in the administration of social insurance. *Roosevelt and Frankfurter, Their Correspondence — 1928–1945,* Max Freedman, ann. (Boston: Little, Brown, 1967), 224.
4. Witte, *Development of Social Security;* Social Security Board, *Social Security in America, The Factual Background of the Social Security Act as Summarized from Staff Reports to the Committee on Economic Security* (Washington: 1937); *Report to the President of the Committee on Economic Security* (Washington: Jan. 1935); Roger S. Hoar, *Wisconsin Unemployment Insurance* (South Milwaukee: Stuart, 1934); Charles A. Myers, "Employment Stabilization and the Wisconsin Act" (unpublished Ph.D. dissertation, University of Chicago, 1939); Perkins, *Roosevelt,* ch. 23; Alpheus Thomas Mason, *Harlan Fiske Stone: Pillar of the Law* (New York: Viking, 1956), 408; Thomas H. Eliot, "The Social Security Bill 25 Years After," *Atlantic* (Aug. 1960), 72–75; Paul

Kellogg, *et al.* to Miss Perkins, Dec. 21, 1934, Roosevelt Memorandum to L. Howe, Feb. 4, 1935, Roosevelt Papers; Roosevelt Press Conferences, Jan. 16, 1935, vol. 5, p. 53. The reports of the CES study groups are in *Social Security in America* except for that on health insurance. The modest CES recommendations on that subject, dated November 6, 1935, appear as Appendix III to Witte's book. There is an unpublished "preliminary draft" of a federal-state system of health insurance approved by the executive committee of the Technical Board. "Final Report on Risks to Economic Security Arising out of Ill Health," Mar. 7, 1935, Committee on Economic Security Papers. The aborted battle over national health insurance is set forth in Daniel S. Hirshfield, *The Lost Reform, The Campaign for Compulsory Health Insurance in the United States from 1932 to 1943* (Cambridge: Harvard University Press, 1970), ch. 2. An interesting historical anomaly is that, in the face of the worst cyclical depression in American history, the New Dealers did not basically view the unemployment insurance and old-age pension systems as "stabilizers," that is, as countercyclical forces to shore up aggregate demand in an economic downturn. For Roosevelt, Miss Perkins, Hopkins, Altmeyer, Witte, and the experts who advised CES, these programs raised essentially moral and social issues. While they were aware of the economic effects, they considered them secondary. Alvin Hansen was the only one who clearly anticipated the stabilizer function, which later became a prime justification for the programs. Interview with Arthur J. Altmeyer, Dec. 1, 1954.

5. Abraham Holtzman, *The Townsend Movement, A Political Study* (New York: Bookman, 1963); John Duffy Gaydowski, "Dr. Townsend and His Plan, 1867–1934" (unpublished M.A. thesis, UCLA, 1970); Dr. Francis E. Townsend, *New Horizons, An Autobiography* (Chicago: Stewart, 1943); Schlesinger, *Politics of Upheaval,* ch. 3; Carey McWilliams, *Southern California Country* (New York: Duell, Sloan & Pearce, 1946), 166–71, 240–313; Witte, *Development of Social Security,* 86. For analyses of the economic defects of the Townsend Plan, see Douglas, *Social Security in the United States,* ch. 3; Nicholas Roosevelt, *The Townsend Plan* (Garden City: Doubleday, Doran, 1936); and Edwin E. Witte, "Why the Townsend Old Age Revolving Pension Plan Is Impossible," Jan. 1935, Committee on Economic Security Papers.

6. Witte, *Development of Social Security,* 75–108; Douglas, *Social Security in the United States,* ch. 4; Eliot, "The Social Security Bill," 73–74; *A Bill to Alleviate Hazards of Old Age . . . ,* Hearings before the House Committee on Ways and Means, 74 Cong., 1 sess. (1935); *A Bill to Alleviate the Hazards of Old Age . . . ,* Hearings before the Senate Committee on Finance, 74 Cong., 1 sess. (1935); Altmeyer, *Formative Years of Social Security,* 3–6; interview with Arthur J. Altmeyer, Dec. 1, 1954; *Railroad Retirement Board v. Alton R. Co.,* 295 U.S. 330 (1935); Roosevelt Press Conferences, July 24, 1935, vol. 6, p. 51; Roosevelt, *Public Papers,* vol. 4, p. 325. The Clark Amendment did not have general industry support. J. Douglas Brown of Princeton, who was in touch with executives of a "number of our very largest

corporations," wrote Senator Wagner on Feb. 22, 1935: "Key industrial executives are not interested in the proposals which the insurance groups are making for contracting out. They see that they have little, if anything, to gain and something to lose." Wagner Papers.

7. Burns, *Lion and Fox,* 202–5; Samuel Lubell, *The Future of American Politics* (Garden City: Doubleday Anchor, 1956), ch. 3, 212; Schlesinger, *Coming of the New Deal,* 506–7; Sherwood, *Roosevelt and Hopkins,* 64–65.

Three

1. Perkins, *Roosevelt,* 3; Sherwood, *Roosevelt and Hopkins,* 71–72.
2. *The Secret Diary of Harold L. Ickes, The First Thousand Days, 1933–1936* (New York: Simon and Schuster, 1953), 194, 244, 434–38; Arthur W. MacMahon, John D. Millett, Gladys Ogden, *The Administration of Federal Work Relief* (Chicago: Public Administration Service, 1941), 28–43; Roosevelt, *Public Papers,* vol. 2, p. 253; *Complete Presidential Press Conferences of Franklin D. Roosevelt* (New York: Da Capo, 1972), vol. 4, pp. 171–72; Corrington Gill, *Wasted Manpower, The Challenge of Unemployment* (New York: Norton, 1939), 178; for the FERA plan to join public works and public employment, see the Emerson Ross proposal to the Technical Board of the Committee on Economic Security, Nov. 5, 1934, Committee on Economic Security Papers.
3. MacMahon, Millett, Ogden, *Administration of Federal Work Relief,* ch. 2; *Emergency Relief Appropriation,* Hearings before the Senate Committee on Appropriations, 74 Cong., 1 sess. (1935); *Congressional Record,* vol. 79, pt. 3, pp. 2382–96; pt. 4, pp. 4364–65; Ickes, *Secret Diary,* 333, 334, 340; AFL, EC Minutes, Feb. 13, 1935, pp. 239–43; Green to all U.S. Senators, Jan. 28, to international presidents, Feb. 14, 1935, Green Papers.
4. MacMahon, Millett, Ogden, *Administration of Federal Work Relief,* ch. 3, 122; Schlesinger, *Politics of Upheaval,* ch. 19; Ickes and Hopkins Memorandum, Oct. 6, 1934, Ickes Papers; John Morton Blum, *From the Morgenthau Diaries, Years of Crisis, 1928–1938* (Boston: Houghton Mifflin, 1959), 235–39; Ickes, *Secret Diary,* 264–66, 378, 382, 410, 422, 424–25, 429, 434–37; Donald S. Howard, *The WPA and Federal Relief Policy* (New York: Russell Sage, 1943), 854.
5. Ickes, *Secret Diary,* 438, 446–48, 455, 458, 460–61; Searle F. Charles, *Minister of Relief, Harry Hopkins and the Depression* (Syracuse: Syracuse University Press, 1963), 125–26.

Four

1. Terkel, *Hard Times,* 161, 353.
2. Robert R. Nathan, "Estimates of Unemployment in the United States, 1929–1935," *International Labour Review* 33 (Jan. 1936), 49–73; Paul Webbink, "Unemployment in the United States, 1930–40," *American Economic Review* 30 (Feb. 1941), 251; *Historical Statistics,* 116, 283, 409; Charles

Frederick Roos, *NRA Economic Planning* (Bloomington, Ind.,: Principia, 1937), ch. 1; Hugh S. Johnson, *The Blue Eagle from Egg to Earth* (Garden City: Doubleday, Doran, 1935), chs. 16, 17; Schlesinger, *Coming of the New Deal,* chs. 6, 12–14, p. 567; Bernstein, *Turbulent Years,* ch. 1; Murray R. Benedict, *Farm Policies of the United States, 1790–1950* (New York: Twentieth Century Fund, 1953), ch. 12; G. Griffith Johnson Jr., *The Treasury and Monetary Policy, 1933–1938* (Cambridge: Harvard University Press, 1939); James Daniel Paris, *Monetary Policies of the United States, 1932–1938* (New York: Columbia University Press, 1938); Joseph E. Reeve, *Monetary Reform Movements* (Washington: American Council on Public Affairs, 1943); Milton Friedman and Anna Jacobson Schwartz, *A Monetary History of the United States, 1867–1960* (Princeton: Princeton University Press, 1963), ch. 8; George F. Warren and Frank A. Pearson, *Gold and Prices* (New York: Wiley, 1935); Arthur D. Gayer, *Public Works in Prosperity and Depression* (New York: National Bureau of Economic Research, 1935), chs. 1, 2; John Maynard Keynes, *The Means to Prosperity* (London: Macmillan, 1933); Marriner S. Eccles, *Beckoning Frontiers* (New York: Knopf, 1951), 104–13; Arthur D. Gayer, *Public Works and Unemployment Relief in the United States* (New York: American Council, 1936), 7; Bernstein, *Lean Years,* 481–84; Perkins, *Roosevelt,* ch. 16; George Martin, *Madam Secretary, Frances Perkins* (Boston: Houghton Mifflin, 1976), 260–63.

3. The national income payments estimates are in the *Survey of Current Business, 1938 Supplement,* the industrial production index in contemporary issues of the *Federal Reserve Bulletin,* federal expenditures in the *Annual Reports* of the Treasury. Nathan's figures are in the article cited above in Note 2.

4. John Maynard Keynes, *The General Theory of Employment, Interest, and Money* (New York: Harcourt, Brace, 1936); R.F. Harrod, *The Life of John Maynard Keynes* (London: Macmillan, 1951); R.F. Kahn, "The Relation of Home Investment to Unemployment," *Economic Journal* (1931), 173–98; *The New Economics, Keynes' Influence on Theory and Public Policy,* Seymour E. Harris, ed. (New York: Knopf, 1947); Lawrence R. Klein, *The Keynesian Revolution* (New York: Macmillan, 1947); Robert Lekachman, *The Age of Keynes* (New York: Random House, 1966); Leonard Woolf, *Sowing* (New York: Harcourt, Brace, 1960), 145; Leonard Woolf, *Beginning Again* (New York: Harcourt, Brace & World, 1963), 25. The Keynes letter to Shaw is in Harrod, p. 462; the concluding paragraph of *The General Theory* is at pp. 383–84; *The Times* obituary is in Harris, p. xxii; the letter to Mrs. Keynes is in Harrod, p. 199; and the Samuelson quotation is from Harris, p. 145.

5. *Survey of Current Business, 1938 Supplement,* 6, 7, *1940 Supplement,* 6, 7, 33; Bureau of Labor Statistics, Bull. No. 1312, *Employment and Earning Statistics for the United States, 1909–60* (Washington: 1961), 2, 474, 488; *Historical Statistics,* 70; Kenneth D. Roose, *The Economics of Recession and Revival, An Interpretation of 1937–38* (New Haven: Yale University Press, 1954); Alvin H. Hansen, *Full Recovery or Stagnation* (New York: Norton, 1938), 278–80, 293, 297; John Morton Blum, *From the Morgenthau Diaries, Years*

of Crisis, 1928–1938 (Boston: Houghton Mifflin, 1959), 269, 384, 386, 393, 394, 402–5, 409, 414–15, 417, 434–35; *The Secret Diary of Harold L. Ickes, The Inside Struggle, 1936–1939* (New York: Simon and Schuster, 1954), 170, 224, 229, 232, 260, 325, 360, 411, 417, 584–85; Arthur D. Gayer, "Fiscal Policies," *American Economic Review,* Supp. (Mar. 1938), 107; Seven Harvard and Tufts Economists, *An Economic Program for American Democracy* (New York: Vanguard, 1938); *Economic Balance and a Balanced Budget, Public Papers and Addresses of Marriner S. Eccles,* R. L. Weissman, ed. (New York: Harper, 1940); Keynes to Roosevelt, Feb. 1, 1938, Roosevelt Papers; Perkins, *Roosevelt,* 225–26; Burns, *Lion and Fox,* 330–36; A. A. Berle, Jr., and Gardiner C. Means, *The Modern Corporation and Private Property* (New York: Macmillan, 1932); Joan Robinson, *The Economics of Imperfect Competition* (London: Macmillan, 1933); Edward H. Chamberlain, *The Theory of Monopolistic Competition* (Cambridge: Harvard University Press, 1933); Gardiner C. Means, *Industrial Prices and Their Relative Inflexibility,* Sen. Doc. No. 13, 74th Cong. (1935); Roosevelt, *Public Papers,* vol. 7, pp. 115–16, 221–48, 305–32; Thurman W. Arnold, *The Folklore of Capitalism* (New Haven: Yale University Press, 1937), ch. 9; *Tolan Committee Report,* 503.

6. Terkel, *Hard Times,* 105–8.

Five

1. *To Establish Fair Labor Standards in Employments in and Affecting Interstate Commerce,* Joint Hearings on S.2475 and H.R. 7200, Senate Committee on Education and Labor and House Committee on Labor, 75 Cong., 1 sess. (1937), pt. 2, pp. 767, 788–89.
2. Leverett S. Lyon and others, *The National Recovery Administration, An Analysis and Appraisal* (Washington: Brookings, 1935); Charles Frederick Roos, *NRA Economic Planning* (Bloomington, Ind.: Principia, 1937); Bernstein, *Lean Years,* 71–72; *Historical Statistics,* 92–93; *Schechter Poultry Corp. v. United States,* 295 U.S. 495 (1935).
3. *Hammer v. Dagenhart,* 247 U.S. 251 (1918); *Bailey v. Drexel Furniture Co.,* 259 U.S. 20 (1922); *Adkins v. Children's Hospital,* 261 U.S. 525 (1923); *Muller v. Oregon,* 208 U.S. 412 (1908); *Atkin v. Kansas,* 191 U.S. 207 (1903); *Holden v. Hardy,* 169 U.S. 366 (1898); *Lochner v. New York,* 198 U.S. 45 (1905); *Bunting v. Oregon,* 243 U.S. 426 (1917); *Schechter Poultry Corp. v. United States,* 295 U.S. 495 (1935).
4. Perkins, *Roosevelt,* ch. XXI; Perkins to Roosevelt, Apr. 17, Roosevelt to McIntyre, May 16, Green to Roosevelt, May 29, Roosevelt to Early, May 30, 1936, Roosevelt Papers; Thomas W. Holland, "The Prevailing Minimum Wage Standard of the Public Contracts Act" (unpublished Ph.D. dissertation, University of Wisconsin, 1939); *Carter v. Carter Coal Co.,* 298 U.S. 238 (1936); *Morehead v. New York ex rel. Tipaldo,* 298 U.S. 587 (1936); Schlesinger, *Politics of Upheaval,* 476–81.

5. For a detailed review of the Supreme Court crisis in relation to labor legislation, see Bernstein, *Turbulent Years,* ch. 13. *West Coast Hotel v. Parrish,* 300 U.S. 397 (1937); *NLRB v. Jones & Laughlin Steel Corp.*, 301 U.S. 1 (1937); *To Establish Fair Labor Standards,* Report of the Senate Committee on Education and Labor, No. 884, 75 Cong., 1 sess. (1937); House Report No. 1452, 75 Cong., 1 sess. (1937); Paul H. Douglas and Joseph Hackman, "The Fair Labor Standards Act of 1938," *Political Science Quarterly* 53 (Dec. 1938), 491–515, 54 (Mar. 1939), 29–55; Perkins, *Roosevelt,* ch. XXI; Jonathan Grossman, "Fair Labor Standards Act of 1938," *Monthly Labor Review* 19 (June 1978), 22–30; Orme W. Phelps, "The Legislative Background of the Fair Labor Standards Act," *Journal of Business* 12 (Apr. 1939); Matthew Josephson, *Sidney Hillman: Statesman of American Labor* (Garden City: Doubleday, 1952), 441–49; Jeremy P. Felt, "The Child Labor Provisions of the Fair Labor Standards Act," *Labor History* 11 (Fall 1970), 477–81; Katharine du Pre Lumpkin, "The Child Labor Provisions of the Fair Labor Standards Act," *Law and Contemporary Problems* 6 (1939), 391–405; Roosevelt, *Public Papers,* vol. 6, pp. 211–14, vol. 7, p. 392; Roosevelt Press Conferences, Dec. 29, 1936, vol. 8, pp. 207 ff., Apr. 13, 1937, vol. 9, pp. 259–60; F. Perkins to M. McIntyre, Dec. 29, 1936, C.F. Hurley to Roosevelt, Feb. 3, 1937, H.H. Lehman to Roosevelt, Mar. 9, 1937, J.J. O'Connor to House Rules Committee, Oct. 13, 1937, J. Farley to Roosevelt, Aug. 3, 1937, T.B. Love to Roosevelt, Oct. 21, 1937, Memo for the Attorney General and J. Edgar Hoover, Nov. 18, 1937, M.T. Norton to Roosevelt, Apr. 29, 1937, Roosevelt to Norton, Apr. 30, 1937, Roosevelt Papers; AFL, EC Minutes, Feb. 12, Oct. 3, Dec. 3, 1937. There is an interesting document in the Roosevelt Papers. Martin Dies, the conservative Texas Democrat who was stepping onto the national stage as chairman of the House Un-American Activities Committee, wrote Roosevelt on Jan. 11, 1938, to propose amendments to the labor standards bill. While there would be national norms of 40 cents and 40 hours, the states would be empowered to reduce the minimum wage to 25 cents and increase maximum hours to 44. In addition, Dies proposed a special arrangement for the oil industry of a daily minimum wage and a biweekly hours maximum. On January 13, Roosevelt wrote the following "Memo for Mac" (McIntyre): "Call up Martin Dies and tell him that any idea of having an individual State vary a national Wage and Hour Bill is not only unsound but would destroy the effectiveness of building up a purchasing power in those sections worst needing it, and the President regards it as the weakest, most dangerous proposition he has ever heard. Tell him further that if we start to legislate for the oil industry, we will be aiding and abetting those people who want to exempt the canners, the cheese factories and the lumber mills, and that is completely unsound."
6. *U.S. v. Darby Lumber Co.*, 312 U.S. 100 (1941); Alpheus Thomas Mason, *Harlan Fiske Stone, Pillar of the Law* (New York: Viking, 1956), 550–56.

Six

1. L. Hickok to A. Williams, Oct. 31, 1935, Hopkins Papers.
2. Donald S. Howard, *The WPA and Federal Relief Policy* (New York: Russell Sage, 1943), the long quote at p. 126; A.W. MacMahon, J.D. Millett, and Gladys Ogden, *The Administration of Federal Work Relief* (Chicago: Public Administration Service, 1941), 13; Lewis Meriam, *Relief and Social Security* (Washington: Brookings Institution, 1946), ch. XII.
3. *Relief of Unemployment through the Performance of Useful Public Works,* Joint Hearings before the Senate Committee on Education and Labor and the House Committee on Labor, 73 Cong., 1 sess. (1933), 44–61; John A. Salmond, *The Civilian Conservation Corps, 1933–1942* (Durham: Duke University Press, 1967); Library of Congress, *Civilian Conservation Corps,* Senate Document No. 216, 77 Cong., 2 sess. (1942); Kenneth Holland and Frank Ernest Hill, *Youth in the CCC* (Washington: American Council on Education, 1942), the long quote is at pp. 11–12; Charles Price Harper, *The Administration of the Civilian Conservation Corps* (Clarksburg, W. Va.: Clarksburg Publishing Company, 1939); Frank Ernest Hill, *The School in the Camps* (New York: American Association for Adult Education, 1935); Perkins, *Roosevelt,* ch. 14; Schlesinger, *Coming of the New Deal,* 337–41. The administrative responsibility for CCC proved valuable to many Army officers. Then Colonel George C. Marshall, Schlesinger notes, organized seventeen camps in the Southwest.
4. Federal Security Agency, *Final Report of the National Youth Administration* (Washington: 1944); Betty and Ernest K. Lindley, *A New Deal for Youth* (New York: Viking, 1938), the quotation is on p. 202; Joseph P. Lash, *Eleanor and Franklin* (New York: Norton, 1971), ch. 45; Palmer O. Johnson and Oswald L. Harvey, *The National Youth Administration* (Washington: Advisory Committee on Education, 1938); Lewis L. Lorwin, *Youth Work Programs* (Washington: American Council on Education, 1941). A young and ambitious politician, Lyndon Baines Johnson, put his foot on the first rung of the political ladder as NYA administrator for Texas. The experience may have influenced the domestic programs developed during his presidency.
5. *Helvering v. Davis,* 301 U.S. 619 (1937); *Steward Machine Co. v. Davis,* 301 U.S. 548 (1937); Schlesinger, *Politics of Upheaval,* 613–15; H.S. Clark to M.A. LeHand, Oct. 20, J.G. Winant to Roosevelt, Sept. 28, Roosevelt to Winant, Sept. 29, Nov. 16, 1936, the "PAY DEDUCTION" notice is in the Social Security Board file, Roosevelt Papers; *Social Security Bulletin, Annual Statistical Supp., 1955,* 48–49; Arthur J. Altmeyer, *The Formative Years of Social Security* (Madison: University of Wisconsin Press, 1966), chs. 2–4; Robert T. Lansdale and others, *The Administration of Old Age Assistance* (Chicago: Public Administration Service, 1939); Evaline M. Burns, *The American Social Security System* (Boston: Houghton Mifflin, 1949), ch. 11; Paul H. Douglas, *Social Security in the United States* (New York: Whittlesey House, 1939), chs. 6–7; Meriam, *Relief and Social Security,* chs. 2–4.

6. The first two volumes of *The Secret Diary of Harold L. Ickes* (New York: Simon and Schuster, 1953, 1954), *The First Thousand Days, 1933–1936* and *The Inside Struggle, 1936–1939,* provide a remarkable inside history of PWA at the top. The specific citations are to vol. 1, pp. 130, 290, 481, 537, and to vol. 2, pp. 78, 189, 668, 669. See also Jack F. Isakoff, *The Public Works Administration* (Urbana: University of Illinois Press, 1938); Harold L. Ickes, *Back to Work* (New York: Macmillan, 1935); J. Kerwin Williams, *Grants-in-Aid under the Public Works Administration* (New York: Columbia University Press, 1939); BLS, Bull. No. 658, *P.W.A. and Industry, A Four-Year Study of Regenerative Employment* (Washington, 1938); Viola Wyckoff, *The Public Works Wage Rate and Some of Its Economic Effects* (New York: Columbia University Press, 1946); Public Works Administration, *America Builds, The Record of PWA* (Washington, 1939); C.W. Short and R. Stanley-Brown, *Public Buildings, Architecture under the Public Works Administration, 1933 to 1939* (Washington: 1939); J.K. Galbraith, assisted by G.G. Johnson, Jr., *The Economic Effects of the Federal Public Works Expenditures, 1933–1938* (Washington: National Resources Planning Board, 1940); John Maurice Clark, *Economics of Planning Public Works* (Washington: National Planning Board, 1935).
7. Altmeyer, *Formative Years,* chs. 2–5; Douglas, *Social Security,* chs. 12–14; Burns, *American Social Security,* chs. 6–7; Harry Malisoff, "The Emergence of Unemployment Compensation," *Political Science Quarterly* 54 (June 1939), 237–58, (Sept. 1939), 391–420, (Dec. 1939), 577–99; Walter Matschek and R.C. Atkinson, *Problems and Procedures of Unemployment Compensation in the States* (Chicago: Public Administration Service, 1939); Walter Matschek and R.C. Atkinson, *The Administration of Unemployment Compensation Benefits in Wisconsin* (Chicago: Public Administration Service, 1937); *Social Security Bulletin, Annual Statistical Supp., 1955,* 12; R.E. Quinn to Roosevelt, Feb. 25, Altmeyer to M.H. McIntyre and James Roosevelt, Mar. 17, James Roosevelt to D.W. Bell, Mar. 22, 1938, Altmeyer to Roosevelt, July 29, 1939, Altmeyer to E.M. Watson, Sept. 29, 1941, Roosevelt Papers.
8. Altmeyer, *Formative Years,* chs. 2–4; Douglas, *Social Security,* ch. 6; Altmeyer to Roosevelt, Sept. 11, 1937, Roosevelt to Altmeyer, Apr. 28, Altmeyer to Roosevelt, Dec. 30, 1938, July 29, 1939, Roosevelt Papers; Martha Derthick, *Policymaking for Social Security* (Washington: Brookings Institution, 1979), chs. 4, 6, 10; *Report of the Social Security Board,* House Document No. 110, 76 Cong., 1 sess. (1939); John J. Corson, "Administering Old-Age Insurance," *Social Security Bulletin* 1 (May 1938), 3–6; J.L. Fay and M. J. Wasserman, "Accounting Operations of the Bureau of Old-Age Insurance," *Social Security Bulletin* 1 (June 1938), 24–28; Lyle L. Schmitter and Betti C. Goldwasser, "The Revised Benefit Schedule under Federal Old-Age Insurance," *Social Security Bulletin* 2 (Sept. 1939), 3–12; Social Security Board, *Fifth Annual Report, 1940,* 173; Social Security Board, *Sixth Annual Report, 1941,* 167, 173, 176; *Social Security Bulletin, Annual Statistical Supp., 1955,* 21, 30, 33. To Altmeyer's distress, in 1939 "ardent Keynesians" in the Treasury, presumably Harry Dexter White

and Lauchlin Currie, expressed agreement with the insurance industry's concern over the growth of the trust fund. They wanted the system to be financed out of general revenues and the size of the pension to change in relation to the business cycle in order to help iron out economic fluctuations. Roosevelt, who was firmly committed to the contributory principle, had no patience with this view. This position, in fact, was a sophisticated restatement of the Townsend Plan. Altmeyer, *Formative Years,* 107–10.

9. *Helvering v. Davis,* 301 U.S. 619 (1937).

Seven

1. Bertram D. Wolfe wrote more or less the same biography of the painter twice: *Diego Rivera, His Life and Times* (New York: Knopf, 1939) and *The Fabulous Life of Diego Rivera* (New York: Stein and Day, 1963). See also Geoffrey T. Hellman, "Enfant Terrible," *New Yorker,* May 20, 1933, 21–24; "Diego Rivera's Mural for Rockefeller Center," *Forum* 91 (Apr. 1934), 224–25; "Rivera's Revolution," *Nation* 136 (May 24, 1933), 573–74; Archibald MacLeish, *Frescoes for Mr. Rockefeller's City* (New York: John Day, 1933). According to Wolfe, Rivera repainted the mural with a fierce Lenin for the old building of the New Workers' School on Fourteenth Street. Uncertain of the future of the structure, he put the work on twenty-one movable panels. A few years later the School dissolved and donated the Rivera to the International Ladies' Garment Workers' Union, which installed eighteen panels at its Camp Unity in the Poconos. The ILGWU, which was strongly anti-Communist, considered the other three too communistic and, evidently, sold them to a New York capitalist. Greta Berman reported that Rivera repainted "Man at the Crossroads" in 1934 for the Palace of Fine Arts in Mexico City, that twenty of the New Workers' School panels have been "lost," and that the sole survivor is in the Museum of Decorative Arts in Lund, Sweden. *The Lost Years. Mural Painting in New York City under the WPA Federal Art Project, 1935–1943* (New York: Garland, 1978), 228.
2. A bibliography of labor novels lists three published between 1920 and 1929. There were seventy-six from 1930 to 1942. This number does not include short stories, drama, or verse. *The Worker in American Fiction, An Annotated Bibliography,* Institute of Labor and Industrial Relations, University of Illinois (Champaign: 1954). The relationship between the Communist Party and American writers during the thirties led to an enormous literature. The decisive work is Daniel Aaron, *Writers on the Left* (New York: Harcourt, Brace & World, 1961). The quote is at p. 292. Elliot Paul, *The Stars and Stripes Forever* (New York: Random House, 1939), 39 ff.; Jack Salzman and David Ray, eds., *The Jack Conroy Reader* (New York: Burt Franklin, 1979), 44–49, 78, 133, 143, 184–86; Albert Halper, *The Foundry* (New York: Viking, 1934), 49, 101, 132, 288, 307–10; Robert Cantwell, *The Land of Plenty* (New York: Farrar & Rinehart, 1934), 17, 70, 78, 96, 98, 106, 108, 114, 172, 174, 252, 272; Walter Havighurst, *Pier 17* (New

York: Macmillan, 1935), 6–10, 77–78, 87; Louis Colman, *Lumber* (Boston: Little, Brown, 1931), 13–14, 184, 289–90, 292; James T. Farrell, *Studs Lonigan* (New York: Modern Library, 1935), vol. 1, 17, 48, 52, 69, vol. 2, 45, vol. 3, 307–8; Wellington Roe, *Begin No Day* (New York: Putnam, 1938), 28, 32, 63, 73–74, 128, 133, 172; Upton Sinclair, *Little Steel* (New York: Farrar & Rinehart, 1938), 30, 133; Nelson Algren, *Somebody in Boots* (New York: Vanguard, 1935), 29, 45–46, 147; Pietro DiDonato, *Christ in Concrete* (Indianapolis: Bobbs-Merrill, 1937), 11, 13, 14, 18, 24–25, 66–67, 108, 109–10, 118, 127, 186, 189, 192, 200–201, 237–40, 273, 285–86, 301; Fielding Burke, *A Stone Came Rolling* (New York: International, 1935), 9, 111, 128–29, 229, 388; Charles B. Givens, *The Devil Takes a Hill Town* (Indianapolis: Bobbs-Merrill, 1939), 18; John Steinbeck, *Of Mice and Men* (New York: Modern Library, 1937), 29–30, 119, 129–30; Jack Conroy, *The Disinherited* (London: Wishart, 1934), 12, 24–25, 41, 47, 49, 52–54, 60, 88–89, 154–55, 195, 247, 291–92; Edwin Lanham, *The Stricklands* (Boston: Little, Brown, 1939), 102, 270; William Attaway, *Blood on the Forge* (New York: Doubleday, Doran, 1941), 40, 42, 45, 47, 49, 52–53, 57, 67, 68, 70–73, 76, 105–6, 128–31, 143; Richard Wright, *Black Boy* (New York: Harper, 1945), 17, 127, 162–66, 174, 179; Jack Conroy, *A World to Win* (New York: Covici-Friede, 1935), 66, 74–75, 189–90, 203, 204, 208, 282–83, 296; John Steinbeck, *In Dubious Battle* (London: Heinemann, 1977), 50, 78; Albert Halper, *The Chute* (New York: Viking, 1937), 7, 31, 68, 204, 245, 279, 490; John Steinbeck, *To a God Unknown* (New York: Covici-Friede, 1933), 59; Edward Dahlberg, *Bottom Dogs* (New York: Simon & Schuster, 1930), 146, 148, 184; Meridel LeSueur's stories of the Great Depression have been collected in *Women on the Breadlines* (Cambridge: West End, 1977) and *The Girl* (Cambridge: West End, 1978); James Agee and Walker Evans, *Let Us Now Praise Famous Men* (Boston: Houghton Mifflin, 1941), 319–48; John Steinbeck, "Johnny Bear" in *The Red Pony and Other Stories* (Cleveland: World, 1938), 161–62; Josephine Herbst, *The Executioner Waits* (New York: Harcourt, Brace, 1934), 288; Ruth McKenney, *Jake Home* (New York: Harcourt, Brace, 1943), 17–20; Thomas Bell, *Out of This Furnace* (Boston: Little, Brown, 1941), 269–71; Edward Dahlberg, *Those Who Perish* (New York: John Day, 1934), 148; John Dos Passos, *U.S.A.* (New York: Harcourt, Brace, 1937), v–vi, vol. 1, 93–96, vol. 2, 421–23, vol. 3, 456–61, 559–61; John Steinbeck, *The Grapes of Wrath* (New York: Viking, 1939), 6, 44, 64, 156, 160–61, 236, 263–73, 280, 291, 319–24; Erskine Caldwell and Margaret Bourke-White, *You Have Seen Their Faces* (New York: Modern Age, 1937); Dorothea Lange and Paul S. Taylor, *An American Exodus* (New York: Reynal & Hitchcock, 1939); Josephine Johnson, *Jordanstown* (New York: Simon & Schuster, 1937); Mari Sandoz, *Capital City* (Boston: Little, Brown, 1939); Leane Zugsmith, *A Time to Remember* (New York: Random House, 1936).

3. Joseph Wood Krutch, *The American Drama Since 1918* (New York: Braziller, 1957); Nicolai A. Gorchakov, *The Theater in Soviet Russia* (New York: Columbia University Press, 1957); Glenn Hughes, *A History of the American*

Theatre, 1700–1950 (New York: Samuel French, 1951), chs. XI, XII, XIII; Robert Ardrey's observations are in the preface to his *Plays of Three Decades* (New York: Atheneum, 1968); Malcolm Goldstein, *The Political Stage, American Drama and Theater of the Great Depression* (New York: Oxford University Press, 1974); Morgan Y. Himelstein, *Drama Was a Weapon* (New Brunswick: Rutgers University Press, 1963); Ben Blake, *The Awakening of the American Theatre* (New York: Tomorrow, 1935); Harold Clurman, *The Fervent Years, The Story of the Group Theatre and the Thirties* (New York: Knopf, 1945); Jane DeHart Mathews, *The Federal Theatre, 1935–1939* (Princeton: Princeton University Press, 1967); Hallie Flanagan, *Arena* (New York: Duell, Sloan and Pearce, 1940); John Houseman, *Run-through, A Memoir* (New York: Simon and Schuster, 1972), chs. 4–6; John O'Connor and Lorraine Brown, *Free, Adult, Uncensored* (Washington: New Republic, 1978); Clarence J. Wittler, *Some Social Trends in WPA Drama* (Washington: Catholic University Press, 1939), 72; William Saroyan, *Three Plays* (New York: Harcourt, Brace, 1939), 17–20; Archibald MacLeish, *Panic* (Boston: Houghton Mifflin, 1935), 4–5, 8–9, 12–14, 46, 65; Sidney Kingsley, *Dead End* in Burns Mantle, *The Best Plays of 1935–36* (New York: Dodd, Mead, 1964), 239–76; Jack Kirkland, *Tobacco Road* (London: Martin Secker & Warburg, 1937); Clifford Odets, *Awake and Sing!* in Harold Clurman, *Famous American Plays of the 1930s* (New York: Dell, 1968), 19–93; Clifford Odets, *Waiting for Lefty,* Marc Blitzstein, *The Cradle Will Rock,* Ben Bengal, *Plant in the Sun,* and Albert Maltz, *Private Hicks* are in William Kozlenko, *The Best Short Plays of the Social Theatre* (New York: Random House, 1939); George Sklar and Albert Maltz, *Peace on Earth* (New York: Samuel French, 1934); Paul Peters and George Sklar, *Stevedore* (New York: Covici-Friede, 1934); Lillian Hellman, *Days to Come* in *Four Plays* (New York: Modern Library, 1942); "Altars of Steel" by Thomas Hall-Rogers was not published but is summarized in M. Laurence Miller, "Original Federal Theatre Protest Plays, 1936–1939," unpublished Ph.D. dissertation, UCLA, 1968; George Brewer, Jr., *Tide Rising* (New York: Dramatists Play Service, 1937); Albert Bein, *Let Freedom Ring* (New York: Samuel French, 1936); *Pins and Needles* was not published, but most of the songs were recorded by Columbia Records.

4. George Biddle, *An American Artist's Story* (Boston: Little, Brown, 1939), 252–95; William F. McDonald, *Federal Relief Administration and the Arts* (Columbus: Ohio State University Press, 1969), chs. 15–19; Richard D. McKinzie, *The New Deal for Artists* (Princeton: Princeton University Press, 1973), McKinzie discusses Erica Beckh Rubinstein's findings on p. 108; Karal Ann Marling, *Wall-to-Wall America: A Cultural History of Post-Office Murals in the Great Depression* (Minneapolis: University of Minnesota Press, 1982); Edward Bruce and Forbes Watson, *Art in Federal Buildings* (Washington: Art in Federal Buildings, 1936); Francis V. O'Connor, *The New Deal Art Projects* (Washington: Smithsonian Institution Press, 1972); *Art for the Millions,* Francis V. O'Connor, ed. (Greenwich: New York Graphic Society, 1973); Lloyd Goodrich, *Reginald Marsh*

(New York: Abrams, n.d.), the quotations are at pp. 30, 34, 142; Norman Sasowsky, *The Prints of Reginald Marsh* (New York: Potter, 1976); Lloyd Goodrich, *Raphael Soyer* (New York: Praeger, 1967); Frank Gettings, *Raphael Soyer, Sixty-five Years of Printmaking* (Washington: Smithsonian Institution Press, 1982); Walter K. Gutman, *Raphael Soyer, Paintings and Drawings,* with a preface by Jerome Klein (New York: Sherwood, n.d.); Raphael Soyer, *Self-Revealment, A Memoir* (New York: Maecenas, 1967), 72–73; Kenneth W. Prescott, *The Complete Graphic Work of Ben Shahn* (New York: Quadrangle, 1973); Ben Shahn, *Paintings and Graphics* (Santa Barbara Museum of Art, 1967); *Rockwell Kent,* Fridolf Johnson, ed. (New York: Knopf, 1982).

5. F. Jack Hurley, *Portrait of a Decade, Roy Stryker and the Development of Documentary Photography in the Thirties* (Baton Rouge: Louisiana State University Press, 1972); Roy Emerson Stryker and Nancy Wood, *In This Proud Land, America 1935–1943 as Seen in the FSA Photographs* (Greenwich: New York Graphic Society, 1973), specific references at pp. 7, 8, 19; Hank O'Neal, *A Vision Shared, A Classic Portrait of America and Its People, 1935–1943* (New York: St. Martin's, 1976); Beaumont Newhall, *The History of Photography,* rev. ed. (New York: Museum of Modern Art, 1982), ch. 13; George Walsh, Colin Naylor, Michael Held, *Contemporary Photographers* (New York: St. Martin's, n.d.); Milton Meltzer, *Dorothea Lange, A Photographer's Life* (New York: Farrar, Straus, Giroux, 1978), quote at pp. 71–72, the story of "Migrant Mother" at pp. 130–33; Walker Evans, *American Photographs* (New York: Museum of Modern Art, 1938); *The Photographic Eye of Ben Shahn,* Davis Pratt, ed. (Cambridge: Harvard University Press, 1975).

6. John Greenway, *American Folksongs of Protest* (Philadelphia: University of Pennsylvania Press, 1953); Liston Pope, *Millhands and Preachers* (New Haven: Yale University Press, 1942), 86–90; Tom Tippett, *When Southern Labor Stirs* (New York: Cape & Smith, 1931), 251, 274; Fred E. Beal, *Proletarian Journey* (New York: Hillman-Curl, 1937), 132; Margaret Larkin, "Ella May's Songs," *Nation* 129 (Oct. 9, 1929), 382–83; "The Winnsboro Cotton Mill Blues" is in Edith Fowke and Joe Glazer, *Songs of Work and Freedom* (Chicago: Roosevelt University, 1960), 74–75; Archie Green, *Only a Miner* (Urbana: University of Illinois Press, 1972); George Korson, *Coal Dust on the Fiddle* (Philadelphia: University of Pennsylvania Press, 1943); Alan Lomax, *The Folk Songs of North America* (Garden City: Doubleday, 1960); Joe Klein, *Woody Guthrie, A Life* (New York: Knopf, 1980); Woody Guthrie, *Bound for Glory* (New York: Dutton, 1943); Woody Guthrie, *California to the New York Island* (New York: Guthrie Children's Trust Fund, 1958); David King Dunaway, *How Can I Keep from Singing: Pete Seeger* (New York: McGraw-Hill, 1981); *Songs of American Labor, Industrialization and the Urban Work Experience: A Discography,* Richard A. Reuss, ed. (Ann Arbor: Institute of Labor and Industrial Relations, University of Michigan, 1983). As Reuss demonstrates, there is an enormous discography of labor songs. A highly selected list follows: John Greenway, *American Industrial Folksongs,* Riverside RLP 607; Pete Seeger,

American Industrial Ballads, Folkways FH 5251; Joe Glazer, *Songs of Coal,* Sound Studios 12-1137; Woody Guthrie, *Library of Congress Recordings* (6 sides), Elektra EKL 271/272; Merle Travis, *Folk Songs of the Hills,* Capitol 48001; Almanac Singers, *Talking Union,* Keynote 106; *Pete Seeger Sings Woody Guthrie,* Folkways FTS 31002; Mike Seeger, *Tipple, Loom & Rail,* Folkways FH 5273. I have deliberately avoided that notoriously metaphysical question: What is a folk song? Or, more basic, who are the folk? These questions are debated at length in the literature and Archie Green discusses them sensibly in his book. I prefer Woody's definition: "A folk song is what's wrong and how to fix it, or it could be whose hungry and where their mouth is, or whose out of work and where the job is or whose broke and where the money is or whose carrying a gun and where the peace is — that's folklore and folks made it up." Klein, *Woody Guthrie,* 169.

7. Klein, *Woody Guthrie,* 135–36, 140–41, 276, 286, 411.

Eight

1. *Historical Statistics,* 22, 23, 70, 95, 99, 393; Robert R. Nathan, "Estimates of Unemployment in the United States, 1929–1935," *International Labour Review* 63 (Jan. 1936), 49–73; Nathan also made estimates of nonagricultural unemployment for the period 1929–1940, *Tolan Committee Report,* 502–3; Clarence D. Long, *The Labor Force under Changing Income and Employment* (New York: National Bureau of Economic Research, 1958), ch. 10; John D. Durand, *The Labor Force in the United States, 1890–1960* (New York: Social Science Research Council, 1948), 96–102; Bureau of Labor Statistics, Bull. No. 1312, *Employment and Earnings Statistics* (1961), 13, 30; Robert S. and Helen Merrell Lynd, *Middletown in Transition* (New York: Harcourt, Brace, 1937); Samuel A. Stouffer and Lyle M. Spencer, "Marriage and Divorce in Recent Years," *Annals* 188 (Nov. 1936), 63–66; Ruth Shonle Cavan and Katherine Howland Ranck, *The Family and the Depression* (Chicago: University of Chicago Press, 1938); Robert Cooley Angell, *The Family Encounters the Depression* (New York: Scribner, 1936); Glen H. Elder, Jr., *Children of the Great Depression* (Chicago: University of Chicago Press, 1974); Mirra Komarovsky, *The Unemployed Man and His Family* (New York: Columbia University Press, 1940); *Tolan Committee Report,* 469; Edwin H. Sutherland and Harvey J. Locke, *Twenty Thousand Homeless Men* (Chicago: Lippincott, 1936); John N. Webb, *The Transient Unemployed,* WPA Research Monograph III (Washington: 1936); John N. Webb and Malcolm Brown, *Migrant Families,* WPA Research Monograph XVIII (Washington: 1938); Walter J. Stein, *California and the Dust Bowl* (Westport: Greenwood, 1973), quote at p. 60; Bernstein, *Lean Years,* chs. 12, 13; Bernstein, *Turbulent Years,* chs. 2–9; Schlesinger, *Politics of Upheaval;* John A. Garraty, *Unemployment in History* (New York: Harper & Row, 1978), chs. 9–10.
2. Bernstein, *New Deal Collective Bargaining; Historical Statistics,* 74, 94; Winifred W. Wandersee, *Women's Work and Family Values, 1920–1940* (Cambridge: Harvard University Press, 1981), ch. 5; Lois Scharf, *To Work and*

to Wed (Westport: Greenwood, 1980); Susan Ware, *Beyond Suffrage, Women in the New Deal* (Cambridge: Harvard University Press, 1981); Gunnar Myrdal, *An American Dilemma* (New York: Harper & Row, 1962 ed.), 205–6, Appendix 6; Harvard Sitkoff, *A New Deal for Blacks* (New York: Oxford University Press, 1978), ix, ch. 12; Samuel Lubell, *White and Black* (New York: Harper & Row, 1964), 53–54; Raymond Wolters, *Negroes and the Great Depression* (Westport: Greenwood, 1970); Herbert Hill, *Black Labor and the American Legal System* (Washington: Bureau of National Affairs, 1977), ch. 3; Schlesinger, *Politics of Upheaval,* ch. 23.

3. Lorena A. Hickok to Hopkins, September 19, 1936, Hopkins Papers; Edgar Eugene Robinson, *The Presidential Vote, 1896–1936* (Stanford: Stanford University Press, 1934), 228, and *They Voted for Roosevelt* (Stanford: Stanford University Press, 1947); V.O. Key, Jr., "A Theory of Critical Elections," *Journal of Politics* 17 (Feb. 1955), 4; Burns, *Lion and Fox,* 284; Schlesinger, *Politics of Upheaval,* chs. 32, 34; Samuel Lubell, *The Future of American Politics* (Garden City: Doubleday, 1956), ch. 3; Carl N. Degler, "American Political Parties and the Rise of the City: An Interpretation," *Journal of American History* 51 (June 1964), 41–59; Kristi Andersen, *The Creation of a Democratic Majority* (Chicago: University of Chicago Press, 1979), ch. 6; Nancy J. Weiss, *Farewell to the Party of Lincoln* (Princeton: Princeton University Press, 1983), chs. 9, 10; Laurence H. Fuchs, *The Political Behavior of American Jews* (Glencoe: Free Press, 1956); J. David Greenstone, *Labor in American Politics* (New York: Knopf, 1969), ch. 2; Harry A. Millis and Royal E. Montgomery, *Organized Labor* (New York: McGraw-Hill, 1945), 232–38; David H. Bennett, *Demagogues in the Depression: American Radicals and the Union Party, 1932–1936* (New Brunswick: Rutgers University Press, 1969); David A. Shannon, *The Socialist Party of America, A History* (New York: Macmillan, 1955), ch. 10; Bernard K. Johnpoll, *Pacifist's Progress, Norman Thomas and the Decline of American Socialism* (Chicago: Quadrangle, 1970), ch. 5; Leonard Leader, "Upton Sinclair's EPIC Switch: A Dilemma for American Socialists," *Southern California Quarterly* 62 (Winter 1980), 361–85; Daniel Bell, "The Background and Development of Marxian Socialism in the United States," in Donald Drew Egbert and Stow Persons, *Socialism and American Life* (Princeton: Princeton University Press, 1952), vol. 1, pp. 355–57, 369–89; Harvey Klehr, *The Heyday of American Communism* (New York: Basic, 1984), ch. 11.

4. William Temple, "The State," in Charles I. Schottland, *The Welfare State, Selected Essays* (New York: Harper & Row, 1967), 23; William A. Robson, *Welfare State and Welfare Society* (London: George Allen and Unwin, 1976), ch. 1, pp. 21–22; Piet Thoenes, *The Elite in the Welfare State* (London: Faber & Faber, 1966), 125, 133; Asa Briggs, "The Welfare State in Historical Perspective," in Schottland, *Welfare State,* 29, 30, 42; Sidney Webb's address was published as Fabian tract no. 159, *The Necessary Basis of Society* (London: Fabian Society, 1923); Marquis W. Childs, *Sweden, The Middle Way* (New Haven: Yale University Press, 1947), chs. 11, 12; J. B. Condliffe, *The Welfare State in New Zealand* (London: George Allen & Unwin,

1959), ch. 7; Richard M. Titmuss, *Essays on "The Welfare State"* (London: George Allen & Unwin, 1958), preface; Charles Frankel, "The Welfare State: Postscript to Emergency," in Schottland, *Welfare State,* 207–9; Sidney Fine, *Laissez Faire and the General-Welfare State* (Ann Arbor: University of Michigan Press, 1956); Gunnar Myrdal, *Beyond the Welfare State* (New Haven: Yale University Press, 1960), 62, 64; Sir William Beveridge, *Social Insurance and Allied Programs* (New York: Macmillan, 1942), 5–6.

5. Lorena Hickok to Hopkins, August 7–12, 1933, Martha Gellhorn to Hopkins, November 5, 11, 19, 1934, Hopkins Papers.

Index

Adams, Ansel, 257, 260–61
Adkins v. Children's Hospital, 122–23, 132, 133
Adkin v. Kansas, 124, 126, 130
Advisory Committee on Allocations, 82
Aged and the New Deal. *See* Social Security Act; Townsend Movement
Agee, James: *Let Us Now Praise Famous Men,* 201–02, 206–07, 262
Agricultural Adjustment Act: passed, 88; payments for basic commodities, 88; amended to make silver legal tender, 89
Agricultural Adjustment Administration (AAA): established to revive agriculture, 28; provides surplus cotton for Hopkins, 40; cotton program and acreage-reduction program unfair to black tenant farmers, 295
Agriculture: excluded from wages, hours, and child labor laws, 138
Aid to Families with Dependent Children (AFDC), 167–68, 290
Algren, Nelson: *Somebody in Boots,* 200
Altmeyer, Arthur J.: and CES, 42, 52, 200; and Perkins, 42, 45; and social insurance, 59, 68; and Social Security Board, 164–65; moves toward federalized social insurance, 181; and extended social security program, 184–85
Alton Railroad case, 69
Amalgamated Clothing Workers, 135
American Association for Labor Legislation (AALL), 44, 47
American Association for Old Age Security, 48
American Federation of Labor (AFL): on jobs for reliefers, 36; supports unemployment insurance, 48; concentrates on enacting NLRA, 67; and wage policies, 79; estimates unemployment, 86; favors reduction of hours, 91; disagrees with CIO over wages-hours bill, 107; lobbies for wages-hours bill, 127; supports wages-hours for women and opposes for men, 122, 135, 138, 139; and the Fair Labor Standards Act, 140, 141; and poor relations with CIO, 245; concerned with company unions,

American Federation of Labor (AFL) (*cont.*)
177; fights antidiscrimination clauses, 295
American Medical Association (AMA), 47, 59
An American Dilemma. See Gunnar Myrdal
Anderson, Sherwood: *Home Town,* 262
Andrews, John B., 44
Anti-lynching bill, Costigan–Wagner, 295
Antitrust enforcement, 113–14, 288–89
Arnold, Thurman W., 113–14
Art: George Biddle, 246–47, 248; Mexican muralists, 246; Edward Bruce, 247–49; National Commission of Fine Arts, 246–47; and "Communist" murals, 249; and cultural nationalism, 249–50. *See also* Federal One; Federal Art Project; individual artists; WPA
Associated General Contractors, 79
Attaway, William: *Blood on the Forge,* 196–97, 201, 204, 205–06, 207, 214

Baker, Jacob, 29, 37
Bane, Frank, 29, 37
Bell, Daniel, 77, 78, 81–82
Beveridge, Sir William, 49, 50, 305
Biddle, George, 246–47, 256
Bilbo, Theodore (Senator), 41
Bituminous Coal Conservation Act, 128–29
Black, Hugo L. (Supreme Court Justice), 91–92, 136–37, 138, 143
Black Tuesday, 105
Blacks: migrating, 11–12, 18, 280; unemployment, 22; relief, 31, 32, 287, 294; and WPA, 154; and CCC, 156–57, 288, 294; theater, 226–27, 234–36, 240–41; women, 290; stratified in the labor market, 293, 294, 295; and union discrimination, 294; discrimination by New Deal agencies, 294; and Federal Theatre, 226–27, 240–41; swing vote to FDR, 31, 295. *See also* Brotherhood of Sleeping Car Porters; Folksongs; Literature; March-on-Washington; Gunnar Myrdal; A. Philip Randolph
Blind: assistance for, 290. *See* Social Security Act
Blitzstein, Marc, 223; *The Cradle Will Rock* (play), 228, 229, 235–36, 237
Bonus Army march, 284
Bourke-White, Margaret, 213, 262
Brandeis, Louis D. (Justice), 123, 129
Brewer, David J. (Justice), 122–23
Brotherhood of Sleeping Car Porters, 294
Brownlow, Louis, 37
Building industry, 89–90
Building trades: and public contracts, 90, 126–28
Buildings, public: murals, 247, 248, 249, 252, 255–57
"Bum blockade," 5, 282
Bunting v. Oregon, 124
Bureau of Labor Statistics: unemployment figures, 17–18, 53, 87, 103, 172, 277
Bureau of Public Roads, 84
Bureau of Unemployment Compensation, 175–76
Burke, Fielding: *A Stone Came Rolling:* 196, 205, 207, 208, 215
Butler, Pierce (Justice), 130–31

Caldwell, Erskine, 223–24, 233–34, 262
California Emergency Relief Administration (CERA), 1–2, 260

Cardozo, Benjamin N. (Justice), 129, 130, 187–88
Carter Family: "Coal Miner's Blues," 268
Carter v. Carter Coal Co., 128–29, 130, 131, 133, 134
Children's Bureau: studies security of children, 53; gets AFDC, 58–59; gets welfare programs, 136, 137; and Norton bill, 143
Child Labor Amendment, 128, 130, 135, 136–37. *See also* Owen-Keating bill; Walsh-Healey Public Contracts Act
Child welfare. *See* Social Security Act
Churchill, Winston, 127
Civilian Conservation Corps (CCC): organization, 155; cost and number of enrollees, 156; efforts to eliminate discrimination, 156–57; and conservation of natural resources, 157–58; conserves natural and human resources, 157–59; shifts to defense projects, 159; popularity of program, 159–60; complaints about education and social integration, 160; related to youth at NYA, 160–61, 288; Mrs. Roosevelt insists women be included, 291
Civil Works Administration (CWA): created, 37; as distinct from PWA, 37–38, 287; achievements and shortcomings, 38; wages and bonus, 38–39; army uses to study mobilization, 39–40; phased out and FERA takes over projects, 40; and the arts, 225, 247; discriminates against women, 291
Clark, Bennett Champ (Senator): and Clark Amendment, 69–70
Clurman, Harold, 222
Collective bargaining, 135. *See also* National Labor Relations (Wagner) Act; AFL; CIO
Commerce clause (U.S. Constitution), 124–26, 133, 145
Committee on Fair Employment Practices (FEPC), 296
Committee on Economic Security (CES), 17, 42, 45; organization, 51; Technical Board on Economic Security, 52; and Advisory Council, 52–53; and unemployment insurance, 53–56; drafts program for the aged, 56–58; develops programs for child welfare and the blind, 58–59; national health insurance killed by AMA, 59; supports public health programs, 59; and the placement of programs, 60; and the signing of Social Security Act, 61; amount and duration of benefits, 178
Committee on Finance, 91
Commons, John R.: influence on policy and students, 37, 43–45, 48, 166, 171; *A Documentary History of American Industrial Society,* by, 44; *History of Labour in the United States,* by, and Associates, 44
Communist Party: supports unemployment insurance, 67; silent on Rivera murals, 192; and writers, 192–93; and the theater, 218–21, 235–43; unemployment demonstrations, 283–84; and Popular Front, 302
Congress of Industrial Organizations (CIO): gains through Wagner Act, 107, 285; disputes with AFL, 107, 138, 140, 285; Communists within, 286; commitment to reelect FDR, 301
Connery, William P., Jr. (Representative), 47, 137

Conroy, Jack: *The Disinherited,* 195–96, 200–01, 204–05, 206; *A World to Win,* 198, 199–200, 208

Construction industry: housing, 87, 104–05

Costigan, Edward P. (Senator): bill for unemployment relief, 24, 25; fight for labor and social legislation, 44

Coughlin, Charles E. (Father): on cheap money, 88–89; extreme political views, 285; and Union Party, 298; attacks Jews and FDR, 301

Crime: alcoholism and theft, 20–21, 279; prostitution, 21; stealing food and coal bootlegging, 283

Cummings, Homer S. (Attorney General), 51, 52

Dahlberg, Edward: *Bottom Dogs,* 200, 201, 210; *Those Who Perish,* 207

Davis, Stuart, 251

Davis-Bacon Act, 127, 128

Davey, Martin L. (Governor), 41

de Kooning, Willem, 251

Department of Agriculture, 32, 53, 56, 60

Department of Commerce, 92

Department of Justice, 113, 128, 137

Department of Labor, 4, 41, 60, 70, 136, 141, 143, 292

Department of the Treasury, 56, 60, 93, 248, 249

Devaluation of the dollar, 88–89

DiDonato, Pietro: *Christ in Concrete,* 195, 200, 205, 206, 208

Dill, Clarence C. (Senator), 41

Dill-Connery bill, 42

A Documentary History of American Industrial Society. See John R. Commons

Dos Passos, John: *U.S.A.,* 19, 211

Douglas, Helen Gahagan (Representative), 4–5

Douglas, William O. (Justice), 109, 143

"Dust Bowl," 2, 269, 273

Eastman Kodak Company, 68

Eccles, Marriner S., 36, 75, 91, 108–09

Economic Security Act: changed to Social Security Act, 67–70

Education: of migrants, 5

Eliot, Thomas, 60, 68

Emergency Relief Appropriations Act of 1935, 80, 103, 196, 288. *See also* FERA

Emergency Relief and Construction Act, 23

Epstein, Abraham, 47–48, 55, 68–69

Equal Rights Amendment, 292

Ethnic groups: support FDR, 299–300

Evans, Walker, 202, 207, 259, 260, 262

Evictions, 20

Ewing, Sherrard, 29

Fair Employment Practices Committee (FEPC), 296

Fair Labor Standards Act: preceded by Walsh-Healey, 128; provisions, 142–43; constitutionality in *U.S. v. Darby Lumber Co.,* 144–45; passage as exception to congressional move to right, 287; limited coverage, 290

Fair Labor Standards bill: hearings, 116–17; FDR sends to Congress, 136; joint hearings, 137–38; Senate committee report, 138–39; killed in committee, 139; FDR calls special session of Congress, 139–40; AFL opposed, 139, 140; Southern opposition, 140; Norton bill and AFL substitute, 140–41; FDR conciliatory to South, AFL, and business, 141; "barebones" bill, 141; and the Court, 144–45

Families: social problems, 20, 21, 34–35, 278–80, 281
Farley, James A. (Postmaster General), 71, 108, 140
Farm Journal: "Farmers to Arms," 140
Farm Security Administration (FSA): study of migrant education, 5; and photography, 257–62
Farmers: migrancy, 4
Farrell, James T.: *Studs Lonigan,* 194–95, 201, 208, 210
Federal Art Project of WPA. *See* Federal One
Federal Bureau of Investigation, 140
Federal Emergency Relief Administration (FERA): 22; unemployment relief, 24–25; and Hopkins, 24–25; policies of, 29–32; becomes CWA, 37–38; replaced, 41; projects, 40–41; exploited by the states, 32, 41; provides funding for CES, 42; shifting from FERA to WPA, 73–74; decision to abolish, 74–78; becomes WPA, 149; experimental program for youth, 160; shelters for transients, 280–81, 282; Hopkins insists on relief for blacks in South, 287; restores public confidence, 288
Federal Employment Stabilization Board, 90
Federal One, WPA Art Project: 225–49, 250–52, 253–55
Federal Reserve Board, 36, 75, 87, 92–93, 107, 108
Federal Theatre Project, WPA: 216–20, 224–27, 228–30; Living Newspapers, 226, 229–30
Fifth Amendment, 122, 123, 130
Fisher, Irving, 88
Flanagan, Hallie, 225, 227–28
Folk songs and singers, themes: textile industry, 262–65, coal mining, 265–69, migrants, 269–74. *See also* Carter Family; Woody Guthrie; Alan Lomax; Ella May Wiggins
Ford Hunger March, 284
Fourteenth Amendment, 122, 123, 124, 130, 131, 132
Frank, Jerome, 56
Frankfurter, Felix (Justice), 45, 126, 132, 143
Fraternal Order of Eagles, 47–48

Galloway, George B., 87
Gallup Poll, 74, 139, 141, 143
Garner, John Nance (Vice President), 41
Gayer, Arthur D., 91
Gellhorn, Martha: reports on unemployment, 22; hired by Hopkins, 32; reports people talk of FDR as if he were Moses, 306–07
General Federation of Women's Clubs, 292
The General Theory of Employment, Interest, and Money. See John Maynard Keynes
Gibbons v. Ogden, 144
Gill, Corrington, 29, 37, 79
"Gold clauses," repudiated, 89
Gold Reserve Act, 89
Gold standard, 88
Gompers, Samuel, 37, 48
Gorky, Arshile, 251
Graham, Frank P., 52, 56
The Grapes of Wrath (film), 262, 270. *See also* John Steinbeck
Graphic Arts Workshop, 250–51
Green, Archie, 265, 266
Green, William, 67, 68, 79, 127, 138, 139, 141
Gross national product, 104
Group Theatre, 221–22. *See also* Federal Theatre; WPA
Groves bill, unemployment insurance: 45, 48
Guthrie, Woody, 1, 5, 19, 270–72, 273–74

Halper, Albert: *The Chute,* 199, 201, 207, 208; *The Foundry,* 193, 203, 205, 206, 215
Hammer v. Dagenhart, 121, 122, 136, 144. *See also* Owen-Keating bill
Harrison, Pat (Senator), 91
Havighurst, Walter: *Pier 17,* 203, 215
Haynes, Rowland, 29
Healey, Arthur D. (Representative), 127, 140
Health, 4
Hellman, Lillian, 241–43
Helvering v. Davis, 164, 187–88
Herbst, Josephine: *The Executioner Waits,* 203
Hickok, Lorena, 32; reports on New York's relief program, 32–35; unemployment relief and labor conditions, 146–48; reports from Pennsylvania, 306
Hillman, Sidney, 135, 138
History of Labour in the United States. See John R. Commons
Hoboes and Wobblies, 4, 211, 269, 280
Hodson, William, 24–25
Holden v. Hardy, 124
Holmes, Oliver Wendell (Justice), 122, 123, 133, 136, 144
Holtzoff, Alexander, 52
Hoover, Herbert (President), 24, 29, 90, 107, 282–83, 284, 298
Hoovervilles, 5, 19, 212, 257, 279
Hopkins, Harry: plan for unemployment relief, 24, 25; as administrator, 25, 27–30, 34; career as social worker, 26; and FERA, 29–32, 60, 74; relationship with Ickes, Hutchins, Wallace, Perkins, 36–37; conflict with Ickes, 37, 76, 81–82; and CWA, 37, 76; wage objectives, 38–39; on white collar projects, 40–41; and CES, 42, 51, 52; bad health, 59; and election, 71; plan for unemployment relief, 71, 73, 75, 76–78; and WPA, 82, 83–84, 112; supports theater projects, 225; supports jobs for blacks, 154, 293–94; and youth, 160–61; and art projects, 247, 250
House Committee on Un-American Activities, 230
House Labor Committee, 138
Houseman, John, 227, 228
Housing: lack of, 4–5
Hughes, Charles Evans (Chief Justice), 125–26, 129, 130, 132–33, 133–34, 144
Hundred Days. *See* FDR
Hunger: among migrants, 4, 19
Hutchins, Robert, 37

Ickes, Harold L. (Secretary of the Interior), 83, 112–13; and PWA, 28, 36, 37, 73–77, 80, 81, 83, 91, 113, 168–70; as administrator, 168–70; conflict with Hopkins, 37, 72, 81, 82–83; and House Appropriations Committee, 78; and development of public power, 80; relationship with FDR, 84–85, 108, 109, 174; attacks monopolies, 111; supports jobs for blacks, 294
Immigrants: voting patterns, 299–300
Index of income payments, 104
Index of Industrial Production, 92–93, 103, 104, 105
Industrial Relations Counselors, 48, 53, 54
Industrial Workers of the World (IWW), 210. *See also* Hoboes and Wobblies
International Ladies' Garment Workers' Union (ILGWU), 222–23, 245

Jackson, Robert H., 111, 113, 136
Johnson, Hugh S. (General), 28, 35, 87, 88, 92, 93, 126

Jones & Laughlin Steel Corp., 133–34

Kazin, Alfred, 22
Kennedy, Joseph P., 82
Keynes, John Maynard, 90, 91, 94–102; *The General Theory of Employment, Interest, and Money,* by, 75, 109–10, 288
Keynesians, 36, 78, 108–09, 111, 112, 288
Kingsley, Sidney: *Dead End* (play), 224, 232–33

Labor Advisory Board, 120
Labor disputes, 31, 285
Labor movement, 284–85
Labor Standards bill, 141–42
Labor Standards Board, 137
Labor unions, 18. *See also* AFL; CIO
La Follette, Philip (Governor), 44, 286
La Follette, Robert M. (Senator), 43
La Follette, Robert M., Jr. (Senator), 24, 25, 44–45, 286
La Follette–Costigan bill, 23, 24
La Guardia, Fiorello (Mayor), 296, 301
Landon, Alf M. (Governor), 131, 165–66, 297, 298
Lange, Dorothea, 1, 2, 19, 213, 258–59, 260, 261–62, 273
Laning, Edward, 256
Latimer, Murray W., 52
Leiserson, William M., 56
Lewis, David J. (Representative), 41
Lewis, John L., 107, 135, 138, 285, 286, 301
Lewis, Sinclair: *It Can't Happen Here,* 226
Life, 257
Literature, 192–93; themes, social and ethnic divisions, 193–98; ambivalence about higher education, 198–200; brutality of work, 200–02; death on the job, 202–03; accidents on the job, 203–05; cutthroat competition and wage cuts, 205–06; unemployment, 208–10; the hobo and the Wobbly, 210–12; Hoovervilles, 212–13; farmworkers, 213–14; unions and strikes, 24, 214–16
Little Steel strike, 107
Lochner v. New York, 124
Lomax, Alan, 270
London Economic Conference, 89
Long, Huey P., Jr. (Senator), 164, 285–86, 298
Look, 257
Lubell, Samuel, 71, 294–95
Lubin, Isador, 52
Lundeen bill, 67, 69

MacArthur, Douglas (General), 284
McCarran, Pat (Senator), 41, 79, 80
McCarthy, Charles, 43
McKenney, Ruth: *Jake Home,* 204–05, 215–16
MacLeish, Archibald, 231–32, 262
McReynolds, James C. (Justice), 134
Maltz, Albert, 220–21, 240
March-on-Washington Movement, 296
Marriage: rates decline, 278–79
Marsh, Reginald, 252–53, 256–57
Marxists, 286. *See* Communist Party
Matisse, 190
Mechanization as cause of transiency, 281–82
Memorial Day Massacre, 228
Mercury Theatre, 229
Mexicans: migratory, and education, 5
Migrants: numbers of, 3; ethnicity, 4; health, 4; income levels, 4; housing, 5; education, 5; segregation, 5; children and women, 18. *See also* John Dos Passos, Woody Guthrie; Literature; Oral histories; John Steinbeck; Tolan Committee; Transiency

Millis, Harry A., 52
Minimum wage: and the South, 116, 120; and child labor, 30, 122–23
Mitchell, Wesley C., 44
Morehead v. New York ex. rel. Tipaldo, 130, 131, 132
Morgenthau, Henry (Secretary of the Treasury), 77, 105, 106, 110, 111; and CES, 51, 52, 56, 61; prefers Hopkins to Ickes, 81; on balancing the budget, 103, 104; on FDR, 108
Murphy, Frank (Justice), 143
Murray, James E. (Senator), 41
Music. *See* Folk songs; individual singers
Myrdal, Gunnar, 93, 305, 306; *An American Dilemma,* by, 292–93

Nathan, Robert R., 17–18, 86, 93, 103, 114, 276, 277, 290
National Association for the Advancement of Colored People (NAACP), 294, 295
National Association of Manufacturers (NAM), 41, 67, 74, 138, 140
National Child Labor Committee, 136
National Commission of Fine Arts, 246–47, 256
National Emergency Council, 17, 36, 82
National health insurance. *See* CES
National Industrial Conference Board, 86
National Industrial Recovery Act (NIRA): drafted, 88; and PWA, 91; codes, 76, 92, 117, 118, 119, 127, 135–36; Title I ruled unconstitutional, 121; and the Court, 121–26, 133–35; and commerce clause (U.S. Constitution), 125–26; fosters union strength, 285
National Labor Relations (Wagner) Act (NLRA), 49; fosters union strength, 107, 153; and the Court, 133, 290; and collective bargaining, 290; affects blacks, 295, 296
National Labor Relations Board (NLRB), 290; and unions, 67, 140; jurisdiction over interstate commerce, 13
National Recovery Administration (NRA): and General Johnson, 28, 35, 88; creates boomlet, 35, 93; announces President's Re-employment Agreement, 118; administrative disaster of, 119–21
National Youth Administration (NYA), 161–64
NLRB v. Jones & Laughlin Steel Corp., 133–34
Norris–La Guardia Act, 45
Norton, Mary T. (Representative), 140
Norton bill, 140–41, 142–43

O'Connor, John J. (Representative), 140
Odets, Clifford: *Till the Day I Die* (play), 219; *Awake and Sing!* (play), 220, 222, 234–37; *Waiting for Lefty,* 220, 222, 235
Ohio: relief agency federalized by Hopkins, 41
"Ohio Plan": for unemployment insurance, 48
"Okies" and "Arkies," 2, 260, 270, 280, 281–82, 301
Old Age Assistance, 166–67
Old-age insurance, 289
Old-age pensions. *See* CES; Social Security Act
Old Age Pensions, Ltd., 65, 67
Oliphant, H. J., 52
Olson, Floyd B. (Governor), 286
O'Mahoney, Joseph (Senator), 114
Oral histories, 5–15, 18–22, 86, 115. *See also* Studs Terkel; Tolan Committee
Orozco, José Clemente, 190
Owen-Keating bill, 121–22

Peek, George N., 28
Peoples, C. J. (Admiral), 78–79
Perkins, Frances (Secretary of Labor): and Hopkins, 24, 25, 37; and Altmeyer, 42, 45; on social insurance and social security, 48, 49, 51, 59; and CES, 42, 51–52, 56, 58, 60, 61; and FDR, 72; and NRA, 117; on wage, hour, and child labor bill, 92, 141; and the Court, 126, 131; and the Walsh-Healey Act, 128, 134; and the Fair Labor Standards Act, 138, 248
Photography. *See* Ansel Adams; Margaret Bourke-White; Walker Evans; Dorothea Lange; Ben Shahn; Roy Stryker
Picasso, 190
Pins and Needles, 223, 245
Pollock, Jackson, 251, 255
Progressive Era, 43, 47
Progressive Movement, 44
Prohibition, 66, 300
Public Works Administration (PWA), 81, 91, 103, 188; projects, 31, 91, 174; budget, 37, 70, 168, 171–72; increases employment, 172–73; and organized labor, 173; wage policy, 173; art projects, 247, 248
Pyle, Ernie, 27

Railroad Retirement Act, 148
Railway Labor Act, 290
Randolph, A. Philip, 295, 296
Recession, 106, 107, 114
Reconstruction Finance Corporation (RFC), 23, 24, 25, 90
Reed, Stanley (Justice), 143
Republican Party, 299
Resettlement Administration (RA), 258
Rice, Elmer, 229–30
Riefler, Winfield, 36, 52
Riis, Jacob, 257
Rivera, Diego, 189–92, 249
Roberts, Owen J. (Justice), 129, 130, 132
Rockefeller, Nelson, 190, 191, 192
Roose, Kenneth D., 105
Roosevelt, Eleanor (Mrs. Franklin D.): on migrant camps, 4; urges program for youth, 160–61; urges CCC camps for women, 291; as role model, 292; argues for jobs, 294; meets with La Guardia and Randolph to head off March-on-Washington, 296
Roosevelt, Franklin Delano (FDR): on relief, 23, 24, 25, 275; on FERA, 23, 25, 35, 72–78, 80; Hundred Days, 25, 28, 72, 89, 286–87, 288; fiscal policies, 27, 52, 91, 105, 108, 109–10, 112, 113, 288–89; and the AAA, 28, 92; and NIRA, 28, 88, 92, 119, 135, 136; and PWA, 28; and CES, 41–53, 55–56, 60–61; and social security, 49, 50–51; leadership, 70–71, 92, 108, 112; on agriculture, 89; and the Court, 107, 108, 126, 131–32, 134–35, 139, 143; politics and reelection, 108, 131–32, 296–99, 300–01; and Walsh-Healey, 127; and wage-hour bill, 139–40, 141; and Fair Labor Standards Act, 142–43; and labor legislation, 286–87; relations with blacks, 294–96; and unemployment, 287–89
Roper, Dan (Secretary of Commerce), 17
Rothko, Mark, 251
Rural rehabilitation: California Emergency Relief Administration (CERA), 1–2

Samuelson, Paul A., 102
Sandoz, Mari: *Capitol City*, 214
Saroyan, William: *The Time of Your Life* (play), 223, 230–31

Schechter case, 121, 124–26, 127, 129, 133, 134
Scottsboro case, 223
Seeger, Pete, 274
Select Committee to Investigate the Interstate Migration of Destitute Citizens. *See* Tolan Committee
Senate Committee on Education and Labor, 116, 127, 138
Shahn, Ben, 251, 255, 260
Share-Our-Wealth scheme, 285–86. *See also* Huey Long
Sherman Antitrust Act, 113
Sherwood, Robert E., 27, 72–73; *The Petrified Forest* (play), 224; *Abe Lincoln in Illinois* (play), 224
Shumlin, Herman, 22
Silver: and cheap money, 88
Silver Purchase Act, 89
Sinclair, Upton, 215, 286, 301–02
Slichter, Sumner H., 23
Smith, Gerald L. K., 285–86, 301
Social insurance, 46–49. *See also* Social Security Act
Social Security Act: and unemployment insurance, 17–18, 41–42, 46–49, 53–56, 175; and Altmeyer, 45; welfare provisions, 29; FDR's attitude toward, 49–51; old-age assistance, 48, 56–58, 165, 166–67, 181–84; and executive order on economic security, 51; constitutionality, 58, 164; and effect on women and children, 58–59; public health and the blind, 59; and work relief, 60, 74; and economic security bill, 60–61; influenced by Townsend, 66; congressional hearings, 67–70; compared to Fair Labor Standards Act, 143; categories of relief, 148; provides AFDC, 167–68, 289–90; assistance programs, 148; exempt workers, 177; benefits, 176–80; unemployment trust fund, 180; federalization, 180, 289; old-age benefits, 181–82; record-keeping, 182–84; 1939 amendments, 186–87
Social Security Board, 164, 175–76, 180–81, 185
Socialist Party, 283, 286, 301–02
Southern States Industrial Council, 116
Steichen, Edward, 257
Steinbeck, John: *The Grapes of Wrath,* 19, 195, 212–14, 262, 273; *To a God Unknown,* 200; "Johnny Bear," 202; *In Dubious Battle,* 202–03, 215; *Of Mice and Men,* 210
Stieglitz, Alfred, 257
Stock market, 105, 111
Stone, Harlan Fiske (Justice), 58, 129, 130–31, 144–45
Strand, Paul, 257
Straus, Jesse Isador, 23–24
Strikes, 107, 153, 228, 283, 285
Stryker, Roy E., 258, 259, 260, 261
Supreme Court, 58, 59, 107, 121, 122, 134, 136, 143, 285, 290
Sutherland, George (Justice), 133
Swope, Gerard, 87

Taft, William Howard (Chief Justice), 133
Talmadge, Eugene (Governor), 294
Tammany Hall, 35, 299
Taylor, Paul S., 1–3, 213, 260
Technical Board on Economic Security, 52, 54–55. *See also* CES
Temporary Emergency Relief Administration (TERA), 23, 24
Temporary National Economic Committee (TNEC), 114
Tennessee Valley Authority (TVA), 80
Terkel, Studs, 18, 19, 20–21, 22, 86, 115
Theater. *See* Federal One; Federal Theatre; individual playwrights
Thirty-hour bill. *See* Hugo Black; Wages-hours

Thomas, Elmer (Senator), 88
Thomas, Norman, 283, 298, 302
Tolan, John H. (Representative), 2–3. *See also* Tolan Committee
Tolan Committee: on migrants, 2, 3, 5–15, 280–81
Townsend, Francis E. (Dr.), 61–66, 285, 298
Townsend Movement, 57, 63–66, 67, 69. *See also* Dr. Francis E. Townsend
Tracy, Dan, 40
Transiency: described, 1–2; caused by unemployment, 280, 281; statistics, 281; among women and in families, 281; communities find unsettling, 282. *See also* Hoboes and Wobblies; Literature; Migrants
Transient Bureau: federal, 7
Transient program. *See* FERA
Tugwell, Rexford G., 52, 56, 87, 88, 258
Treasury Relief Art Project, 247, 248

Unemployed Citizens League, 283
Unemployed Cooperative Relief Association, 283
Unemployment insurance, 41, 48, 175. *See also* Social Security Act
Unemployment: statistics, 17, 186–87, 92, 103, 276–78; and loss of morale, 21–22; nonagricultural, 114; causes social disorganization, 278–79, 281; and demonstrations, 283. *See also* AAA; CCC; CWA; PWA
Union Party, 298, 301
Unions, 275. *See also* AFL; CIO
United Mine Workers, 301
United States Chamber of Commerce, 67, 74, 87, 138, 140
United States Steel, 18
Urban League, 294, 295
U.S. Office of Education, 159
U.S. Public Health Service, 59, 60
U.S.S. *Enterprise,* 80
U.S.S. *Panay,* 107
U.S.S. *Yorktown,* 80
U.S. v. Darby Lumber Co., 144–45

Vandenberg, Arthur H. (Senator), 183
Veblen, Thorstein, 44
Veterans Bonus March. *See* Bonus Army march
Vinson, Fred (Representative), 68

Wage determination: for relief programs, 32; in CWA, 38–39
Wages-hours: thirty-hour bill, 92; forty-hour week and hours of work, 119, 123, 128, 129–30; in building trades, 127; and children, 136, 137–38, 141; wage rates, 278. *See also* NIRA
Wagner, Robert F. (Senator): supports La Follette–Costigan bill, 24, 25, 44; introduces unemployment insurance bill, 41, 49, 61, 90, 117
Wagner Act. *See* NLRA
Wagner-Lewis bill, 54, 55
Walker, Frank, 82, 84
Wallace, Henry A. (Secretary of Agriculture), 37, 51, 52, 56, 61, 112
Walsh, David I. (Senator), 127
Walsh-Healey Public Contracts Act, 127–28, 173
War Industries Board (WIB), 87
Washington Post, 68
Welfare programs. *See* Social insurance; Social Security Act
Welfare state, 302–06
Welles, Orson, 227, 228
West Coast Hotel Co. v. Parrish, 132
Weston, Edward, 257
White, Walter, 295
Wiggins, Ella May, 264
Wolfe, Thomas, 1, 3
Williams, Aubrey, 29, 36, 37, 52

Willkie, Wendell, 22, 28, 101
Witte, Edwin E., 45, 52–53, 56, 59, 60, 61, 66, 69–70
Women: as prostitutes and migrants, 18, 280; single, 35; minimum wage and wage discrimination, 120, 122–23, 124, 130, 290–91; equal pay for equal work, 139; discriminated against by CWA, FERA, PWA, WPA, 286, 288, 291; New Deal does little to help, 290–92; more black than white working, 299; many vote for first time, 300. *See also* Literature; individual women
Women's Trade Union League, 292
Woodin, William H. (Secretary of the Treasury), 36
Work ethic, 32
Work-sharing, 18
Workmen's compensation, 47. *See also* Social insurance; Social Security
Works Progress Administration (WPA), 28, 102, 148; *vs.* PWA, 82–84; established, 112, 149; arts program, 149; funding, 149–50; projects, 150–51; employment figures, 151; FDR's ideas on, 152; antidiscrimination program, 154; accomplishments, 154–55; "boondoggling," 154–55; Negro Theatre Project, 227; and blacks, 287, 295; programs, 287–88
Wright, Richard: *Black Boy,* 197–98, 262